Fernand Salentiny

Encyclopedia of World Explorers

From Armstrong to Shakleton

Edited by
Werner Waldmann

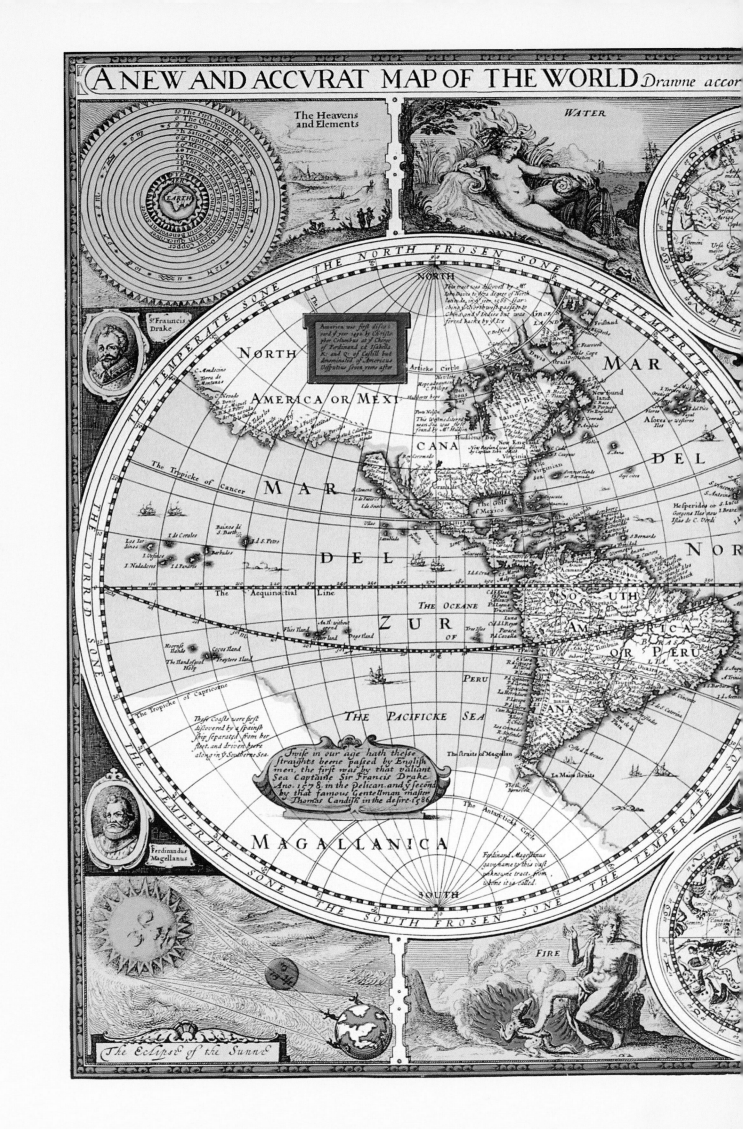

A NEW AND ACCVRAT MAP OF THE WORLD Drawne accor

The Heavens and Elements

WATER

THE NORTH FROSEN SONE

NORTH

St Fraucis Drake

NORTH

AMERICA OR MEXI

MAR

CANA

DEL

MAR

DEL

NOR

ZUR

The Aequinoctial Line

THE OCEANE

SOUTH

AMERICA

OR PERU

PERU

ANA

The Tropicke of Capricorne

THE PACIFICKE SEA

The Straits of Magellan

Ferdinandus Magellanus

MAGALLANICA

The Antarcticke Circle

SOUTH

THE SOUTH FROSEN SONE

THE TEMPERATE SONE

FIRE

The Eclipse of the Sunne

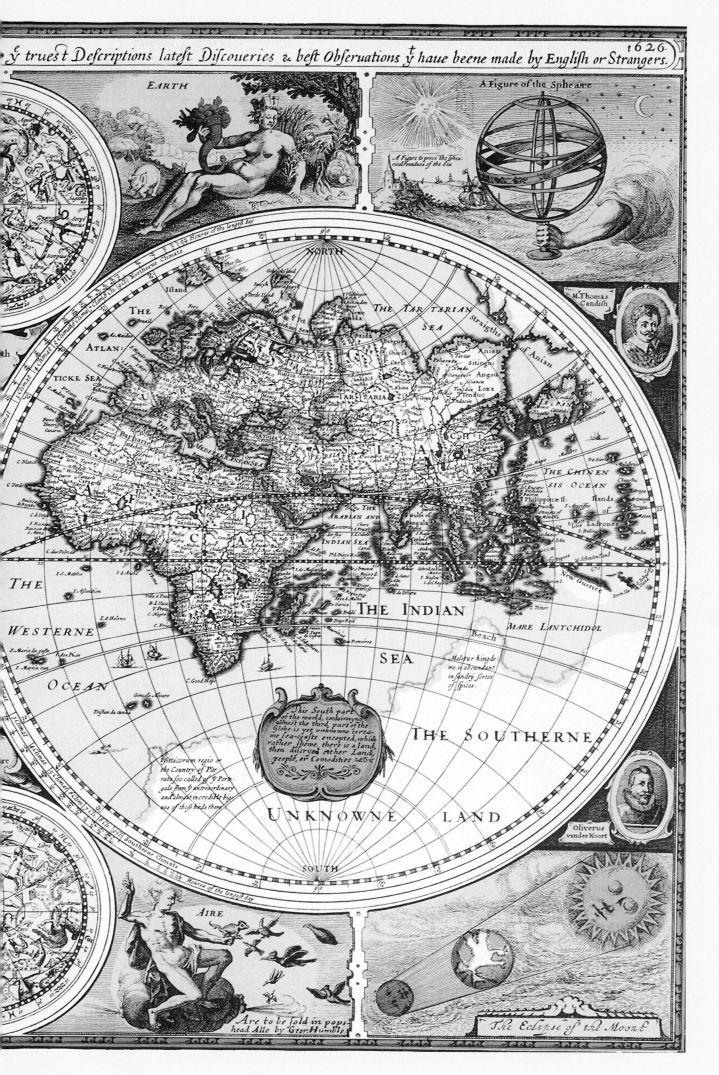

The world as it was known in the early 17th century.

Conception and realization: MediText, Stuttgart
Translation: Beate Gorman, Dr. Brendan Donnellan
Copy editing: Andrew Leslie, MediText
Cover picture: © Getty Images, München

Printing: Neue Stalling, Oldenburg

© 2002 DuMont monte Verlag, Köln
(Dumont monte, UK, London)

ISBN 3-8320-7125-3
Printed in Germany

Contents

UNBOUNDED CURIOSITY

People have always been attracted by distant lands. Even the early humans were not content to spend their time in the one place: On the lookout for a new, more favourable place of abode and, particularly new hunting grounds, they constantly traveled throughout their region. However, the more civilized mankind became, the more pronounced was the urge to travel further and further afield and to explore unknown distant regions. Of course, these explorers were not solely motivated by the pure desire to explore or the love of adventure: In most cases this urge for discovery and exploration was backed by very real economic and political interests.

The increasingly well-organized communities were forced to find new living space for their inhabitants and to exploit additional sources of food and mineral resources. Traveling on foot or with the help of draught animals was a tiresome and difficult exercise. The most important physical features in these voyages of discovery were the rivers, on which the explorers could travel quickly and comfortably. In most cases the rivers flowed into the sea. And the oceans of course had their own attraction, conjuring up images of new, enticing worlds.

Most expeditions set out in several ships, of which often few or even none returned.

For millions of years, people wandered around the planet aimlessly and only driven by instinct; however, this changed with the advent of the early high cultures. Even the Egyptians built ships and sailed to foreign shores, where they made vassals of the inhabitants and took possession of their riches.

The history of discovery is largely a history of conquest. It begins at the start of the 3rd century BC when Egyptian ships reached – by chance, of course – a legendary rich country that the seafarers called Punt. This was probably what we now know as Somalia. Apart from the fascinating tales of the experiences of the men there, the rulers at home were, of course, also interested in the souvenirs that the travelers brought back with them in the holds of their ships: spices, incense, gold – there is even mention of dwarves.

The inhabitants of coastal areas were more or less predestined to explore the seas systematically. They simply sailed along the coast, even when it took months or years. In this way the Phoenicians and Greeks were soon able to explore the Mediterranean and the surrounding regions. In this context, we should perhaps remember one of the most important world explorers – Alexander the Great – who brought back an immense amount of information for the scholars at home, in order to expand the world view of classical antiquity.

THE DESIRE FOR ADVENTURE AND LUST FOR POWER

One should not be under any illusion as to the motives of these explorers well into modern times. They were adventurers hungry for experience, who found life at home too restrictive and felt that they had to live a life of constant danger; fanatical missionaries with an urge to bless distant peoples with their religions; and of course power-hungry vassals of the various ruling houses who were keen to gain political influ-

ALEXANDER the GREAT.

and women who filled in the blank spaces in the atlas continue to explore remote regions of the Earth in order to discover its last remaining secrets. In many cases these are fine details such as rare fauna or flora that have to be examined or historical relics of ancient cultures hidden under the thick foliage of the jungle. But even the realms of the mountains and oceans still have many secrets that can only be drawn from the darkness of time with modern technology. These days, it is especially exciting to read the old reports of the discoverers and seafarers and to accompany them in spirit on their arduous, brave journeys.

Many ships came to grief in storms or ran aground on reefs. This contemporary engraving depicts such a dramatic situation, in which there were rarely survivors.

ence and increase their wealth. The Spaniards' brutal occupation of the Aztec kingdom is one of the most outstanding examples.

The 18th century was the period when Europeans systematically filled the last blank spaces on the maps of the world – and above all served state economic interests with a rigorous policy of colonization. Although one of the best-known explorers, James Cook, displayed a secure instinct when it came to dealing with the native populations he encountered, he also fulfilled the dreams of the power-hungry British admiralty. The country that financed such expeditions wanted a good return on its money. It took personalities of integrity such as Alexander von Humboldt and of course also a certain zeitgeist to cultivate pure scientific curiosity. In any case, Humboldt's major expedition to South America ushered in the era of scientific exploration of foreign countries and peoples. Nowadays, very few parts of the world still remain to be charted. But even today, descendants of these bold men

CONQUERORS, ADVENTURERS AND EXPLORERS

The history of exploration of the Earth is an exciting panorama of human curiosity, desire for adventure and scientific meticulousness. Even the early cultures felt drawn to explore the oceans in their fragile wooden ships, hoping to find a legendary country somewhere in the great unknown. Later, Columbus and Cortez showed the world the true reason for their and their masters' desire to discover new lands: Their aim was to subjugate foreign peoples in order to increase their own power. This history, which in many cases is characterized by complete disregard for human life, has only attracted scientific interest in recent times.

THE KEY FIGURES

When conversation revolves around the great seafarers and explorers of the past, the name Columbus is bound to come up at one point or another. While this Genoese adventurer is one of the numerous key figures in the history of the European search for foreign peoples, he was (and still is) described in many history books as a cartographer or even a mathematician, although even after his fourth and last passage he still believed he was in the realm of the Grand Kahn. However, from a geographical point of view the bold undertakings of Diaz, Cabral and Vasco da Gama – to mention just the most important explorers of Columbus' era – were, at the very least, equal to Columbus' achievements. Taking Columbus and thus the second half of the fifteenth century as the starting point for the history of exploration would be oversimplifying the historical facts.

The first regular contact between the "civilized" Europeans and the "non-civilized" inhabitants of North America (as one was in the habit of saying in the Old World, regardless of what was understood to be "civilization" in the Late Middle Ages) was not in 1492 on the well-populated islands of the Caribbean, but much, much earlier, and in the far north of the continent.

Almost five hundred years before Columbus' journey to Central America a highly significant historical event took place not far from the northern arctic circle. The Norwegian Eric "the Red", who had been banished from Iceland for the crime of murder, set off with a handful of loyal followers in an open rowing boat into the as yet uncharted waters of the North Atlantic, rounded Cape Farvel, Greenland's southernmost tip, and then headed northwards, landing on the west coast of Greenland, which from a geographical point of view belongs to the American continent. Here he founded two settlements, the western (Westbygd) and the eastern settlement (Ostbygd). Far removed from feudal Europe, Eric ruled this colony more or less as his private property, issued and laid down the law. Eric had set up the first European "State" in America. At the same time, this represented the first and – for the next six hundred years – last peaceful penetration of the American continent. Eric's sons, Leif, Thorwald and Freydis, advanced to what today are the Davis Strait and Baffin Bay, crossed the eastern part of Labrador and traveled along the coast of Newfoundland. It is quite possible that one of them even reached what we now know as Quebec. Knowledge of the explorations that took place in these waters around 1000 AD was mainly based on assumptions; after all, the Vikings did not keep logbooks, nor did they write reports of their travels. At least we know that these journeys were technically possible in those days.

Eric's attempt to gain Western Greenland for a permanent settlement foundered in view of the inhospitable nature of the land, the armed resistance of the Inuit, the disinterest of his countrymen in Iceland and Norway, and last but not least a sudden change in climate, which caused many deaths among the settlers. When Greenland came under Norwegian rule in 1261, the rest of Europe paid little heed to these events.

Eric's enterprise was that of a bold lone wolf. It was of no particular strategic consequence, since at that time no one in Norway realized that Greenland could be used as a stepping-stone for the exploration of the Canadian Arctic.

THE PORTUGUESE

Three years after Greenland's incorporation under the Norwegian crown, Portugal became a nation state through the expulsion of the last Arabs from Algarve (southern Portugal). It was to take more than two hundred years before Spain was able to completely rid itself of the Moslem foreign rule. This situation gave the Portuguese significant economic, political and strategic advantages in acquiring overseas possessions.

This woodcut shows the landing of Columbus' caravels on the island of Guanahani in 1492.

This engraving from the early 17th century shows an Indian warship fitted with a ram; the Portuguese used similar vessels for the transport of goods.

Italy, central Germany, southern Sweden, central England and in the Liège-Cologne region. This industry had allowed fleets to be built. Besides, Portugal had neither a moneyed domestic market nor a lucrative export market.

But just two decades after the liberation from Islamic rule, Diniz the "Enlightened" or the "Just" (el justo) ascended the Portuguese throne. He gave Portugal's economy the first impulses it so sorely needed. The next rulers, Alphonso V, Peter I and Ferdinand I, continued the economic policies initiated by Diniz.

The succession to the throne of João I, from the house of Aviz, marked the beginning of Lusitania's rise to a colonial world power. By the time Johan I died after ruling for 48 years, Portugal's seafarers had reached the River Zaire (Congo) and gathered the first specific information about Central Africa (in particular about the empire of the archpriest John, who was to all intents and purposes the Ethiopian king).

However, the Portuguese economy in the late Middle Ages was not in a position to enable King Alphonso III to enforce powerful foreign policies. The centers of the metal processing industry were not in Portugal but in the Alps, northern

The actual foreign expansion came under Henry the Seafarer, who withdrew from court in

Drastic measures were used to maintain discipline on board: This woodcut from the mid-16th century depicts the various fates of sailors accused of mutiny.

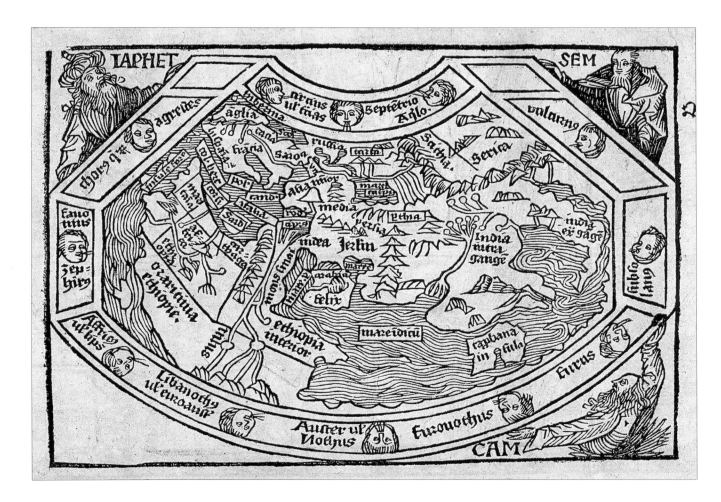

In the 16th century, the prevailing concept of the Earth and its land masses was still very vague. In this world map of Ptolemy, the individual continents play a minor role; more important are the figures depicted in the margins.

1419 (mainly because he had virtually no opportunity of succeeding to the throne in those days) to Sagres, on the southernmost tip of Portugal, where he drafted the plan for the future Portuguese empire. He established two main directions of thrust: taking over the Atlantic islands as maritime bases and circumnavigating South Africa, which would secure access to the lucrative spice trade.

In 1415 Portugal took over the first Arabian base of Ceuta; Lisbon had gained its first military foothold on the "black" continent. Three years later, the colonization of Porto Santo and Madeira was begun by the seafarers Zarco and Teixeira, and by 1427 Portugal came a step closer to the American continent by taking possession of the Azores. The successful policy of "island and cape hopping" had been initiated. While Portugal's attempt to conquer the Canary Islands in 1425 was unsuccessful, on the orders of Henry the Seafarer Gil Eannes sailed around

Cape Bojador in 1433 and Baldaya was able to reach Porto Galé via this cape. In 1440 Goncalves reached Rio Ouro. However, with his last advance one of the darkest chapters of Portuguese (and European) colonial history began. Slave trading between the Christian Portuguese and the Arabs, who were regarded as religious enemies, produced lucrative profits.

Disregarding the losses of ships and highly qualified captains, the Portuguese advanced step by step towards the Cape of Good Hope. Around 1441 the caravel, a ship constructed especially for the stormy Atlantic, provided completely new technical opportunities for the voyages of exploration. By 1448 Portugal had built its first fort in the Bay of Arguin (Guinea coast) and in 1455 Ca da Mosto set out on the first scientific expedition to the Cape Verde Islands.

When Henry the Seafarer died in 1460, a total of 3,000 km (1,860 miles) of the west African coast were in Portuguese hands. When the Mina

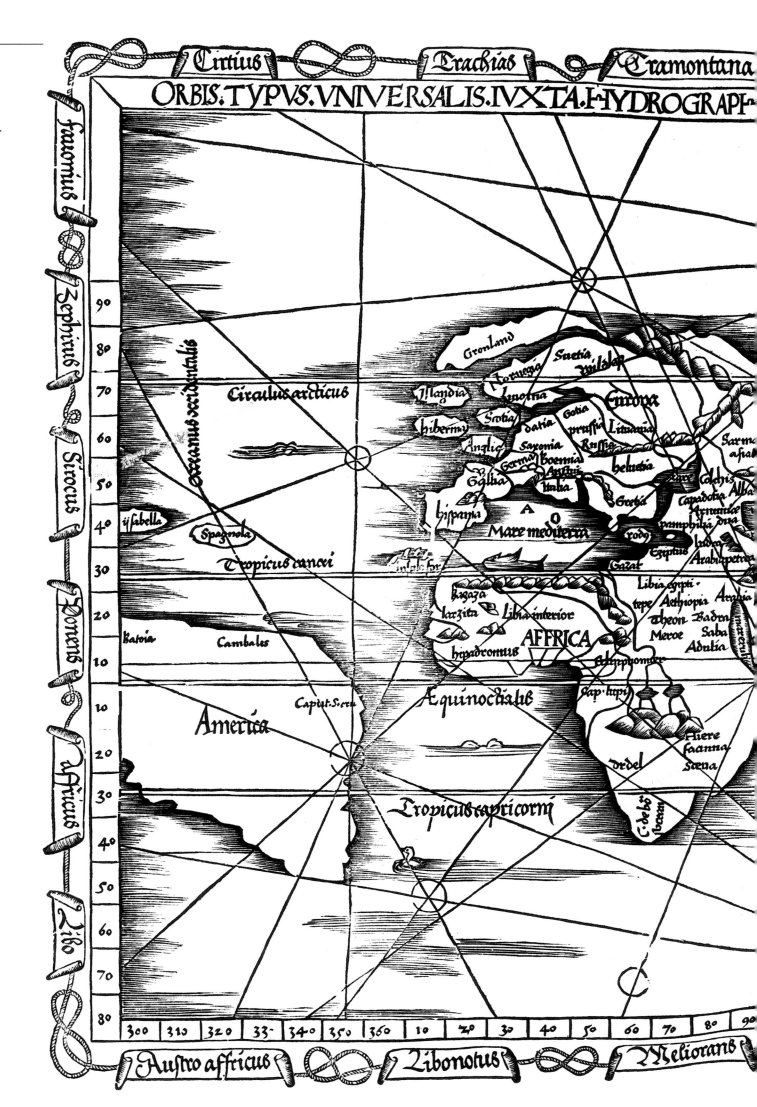

The Greek Claudius Ptolemy created the most important atlas of antiquity. His view of the world held sway for a very long time; accordingly, it proved difficult to correct his erroneous assumptions over the course of the subsequent centuries.

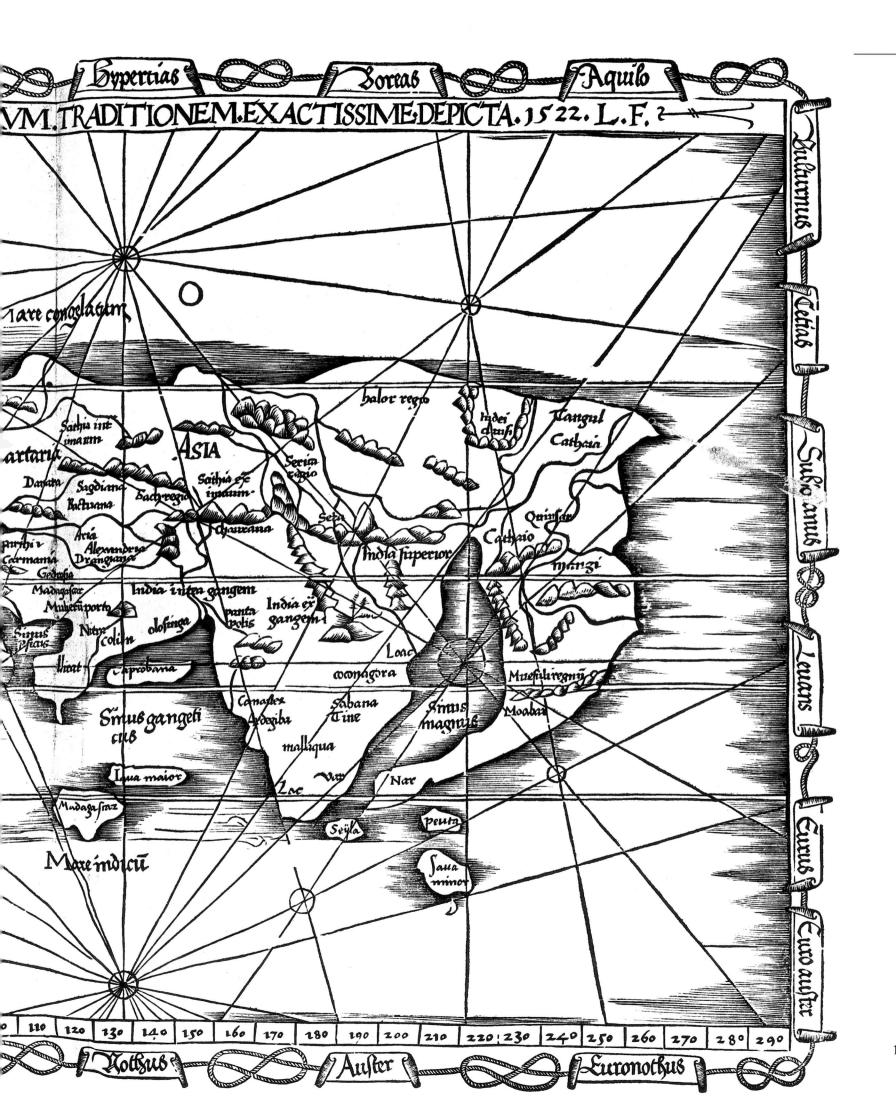

fort was erected on the Gold Coast it was only a matter of time before the Portuguese would reach the southernmost tip of Africa. In 1488 Bartholomeu Diaz circumnavigated the stormy cape and by the end of the fifteenth century Vasco da Gama, through his historically significant journey, had broken the Arabian monopoly in spice trading. Portugal had entered the lucrative pepper trade. However, to be able to emerge victorious from the beginning "pepper war", in addition to strong artillery Portugal needed the personal strength of Albuquerque. Establishing a military base on Goa (west coast of India), setting up fortified trading posts along the Malabar Coast and conquering Hormuz, the "Pearl of the Orient", as the town was described in those days, allowed the Portuguese to navigate the shipping routes in the Indian Ocean and brought a regular income for Lisbon.

After the Treaty of Tordesillas (1494) had been signed, in which the two Iberian states marked out their respective areas of interest, the first weakness in the previously unbroken development of fortifications along the Lisbon–Cape–Goa line became apparent. By turning to Brazil, the gradual decline of Portugal's eastern colonies was set in motion. In regard to its economic means, Portugal had stretched its resources too far. Not even profits of up to 500 per cent per ship's spice cargo could help Portugal surmount the financial problems with which Lisbon was permanently faced in the second half of the sixteenth century. Instead of consolidating the colonial empire in Africa, which was after all quite substantial by that time, Portugal continued to advance still further despite its weak economical footing. The incredibly long route around the Cape of Good Hope to Macao, the most distant colony in the Far East, the loss of entire flotillas to the forces of nature and the military campaigns that Portugal almost constantly had to wage against the Arabs to maintain some degree of safety on the "spice routes" – it was virtually impossible for the demograph-

The map of America from the first scientifically precise world atlas by Gerhardus Mercator, of which the first part appeared in Amsterdam in 1585. Mercator did not live to see the publication of his complete work.

ically (just one million inhabitants) and above all economically underdeveloped Portugal to survive in the long term in view of such hardship. The dawning of the so-called "Golden Age" (1383–1580) had already taken place sixty years before, as Portugal's overseas withdrawal set in. The larger the Portuguese Empire (and later also the Spanish) grew, the poorer the mother country became. For decades on end, its investments far exceeded the income from its colonies. Before Portugal was able to reap the fruits of its foreign investments the British, French and Dutch appeared on the scene and took almost all Portugal's bases from them, from Gibraltar to Singapore. Another factor in Portugal's downfall was that the expansion of its colonies was affected by the Spanish foreign rule in the country from 1580 to 1640.

THE SPANISH

Around the turn of the sixteenth century, Portugal's sister nation Spain entered the stage of colonial rule. According to the global distribution plan of Tordesillas (and the pontifical decree "Inter Caetera"), the Spanish had a free hand in Central and South America with the exception of Brazil. But the alliance of the two kingdoms of Castilia and Aragonia that had been brought about through the marriage of Ferdinand and Isabella (1469) paved the way for the complete reconquista (reconquest). Although from a demographic and economic viewpoint, Spain had become a much stronger national state than Portugal once the Arabs had been driven out, even several years after the reconquista the Catholic ruling couple had limited resources to carry out an effective foreign policy. Columbus' first crossing was only made possible by the support of the financially powerful Pinzón group.

Like the Portuguese, the Spanish secured a strategic base on the route to America by conquering the Canary Islands (1479). Almost all seafarers dropped anchor here before beginning their journeys of exploration to the American continent. In 1492 Columbus undertook his journey to the Central American island world and landed on San Salvador; this may have been good propaganda, but the venture was not adequately prepared in technical terms.

Almost twenty years after Columbus' voyage the entire Caribbean islands were in the hands of the Spanish crown, Pinzón had advanced almost to Rio de la Plata, and Balboa had reached the Pacific Ocean (1513). Through its overseas expansion Spain had risen to become the second world power, but the precious metals which had been hoped for and were urgently needed were still lacking. Columbus had deliberately misinformed the Spanish crown by making false statements about the enormous quantities of gold and silver to be found. It was not until Cortez' trek to Tenochtitlán (Mexico City) and the conquest of the Aztec empire and destruction of the Inca empire in Peru by Pizarro that Spain was able to escape certain national bankruptcy (which nevertheless still had to be declared in 1557, 1575 and 1596). Parallel to this unexpected wealth, which was especially noticeable in Castilia (Seville, Toledo, Burgos and Leon), but not in Aragonia, there was a spate of price increases, an outflow of gold to northern Europe through the luxury purchases by wealthy Spaniards and a reduction in the population, mainly in central Spain. Many young Spaniards, impoverished noblemen and profit-hungry merchants turned their backs on their mother country. The New World offered not only wealth, but also a marked increase in freedom. Even more disastrous for Spain was the extravagance of its rulers, which reached an absolute pinnacle under Philip II.

Spain had squandered its powers just fifty years after its promising entry on to the colonial scene. The expansion policies in Europe and in the colonies, a so-called "war on two fronts", was unbearable for the national economy.

Around this time Britain, France and Holland appeared as tough competitors against Spain in the battle for possession of the world.

THE BRITISH

Four years after Spain's pitiful attempt to force Britain on to its knees by the "invincible" Armada, Britain founded the colony of Virginia on the east coast of America. In 1609 it occupied the Bermuda Islands and in 1627 Barbuda. Albion's power of thrust bore out the strategic value of these bases in the zones still occupied by Spain and the fact that Britain intended to become a colonial power at Spain's (and Portugal's) cost, regardless of the long outdated Treaty of Tordesillas. Drake's organized privateering forays, particularly against the Spanish silver ships, are highly characteristic of Britain's initial period as a colonial power.

Individual entrepreneurs from Bristol were already embarking on trading missions to the Gulf of Guinea and to Brazil. The East India Company, founded in 1600, developed lucrative business with Indian trading companies, to the disadvantage of the Portuguese. By 1633 the British had settled in Bengal and just five years later in Honduras.

Depending on the strength or weakness of the respective colonial opponents, the direction of thrust went eastwards or westwards. In 1647 the British set up trading offices on the Bahamas and in 1655 on Jamaica, in the midst of the Spanish zone of influence. The British drove the Dutch away from the North American coast. New Amsterdam, which had been founded in 1612, became a British harbor town in 1664 and was renamed New York. The Treaty of Utrecht (1713) gave Britain Acadia (the eastern part of Canada), Newfoundland and Gibraltar, and the Treaty of Paris (1763) gave the British India (with the exception of the French trading offices), Canada, Florida, the islands of Grenada, Tobago, St. Vincent and Senegal (with the exception of Gorée). From that

A typical 18th-century ship (frontispiece to Père Fournier's "Hydrographie").

Facing page: This illustration from the book of the Austrian Benedictine monk Philoponus shows that the explorers were not merely interested in discovery, but felt obliged to introduce the Christian faith to the local inhabitants, if necessary with force.

point on the British Empire experienced a true colonial "escalation". Trafalgar made Britain ruler of the seas. The Second Treaty of Paris (1815) extended what was already the world's greatest colonial power by the island of Ascension, the Cape of Good Hope, St. Lucia (Caribbean Sea), Mauritius (Ile de France), the Seychelles (Indian Ocean), Malacca, Ceylon and Malta.

The turning point did not come until after the Second World War. India's independence in 1947 was the first step in Britain's general withdrawal from overseas.

THE FRENCH

At the time that the Spanish were conquering entire empires in America with just a handful of conquistadors, French fishermen from St. Malo and Honfleur (Channel coast) were already making long journeys to the waters of Newfoundland where fish were in abundance.

The first systematic attempts at colonization were made by Jacques Cartier. However, as the expected flood of settlers did not take place, France had to postpone its plans of increasing its overseas powers. The foundation of the states of Port Royal (1604) and Quebec (1608) increased France's chances of ensuring a place in the division of North America.

In 1626 France set up trading offices on Santo Domingo (Haiti), and shortly afterwards on Martinique and Guadeloupe. France had entered the field as a new and dangerous competitor for both the Spanish and the British.

Colbert, "Minister for Colonial Affairs" under Louis XIV, provided French colonialism with the necessary economic backing through the foundation of the "Compagnie des Indes Occidentales" (West Indian Trading Company) and the "Compagnie des Indes Orientales" (East Indian Trading Company). However, the treaties of Utrecht and Paris dealt France something of a hard blow in respect of its overseas possessions in Asia and America.

France's colonial future lay in Africa. In 1830 Algeria was conquered, nine years later a trad-

Apostoli eliguntur et mittuntur

fide Christi eruditur Baptizantque.

Fra, Buillyua por Vicario del Papa con Breue Apostolico.

Fray Buill começaron la conuersion de los Indios Bauli Zaron

Isla Haity siue Spaniola
Isla Deseada
Isla Dominica
La Vega

Admiral C.Colon.

ayles priseron martyrio por quebra los Idalgos

S. Cruz que passo Fray Buill en la Vega.

Idala prostra, nunc ac Martyrum pro fide Christi coluint.

San tium miraculossin Crucis signum erigunt

Thomas Botius Eugubinus S. Congregationis Oratory in Vrbe Roma Presbyter Primo signorum vera Ecclesia tomo affirmat. Primus Euangelij raco fuit Indiæ Occidentalis Fr. Buill Catalonus ex Ordine S. Benedicti quem Papa Alexander sextus Sacerdotibus duodecim præfecit, suasque in ijs Regionibus illi partes mandauit. Auspicijs Ferdinadi et Isabella Regibus Hispaniæ Classe armata instructa in Americam transfretarunt Calend. 14 Septembr. Anno Christi: 93

REVERENDISSIMO AC NOBILI DOMINO, MONASTERII SEITTENSTÖTTENSIS IN CTI BENEDICTI, ABBATI VIGILANTISSIMO CTORI CLARISSIMO DOMINO SVO GRATIOSIS: LOPON, ANNO SA:

DOMINO CASPARO PLAVTIO MO AVSTRIA INFERIORI ORDINIS SAN. THEOLOGO AC PHILOSOPHIÆ DO SIMO D.D. DON FR. HIERONYM, PHI LVTIS. 1622.

The adjacent engraving gives a graphic account of the legendary voyage of St. Brendan, while the illustration below conveys to the European beholder the atrocities of the barbarians: human sacrifice, cannibalism and idolatry.

Facing page: Somewhat more accurate were the depictions of exotic fauna in Johann des Bry's "India orientalis".

ing company was opened in Gabon, in 1842 the Ivory Coast was occupied, in 1865 Senegal was "pacified" and in 1857 Dakar was founded on the West African coast. At the same time, France gained a foothold in New Caledonia; and the Marquesas Islands and Tahiti in the Pacific

VII.
CONTRAFACTVRA QVO-
RVNDAM ANIMALIVM, IN INDIA
celebrium.

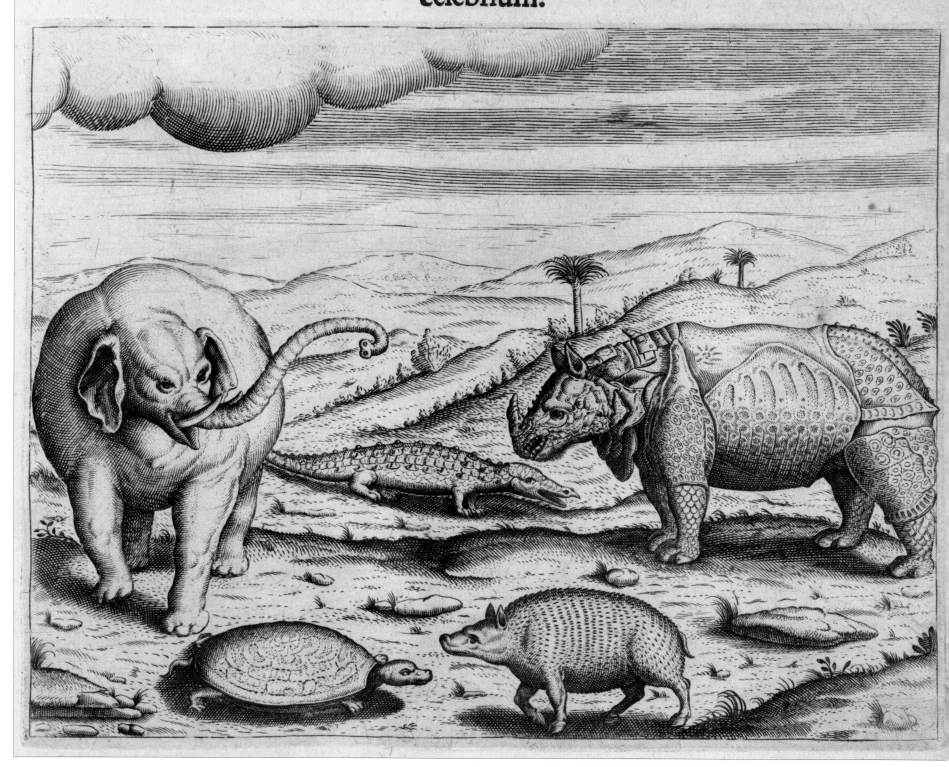

When the great sailing ships dropped anchor on the shores of distant lands such as Tahiti, shown here, they had to be overhauled by the crew. Parts of the rigging were removed, as were with the cannons, and the sides of the ships were cleaned of algae and mollusks.

became so-called French "protectorates". The chain of acquisitions and conquests did not begin to diminish until the 1930s. When Syria was finally granted independence in 1941, this was in fact the first step in the decline of French colonialism.

THE DUTCH

Holland, which was small from a territorial point of view but nevertheless dynamic and a significant seafaring nation, also secured itself a large colonial empire. The main aim of the "East India Company", founded in 1602, was to compete against Spain and Portugal. In 1605 the Dutch settled on the Moluccas, in 1607 on Celebes and in 1613 on Timor. Batan was founded in 1619. The Dutch advance to the North American east coast was only a short-lived affair. The British were not prepared to put up with any competition whatsoever. Also short-lived were the occupations on the west coast of Formosa (1624) and

Brazil (1624-1654). In 1632 Holland penetrated Spain's zone of interest and occupied Curaçao. Through the Treaty of Breda these territories were taken over by Surinam. In 1815 Holland became a world power through its re-occupation of "Dutch India" (Indonesia with the exception of Java). The Second World War gave Indonesia its independence and brought autonomy to the Dutch Antilles.

THE ITALIANS

Less heeded and less significant than the overseas endeavors of Spain, Portugal, Britain, France and the Netherlands were the colonialization attempts of the Italians. The reasons why they were powerless against the global distribution plans of the other European countries in the sixteenth, seventeenth and eighteenth centuries lay in the centuries-old political structure of the peninsula. Nine years after Italy's first autonomous statehood through Cavour (1861),

The explorers made only fleeting sketches of the exotic landscapes, which were later elaborated on by artists; the disadvantage of this method, of course, was that the artists had never seen the motifs with their own eyes. The advent of photography put an end to this situation. The two African landscapes shown here were photographed on black-and-white plates and subsequently colored by a lithographer.

the Italians occupied the Bay of Assab (a harbor on the Red Sea), which they then used as a point of departure for their African expansion. In 1885 Turkey ceded Massaua (northern Ethiopia) to Italy and in 1889 the Treaty of Uccialli gave Italy the so-called "moral" protectorate over Abyssinia. In 1890 Italy founded the colony of Eritrea and in 1905 Somaliland. 1912 saw a significant territorial expansion of the Italian empire: It was joined by Tripolitania and Cyre-

This uncritical depiction of a South American slave market in no way gives a true representation of the terrible reality. Contemporary Europeans regarded slavery as legitimate.

Chained and herded together like animals, the natives were transported to Europe as "illustrative material". The few foot fetters to be seen here fail to give a true picture of the horrendous conditions below deck.

naica. In 1926 Italy acquired Djuba (south of Italian Somaliland), and in 1931 the Al Kufrah Oasis in Libya. Only four years later the whole of Libya and, in 1936, Abyssinia were in Italian hands. Italy's colonial power, built on economically rather insignificant territories, practically ceased to exist in 1941.

THE GERMANS

Germany acquired its colonies at an even later stage than Italy. In 1897 it secured Kouatchou, the Carolina and Mariana Islands in the Pacific and settled in Togo, Cameroon, German Southwest Africa and German East Africa. The First World War put an end to this very brief period of colonization.

THE RUSSIANS

The conquest and penetration of Siberia took place more or less in the background of world and colonial politics. This was initiated by the Stroganovs, a pioneering family from Novgorod. The military conquest ran more or less parallel to the economic penetration. A great deal of credit must go to the Cossack Jermak Timofeyevich, who served the Stroganovs. The subjugation of Siberia on the orders of the Moscow central government was carried out in a number of stages. When one region had been liberated, troops immediately began building "ostrogs" (fortified settlements), which soon developed into cities and trading centers.

In this way, the town of Tobolsk (1587) was founded at the confluence of the rivers Ob and Irtysh, Tara (1594) was established on the Irtysh, Surugt (1594) on the Ob, Obdorsk (1595) east of the Ob estuary, Tomsk (1604) on the Ob, Turuchansk (1607) on the estuary of the lower Tunguska in Yenisei, Jakutiske (1632) on the Lena, Okhotskoya (1649) on the Sea of Okhotsk, and Nershinsk (1658) and Albasin (1665), to mention just the main centers.

The Treaty of Nershinsk (1689) consolidated the border between Russia and China. Without possessing the Kamtshatka peninsula or the outermost region of northern Siberia, the Czar had the largest empire in the world in terms of sheer size.

The business-minded Stroganovs extracted considerable quantities of salt from the "territory of the cold", which sold exceptionally well even in Italy. The well-to-do czar's court and the boyars (noble classes) were good customers for the many rare furs from the region.

CONQUERORS, ADVENTURERS AND RESEARCHERS

Our attempts so far to illustrate to our readers the foreign policies of the most powerful European countries in broad outlines shows that "becoming acquainted" was anything but peaceful in those days. However, simply placing the blame on the so-called "conquistadores", whether they went by the name of Cortez, Pizarro or Jermak, would be completely wrong and would distort the historical facts.

These people were soldiers with their own moral standards, not honorable crusaders, and most certainly not good Samaritans. They were in the service of a ruler who awarded them with titles (most of which had no political value) and gave them exceptionally vague codes of conduct, usually in the form of a memorandum. And these conquerors and explorers made use of these "decrees" in accordance with the diverse situations they found themselves in. And we hardly need mention that these adventurers made full use of their special rights as soon as they were away from the control of their rulers.

Rivalry among the conquerors, their urge to gain riches quickly, their individual struggles for more and more power over the newly discovered territories and their unscrupulous behavior towards the American native peoples gave rise to centuries of rightful criticism, which

SINEESE UROUWEN
Mulieres Chinenses.

The engravings of the Dutchman Johan Nieuhof conveyed a harmonious, peaceful image of China to the astounded Europeans. Rather than inventing wondrous creatures, Nieuhof provided accurate, detailed documentation of the country and its inhabitants.

SINEESE MANNEN.
Viri Chinenses.

was principally directed at the conquerors and adventurers themselves. However, censure of the rulers in whose service they operated was less severe, regardless of country or religion. But we should bear in mind that it was they who issued the "privileges" to these broadswords, who above all brought their masters wealth and political and personal prestige, which many of them urgently needed, depending on the political situation in their respective countries. In those days there was no international public law in existence that would have improved the political moral attitudes of the two parties involved. However, a comparison with the twentieth century will readily show that in quite a number of respects, the "encounter of the civilizations" would not have been much milder in more recent times.

What encouraged the Portuguese, followed by Spain, Britain, France, the Netherlands, Belgium, Germany and Italy, to reach out to foreign and unknown lands across the seas?

In many history books, improvements in the compass are given as the main reason behind this urge to explore foreign lands. This may be true to a certain extent; but the Vikings had no maritime instruments whatever and still they were able to overcome vast distances on the open seas. Moreover, they did this in open rowing boats.

Let us look back to the fifteenth century. Under King João I the Portuguese began systematically settling in northern Africa. The campaign was religiously motivated at first: for centuries, Islam had economically exploited southern Portugal. The task was now to fight Islam in its "own" country; there was thus no alternative but to go to Africa with a naval fleet and an army.

The first large-scale conflict was in Ceuta, more or less on the edge of the Sahara. Here the Portuguese did not just come into contact with a culture that they knew, Islam, but also with the wholesalers who came to Fez from Gao on the

European encounter with the inhabitants of Brazil: This scene was documented by Moritz Rugendas in his work "Picturesque Travels through Brazil" from 1835. Noteworthy is the patronizing attitude of these explorers towards the "savages".

Niger via Timbuktu, Wadan (a trading center around 600 km or 370 miles northeast of Timbuktu) and via Sidi Moussa (a market town approximately 600 km south of Fez), to barter their products and exchange news. These merchants were the most important bringers of news during the Middle Ages.

Taking part in the "Sahara market life" and fighting Islam were the two primary goals of Portuguese expansion.

When Vasco da Gama set out on his journey to Calicut, his motives were still the same. The only difference was that on the one hand, the military deployment was larger and on the other hand, the territorial and economic profits were considerably higher. Islam was still Portugal's major enemy and also put up resistance to the Lusitanian expansion in the orient.

The nation-state egotism of the two Iberian countries, which reached its culmination under the Catholic monarchs Ferdinand and Isabella, enticed the Castilians and Aragonians to engage in even fiercer armed combat than the Portuguese in building up an empire. Spain was able to take possession of the Central and South American regions with their many gold and silver mines. Greed for these precious metals especially spurred the Spanish on in their search for more and more mines.

Another reason for the urge to explore the "New World" (especially the Iberians) was the missionary zeal which the explorers and their rulers liked to express in the newly claimed overseas territories. In those days it was a matter of course for the Catholic (and later also the Anglican) rulers to consistently convert all their subjects to Catholicism (or Anglicanism) soon after taking possession of the newly gained territories – which, incidentally, was carried out with all due "legal" pomp and ceremony. All voyages of discovery were placed under the sign of the Cross. Territorial gains for the Portuguese and Spanish, later also for Britain and France, meant spreading their country's religion (and growth

in the religious power of the Pope if these were Catholic countries).

At the close of the Middle Ages, the European rulers' desire for political, economic and religious power triggered a veritable wave of overseas invasions. Their campaigns headed in a westerly direction and around Africa because Islam blocked the Near East as an access route to the Far East. Liberating the land route to India would have required the mobilization of all "western" forces and, at the same time, this would have amounted to an all-out confrontation between western Europe and the Middle East. However, western Europe was neither willing nor able to do this. The Crusades are one example of this political and military incompetence of western Europe.

Parallel to the discoveries and conquests in America, Asia and Africa by the western Europeans, there was a shift of both economical and political power in the Mediterranean region. The maritime trading republics of Venice and Genoa, whose fortunes were very closely connected to the Arab exchange of trade, were the two prime casualties of the Portuguese "pepper war". This wasnot merely because shifting the trade routes to the Atlantic represented a serious economic setback for them – Lisbon and Seville also dictated the prices for the precious metals and spices. This was nothing less than a humiliation for these two cities, as merchants from the north now sought their ways on the Tejo and the Guadalquivir.

Up until now the discourse has largely centered around national-state rivalry, the spice wars, which were fought with quite bitter severity, the downfall of the Central and South American cultures following the advent of the Spanish conquistadors, the overseas economical and political aspirations of European countries – in other words, around national-state arrogance and expedient political egotism. Thus, the fifteenth and sixteenth centuries were principally the era of adventurers.

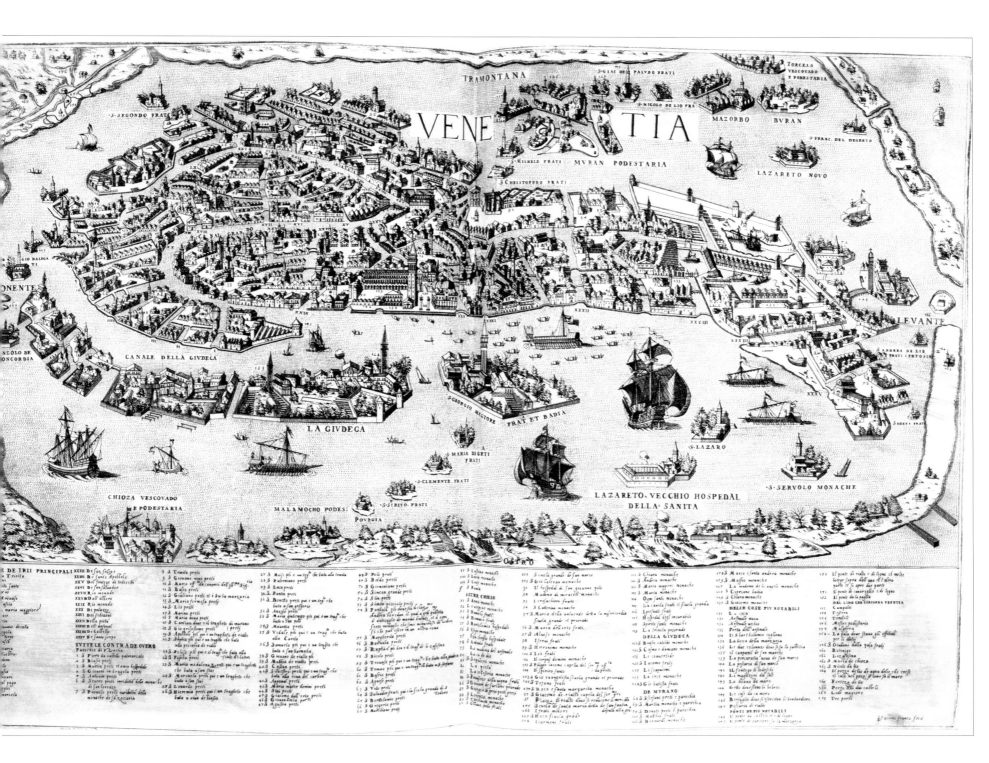

On the other hand, the centuries to follow – the seventeenth, eighteenth and nineteenth, and even the twentieth century – were characterized by the actions of scientific researchers.

These researchers, whether sponsored and commissioned by governments or financed by private patrons, achieved a great deal for the advancement of science. Each and every one of their findings represented some form of progress in the areas of geography, zoology, botany, ethnography or glaciology. Most of these researchers and explorers were lone wolves who set out to make discoveries purely in the name of science; of course, they would also have had a certain love of adventure.

As regards the following section of the history of research and exploration, I have attempted to summarize it as far as possible into geograph-

Venice was a hub of activity in overseas trade. This illustration shows great attention to detail in the representation of the individual buildings.

ical and chronological blocks. It is also intended as a supplement to the alphabetically structured individual biographies, which can be found further on in this encyclopedia.

A VOYAGE THROUGH THE HISTORY OF EXPLORATION

The first people to be gripped by the excitement of travel and to leave Europe were generally pilgrims. The travel reports that they personally wrote or had written by others are often full of contradictions and geographical untruths, for instance the report from the Irish monk Brendan who claimed that he discovered the Azores in the sixth century.

During the seventh century, the French theologian Arkulf visited Palestine and other countries of the region; however, he did not describe his travels in detail.

In the ninth century, the Venetian Sanudo undertook four to six journeys to the Near East. He left for posterity a description of this part of Asia, which was virtually unknown from a geographical point of view in those days.

The pilgrims were followed by the legations from the French king Louis the Pious. The most important of these "travel diplomats" and negotiators was the resourceful Carpini.

Laurentius of Portugal, a Franciscan monk, was by Pope Innocent IV to the court of the Mongol ruler Batu (a nephew of Genghis Khan) on the Volga. Laurentius' travel diaries, written by Carpini, provide the first specific references to life and conditions in Russia in those days.

The Franciscan monk John of Montecorvina traveled across China in 1288 and died before returning from the "Middle Kingdom".

The Spaniard R. G. de Clavijo was sent by Henry III of Castilia to visit the powerful Mongol emperor Tamerlan, who held court in Samarkand in 1404. His records are more prosaic than those of his predecessor. Interesting, however, are his descriptions of the town of Samarskand-

skiy, which completely coincide with the geographical conditions at that time.

The Florentine merchant Pegoletti journeyed from the Sea of Asov via the old trade route right across Asia, finally ending up in China; his reports abound with practical and behavioral recommendations for merchants who traveled to the Far East in those days. And the name Marco Polo speaks for itself.

The Late Middle Ages belonged to the governmental and royal envoys and the merchants as travelers and observers of foreign customs and habits, but the era was also characterized by the pure spirit of adventure.

A German by the name of Hans Schiltberger from Munich served as a soldier under Tamerlan and in the course of his duties traveled across extensive parts of Asia known in those days as the "Golden" and "White Hordes".

N. Conti, from Venice, settled in Damascus while he was still quite young, learned to speak the Arab language and journeyed throughout the lands around the Persian Gulf. As "punishment" for his temporary fall from Christianity, when he returned to Rome, the Pope commanded him to write a detailed travel report.

But the Far North also received its fair share of attention. The Norwegian Ottar is said to have traveled across Lapland in the ninth century and to have researched the shores of the White Sea. According to the sagas (Scandinavian heroic sagas), Nadod, a Norwegian pirate, was driven on to the east coast of Iceland by a storm. The Norwegian Ingølfer, banished from his homeland because he had committed murder, sailed to Iceland and, in 874 AD, founded Reykjavik.

Besides the European travelers and adventurers, Arabian globetrotters also set out to explore strange lands and cultures.

Sallam, an interpreter at the court of the Caliph of Baghdad, was commissioned by his master to explore the banks of the Caspian Sea in the ninth century. During the tenth century Ibn Khordadbeh, Istakhari and Ibn Haukal traveled across almost all of the regions of Africa and Asia that were under Islamic rule at the time. In 921 AD Ibn Fadlan undertook a journey to the Volga, in order to convert the Bulgars who were settled there (Volga Bulgars) to Islam. The celebrated cartographer Idrisi from Ceuta journeyed throughout all the Mediterranean countries during the twelfth century and provided the first overview of the known world at that time. Ibn Battuta traveled both to Southeast Asia and to West Africa.

The fifteenth and sixteenth centuries were characterized by the significant undertakings of the Portuguese and Spanish. The west and east African coasts, Indonesia, the Caribbean islands and South America were discovered and explored. These two centuries also saw the first advances made into Arctic America. The search for the Northwest Passage had begun in earnest.

In 1472, two Danish pirates by the names of Pothorst and Pining were commissioned by the Danish king Christian I to sail to the east coast of North America, where they discovered Newfoundland and the Gulf of Saint Laurence. The Cortereal brothers are even said to have reached the 60° northern parallel. In 1523, the Florentine Verrazano explored the Labrador region on the orders of the French king Francis I, with the aim of finding the Northwest Passage. The Portuguese E. Gomez charted the first map from the coast of Florida to Labrador in 1525.

The first circumnavigations of the world were also carried out in the sixteenth century. Magellan (whose world circumnavigation ended on the Philippines) was followed in the next century by Cavendish, Dampier, Anson, J. Byron, S. Wallis, Cook and Carteret, all from Britain, the Frenchmen Bougainville, and Dupetit-Thouars, the Russian Kotzebue, O. van Noort and Roggeveen from the Netherlands and the Italian G. Carelli. The objective of these global circumnavigations, apart from hydrographical research of the world's oceans, was to define the major shipping lanes.

CAPTAIN COOK

London Published as the Act directs Sept 20 1800 by J Wilkes

The tangle of islands north of Australia, the Sandwich Islands, the New Hebrides, the Ladrones and the Society Islands (all located in the Pacific), were already explored in the sixteenth century by the Spaniards J. de Grivalja and P. de Alvarado (New Guinea), R. López de Villabolos (Carolinas, Philippines), Y. Ortíz de Retes (New Guinea), A. de Mendaña (Solomons, Marquesas), P. F. Quiroz (New Hebrides) and

Captain Cook was England's most famous and significant seafarer and explorer.

Torres (the strait between New Guinea and Australia), by the Englishmen Gilbert and Marshall (Gilbert Islands and Marshall Islands) and by L. I. Duperry from France (Dumont d'Urville Island).

The Australian coast and Tasmania were mainly explored by the Dutch. W. Janszoon reached the Gulf of Carpentaria. D. Hartog discovered the "Eendracht coast", and J. Carstenz dropped anchor in "Arnhem Land". P. van Nuytz was driven by a storm on to the coast of New Holland. G. Th. Pool explored the shores of New Guinea, and Abel Tasman discovered "Van Diemen's Land", which is now known as Tasmania. From Britain, M. Flinders proved that Tasmania was an island, and G. Bass, another British seafarer and compatriot of Flinders, went on land at "Botany Bay" (one of the first areas of Sydney to be settled).

Indonesia was visited by the Portuguese V. Lourenzo (1526, Borneo), M. Pinto (1540, Sunda Islands) and by the Spaniard L. de Legazpi (1567, Philippines) and his companion Urdañeta (1565, Moluccas).

During the sixteenth century the south Atlantic and the Magellan Strait were the operational field of the Spaniard J. Ladrilleros, Hawkins and Davis from Britain (Falkland Islands), the Dutch Mahu, Gerrits, Cordes, Wert and Adam and the Belgian Le Maire ("Le Maire Strait") and his companion Schouten.

In the sixteenth century, the west coast of South and North America and the Northwest Passage were the destinations of the Spanish, represented by Quevara (the coast of what is today Chile), J. R. Cabrillo (California), Juan Fernández (Juan Fernández Islands, west of Santiago de Chile), J. de la Fuca (Strait of Vancouver) and the Russian Chirikov (the coast of Alaska).

Exploration of the Sahara and the Niger Basin was initiated in 1798 by the German explorer Hornemann, who came as far as Mursuk (1801). J. Fremdenburgh, another German, traveled along the Fessan. The British explorer G. F. Lyon brought back the first information about the Tuaregs to Europe. J. Richardson, a British missionary, explored large parts of the desert as part of an alliance with the Germans Overweg and Heinrich Barth. However, the most significant researchers and explorers were the French, with Duveyrier, Foucauld and Caillié. The German Africa explorer Gerhard Rohlfs earned himself a reputation through his geographical and ethnographic exploration of Morocco, the western Sahara and Libya.

In the course of the nineteenth century and at the start of the twentieth, the Sahara Desert was explored above all by people such as the French Foureau (Tassili N'jjer), Lamy (Chad), Gentil (Morocco), Gautier (western Sahara), Guillo-Lohan (Hoggar), Laperine (Adrar), Nieger (western Sahara), Cuny (Libyan coast), Dournaux-Dupère and Joubert (western and central Sahara), V. Largeau (Hoggar), P. Soleillet (Tuat Oasis), Palat (South Oranais), the German Oskar Lenz (Atlas Saharian, Tindouf Oasis) and the French Haardt and Audoin-Dubreuil (central Sahara), Monod and Lhote (southern Algeria).

The search for the sources of the Niger was initiated as early as 1699 by the French medical practitioner C. Poncet, who had settled in Cairo. Accompanied by the Jesuit priest Xavier de Bredevent, he proceeded as far as Dongola, the ancient capital of Nubia. Between 1792 and 1796 the British archaeologist W. G. Browne advanced into Darfur and was the first to identify the Bahr al Abjad as the principal tributary of the Nile. In the year 1824, the German explorer E. Rüppel investigated approximately 90 km (55 miles) of the White Nile, and Dr. Werne, another German explorer of Africa, reached the No Swamps, which had never before been seen by a European. The Austrian consul in Khartoum, T. von Heuglin, the German Africa explorers Georg Schweinfurth and Gustav Nachtigal, A. Tinné from the Netherlands, and the Italian explorers Miani and Piaggia also investigated an extensive region between the White Nile and the Blue Nile.

The heart of Africa and its great lakes, the so-called "African inland sea", was the particular interest of the British explorers Burton, Speke, Grant, Baker, Lugard, Gordon, Stanley and Livingstone, but also of the Germans Eduard Schnitzer (Emin Pacha) and the Duke of Mecklenburg and Oskar Baumann from Austria.

Abyssinia and Somaliland were the early destinations of the Portuguese explorers Payva (1487), Calvao (1515), R. de Lima (sixteenth century), Paez (who discovered the sources of the Blue Nile in 1615), the Swiss Burckhardt (nineteenth century) and the French brothers d'Abbadie. They were followed by the German explorers Ludwig Krapf, Erhardt (an important cartographer), Karl-Klaus von der Decken, J. Pfeil and Hans Mayer, the Hungarian S. Teleki and the Italians Cecchi, Chiarini, Giuletti, Borelli and Bottego.

The exploration of Lake Chad and the surrounding region as well as the sources of the Niger was the work of the British Houghton (1789), Mungo Park (1800), Baikie (1857–1864), Lander (1832–1834), G. Laing (1822), Dr. Denham (1821–1824), Clapperton (1821–1824), the French L. G. Binger (1886) and E. Gentil (1895–1898), the German-Russian Eduard Robert Flegel and the Germans Eduard Vogel, Heinrich Barth and Adolf Overweg. As early as 1494 the Portuguese Diego Cão traveled up the Congo (which in those days was still known as Zaire) from the Atlantic, followed by the Italians Cavazzi (sixteenth century), Placenca (1667) and Zuchelli (1696), Frenchmen Belloni du Chaillu (1855) and Brazza (1881), who explored the River Gabon, the Belgians Coquilhat, A. Thys (1887) and Van Gele (1889) and the Germans Wissmann and Dr. L. Wolf (1883, on commission from the Belgian king Leopold II), who investigated the region that was later to become the Republic of Congo.

In 1798, L. E. Almeida, from Portugal, attempted the first east-west crossing of central Africa, while the Hungarian Magyar reached the lower Congo and the River Kasai on the upper Zambezi from Bihé (1847–1852).

The Swede Sparrmann (1772–1776, Mosselbaai) and Wahlberg (1841, Vaal), the German explorer Karl Mauch (1871, Limpopo and Zimbabwe) and the Frenchman Grandidier (1865) explored the region of southern Africa in particular.

Great scientific undertakings right across Africa were carried out by the Portuguese Coimbra (1814–1824, Moçambique-Benguela), Serpa Pinto (1852, Zanzibar-Benguela), J. d. Silva, R. Ivens and H. Capelo, the British Bruce, Livingstone, Stanley and Cameron and by the German Africa explorer Gerhard Rohlfs.

Before North America was explored from a scientific aspect, it had suffered a military conquest. From 1532 to 1535, the Spaniard A. Nuñez (Cabeca de Vaca) traveled back and forth around the Mississippi, the Arkansas, the Arizona and the Colorado. Hernando de Soto trekked through Florida on his search for precious metals and reached the Mississippi, where he died of fever in 1543. Fr. V. de Coronado reached the Colorado and, from 1541 to 1542, explored Texas. In 1595 J. d'Onate explored the Río del Norte.

The camps of the scientific explorers had little to offer in the way of comfort. This historical photograph from the turn of the last century shows a tent from the Duke of Mecklenburg's African expedition.

In 1565 the two Frenchmen Jean Ribaut and Landonnière, together with 400 settlers and soldiers, settled in Florida and founded a Protestant colony.

During the sixteenth century the Mississippi Basin was explored by the well-known French America explorers Cavelier de la Salle, Marquette and Jolliet, Hennepin, Le Moine d'Iberville, the Mallet brothers and the British Jonathan Smith (the founder of Jamestown), William Penn and James Finley.

Canada attracted scientific explorers as early as the seventeenth century. For instance, in 1679 the Frenchman Dulhut reached what is today known as Winnipeg and L. J. La Vérendrye advanced as far as the Saskatchewan in 1749.

Commissioned by the Hudson Bay Company, Groseilliers and Radisson explored eastern Canada (in the mid-seventeenth century), H. Kelsey explored Lake Winnipeg (1690), J. Knight researched the northeastern region of Canada (1719), W. Pink (1766-1773) explored the Churchill River, S. Fraser (1807) the river that was later to bear his name; Fraser advanced as far as the Pacific.

Scientific expeditions through Canada were undertaken by the British geologist C. Lyell (1841), who explored Nova Scotia, the Canadian geologist J. W. Dawson (who researched the Red River and Lake Winnipeg in 1857) and G. M. Dawson, who explored British Columbia. From 1877 to 1890 R. Bell traveled extensively throughout Labrador.

The Rocky Mountains were investigated by the celebrated American explorer John Charles Frémont (1841–1846), the New York fur dealer John Astor (1809) and his companion Stuart (1812–1813). Further expeditions were carried out by J. Newberry-Strong (1851), J. W. Powell (1869–1872), Crawford (1871) and V. F. Hayden (1867). These research expeditions, which primarily served to examine the mountains' geological properties, were also aimed at finding valuable fur-bearing animals.

Primeval forest in the province of Rio de Janeiro: The routes taken by the explorers frequently took them through dense jungle and woodland. This idyllic representation gives no impression of the dangers and tribulations with which the explorers were constantly faced.

As early as 1711 the Russian P. Popov described Alaska in great detail. After Popov, America's largest northern peninsula was explored by the Russians Chestakov (1726), Fedorov (1730), Bering (a Dane in Russian service) and by Chirikov (1741) and Lavashev (1764–1771). In 1883 Mount St. Elias was conquered by F. Chvatka, who was followed in 1897 by the Duke of Abruzzo.

In the fifteenth century in addition to the military conquest, South America was peacefully penetrated by the Spanish. Under conditions of extreme hardship, Francisco de Orellana was the first European to travel along the entire Amazon to the point where it flows into the Atlantic (1541). The German missionary Samuel Fritz explored almost the entire Amazon Basin in the years from 1686 to 1707. The French La Condamine and Saint-Hilaire, Humboldt's friend, as well as the French botanist A. Bonpland, the Portuguese A. R. Ferreira (1783–1793), Spix and Martius (1817–1819), the Russian Langsdorf (1824), the British explorer Chandless (1862–1869) and the French ethnographer Lévi-Strauss (1939) explored the Brazilian rainforest.

The Guyana Plateau was mainly explored by the French physician J. Crevaux (1876–1882) and by the Czech explorer E. S. Vraz (1889–1893). The area that is now Argentina was the major research destination of the explorer F. Moreno (1874), while the German H. Burmeister traveled extensively throughout Uruguay from 1856 to 1861.

As early as the sixteenth century the Italian L. di Barthema undertook the journey from Damascus to Mecca and Medina. He was the first European ever to set foot in either of the two holy Islamic cities. After his ship had been wrecked in 1505, the Portuguese captain Gr. da Quadras reached Baghdad, Basra and Hormuz from the Yemenite coast, although he suffered inexpressible hardship on the way. A British traveling merchant by the name of Jourdain traveled throughout southern Yemen in 1610. Apart from

Carsten Niebuhr, who is probably the best known Yemen explorer, the Arabian peninsula and in particular Yemen and Hadhramaut, were explored by the German scientist U. J. Seetzen from 1802 to 1807, the British Captain G. F. Sadlier (1819), the British explorers Moresby and Haines (1831–1834), J. Wellsted (1835), G. Palgrave (1862), the Finn G. A. Wallin (1848), Juray-Juray (1862) from Syria, the British geologist J. Th. Bent and his wife (late nineteenth century).

In the seventeenth century exploratory expeditions to Afghanistan, Persia, Syria, Palestine were organized by the German E. Kaempfer, Elphistone (1808) from Britain, the Hungarian A. H. B. Vambéry (late nineteenth century, in search of the origins of the Hungarian language), the American E. Robinson (1838), the French archaeologist H. Waddington (1850–1860) and the Russians Chikachev (1847–1858) and Pastuchov (1890).

India, the Himalayas, Nepal and Tibet were the subject of the exploratory work of the French F. Pyrard (1602), J. B. Tavernier (1632–1638), the British R. Knox (1657–1679), Dr. Fr. Buchanan (1794–1802), Major W. Lambton (1800), W. Moorcroft (1812), Sir George Everest (1813–1817) and two German researchers, the Schlagintweit brothers.

The Jesuit priest A. Rhodes visited Indochina between 1619 and 1627. Commissioned by the ruler of Cochin China, the French J. M. Dayot prepared a map of the coast of Annam. The British military physician J. Crawford explored Burma, Laos and Siam between 1826 and 1837. From 1858 to 1861, the French natural scientist H. Mouhot undertook a scientific expedition through Siam and Cambodia and discovered the ruins of Angkor. A. Bastian, a German explorer, was the first European to explore the Malacca peninsula. In 1866 Frenchman Doudart de Lagrée explored the Mekong River. Over the course of a quarter of a century, Auguste Pavie explored the whole of Indochina (1870–1895), and the French

Prince of Orleans died in 1901 after undertaking a lengthy expedition through the Tonkin, in Saigon.

Besides the missionaries Ricci, Schall, Goes, Naverette (sixteenth and seventeenth centuries), the Hungarian geologist Cholnoky (1896–1898), the French Legendre and Dessidier (early twentieth century) and the German explorer Richthofen gained widespread acclaim for their scientific expeditions to southern and central China.

Mongolia and Tibet were visited by the British explorers G. Bogle (1774) and S. Turner (1783) as well as by Russian explorers and scientists such as P. Semenov (1857), P. Potanin (1861–1892), Olga and Alexis Fedchenko (1860-1868), Pievzov (1888), the Grum-Grchimailo brothers (1889), and by Valikanov (1858) and Sapochnikov (1902). In the period from 1868 to 1872, the British explorer E. Ney examined the Great Wall of China, while A. Stein (also from Britain) explored the Gobi Desert, and Sven Hedin from Sweden is regarded as the most knowledgeable expert on Asia of the nineteenth and twentieth centuries.

The Cossack Jermak Timofeyevich was responsible for both the military and the scientific exploration of Siberia in 1577. He was followed by the Russians I. Moskvitine, who had already reached the Sea of Okhotsk in 1639, W. Paiarkov (1643, Amur), Khabarov (1653, Oleka River), F. Baikov (1654, Gobi Desert), Fedorov (1732, northeastern Siberia), Gvozdev (1732, Kamchatka), Muraviev and Pavlov (1735, the Archangel region), Malyguine (1736, Obi River), Cheljuskin (1742, Cape Cheljuskin), Ladrintsev (1889, Tola River) and Skolietov (1874, Amur Basin).

Other European researchers also took part in the scientific exploration of the sheer vastness of Siberia, such as the Germans B. D. G. Messerschmidt (1719, scientific expedition through Siberia), Steller (1737–1745, Tomsk, Yenisei, Kamchatka), J. G. Gmelin (1733–1749, Lake Baikal), A. Erman (1828-1829, Ural to Kamchat-

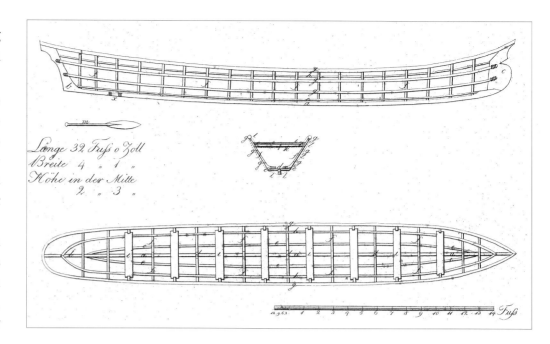

Länge 32 Fuß 0 Zoll
Breite 4 " 1 "
Höhe in der Mitte
2 " 3 "

ka) and Alexander von Humboldt. British explorers were also involved, such as J. D. Cochrane (early nineteenth century, Urals to Jakutiske), as were the Finnish explorer M. A. Castren (1843–1850, Urals, Altay mountains) and the Swede F. S. Strahlenberger (1709–1721).

Japan was discovered more or less by accident in 1542 by the Portuguese A. de Moto. Seven years later, the missionary Franz Xaver reached the Japanese islands. We are indebted to him for the first comprehensive reports from Nippon, which was hostile to Europe at that time. Engelbert Kaempfer visited Yeso in 1630, and the German explorer Fr. v. Siebold settled as a physician in Japan in 1823. He is regarded as the first scientific explorer of this Far Eastern empire.

The first governor of New South Wales, A. Philipp, founded the colony of Port Jackson on the east coast of Australia (1787) with several convicts who had been released on probation. The settlement of the fifth continent had now started on the southeast coast, albeit rather hesitantly at first. J. Oxley (1812–1823), M. Currie (1823), A. Cunningham (1827) and Th. L. Mitchell (1831–1845) explored the eastern and southern parts of Australia.

Central Australia was opened up from a scientific point of view by Charles Sturt (1829-

In his travel report from the years 1803 to 1807, Georg Heinrich von Langsdorff documented the refined design of the canoes he had seen in Alaska.

1844), Burke O'Hara, Gray (1861), Wills (1852–1861), King (1861) and, above all John McDonald Stuart; western and southwestern Australia were explored by S. G. Grey (1838–1841), E. J. Eyre, A. C. Gregory (1845–1865), J. W. Gregory (1901), J. Forrest (1869), R. Austin (1854) and S. Hart (1872–1875). Expeditions to the north and northwest of the country were organized by Friedrich Wilhelm Ludwig Leichhardt (1842 to 1848), Buchanan (1878), A. Forrest (1869–1879) and Calvert (1896).

In 1585, five hundred years after Eric's attempts to colonize Greenland, the British seafarer J. Davis risked an advance to Greenland's west coast, which he named "Land of Desolation". The Dane Hans Egede undertook a large-scale ethnographic exploration through Greenland from 1721 to 1736, and we can thank William Scoresby from Britain for the first glaciological report from the world's largest island (1807–1822). Special merit goes to the British explorers W. Baffin, Hudson, Button, Bylot, James, Ghillham, J. Ross, J. C. Ross, Sabine, Franklin and Parry for their exploratory work in and around Greenland.

The "Search for Franklin" (after the lost British Arctic explorer J. Franklin) was also a race to find the Northwest Passage. Apart from the British physician Dr. J. Rae (1864–1869), the American Ch. F. Hall (1864–1869) and the Briton McClintock (1848–1852, 1857), R. McClure was the most successful. He conquered the entire length of the Northwest Passage (1853).

The nineteenth century saw intensive exploration of the Canadian Arctic. The British explorer J. Richardson (1848, with Dr. Rae from the Mackenzie River to Cape Krusenstern), Sir G. Back (1823 and 1833, the region to the north of Slave Lake and Whale River), Dease, Simpson and William, the last three employees of the Hudson Bay Company (HBC), the American Hayes (1869, Ellesmere and Grinnell Islands), the British whaler J. Palliser (White Fish River and Kaministikwia, 1857), as well as Stefansson and Rasmussen are regarded as the true pioneers of this immeasurably large territory of the North American subcontinent.

In 1553 the British explorer H. Willoughby set out on a journey to the White Sea, with the intention of discovering the Northeast Passage. He probably reached the twin island of Novaya Zemlya; neither he nor his companions returned from this undertaking. Also in 1553 R. Chancellor, a fellow countryman of Willoughby, landed close to Archangel, but he then decided to carry on to Moscow when he realized that it was not possible to advance further at that time. S. Burrough, another British seafarer, discovered Lake Kara and carried on to reach Vaygach Island (1556). On the orders of Queen Elisabeth I, the British seafarers Pett and Jackman repeated Burrough's journey, however without success (1580). The Dutch explorer Willem Barents attempted the breakthrough in 1594; however, he and part of his crew were killed while returning from Novaya Zemlya in the direction of the Kola peninsula.

In 1676, the Briton Wood was commissioned by the English king Charles II to make an attempt to reach China via the Northeast Passage; however, he was forced to give up this attempt not far from Novaya Zemlya.

The Russian admiral F. P. Lutke explored the west coast of Novaya Zemlya and the land of the Chukchi. The Austrian Count Wilczeck reached a latitude of 78° 48' N (1871), while the British Captain Viggins discovered the mouth of the Yenisei (1874). However, the victor in the race to conquer the Northeast Passage was the Swede Nordenskiöld.

In 1913 the Russian Vilkitski was the first to pass the Northeast Passage from east to west, and 19 years later the Russian mathematician and Arctic explorer Otto Schmidt required just three months to conquer the Northeast Passage from Archangel to the Bering Strait.

The race for the North Pole was started in 1587 with the advance of the Briton J. Davis, who reached a latitude of 72° 12' N. The British

Exploration of the Arctic and Antarctic waters called for courage and endurance. The ships frequently had to fight their way through pack ice on their return to the open sea.

Drawings and photographs from Fridtjof Nansen's Norwegian Arctic expedition of 1893-1896. Huskies were essential for travel over the expanses of ice. The photograph below shows how the explorers whiled away the evening hours.

explorer Hudson went still further in 1607, reaching 80° 23' N, and in 1806 Scoresby reached 81° 30' N; Parry managed 82° 47' N in 1827. In 1895 the Norwegian Nansen (drifting) reached a latitude of 86° 12' N and in 1900 the Italian Cagni went as far as 86° 34' N. On 6 April,

1909, the American explorer Peary reached the North Pole on foot and in 1926 the American Arctic explorer Byrd was the first to fly over the North Pole.

In addition to the "traditional" North Pole explorers, others are remembered for their special services in regard to Arctic research, such as Marckham from Britain (1881, 83° 20' N), the American G. W. de Long (1879, reached the "De Long Islands"), the German Air Captain Eckener (1931, Arctic flight in a Zeppelin), the Russian Otto Schmidt (1937, flew a plane from the Rudolf Islands and landed not far from the North Pole), the Russian Arctic explorer Papanin (1937, set up a scientific station near the North Pole), the Russian pilot Levanevski (1936, first flight from Moscow to San Francisco via the North Pole) and Baidukov, Beliakov and Chkalov (1937, first flight from the Soviet Union to the USA via Greenland).

Two years after J. Davis' attempt to reach the North Pole, the Dutch Gerrits (1589) sailed from Holland to the southern Atlantic, where he discovered the South Shetlands or Graham Land. It was not until 220 years after Gerrits' journey that the South Shetlands were rediscovered by Briton W. Smith. Frenchman Bouvet de Lozier, who was convinced of the existence of a southern continent, discovered an island during his journey of exploration to the Antarctic, which he named "Bouvet Island"; however, ice prevented him landing. Guyot and Duclos, seafarers from Brittany, discovered "St. Peter Island" (South Georgia). In 1771, Marion-Dufresne, a French

From Amundsen's logbook: At the left are compass bearings for the route from Framheim to the supply depot; the table at the right shows the positions of the measuring posts.

Amphibian aircraft not only flew beyond the Arctic Circle, they were also capable of landing on the ice. The engines had to be securely covered in order to be restarted in the freezing conditions.

the Norwegian Amundsen was the first person to reach the South Pole; he was followed by Scott, from Britain on 18 January, 1912. For Scott and his few companions, this undertaking in the Antarctic proved fatal. The American pilot Byrd flew over the South Pole with companions Belchen, McKinley and June for the first time on 28 November, 1929.

Significant scientific expeditions to the Antarctic were carried out in 1873 by the German South Pole researcher E. Dallmann, Belgian M. de Gerlache (1897–1899), German Erich Dagobert von Drygalski (1901), the Swede Nordenskiold (1901–1903), Dr. W. S. Bruce from Scotland (1904–1911), Norwegians Rijser-Larsen (1929–1931), Isachsen and Christensen (1931), the American Byrd (1946–1947, Ross Sea) and the British scientist Fuchs (1957–1958, Weddell Sea to the South Pole).

Antarctic exploration flights were carried out at the start of the twentieth century. The German Antarctic explorer Drygalski crossed Emperor William II Land in a balloon (1902), the Norwegian pilot B. Belchen (with J. Byrd, McKinley and H. June) flew over the South Pole (28 November, 1929), the aviator Eielson flew over Graham Land and Peter I Island in 1928, and the American Ellsworth (with Canadian pilot H. Kenyon) explored a large part of western Antarctica. In 1938-1939 German exploration flights were carried out over New Swabia (northern Antarctica), for the first time with a catapult start.

Up until now we have only discussed Europeans and Arabs exploring unknown lands and peoples. But there were also travelers from other regions and directions, for instance from the "Middle Kingdom", where explorers set out in a westerly direction, without quite reaching Europe. From 399 to 414 AD, Fa Hien, an itinerant Chinese monk, undertook an extended pilgrimage and exploratory journey through Asia, reaching Lop Nur Lake and the town of Kotan. Huan Tsang, another Chinese monk, explored the Pamir Mountains in China and the Altai Moun-

marine officer, undertook an extensive journey to the waters of the Antarctic. Another Frenchman, Kerguélen de Trémarec, while searching for "Lozier-Bouvet Island", discovered the Antarctic outposts, the "Kerguélen Islands". In 1772 James Cook reached a latitude of 71° 10' S.

The first expeditions to the Antarctic were carried out by two British whalers, Palmer and Powell; in 1820, they found the South Orkney Islands. The Russian Bellingshausen reached 69° 30' S and landed on two unknown islands which he named "Peter I" and "Alexander I" (western Antarctica). In 1821, the Englishman Weddell pushed forward to 74° 15' S (Weddell Sea), the American Morrell, in the service of the London merchant Enderby, crossed the 65° 7' S parallel, explored the islands of Adelaide and Biscoe as well as Graham Land (1830–1831), Briton J. Balleny, also in the service of the Enderbys from London, discovered the "Balleny Islands" (1839), H. Foster, also from Britain, explored the South Shetland Islands (1829), and American C. Wilkes charted the coast of East Antarctica from 1840 to 1842.

The race for the South Pole began in 1774 with James Cook, who reached a latitude of 71' 10' S. In 1899, Norwegian E. Borchgrevink crossed 78° 5' S and the Briton Shackleton got as far as 88° 23' S in 1909. On 15 December, 1911,

*Photographs from
Nansen's report
"In Night and Ice",
published in 1897*

tains in Mongolia and visited the Buddhist shrines of India, especially those of Bénarès. His journey lasted from 629 to 645 AD, and his travel report provides the first specific references to early India. "Voyages of discovery" and expeditions from other distant countries to Europe are not without a certain attraction. For instance, one sees the Europe of the 1870s from a completely different perspective on reading the curious travel diary of the Persian Shah Nasreddin (1873).

The history of discovery would not be complete if a few words were not dedicated to the European "cooperation" in the fifteenth and sixteenth centuries. Many talented seafarers and pilots came from Florence and Pisa, Genoa and Venice. They entered the service of Portugal and Spain, where there was a constant demand for well-trained, daredevil sailors. Others came from Germany, such as Martin Behaim from Bohemia, who captained Cão's ship safely to the Gulf of Guinea (1482–1486) and provided cartographic material. The ships of the Portuguese and Spanish had an international crew. Besides Castilians and Aragonians, the Basques, Italians, French and British sailors took part in these crossings. In those days, anyone who felt a particular urge to travel abroad or for whom things got too hot for comfort in their homeland signed on in Lisbon, Seville or Cadiz. In view of the hazards

The Seafarers' Monument in Lisbon, Portugal

that the sailors faced in the course of these undertakings, the wages were quite modest; but every journey into the unknown brought the promise of bounty.

Germany did not just provide experienced pilots and cartographers. Families such as the Fuggers, Welsers, Gossenbrots, Höchstetters and Hirschvogels, important merchant bankers with global networks in those days, contributed financially to the development of the Spanish colonies. The German conquistadors Sayler, Ehringer, Hohermut, Alfinger, Federmann and Philipp von Hutten traveled back and forth through Venezuela's rainforest in their search for precious metals – with the agreement of the "India Council" of Seville.

It goes without saying that the history of discovery and exploration was anything but a romantic adventure. The above descriptions should make it quite clear which power-political and scientific motives were the mainsprings behind these individual daredevil, epoch-making and, more often than not, catastrophic undertak-ings. But in spite of this we still find a certain attraction in the harsh wind of the centuries in which traveling was a hazardous venture into the unknown, described in the following life stories of some famous and some not so famous explorers and seafarers, discoverers and con-querors and last but not least, the real adventur-ers and globetrotters, the pirates and buccaneers who sailed the Seven Seas.

The following articles, like the summarizing contributions in this book, were prepared to a great extent on the basis of authentic source material. However, historical travel and research literature does not always agree on data and facts or on the spelling of place names and the like. Where these refer to factual statements, they have been checked and standardized where pos-sible. On the other hand, a certain amount of freedom was taken in regard to spelling and naming according to the individual reports, as a consistent equalization across centuries and nations could not possibly take account of the many and diverse testimonies.

SEAFARERS AND EXPLORERS FROM A TO Z

This section presents the most significant seafarers and explorers of our Earth, in alphabetical order from William Adams to Ferdinand Graf von Zeppelin. In addition to biographical dates, the achievements of the individual explorers are described in detail. Extensive suggestions for further reading are an invitation to find out more about these figures of world history.

A

ADAMS, WILLIAM

British seafarer, born 1564 in Gillingham (Kent), died 1620 in Japan.

In 1598, in the position of helmsman, Adams set out with a fleet of five ships from the Dutch island of Texel on a journey to the Far East. The "Erasmus" was shipwrecked, but Adams was able to reach the Japanese mainland. He then built ships according to British designs for Iye-yasu, a shogun (one of the military dictators who ruled Japan from 1192 to 1867). William Adams died in Japan and was buried in the town of Yokosuka.

Adams was the first Englishman to gain high honor in the Japanese imperial court.

Further reading
T. Rundall, The letters of W. Adams, 1611-1617. Memorials of the Empire of Japan. London 1850
C. W. Hillary, England's earliest introduction to intercourse with Japan: the first Englishman in Japan (William Adams) 1600-1620. London and Felling-on-Tyne 1905
The Log-Book of W. Adams, 1614-1619, with the journal of Edward Saris and other documents relating to Japan, China etc. Edited with introduction and notes by C. J. Purnell. London 1916

ALBUQUERQUE, AFFONSO DE

Portuguese seafarer, Viceroy of Portuguese India (East India), born c. 1453 in Alhandra (near Lisbon), died 1515 in Goa (Malabar coast).

The Portuguese Affonso de Albuquerque's conquests helped to make Portugal the leading economic power of the world.

Affonso de Albuquerque's historical "career" did not begin until the start of the sixteenth century, when King Manuel I named him successor to Almeida, the first Viceroy of Portuguese India.

Using force, cunning and diplomatic skill, Albuquerque created an empire that stretched from the Malabar coast right across Malacca to Indonesia. The method of controlling such an enormous territory was the same that had been used on the coast of Africa: landing at favorable positions, setting up pillars of rock bearing coats of arms ("padraos"), constructing forts, leaving behind a small dynamic occupation force and creating trading relationships with the hinterland.

Albuquerque knew that a periodical fleet display would not be sufficient to occupy the Persian Gulf, but that this required a proper military campaign. This undertaking called the Egyptians into action along with the Arabs and their trading partners, the Venetians. The Sultan

of Egypt even threatened to destroy the Holy shrines of Jerusalem. Manuel ignored all the warnings of the royal council, equipped a 2,500-strong army and commissioned Albuquerque with the bold undertaking, which was initiated with a surprise attack on the East African coast. The Arabian fleet was destroyed in the naval battle of Diu (Gujrat). The Portuguese subsequently blocked the Red Sea, defeated the Imam of Masqat, and with the help of Hindu troops, Affonso de Albuquerque conquered the commercial metropolis of Goa in 1510. In doing so he secured the spice monopoly for Portugal for many years to come. However, an attack he lauchned on Mecca proved unsuccessful. The rulers of Siam, Sumatra and Java were forced to pay high tributes. Two of Albuquerque's officers, A. de Abreu and F. Serrao, made successful advances to Bali and the Moluccas in 1511.

Under Albuquerque, Goa became the economic and political center of Portuguese India. His political power was based above all on the superiority of the Portuguese weapons (mainly the ships' artillery), on the speed with which he could move his troops from one place to another, and on the lack of unity among the Arab princes.

Despite the permanent financial problems of the Portuguese crown, Albuquerque also expanded the schooling system. Law and finance were in the hands of the local public servants. Marriage between Portuguese men and Indian women was allowed; however, the women were required to convert to Christianity. Portuguese women were not permitted to settle in Goa. The spread of the Portuguese language in the Indian Empire was pursued with all means at their disposal. Albuquerque also founded a senate; however, only Portuguese citizens were eligible for election.

At the time of the death of Affonso de Albuquerque in 1515, Portugal was the world's first politico-economic power and ruled part of the Atlantic, the Indian Ocean and the western Pacific.

Further reading
C. Pereyra, *La conquête des routes océaniques d'Henri le Navigateur à Magellan, Paris 1923*
G. de Raparaz, *La época de los grandes descubrimientos españoles y portugueses. Paris 1923*
A. Kammerer, *Les guerres du poivre, les Portugais dans l'océan Indien et la Mer Rouge au 16e siècle. Le Caire 1935*

ALDRIN, EDWIN

US American astronaut, born 1930 in Montclair (New Jersey).

The Westpoint graduate was employed by the US Air Force as a pilot and engineering officer before joining NASA in 1963, where he was trained as an astronaut. In 1966, together with

The American Edwin Aldrin was the second man, after Neil Armstrong, to set foot on the surface of the moon.

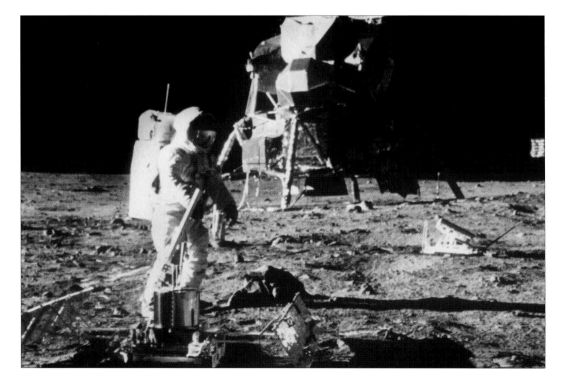

James Lovell, he flew the space capsule "Gemini 12". Between 11 and 15 November, the two astronauts tested the maximum stress that the human body can take in space. During the flight, Aldrin spent a total of 126 minutes outside the capsule, which at that time was the longest maneuver ever to have been carried out in space. From 16 to 24 July, 1969 he was pilot of the moon landing module in "Apollo 11" and set foot on the surface of the moon just 20 minutes after Neil Armstrong, the first man to set foot on the moon.

In 1971 Aldrin left the NASA and returned to the US Air Force as a commanding officer. He was thus the first astronaut to return to military service, although he retired from this in 1972. After various consulting activities, Aldrin accepted a lectureship at the University of North Dakota from 1985 to 1988.

Alexander the Great's campaigns also took him to Egypt. This photograph shows the Pyramids of Gizeh.

Further reading
E. Aldrin, Return to earth. New York 1973
E. Aldrin/M. Mc Connell, Men from earth. New York 1989
N. Armstrong/E. Aldrin/M. Collins, Wir waren die Ersten. Frankfurt/M. 1970

ALEXANDER THE GREAT

King of Macedonia, general and conqueror, born 356 BC in Pella, died 323 BC in Babylon.

Alexander the Great was a pupil of Aristotle. He secured his position of power in Greece through fast attacks. In 334 BC he started his campaign against the Persians, which he won in 333 BC near Issos (in present-day Turkey). Alexander then carried on across Syria to Egypt, a region which was already familiar to the Greeks, and defeated the Persians once more in 331 BC during his return to Macedonia. In 330 BC he conquered Babylon, Susas and Persepolis. Alexander was proclaimed King of Asia and subsequently set out to conquer and rule the entire Persian empire. His subsequent campaign eastward led him to Kabul and in winter 330 BC Alexander and his troops overcame the Hindu Kush Mountains. Bactria (north of the Hindu Kush Mountains) and Samarskandskiy subsequently fell into his hands and in 327 BC he crossed the Indus into India. At that time it was believed that the Indus was a source of the Nile because it was infested with crocodiles, which were only known in Egypt up until that time. Alexander advanced to the Himalayas, but his forces mutinied and forced him to retreat. Alexander and his troops went by ship as far as the Indian Ocean, where they disembarked and took the overland route westward. Alexander the Great never saw his homeland again; he died of malaria in 323 BC in Babylon.

During the period from 334 to 323 BC Alexander the Great's empire covered almost the entire world known to Egypt at that time; however, after his death it soon dissolved (struggle for succession). Despite this, during his rule he had the honor of gaining invaluable new knowledge of distant lands, foreign peoples, hitherto unfamiliar religions (Buddhism), and exotic flora and fauna. At the same time he paved the way for the creation of global trading and global traffic. Besides, he founded more

Alvarado attacks the Aztecs, who have gathered for a feast.

than 70 towns, which expedited the spread of the Greek language and culture.

Further reading
J. F. Fuller, Alexander der Große als Feldherr. Stuttgart 1961
G. Wirth, Alexander der Große. Reinbek 1973
P. Högemann, Alexander der Große und Arabien. Munich 1985
W. Will, Alexander der Große (Geschichte Makedoniens), Volume 2. Stuttgart 1986
M. Grillandi, Alexander der Große und seine Zeit. Klagenfurt 1987
J. Seibert, Alexander der Große. 3rd unabridged edition Darmstadt 1990
F. Hampl, Alexander der Große, ed. D. Junker. 3rd extended edition Göttingen 1992
S. Lauffer, Alexander der Große. Reprint, Munich 1993
I. Schifman, Alexander der Große. Leipzig 1994
Nicholas Hammond: Alexander der Große. Berlin 2001

ALVARADO, PEDRO DE

Spanish conquistador, born c. 1485 in Badajoz, died 1541 in Guatemala.

In 1517 Pedro de Alvarado took part in an exploratory expedition to investigate the Mexican Yucatan peninsula. From 1519 to 1521 he served under Cortez, the conqueror of the Aztec Empire. When Cortez undertook a punitive expedition from Tenochtitlán (Mexico City) to Guatemala in order to prevent his subordinate, the conquistador Panfilo de Narvaez, conquering and establishing his own empire, Alvarado represented Cortez in the Mexican capital. His harsh measures triggered an uprising among the capital's population and led to the siege of

Tenochtitlán by thousands of Aztec warriors. Cortez set out for Tenochtitlán to help Alvarado; however, he was forced to flee the capital with Alvarado, leaving behind his entire artillery. During this retreat Alvarado saved himself with an enormous leap over a wide trench which was part of the town's fortifications and which has since borne the name of "Salto Alvarado".

From 1523 to 1527 Alvarado carried out a warlike expedition to Guatemala and founded the colonies of Guatemala de Vieja and Porto de la Posesión. Three years later Charles V appointed him governor of Guatemala. Alvarado died in 1541 during a voyage of exploration to southern Mexico.

Further reading
G. B. Ramusio, Primo (Terzo) Volume delle Navigationi. Venice 1563
A. de Herrera Tordesillas, Drie verschyede togten ... in West-Indies. De eerste door F. de Garay, de tweede door P. d'Alvarado van Mexiko na Guatemala. Without place of publication 1707
C. Fernández Duro, Las Joyas de Isabel la Católica las naves de Cortés y el salto d'Alvarado. Madrid 1882
A. de Altoaguirre y Duvale, Don Pedro de Alvarado conquistador del Reino de Guatemala. Madrid 1927

AMUNDSEN, ROALD ENGEBREGT GRAVNING

Norwegian polar explorer and the first man to reach the South Pole, born 1872 in Borge (Ostfold), died 1928 in the Arctic.

Roald Amundsen studied medicine at Christiana University (Oslo). In 1889 he abandoned his studies and turned his attention to polar research. In 1893 he signed on as a sailor on the whaler "Magdalena". From 1897 to 1899 he accompanied the Belgian Antarctic researcher de Gerlache on his journey to the South Pole; this was Amundsen's first winter in the Antarctic.

In 1901 Amundsen studied in Wilhelmshaven, Potsdam and Hamburg, where the well-known scientist Prof. Neumeyer instructed him in geomagnetism. In that same year, thanks to the generous support of several sponsors, Roald Amundsen was able to purchase the 47-ton whaler "Gjöa". He equipped the ship with a powerful engine, had it appropriately equipped and in 1903, accompanied by just six men and with provisions for five years, undertook his first northern voyage of discovery. In three months he was able to travel the full length of the Northwest Passage from the Atlantic to the Pacific.

In 1910 Amundsen came up with the idea of sailing as far as the Bering Strait in Nansen's "Fram" in order to reach the North Pole from

Roald Engebregt Amundsen

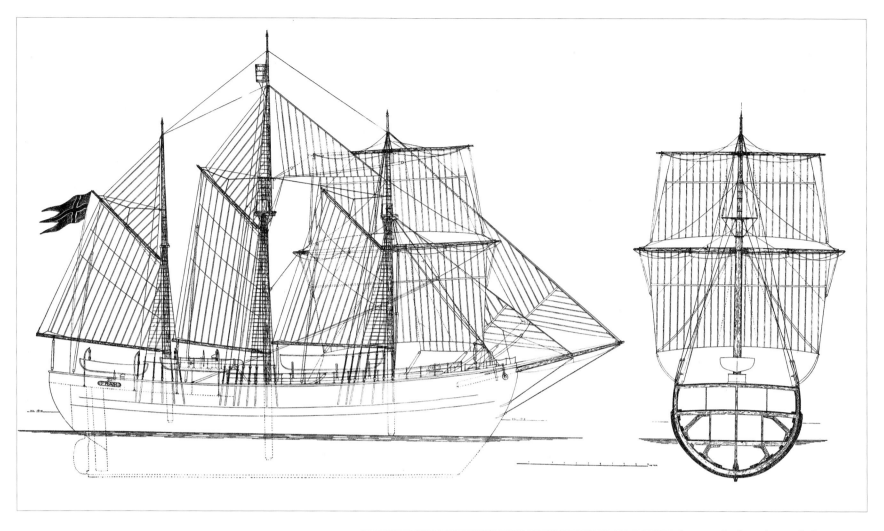

there. However, when he received the news that the British polar explorer Scott was already on his way to the South Pole, Amundsen changed his plans and set his sights on arriving there before him. Scott's and Amundsen's expeditions were both heading for the South Pole in 1911, the only difference being that Scott knew nothing of Amundsen's objective. Once Amundsen had passed the Antarctic Circle, he headed towards "King Edward VII Land". However, as Japan had laid claim to this area for research purposes, Amundsen changed direction and set up camp on the great ice barrier between "King Edward VII Land" and "Victoria Land". From "Whale Bay", discovered by the British polar explorer Shackleton and named by Amundsen, he set out on his historical trek to the South Pole. After preparing his expedition carefully, he gave the signal to start on 19 October, 1911.

A drawing of the "Fram" (above), and the ship in the drift ice (below).

By 5 November, he and his four companions and fifty dogs had reached the 82° S parallel. After a two-day rest, the trek continued. Fifteen days later he had reached 85° 36' S, and on 7 December he had broken Shackleton's record (88° 23' S). On 13 December the expedition passed 89° 37' S and on 14 December Amund-

The airship "Norge"

sen had reached his goal – four weeks before Scott. After hoisting the Norwegian flag, Amundsen claimed the land around the North Pole for his country and named it "King Haakon VII Plateau". The expedition set out on its return journey on 17 December and after just 39 days Amundsen had reached Whale Bay again with no particular difficulties.

After returning from his successful South Pole expedition, Amundsen took up his old plan once more – to set out from the Bering Strait in search of traces of the "Jeannette", which had sunk in the East Siberian Sea in 1881 due to the pressure of the ice, and then to allow his ship to drift with the ice in the direction of the North Pole with the so-called "Fram drift". It was a repeat of Nansen's venture. However, the outbreak of the First World War prevented him from setting out. It was not until the summer of 1918 that Amundsen was finally able to leave Norway on the "Maud", the successor of the "Fram". The expedition also took an aircraft. After spending two winters on the Siberian coast, Amundsen was able to set out in the di-

rection of the North Pole from Nome in Alaska. However, unfavorable ice conditions forced him to abandon his plan. It was 1922 before he could make a second attempt on the "Maud" from Point Hope in Alaska. Amundsen himself did not take part in this attempt. After drifting for two years, the "Maud" only reached the New Siberian Islands between the Laptev Sea and the East Siberian Sea. Because the "Fram drift" was known from that point onwards, the "Maud" freed itself from the ice and sailed to Alaska.

In 1925 Amundsen came up with the idea of flying over the North Pole in an aircraft. On 21 May of that year, he started out from Kings Bay (Spitsbergen) with an airplane provided by millionaire and polar explorer Ellsworth. However, approximately 250 km (155 miles) before reaching his target Amundsen was forced to make an emergency landing. It was not until 15 June that he was able to make the return flight to Spitsbergen.

One year later Amundsen, the American Ellsworth and the Italian Nobile attempted to reach the North Pole in an airship built by Nobile, the

"Norge". On 7 May, 1926 Nobile landed on Spitsbergen. The American polar researcher Byrd was also in Spitsbergen at that time. Byrd beat Amundsen in flying over the North Pole by 48 hours. After Byrd's victorious return Amundsen, Nobile and Ellsworth together with 13 other crew members set out to fly over the North Pole on 12 May. After ten days they crossed the North Pole, set course for Alaska and landed safely in the township of Nome (900 km or 560 miles from Anchorage).

On 23 May, 1928 Nobile attempted to repeat this flight with a purely Italian crew. The airship ended up in a snowstorm and was forced to make an emergency landing. It was not until 15 days after this incident that Nobile was able to request assistance via radio. Amundsen immediately set out on a search expedition with the two French pilots Guilbaud and de Cuverville to save Nobile and his crew. On 18 June search planes found the wreckage of Amundsen's plane in the Barents Sea.

Along with Byrd and Scott, Amundsen was one of the greatest polar explorers of the twentieth century. His success in the race to be the first to reach the South Pole can be attributed above all to his detailed preparations. Even the proud Lord Curzon paid tribute to Amundsen's achievements before the "Royal Geographical Society" in London.

Left: the iced-up entrance to the cabin; Above: The crew assembled in the cabin in the evening

Further reading
F. Nansen, Northern Water. Capt. R. Amundsen's oceanographic observations in the Arctic Seas in 1901. (Skrifter udgive af Videnskabs – Selskabet i Christiana. Mat. naturv. Klasse 1906, No 3)
R. Amundsen, Die Nordwestpassage. Meine Polarfahrt auf der Gjöa 1903-1907. With an appendix from first lieutenant G. Hansen. The only authorized translation from Norwegian by Pauline Klaiber. Munich 1908
R. Amundsen, The South Pole. An account of the Norwegian Antarctic Expedition in the "Fram" 1910-1912. London 1912
–, Nordostpassagen. Maudfaerden langs Asien kyst, 1918-1920. H. U. Sverdrups
ophold blandt Tsjukjerne Godfred Hansens Depotekspedition, 1919-1920. Christiana 1921
–, My Polar Flight. London 1925
–, My life as an explorer. London 1927
The Scientific Results of the Norwegian Arctic Expedition in the Gjöa 1903-1906, under the conduct of Roald Amundsen. 3 volumes. Oslo 1930-1933
A. A. Michieli, Roald Amundsen. Turin 1938
Bellamy, Patridge, Amundsen (A biography with portraits) Without place of publication 1953
H. Hansen, Gjennom isbaksen; Atten ar med Roald Amundsen. Without place of publication 1953
K. Holt, Scott – Amundsen. Wettlauf zum Pol. Revised version Vienna 1979
R. Huntford, Scott & Amundsen. London 1979
R. Amundsen, Die Eroberung des Südpols 1910-1912. 2nd edition Stuttgart 1987
P. Marc, Amundsen und Scott am Südpol. Zurich 1992
D. Brennecke, Roald Amundsen. Reinbek 1995

Salomon August
Andrée's balloon

ANDERS, WILLIAM ALISON

US American astronaut, born 1933 in Hong Kong.

William Anders was part of the crew of the space capsule "Apollo 8", in which he and fellow astronauts Frank Borman and James Lovell were the first to circle the moon. In view of his scientific knowledge, Anders was given the task of assessing the type and significance of the radiation that the astronauts could face. The "Apollo 8" mission reached its climax on 24 December, 1968 when, once the flight pattern had been stabilized, the capsule was able to orbit the moon ten times in the following 20 hours. "Apollo 8" set out on its return to Earth on 25 December. On the following day the astronauts landed in the Pacific between Hawaii and Samoa. The entire world was able to witness this first circling of the moon in five live television transmissions. The flight on board the "Apollo 8" was Anders' first and last space mission.

William Anders left the NASA astronaut group in 1969 and worked in various public committees. He served as ambassador to Norway from 1976 to 1977.

ANDRÉE, SALOMON AUGUST

Swedish polar explorer, born 1854 in Grenå, died in 1897 on the island of Vitå, Svalbard (Spitsbergen).

Andrée was an engineer. In 1892 he was honored by the Swedish Academy of Sciences for his research work into improving aviation technology. When Nordenskiold asked Andrée in 1895 if it would be possible to reach the North Pole in a balloon, the engineer with a passion for aviation did everything in his power to realize this goal.

Andrée's planned undertaking was well accepted by the Swedish government. The king and the industrialist Alfred Nobel financed almost the entire expedition. In June 1896 the Swedish freighter "Virgo" set the crew and its equipment on land on the "Island of the Danes" (Spitsbergen). When no favorable wind had arisen by August, Andrée's companion Erkholm persuaded the researcher to postpone the balloon trip. On 11 July, 1897 Andrée was finally able to put his bold plan into action. With a crew of three on board (Andrée, Fraenkel and Strindberg) the balloon "Oernen" (eagle) started from the "Island of the Danes" and headed towards the North Pole. On 16 July, a whaler working in these waters received Andrée's position, 82° 2' N and 15° 15' E, and the news: all fine on board. But this was the last that was heard of Andrée and his companions.

It was not until 1930 that a search expedition led by Dr. Gunnar Horn found the bodies of the North Pole explorers. From the balloon's log it was evident that lack of wind had forced them to land the balloon on the island of Vitå and to spend the winter there. Because they had inadequate clothing and not enough to eat, the three met a terrible end.

Further reading
C. F. G. Anderson, S. A. Andrée, hans följesla-gare och hans polarfärd, 1896-1897. Stockholm 1906
G. P. Putnam, Andrée. The record of a tragic adventure. New York 1930
W. Baumgart, Andrée. Ein Kampf um den Pol. (Edited by M. Lloyd. Blackie's Graded German Texts.) London and Glasgow 1938

ARMSTRONG, NEIL

US American astronaut, born 1930 in Wapakoneta (Ohio).

Neil Armstrong was originally a marine pilot. He completed his aircraft design studies in 1955 and became a test pilot, among other things for the rocket research aircraft "X 15". In this aircraft he reached heights of up to 60 km (37 miles) and speeds of more than 6,700 km/h (4,160 mph). In 1962 he joined NASA and in 1966, as commander of "Gemini 8", carried out

Neil Armstrong became famous not only as the test pilot of the legendary rocket-propelled aircraft "X15", but also as the first man on the moon.

In November of the same year a second crew took off for the moon. The photograph shows one of the astronauts of this Apollo 12 mission.

the first coupling rendezvous. In July 1969 he commanded the spaceship "Apollo 11", which started from Cape Kennedy on 16 July at 1:32 p.m. GMT on the tip of a 111 meter (364 foot), 3,100 ton and 155 million horsepower Saturn V rocket. "Apollo 11" was to take Earth's inhabitants to the moon for the first time in the histo-

ry of mankind. On 19 July the spaceship circled the moon; apart from Armstrong, fellow astronauts Edwin Aldrin and Michael Collins were on board. On 20 July the moon landing module "Eagle" containing Armstrong and Aldrin successfully separated from the command capsule, which Collins continued to fly around the

moon. At 8:17 p.m. the two astronauts reached the surface of he moon in what had been a precise landing maneuver. After a period of several hours in the landing craft, the astronauts began making preparations to leave it. On 21 July, at 2:56 a.m. GMT Neil Armstrong was the first human being to set foot on the moon, and Edwin Aldrin followed him a short time later. The two astronauts spent 22 hours on the moon. A two-hour walk was transmitted live to the Earth from a camera that they carried with them. According to estimates, this event was watched on television by 500 million people throughout the world – the same number that had witnessed the launch.

President Richard Nixon made the first telephone call to the moon. On 21 July, the astronauts began their return to Earth by igniting the return stage. At 9:35 p.m. the moon landing module was successfully re-coupled with the mother ship "Columbia", into which the astronauts climbed. The moon landing module was then ejected into space, and the "Apollo 11" mission ended successfully on 24 July with the spaceship's splashdown in the Pacific.

Neil Armstrong left the NASA in 1971 and began lecturing at various universities. After the "Challenger" catastrophe in 1986, Armstrong was appointed to the committee that was established to discover the causes of this accident.

Further reading
N. Armstrong/E. Aldwin/M. Collins, Wir waren die ersten. Frankfurt/M. 1970

In the Apollo 15 mission of 1971 a moon vehicle was used for the first time.

Chronicle
The moon landings

July 1969 On 16 July, the three-man team consisting of N. Armstrong, M. Collins and E. Aldrin start the first manned moon landing within the scope of the Apollo 11 mission (20 July). The astronauts' walk on the moon is broadcast on television throughout the world. After an overall period of almost 196 hours the team returns to Earth on 24 July.

Nov. 1969 The Apollo 12 mission is launched on 14 November. It reaches the moon on 19 November. The three astronauts' walk on the moon cannot be broadcast to Earth because sunlight has damaged a camera.
On 24 November the team returns to Earth with 43 kg of material collected from the moon.

April 1970 The Apollo 13 mission (11 to 17 April) fails due to technical problems.

Jan. 1971 A handcart is used for the first time on the moon within the scope of the Apollo 14 mission from 31 January to 9 February.

July 1971 A moon vehicle is transported for the first time on the Apollo 15 mission (26 July to 7 August). The vehicle is able to reach a speed of 20 km/h (12 mph) and weighs approx. 200 kg (440 lb). During the return flight the astronauts spend around 38 minutes outside the space capsule.

April 1972 The Apollo 16 mission starts on 16 April. A moon vehicle is also available for this moon landing. The landing (20 April) has to be postponed for several hours due to difficulties with the thruster. The team bring back 95 kg (210 lb) of moon substance on 27 April.

Dec. 1972 The last moon landing takes place on 11 December within the scope of the Apollo 17 mission. The start is delayed by around three hours. Besides the two astronauts (E. Cernan and R. Evans) the team includes selenologist H. Schmitt, who spends almost 75 hours on the surface of the moon. The capsule returns to Earth on 19 December.

ATLASSOV, VLADIMIR

Russian explorer and conqueror, born c. 1650, died 1711.

Until 1697 Atlassov was a government representative in an "ostrog" (a fortified colony) in the region of Jakutisk, when he received news of the Kamchatka peninsula and its inhabitants, the Koryaks. On gaining this information, Atlassov came up with the bold plan of conquering the large peninsula for the central government in Moscow, a plan which he shared with the governor of Jakutiske. After a great deal of hesitation, the governor gave Atlassov permission to conquer the peninsula for the Czar.

Accompanied by 60 Cossacks and 60 local soldiers, Atlassov reached the Sea of Okhotsk and advanced to the Kamchatka River, where he forced the Koryaks to pay tribute. In July he set up an ostrog and erected an immense cross.

Atlassov conveyed the first news about the existence of the Kurile Islands. In 1701 the Cossack leader brought the first Japanese with him to Kamchatka. With incredible accuracy Atlassov carried out regular studies on the geography of Kamchatka. He received a prison sentence for an attack on an influential Russian businessman, but was soon released from prison and appointed commander in chief of all Cossacks on the peninsula. 1705: creation of the ostrogs of Bol'sheretsk (west coast). 1707: Cossack uprising and Atlassov's flight to the ostrog of Niyné-Kamtchatsk, where he was murdered under mysterious circumstances.

Through Atlassov's bold undertaking, the Czar's power had extended to the shores of the Pacific.

Further reading
Y. Semionow, La conquête de la Sibérie du IXe siècle au XIVe siècle. Paris 1938

Aerial photograph of the Karimski volcano, Kamchatka

John James Audubon

Above and right: Two of the numerous pictures of birds and plants which Audubon painted.

AUDUBON, JOHN JAMES

American natural scientist and painter of animals, born 1785 in San Domingo/Haiti, died 1851 in New York.

Audubon, of French heritage, spent his youth on Haiti and in France. He arrived in North America in 1803, where he worked as a merchant until 1819. He subsequently made numerous trips throughout North America as far as Labrador and especially dedicated his life to studying birds. Audubon is the founder of ornithology in the US and made a significant contribution to the discovery of North America's nature.

Audubon showed interest in ornithology from a very early age; he frequently painted the birds of the east and south of the United States. He financed his travels by giving painting lessons, and it was not long before he had produced sufficient material for publication. Audubon's drawings of birds appeared in ten large-format volumes. By virtue of their artistic perfection, they were immediately hailed as a masterpiece; today, the original publications are coveted collector's items.

Further reading
H. Reichholf-Riem, Audubon's Birds.
Cologne 1993
J. J. Audubon, Vögel Amerikas. Hanau
1994

B

Siberian Islands between the East Siberian Sea and the Laptev Sea. All three ships were then driven in a northwesterly direction. During this exceptionally critical time Badigin, who had previously been second helmsman on the "Sadko", took over command of the "Sedow". When the "Malyguin" and the "Sadko" were freed from the ice masses on 28 August, 1938, the damaged "Sedov" was forced to remain at a position of 83° 6' N and 138° 24' E and was set

BACK, SIR GEORGE

English explorer and seafarer, born 1796 in Stockport (Cheshire), died 1878 in London.

George Back joined the Royal Navy at the tender age of twelve. Several years later as a marine soldier, he fought against the Spanish in North America. In 1818 he took part in Buchanan's Spitsbergen expedition and in 1819, together with John Franklin, he explored the Coppermine River. In the spring of 1834 he explored the entire course of the Great Fish River, which was later also called Back River. He was awarded a medal by the Royal Geographical Society for his services.

In 1839 Back, who had retired in 1836 for health reasons, was knighted. In 1857 Sir George Back was promoted to the rank of Admiral.

BADIGIN, CONSTANTIN SERGEVITCH

Russian marine officer and polar explorer, born 1910.

Badigin made his appearance in the history of North Polar exploration when he commanded the polar steamship "G. Sedov" from 1939 to 1940 (named after the Russian polar explorer Georgi Sedov) during its famous drift journey through the Arctic Ocean. In 1937, the "Sedov" had been trapped by ice along with another two ships, the "Sadko" and the "Malyguin", due to the unfavorable conditions close to the New

Expedition to the North Pole

up as a drifting North Polar station. The crew consisted of fifteen men. On this drift the "Sedov" reached a latitude of 86° 39.5' N on 29 August, 1939 and thus broke the record held by the "Fram".

On 8 January, 1940 the "Sedov" was released from its icy prison by the icebreaker Stalin. The drift had lasted a total of 812 days. The scientific results of the "Sedov drift" were also significant. Badigin had not merely supplemented Nansen's and Papanin's observations, but also carried out a whole series of oceanographical, meteorological and geomagnetic measurements in the Arctic Ocean. The ice measurements taken by the "Sedov" proved especially useful for polar shipping.

Further reading
K. Badigin, Die Drift des Eisdampfers Georgi Sedow. Without place of publication, 1946 (German Edition)

BAFFIN, WILLIAM

British seafarer and explorer, born c. 1584 in London, died 1622 off the coast of Hormuz (Persian Gulf).

In 1612, as head pilot of the "Patience" Baffin accompanied the explorer J. Hall into Arctic waters in an attempt to find the Northwest Passage. During this expedition Hall was killed by an Inuit and Baffin wrote the expedition report. One year later, he sailed to Spitsbergen on commission from the Moscow Society in an attempt to discover new fishing grounds.

In 1615 Baffin set out for the Arctic once more with Captain Bylot on the "Discovery". From Hudson Bay, which they thoroughly researched, they traveled along the Davis Strait to "Baffin Bay", where they discovered the Smith, Lancaster and Jones Sounds. Baffin doubted that it was possible to reach the Pacific via the Northwest Passage and proposed to the British Admiralty that he should make an attempt from east to west in order to reach Hudson Bay from the Pacific.

Following these journeys of discovery to the North Pole, Baffin concentrated on Asia, and on commission from the "East Indian Company" he visited Surat (north of Bombay) and sailed the Red Sea and the Persian Gulf. In 1620 he came to the aid the Shah of Persia in driving the Portuguese out of Hormuz. Baffin was fatally wounded during an attack on Qeshm (off the coast of Hormuz).

William Baffin was the first seafarer to undertake a serious attempt to determine the extent of the oceans in longitude with the help of the heavenly bodies. A strait between the Davis Strait, the Lancaster and Smith Sounds and a large island to the north of the Labrador peninsula bear the name of this early Arctic explorer.

Further reading
Cl. R. Markham (ed.), The Voyages of William Baffin 1612 to 1622. London 1881

BAIKIE, WILLIAM BALFOUR

British Africa explorer, born 1825 in Kirkwall (Orkney Islands), died 1864 in Sierra Leone.

After completing his medical studies in Edinburgh, Dr. Baikie joined the Royal Navy. As ship's physician and natural scientist, he took part in an expedition on the Niger on the exploration ship "Pleiad". When the commanding officer of the ship died in the vicinity of Fernando Póo Island, Baikie took over the command, sailed up the Niger and the Benue and reached Garuouat, not far from Yola, the "capital" of Adamaoua (mountainous country in Cameroon).

In 1857 Baikie undertook a second expedition on the Niger. On board the "Dayspring" he sailed into the Nun branch of the Niger Delta, reached the confluence of the Benue and the Niger, where he had to abandon his steamship. It was not until a year later that Baikie and his companions reached Fernando Póo. From 1859 to 1864 the ship's physician explored the land of the Nufi, and visited Bida (a town in central Nigeria) and Kano (in the northern part of Nigeria).

Credit goes to Baikie for his scientific exploration of the Niger and the Benue (the main tributary of the Niger), his collection of valuable material documenting the geographical conditions of Sudan, as well as his successful battle against malaria using quinine.

Further reading
Dr. W. Baikie, Narrative of an exploring voyage up the rivers Kwora and Benue. London 1856
–, Observations on the Hausa and Fulfude languages. London 1861
Petermanns Mitteilungen. Gotha/Editions 1855, 1857, 1859, 1861-1864

BAKER, SIR SAMUEL WHITE

British Africa explorer and discoverer, born 1821 in London, died 1893 in Sandford Orleigh (Devon). After completing his studies in Britain and Germany, Baker founded an agricultural colony on Ceylon. In 1861, together with his wife Florence he set out for Central Africa to discover the sources of the Nile. From Khartoum they reached Gondokoro (from where the Nile is navigable). There they met the two British Africa explorers Grant and Speke.

On their advice, Baker and his wife traveled through the Nyanza region. Pursued and threatened by Arabian slave traders and black potentates through the lands of the Obbos and the Madi (a tribe living north of Lake Albert), the two bold explorers eventually discovered the Luta Nzige on 14 March, 1864, which they named after the husband of Queen Victoria "Albert Nyanza". They then traveled along this lake to the mouth of the River Somerset, which had already been explored by Grant and Speke; this river was given its name by Baker. Although they could not find the outflux of Lake Albert, Baker assumed that it flowed into the Nile. In 1869 Baker returned to East Africa on commission from the Khedive Ismail Pacha in order to annex the region, which had in the meantime been explored, and to further explore the Nile in the central African region. Both the military and geographical results of this extensive undertaking fell well short of the goals that had been set.

Further reading
S. W. Baker, Eight Years Wanderings in Ceylon. London 1855
Petermanns Mitteilungen. Editions 1863-1866
Zeitschrift der Gesellschaft für Erdkunde zu Berlin. 1866
S. W. Baker, The Albert Nyanza. Great Basin of the Nile and Exploration of the Nile Sources. London 1867 (German version, Jena 1867)
–, The Nile tributaries of Abyssinia. London 1867
R. Hall, Die Liebenden auf dem Nil. Berlin 1981.

BALBOA, VASCO NUÑEZ DE

Spanish explorer and conquistador, born 1475 in Jérez de los Caballeros (Estremadura), died 1519 in Acla (Panama).

Balboa had settled as a planter in Haiti, and would probably have stayed there, if his financial backers had not forced him to go on new campaigns of conquest.

After wasting away his fortune and in order to escape his creditors, Balboa headed for Central America: He took part in an expedition led by Batistas, another conquistador, to the southwest coast of the Caribbean Sea and settled as a planter on Haiti. In order to escape the demands of his creditors a second time, he accompanied A. de Ojeda, a Spanish adventurer, on his military campaign and particularly distinguished himself in his leadership of the troops.

In 1510 on Balboa's initiative, the new colony of Santa María la Antigua del Darien was established (in the eastern part of the Central American land bridge, which is now Panama). As a result, he was promoted to General Captain and Governor of the new settlement. From here Balboa undertook his historical trek to the Pacific. On 7 September, 1513, accompanied by 190 Spaniards and a large pack of bloodhounds – which he set on insubordinate Indians during his expedition – he trekked through the rainforest and, after an extremely strenuous journey, on 29 September, 1513 reached the "Mar del Sur" (Southern Sea) in the Bay of San Miguel, which he took into his possession with great pomp in the name of the Spanish king. Because of this, Balboa is regarded as having discovered the Pacific Ocean.

Barents and his companions wintered in this cabin in Novaya Zemlya.

On his return to the settlement in Darien he became involved in a serious argument with the newly arrived and nominated governor Pedro Arias Davila (Pedrarias) as a result of their political differences. Although Balboa had married Pedrarias' daughter to put the matter to rest, Pedrarias accused him of plotting against the Spanish crown and he was beheaded with the help of the jealous Pizarro.

Vasco Balboa's death meant the loss of one of Spain's best and most competent political and military leaders in the "New World". A district and a town in the canal region are named after him.

Further reading
Ruíz Obregon y Retortilla, Vasco Nuñez de Balboa. Historia del descubrimiento del Oceano Pacífico. Barcelona 1913
Manuel J. Quintana, La Vida de Vasco Nuñez de Balboa (Edited with notes and vocabulary by G. Griffin Brownell) (International Modern Language Series). Without place of publication 1914
A. Strawn, The Golden Adventures of Balboa. London 1929

BARENTS, WILLEM (BARENDZ)

Dutch seafarer, born c. 1550 on the island of Terschelling (Netherlands), died 1597 on Novaya Zemlya (Barents Sea).

Willem Barents' research activities first began in 1594, when he undertook his first trip to the West Siberian Sea in search of the Northeast Passage. Accompanied by commanding officers Nai and Tetgales, Barents intended to circumnavigate the northern tip of Novaya Zemlya and from there to advance to Lake Kara. While Nai and Tetgales were successful in reaching Lake Kara, Barents, who was sailing separately in the East Spitsbergen Sea, was forced to turn back within sight of Novaya Zemlya because of the enormous masses of ice. In spite of this lack of success Barents had sailed around 2,500 km (1,550 miles) in the "Barents Sea" and made quite a number of important hydrographical discoveries.

Encouraged by van Linschoten, another Dutch seafarer, the Dutch government equipped a fleet of seven ships and commissioned Barents to make a second journey to the Arctic Sea to establish trade relationships with China via the northeast passage. However, Barents had to abandon his expedition because of ice masses near Pet Strait (also known as Jugor Strait).

In 1596, in the position of first helmsman and accompanied by two other Dutch sailors, J. v. Heemskerck and J. C. Rijp, Barents made a third attempt to discover the northeast passage. Sailing in a northerly direction, he happened upon an island that he named "Bear Island" before carrying on along the west coast of West Spitsbergen, which he believed to be the coast of Greenland. While Rijp returned to the Netherlands, Barents and Heemskerck continued their journey and were able to sail around Cape Nassau on Novaya Zemlya. But then their ship became trapped by ice. They constructed a dwelling out of driftwood and spent the winter on Novaya Zemlya, which ended with the tragic death of Willem Barents. It was only with a great amount of effort that Heemskerck and twelve crewmen managed to reach the island of Vaygach, from where they were rescued by Russian fishermen.

Barents and his crew were the first seafarers to be forced to spend the winter so far north. The "Barents map" is the first polar map without the supposed land masses of the North Pole. An island in the Spitsbergen group, the northern part of Novaya Zemlya ("Barents Land") and the section of sea between the East Spitsbergen Sea and Lake Kara bear the name of this highly significant polar explorer.

Further reading
W. Barents, Deliniato cartae trium navigationum per Batavos ad Septentrionalem plagem Norvegia Moscovia et Nowa Zembla et per fretum Weijgatis Nassovieam dictum ac juxta

Groenlandian. Autore Wilhelmo Bernardo. In: Bry, Johann Theodor de: (Collectio peregrinationum in Indiam orientalem. Fictitious title.) Part 3. Frankfurt 1601

J. Ch. Adelung, Geschichte der Schiffahrten und Versuche, welche zur Entdeckung des Nordöstlichen Weges nach Japan und China von verschiedenen Nationen unternommen wurden. Halle 1768

W. Y. Bontekoe van Hoorn, Die gefahrvolle Reise des Kapitän Bontekoe und andere - Logbücher und Schiffsjournale holländischer Seefahrer des 17. Jahrhunderts. Tübingen 1972

BARROS, JOÃO DE

Portuguese seafarer and author, born 1496 (1497?) in Lisbon, died 1562 (1570?).

Barros came from a family of civil servants and grew up at the court of King Manuel I. As a civil servant he gathered a wealth of experience working abroad and later was in charge of foreign trading from the port of Lisbon. He was commissioned by the king to colonize the Brazilian province of Maranhão; however, his fleet sank just off the coast of Brazil. His time abroad gave him the wealth of experience that he was able to use in his literature. He also wrote books that were intended to help educate the colonized peoples – for example a textbook of Portuguese grammar.

Joao de Barros was also an important historiographer. His first work, the "Crónica do Imperador Clarimundo", appeared in 1520. His numerous chronicles documented Portugal's rise to a colonial power with an impressive use of sober, detailed research.

IOAM DE BARROS

BARTH, HEINRICH

German Africa explorer and geographer, born 1821 in Hamburg, died 1865 in Berlin.

Barth studied archaeology, comparative geography and philology at Berlin University. He was influenced by romanticism from an early age and obtained a doctorate in philosophy. In 1845 Barth undertook a major archaeological expedition to the countries of the Mediterranean and visited Morocco, Algeria, Tunisia and Libya. At the border to Egypt he was wounded by the bullet of a desert bandit and robbed of his possessions. After recovering from this exertion in Alexandria, he then traveled through Palestine, Syria, Cyprus and Rhodes. In 1848 he was commissioned to lecture on the characteristics of Africa's soil at the University of Berlin.

On the recommendation of his former professor, K. Ritter, Barth was commissioned by the British government to participate in an expedition to Sudan led by J. Richardson. The objective of this undertaking was to open up new trading routes and to fight slavery. The Geographical Society in Berlin also proposed that the young German geologist Overweg take part in the expedition.

In 1850 the expedition set out from Tripoli and reached Mursuk (in southwestern Libya) with no great difficulty. On 18 July, the three scientists reached Ghat (Rhat). Their next destination was Agadès, a town on the edge of the as

time afterwards E. Vogel, still a novice among the Africa explorers, was murdered in the Sultanate of Wadi.

Barth's long journey began on 24 March, 1850 and ended on 27 August, 1855. He was celebrated in great style on his return to Europe. Alexander von Humboldt wrote that Barth had "opened up a new world". Several years later, the British government awarded him the Order of the Bath; however, the full professorship that he had hoped for was not to be. The government refused to appoint him as German Consul in Damascus, and he failed to be accepted into the Royal College of Sciences. It was not until 1863 that he was awarded a senior professorship at the University of Berlin.

Barth attempted in vain to clarify the fate of the young German explorer E. Vogel. His health deteriorated rapidly so that he was unable to start either of the two planned major works on Africa and the Mediterranean countries. The great explorer of Africa died in 1865 as a result of a rupture of the stomach lining.

Heinrich Barth is regarded as the model explorer of Africa. In the face of all manner of difficulties, he made astoundingly precise geographical and topographical findings in the hitherto unknown region between Lake Chad and the Niger. As a result of his work many blank areas on the map of central Africa could finally be filled in.

Heinrich Barth is considered to be one of the most profound explorers of Africa. His geographical and topographic works show an impressive scientific precision which was unusual at that time. He died at the comparatively young age of 44.

yet unexplored Aïr Mountains, which they again reached without incident. They were given a friendly welcome by the Moslem inhabitants. The three travelers separated shortly afterwards, since the two Germans had accused the Englishman of being deliberately negligent. Richardson died not far from Kuka on Lake Chad. Barth and Overweg continued from Kuka to Adamaua (mountainous country in central Cameroon) and reached Yola on the River Benue (a tributary of the Niger) before returning to Kuka.

In Europe, Barth was thought to be missing, so the British government sent the German Africa explorer E. Vogel in search of him. But Barth arrived in Kano, reached the Niger via Katsina and Sokota and, on 7 September, 1853, became just the third European to enter the legendary Timbuktu. After remaining there for six months (the inhabitants believed him to be the son of the murdered British major Laing), he had to leave the town. He returned to Kuka via Kano, where he met E. Vogel. Because of bad health Barth was forced to return to Tripoli. A short

Further reading
Monthly reports from the Berlin Geographical Society. 1852
T. E. Gumprecht, Barths und Overwegs Untersuchungsreisen nach dem Tschadsee und in das Innere Afrikas. Berlin 1852
Journal of the Royal Geographical Society. London 1854
H. Barth, Wanderungen durch die Küstenländer des Mittelmeeres, ausgeführt in den Jahren 1849-1855. 5 volumes. Gotha 1857-1859
–, Reisen in Nord- und Zentralafrika in den Jahren 1849-1855. 5 volumes. Gotha 1858 (excerpt, 2 volumes. 1860)

–, *Sammlung und Bearbeitung zentral-afri-kanischer Vokabularien in deutscher und englischer Sprache. Gotha 1862*

v. Schubert, Heinrich Barth, der Bahnbrecher der deutschen Afrikaforschung. Berlin 1897

E. Banse, Große Forschungsreisende (reference to Barth). Munich 1933

–, Unsere großen Afrikaner (reference to Barth). Berlin 1940

H. Schiffers, Die große Reise. Dr. Heinrich Barth, Forschungen und Abenteuer 1850-1855. Minden 1952

Heinrich Barth. Im Sattel durch Nord- und Zentralafrika. Reisen und Entdeckungen in den Jahren 1849-1855, published by R. Italiaander. Mannheim 1967

Heinrich Barth: Ein Forscher in Afrika, ed. H. Schiffers. Stuttgart 1967

Heinrich Barth. Die große Reise. Forschungen und Abenteuer in Nord- und Zentralafrika 1849-1855, edited by H. Schiffers, Tübingen 1977

BARY, ERWIN VON

German Africa explorer, born 1846 in Bavaria, died 1877 in Ghat (Libya).

Bary came from a French family which had emigrated to southern Germany in the seventeenth century. He studied medicine and the natural sciences. Lectures on Barth's and Duveyrier's travel reports about the Sahara awakened in the young Bary the calling to be an explorer. He learned the Arabian and Tuareg languages ("Temacheq"). He spent some time on the island of Malta before crossing to Tripoli, where he undertook several "exploratory journeys" on the edge of the Sahara.

In 1876 the Berlin Geographical Society commissioned him to carry out a major expedition to Sudan, mainly to explore the Hoggar (a massif in the Sahara). With just a small caravan and pretending to be a Turkish physician, Bary, accompanied by a merchant from Tripoli, reached Ghat without incident.

Bary was forced to postpone his plan of exploring the Hoggar because of tribal feuding among the Tuaregs. Instead he explored the Tassili N'jjer (a rocky desert in the central Sahara).

On his return to Ghat, Bary was warmly welcomed by the Turkish governor of the town. As he was still unable to penetrate the Hoggar, he decided to make an excursion to the massif of Aïr – a trip that took a whole year. Here he was robbed of his entire possessions by Tuaregs and returned to Ghat without a penny to his name.

Bary died suddenly one evening after dining at the Turkish governor's residence. It was never ascertained whether he had been poisoned on the orders of the Turkish governor or whether he had simply succumbed to the exertion of his journey in the Sahara.

In the course of just two years of exploration in Sudan, Bary was able to gather a large amount of geographical and ethnographical information, in particular concerning the Tassili N'jjer massif.

Further reading
Bary, Erwin de, Le dernier rapport d'un Européen sur Ghât et les Touaregs de l'Aïr. Journal de voyage d'Erwin de Bary 1876-1877. Traduit et annoté par Henri Schirmer. Paris 1898

BASTIAN, ADOLF

German explorer of Australia, Asia, America and Africa and also an ethnologist; born 1826 in Bremen, died 1905 in Port of Spain (Trinidad).

After training to become a ship's physician, Adolf Bastian succumbed to his fondness for travel and urge to explore. He set out for Australia in 1851, where he visited the goldfields. From Australia he set sail for New Zealand, which he explored, and then crossed the Pacific, landing in Peru. He remained for a long time in the town of Cuzco, the former spiritual and political capital of the Inca Empire. He then traveled to the Mississippi and the Missouri via the West Indies and reached Mexico, where he visited the ruins of the former great Aztec confederation. In California he boarded a ship, crossed the Pacific a second time and reached China, the Indian subcontinent, the Malaysian

The German Adolf Bastian went down in history as an explorer of Africa, but in fact he traveled and researched the entire world – apart from the Arctic and Antarctic.

Adolf Bastian also roamed through Mexico, where he was particularly fascinated by the old Indian cultures. The photograph shows Chichén Itzá, the ceremonial center of the ancient Mayan culture in North Yucatán, Mexico.

Archipelago, Calcutta, crossed the Deccan and then reached Bombay. In the course of his trek through the Near East, Bastian thoroughly investigated the ruins of Babylon and Nineveh and finally set out for Cairo, the former Memphis, via Syria and Palestine, where he remained for several months. He subsequently traveled along the Nile, rode a camel through the desert along the Red Sea, boarded a ship in the port of Mocha in what is today Yemen and reached Africa. In Africa, he explored Zululand, the Congo, West Africa, Liberia, Sierra Leone and Sengambia. In 1859 Bastian returned to Germany to evaluate his geographical, ethnographic and geological material. His journey had taken eight years.

Adolf Bastian's second major expedition lasted four years (1861–1865). This journey him to the Indian subcontinent, which he explored from Mandalay in central Burma as far as Saigon. On this expedition, his principal interest was the study of the Thai languages. From 1863 to 1865 he investigated the Malaysian islands. After visiting Japan he returned to his homeland via Beijing, Manchuria, Inner Mongolia, the Gobi Desert and Siberia. The result of this journey of discovery was a thorough knowledge of the religions and languages of various Asian peoples.

In 1873 Bastian was elected Chairman of the "German Society for the Exploration of Central Africa". Later the same year, he set out on a brief expedition to the Loango coast (Angola). In 1875 and 1876 he again explored South America, where he visited Peru, Ecuador, Columbia and Guatemala, and returned to Germany via the United States. In 1878 he undertook a further major expedition to Asia. Via Baku on the Caspian Sea and Teheran he traveled throughout the Indian subcontinent, the Malaysian Archipelago, Australia, California, Oregon, reached New York and finally ended up in Yucatán. In the course of various travels that he undertook from 1889 to 1891, Bastian explored the Caucasus, Turkestan, Armenia, the Indian subcontinent and Tasmania. Five years later, he traveled once more to the Malaysian Archipelago and East India. His last journey took him once more to the region that is now Pakistan and to the island of Ceylon.

During his exceptionally active life of exploration, Adolf Bastian traveled the whole world with the exception of the Arctic and Antarctica. He is regarded as the founder of ethnology: in order to research the development of the human race, Bastian especially studied the habits and customs of the so-called "natural peoples".

Further reading
A. Bastian, Ein Besuch in San Salvador, der Hauptstadt des Königreichs Kongo. Without place of publication 1859

–, Der Mensch in der Geschichte. Without place of publication 1860
–, Die Völker des östlichen Asien. 6 volumes. Without place of publication 1866-1871
–, Das Beständige in den Menschenrassen. Without place of publication 1868
–, Die Deutsche Expedition an der Loangoküste Afrikas. 2 volumes. Without place of publication 1874-1875
–, Die Kulturländer des Alten Amerika. 3 vols. Without place of publication 1878-1879
–, Kontroversen in der Ethnologie. 4 volumes. Without place of publication 1893-1894
K. Th. Preuss, Adolf Bastian und die heutige Völkerkunde. Bässler-Archiv Without place of publication 1926
–, Die heilige Sage der Polynesier. Kosmogonie und Theologie. Reprint of the Leipzig 1881 edition, Without place of publication 1986
–, Indonesien oder die Inseln des Malaysischen Archipels. Reprint of the 1884-1894 edition,

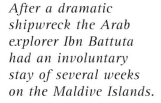

After a dramatic shipwreck the Arab explorer Ibn Battuta had an involuntary stay of several weeks on the Maldive Islands.

without place of publication 1987
–, Ein Besuch in San Salvador, der Hauptstadt
des Königreichs Kongo. Münster 1988

BATES, HENRY WALTER

British biologist and South America explorer, born 1825 in Leicester, died 1892 in London.

Traveling together with Alfred R. Wallace, in 1848 Bates set out for the region around the mouth of the River Amazon in Pará (northern Brazil). They intended to finance their expedition by catching and selling rare insects. However, while Wallace returned to England after four years, Bates continued to explore the Amazon – in spite of illness – until 1859, longer than any other white man before him. In addition, he returned to England with approximately 14,000 zoological and botanical specimens, 8,000 of which had been unknown at that time.

BATTUTA, IBN

Arabian world traveler, born 1304 in Tangier, died 1377 in Fez.

Battuta studied Islamic legal science. Gripped by the desire to travel, he set out for Alexandria in 1326. The purpose of his journey was not to discover unknown lands; rather, he wanted to convince himself of the splendor and beauty of Islamic holy places.

From Mecca, Battuta traveled to Jerusalem and Tabriz (Iran), before returning to the city of the prophets. A short trip took him to Hormuz on the Persian Gulf. His next visit was to Astrakhan on the Caspian Sea, from where he returned to Rabat via Constantinople accompanied by the daughter of the Byzantine emperor Andronicus III. His first journey had been of eight years' duration.

On his second journey he visited the Indian subcontinent. In Delhi he practiced his profession as a judge. The Sultan trusted him so much that he placed him at the head of a legation to the court of the Mongolian ruler in Beijing. On the route to Bengal he was robbed and taken captive, but was able to escape and then attempted to reach China by sea. He suffered shipwreck on this voyage and was forced to spend many months on the Maldives (southwest of the southern tip of India), before continuing on to Sumatra and Java. He traveled along the Mekong Delta, eventually reaching China, and arrived in Beijing in good time to attend the burial of the Great Khan. After twenty years' absence, the jurist returned to his home town of Tangier via Canton and the "world port" of Hangzhou, where the globetrotter was warmly greeted by Sultan Abu Iman.

In 1352 Battuta undertook a third journey to northern and central Africa, which at that time was under Islamic rule. Battuta visited Mali, the "capital" of the Niger region, Timbuktu, which did not particularly impress him, and the East African coastal towns of Mombassa and Kilwa, returning to Fez via Gao (Niger), the Hoggar and the Atlas Mountains, where he dictated his travel report to his biographer Ibn Djozay.

Besides Marco Polo and Wilhelm von Ruysbroek, Battuta is one of the three great medieval globetrotters. Within the space of just 25 years, he covered the unbelievable distance of 100,000 km (60,000 miles) right across Asia, Africa and Europe. Apart from a few chapters, his travel reports are true accounts and are still today seen as the standard work of Arabian travel literature.

Further reading
Kosegarten, De Mohamede Ebn Battuta, Arabe, Tingitano eiusque itineribus. Jena 1818
S. Lee, Travels of Ibn Battuta. London 1829
M. Cherbonneau, Voyage du Cheik Ibn Batoutha à travers l'Afrique septentrionale et Egypte. Paris 1852
Ibn Battuta, Voyages, traduits par Defrémery. Paris 1853-1858
Bl. Tapier, Les voyages Arabes au moyen âge. Paris 1937
Ibn Battuta, Reisen ans Ende der Welt, 1325-1353, republished by H. Leicht. Tübingen 1974

BAUMANN, OSKAR

Austrian explorer, born 1864 in Vienna, died 1899 in Vienna.

In 1885 Baumann accompanied the German explorer Oskar Lenz on his Africa expedition, traveled along the Upper Congo and explored the island of Fernando Póo in the Gulf of Guinea.

While he was on an expedition through East Africa in 1888 together with Hans Meyer, a German explorer of Africa, he was taken captive by Arabs and later released on payment of a ransom.

In the course of an extensive journey which he undertook from 1889 to 1893, Oskar Baumann discovered Lake Manjara and Lake Eyassi (a salt lake in the north of present-day Tanzania) along with the sources of the Kagera, the main tributary of Lake Victoria.

Further reading
O. Baumann, Eine afrikanische Tropeninsel:
Fernando Poo und die Bube. Vienna 1888
–, In Deutsch-Ostafrika während des Auf-
standes. Vienna and Olmütz 1890
–, Usambara und sein Nachbargebiet. Berlin
1891
–, Durch Massailand zur Nilquelle. Reise
und Forschung der Massai-Expedition
des deutschen Antisklaven-Komitees. Berlin
1894

BEEBE, CHARLES WILLIAM

American zoologist and deep sea explorer, born 1877 in New York, died 1962 in Trinidad.

Together with the engineer Otis Barton, Dr. Charles Beebe developed a completely new type of diving device: a 2.7-ton steel sphere ("bathysphere"). This was suspended from a steel hawser and was connected to the ship by a telephone line. Near the Bermuda Islands on 15 August, 1934 Beebe and Barton succeeded in reaching the previously unattained depth of 923 meters (3,028 feet); Beebe was able to observe and photograph many hitherto unknown deep sea creatures.

Beebe was the first to reach a depth of 923 m (3,028 ft) near the Bermudas, in his diving sphere "Bathysphere", which he constructed himself.

BEECHEY, FREDERICK WILLIAM

British polar explorer and geographer, born 1796 in London, died 1856 in London.

Son of the painter S. W. Beechey. He joined the Royal Navy when he was just ten years old and at the age of fifteen took part in a battle off the island of Madagascar. In 1818 Frederick Beechey accompanied the polar explorer J. Franklin in his unsuccessful search for the Northwest Passage, and in 1819 he accompanied the Arctic explorer E. Parry on an expedition to the northern waters.

It was not until 1825 to 1828 that he was able to undertake an expedition on his own to the North American Arctic, as commanding officer of the "Blossom".

One of the small islands off the southwest coast of the Devon Islands (Barrow Strait) as well as a lake (not far from the northern arctic circle) in Canada bear the name of this polar explorer.

Further reading
Fr. W. Beechey, Narrative of a Voyage to the
Pacific and Bering's Strait. London 1831
–, Voyage of Discovery towards the North
Pole, performed in H. M. S. Dorothea and
Trent, under the Command of Copt. D. Buchan.
London 1843

BEHAIM, MARTIN

German seafarer, cartographer and globe maker, born c. 1460 in Nuremberg, died 1507 in Lisbon.

Behaim (Martin de Bohemia – the name of his adopted country) lived for some time in Bohemia. He is said to have been a pupil of the well-known Regiomontanus (Johannes Müller). In 1481 he emigrated to Portugal and became a member of the Lisbon "Juntas dos Mathematicos" under the leadership of King John II.

Accompanied by the Portuguese sailor Diego Cão ("dog"), Behaim, in the position of helmsman and cartographer, undertook a journey in 1484 to the Gulf of Guinea, during which the island of Annobon (now Spanish) was discov-

Martin Behaim created the first globe, which can now be admired in the Germanic National Museum in Nuremberg. However, not all the details are correct. Particularly the East African coast is marked imprecisely.

ered. At Cabo Agostino and Cabo Negro they erected coats of arms in stone (padraos) and continued to the mouth of the Congo, where they asked everyone they could about the land of the Abyssinian ruler. After six months of exploration, the expedition returned to Portugal.

From that point onwards, Martin Behaim was highly respected in Lisbon. Nevertheless, for political reasons he was not permitted to take part in any further expeditions. He then settled permanently on the Azores and concentrated on cartography.

Behaim spent the years from 1491 to 1493 in Nuremberg in order to settle an inheritance matter. During his stay there he made a globe (the oldest existing globe today) on which the Portuguese occupancies on the West African coast are shown in detail. However, the East African coast does not correspond to the geographical situation as we know it today. Before leaving Germany, Behaim instructed the Nuremberg mechanic Kalperger in globe-making. Behaim died in hospital during one of his regular visits

to Lisbon. Behaim's principal achievements lie in the field of cartography. His globe (today in the Germanic Museum in Nuremberg) is the earliest specific evidence of the Portuguese advance towards the Cape of Good Hope. Whether Behaim was in fact a pupil of Johannes Müller still remains to be established conclusively.

Further reading
C. G. von Murr, Diplomatische Geschichte des portugiesisch berühmten Ritters Martin Behaim. From original documents. Nuremberg 1778
F. W. Ghillany, Der Erdglobus des Martin Behaims vom Jahr 1492. Nuremberg 1842
–, Geschichte des Seefahrers Ritter Martin Behaim nach den ältesten Urkunden bearbeitet. Nuremberg 1853
Reichenbach, Martin Behaim. Without place of publication 1889
S. Guenther, Martin Behaim. Without place of publication 1890
E. Ravenstein, Martin Behaim, his life and his globe. Without place of publication 1908
J. Bräunlein, Martin Behaim. Legende und Wirklichkeit eines berühmten Nürnbergers. Bamberg 1992

Sir Edward Belcher's work as an Arctic explorer is noted above all for its high level of scientific precision.

BELCHER, SIR EDWARD

British polar explorer, born 1799 in Halifax (Nova Scotia), died 1877 in London.

Edward Belcher was a marine officer. In 1825 he accompanied the polar explorer F. W. Beechey on his expedition to the Pacific, and from 1836 to 1842 he circumnavigated the world in the "Sulphur". In 1852 he was commissioned to carry out a large-scale expedition in search of the missing John Franklin. On his return to the Beechey Islands, Belcher's ships "Intrepid" and "Pioneer" were trapped by ice. He then used a sledge to explore the Penny Strait (between Bathurst Island and Devon Land) and advanced as far as Jones Sound, which was almost free of ice.

On his return to England Belcher was charged with leaving his ship unlawfully but was found not guilty.

While Belcher found absolutely no trace of the John Franklin expedition, his geographical findings in the Arctic Circle were highly valuable from a scientific point of view. An island in Hudson Bay is named after him.

Further reading
E. Belcher, Narrative of a Voyage Round the World on H. M. S. "Sulphur". London 1843
–, Narrative of a Voyage of H. M. S. "Samarang". London 1848
–, The last of the Arctic Voyages. London 1855

BELLINGSHAUSEN, FABIAN GOTTLIEB VON

Russian polar explorer and discoverer, born 1778 in Hoheneichen (Osel Island), died 1852 in Kronstadt (St. Petersburg).

On completion of his studies at the naval academy in Kronstadt, Fabian Bellingshausen entered the service of the Imperial Russian Navy in the year 1797. In 1819 he was commissioned by Czar Alexander I to explore the Antarctic. With two ships the scientifically trained seafarer set out to investigate the Antarctic waters and discovered two islands, which he named "Peter I" and "Alexander I" (both of which are located in the "Bellingshausen Sea"). During his bold advance into as yet uncharted waters he reached the 60° S parallel in 1821 and subsequently returned to Kronstadt from his successful undertaking: He had in fact circumnavigated Antarctica, although without actually having set foot on the icy continent. Fabian Bellingshausen concluded his career as a military governor of Kronstadt.

The part of the ocean south of Graham Land (West Antarctica) bears the name of this significant Antarctic explorer.

Further reading
Hakluyt Society, Voyage of Captain Bellingshausen to the Antarctic Seas, 1819-1821. London 1945

BELZONI, GIAMBATTISTA

Italian Africa explorer and archaeologist, born 1778, died 1823.

While still young, Belzoni traveled through Italy, England and Holland and in 1815 he set out for Egypt, where he was responsible for transporting ancient relics to national museums. During his time in Africa he explored Nubia, the tombs of Abu Simbel (two important rock temples of Ramses II on the Nile in Upper Egypt) on his own, examined the Chephren Pyramids, dug for buried treasures in the "Valley of the Kings", undertook a journey to the Al-Faijum basin, crossed the Libyan Desert and reached the El Kassar Oasis, which he mistook for the Ammon Oasis.

Giambattista Belzoni's final objective was to discover the sources of the River Niger. However, without having achieved this goal the Italian explorer, who had in the meantime made a name for himself as a world-famous antique collector, died in Gato of a tropical disease at the age of only 45.

Further reading
G. Belzoni, Narrative of the Operations and Recent Discoveries within the pyramids, temples, tombs and excavations in Egypt and Nubia. London 1820
J. F. Dennett, The voyages and travels of Capt. Parry, Franklin, Ross and Mr. Belzoni (Selected by Captain J. F. Dennett). London 1826

BERING, VITUS JONASSEN

Danish seafarer and explorer, born 1680 in Horsens (Jutland), died 1741 on Bering Island.

From an early age Bering was in the service of the Dutch East India Company. In 1722 he met the Russian admiral Seniavin and accepted the favorable offer from the Imperial Russian Admiralty to sail in its service.

For many years both the Czar and the Archangel merchants had been very interested in developing economic and political relationships with North America and China. However, in order to ensure the success of this venture, the geographical relationship between Asia and North America first had to be determined.

In 1725 Beringundertook a scientific expedition to the Kamchatka peninsula and from there searched and charted the channel. Accompanied by M. Spanberger, a Danish naval lieutenant, and A. Chirikov, a Russian seaman, the expedition took two years to reach Kamchatka by the overland route. Two ships were built, the "Fortuna" in Ochotsk (East Siberian coast) and the "St. Gabriel" in Petropavlovsk (Kamchatka). On 13 July, 1728 Bering sailed from Kamchatka in a northerly direction, circumnavigated Cape Chukotskiy, discovered an island that he named "St. Laurence" and reached Chukchi Sea via the Bering Strait, which is named after him. Violent storms forced him to turn back. On arrival in St. Petersburg, Bering insisted that he had reached 67° 11' N. The Russian Admiralty was disappointed in the results of Bering's expedition as the Dane was unable to provide them with any specific information about Alaska.

Thanks to his favorable relationship with Count Golovin and government minister Count Ostermann, Bering was now commissioned with the geographical exploration of the northwest coast of North America and eastern Siberia. With two ships, the "St. Peter" and the "St. Paul", Bering set course for the west coast of North America, accompanied by the scientist G. W. Steller and the French geographer L. Delisle de la Croyère. While the "St. Paul" under the command of Chirikov was lost, Bering discovered the Aleutians and on 20 July, 1741 caught a glimpse of Mount St. Elias (Alaska), North America's third-highest mountain. Sailing along the Alaskan peninsula, he discovered further islands, which are today known as the Andreanov Islands. When the Russian first mate Chumagin died of scurvy on an island, Bering named it after him. However, in the meantime a large part of the crew had come down with scurvy and the September storms had set in. It was only under a great deal of hardship that Bering reached the island that bore his name (today: Comandorskiye Ostrova), where he died of exhaustion on 13 August, 1741. Of the 76 men who started out on the expedition, only 46 reached Petropavlovsk.

Vitus Jonassen Bering is credited above all with rediscovering the strait between Alaska and Siberia.

Further reading
G. P. Müller, Voyages et découvertes faits par les Russes le long des côtes de la mer glaciale et sur l'océan oriental tant vers le Japon que vers l'Amérique. Amsterdam 1766
P. Lauridsen, Vitus J. Bering og de russiske Opdagelsesrejser fra 1725-1743. Copenhagen 1885
F. A. Golder, Bering's Voyages. An account of the efforts of the Russians to determinate the relation of Asia and America. 2 volumes. American Geographical Society Research-Series No 1. New York 1922
Y. Semionov, La Conquête de la Sibérie du IXe siècle au XIXe siècle. Paris 1938

The merits of the Dane Vitus Jonassen Bering lie above all in his rediscovery of the straits between Alaska and Siberia.

BÉTHANCOURT, JEAN DE

French seafarer and colonizer, born c. 1360 in Grainville, died c. 1425.

In 1402 the impoverished nobleman Jean de Béthancourt decided (possibly on the recommendation of the French king Charles VI) to determine whether the Canary Islands would be suitable for systematic settlement. On 1 May, a flotilla consisting of around a hundred settlers left the French port of La Rochelle on the Atlantic. Three clergymen along with the chamberlain of the Duke of Orléans, Gardife de la Salle, and the chronicler P. Bontier also took part in this venture.

Béthancourt took possession of the islands of Lanzarote, Fuerteventura, El Hierro and Gomera for France and in return received the honorary title of "King of the Canary Islands".

The financial malaise of the French court, which was caused primarily by the huge expenses for the Hundred Years War, put paid to the plan of a permanent settlement. Towards the end of the fifteenth century hardly anything was left of this attempt at colonization.

A military occupation of this important Atlantic base by the French would have completely altered the course of colonial history.

From an ethnological point of view, Béthancourt's expedition was especially interesting. It produced a great deal of information about the customs and way of life of the Guanch tribe (the indigenous people of the Canary Islands), for instance the fact that they embalmed their dead before laying them to rest in caves. In 1770 more than a thousand such mummies were found in a large grotto. A possible early connection to the Egyptians in view of this embalming technique is yet to be established.

Further reading
Voyageurs anciens et modernes ou choix des relations de voyages, les plus intéressantes et les instructives, avec biographies, notes et indications par M. Edouard Charton. Paris 1857
G. Gravier, Le Canarien. Rouen 1874

BINGER, LOUIS GUSTAVE

French Africa explorer, born 1856 in Strasbourg, died 1936 in Isle-Adam (Seine-et-Oîse).

Louis Gustave Binger began his career as an explorer at the age of 21 when he traveled along

Lanzarote, one of the Canary Islands, was discovered by the Genoese Lancelotto Malocello in 1312. Béthancourt was later to inspect the island for its suitability for settlement. Béthancourt did not know the fascinating landscape of lava and ash of today (photographs left and on the next page). The present Lanzarote was only created in 1730 by mighty volcanic outbreaks.

the entire loop of the Niger, starting from Bamako (Mali). Within the space of two years, he covered about 4,500 km (2,800 miles), wandered through the regions of the Mossi and Kong and reached the town of Grand-Assam on the Ivory Coast in 1887. Louis Binger discovered that the area between the Kamoe and Niger Rivers with the towns of Kong, Bobo Dioulasso and Djenné, rich in tropical woods and precious metals, could have become France's wealthiest

colony. This assertion naturally called the British and Germans into action, who were also greatly interested in this rainforest region with its wealth of raw materials.

Binger was the first European scientist to explore the Niger from its large loop to its mouth. A town on the Ivory Coast bears the name of this explorer.

Further reading
L. G. Binger, Du Niger au Golfe de Giunée
par les pays de Kong et de Mossi (1887-1889).
Paris 1892

BLIGH, WILLIAM
English seafarer, born 1754 in Plymouth, died 1817 in London.

In 1776 Bligh accompanied James Cook as helmsman on his third circumnavigation of the world.

In 1787 he was instructed by the British admiralty to transport the breadfruit tree and other plants of the South Pacific to the Antilles in order to acclimatize and grow them there. On his voyage east of Australia he discovered a group of islands in the southern region of New Zealand that he named "Bounty" after his ship. Afterwards William Bligh continued on to Otaheite (Tahiti), went ashore and collected rare plants together with the scientists that accompanied him.

During this extended sojourn the other members of the crew indulged in dalliance with the female inhabitants of Otaheite – against Bligh's strict orders. Soon after their departure, a mutiny broke out under the leadership of the sailor Christian Fletcher (the famous mutiny of the Bounty). Together with 18 sailors, Captain Bligh was marooned in an open boat only 23 feet (8.4 meters) long, not far from the Island of Tofua, of the Tonga Group.

After a odyssey lasting an entire month, Bligh managed to reach the Portuguese island of Timor in June 1789 together with his companions. Soon after his return to England he demanded that court action be taken against the mutineers, but also against his supervising officers whom he accused of weakness of character during the rebellion.

In the meantime, the "Bounty" had landed on the small island of Pitcairn (southeast of the Paumotu or Tuamotu Group in the Pacific Ocean). After a brief sojourn on this luscious island, the mutineers were overpowered by the crew of an English warship and were tried by court martial.

In 1805 Bligh was appointed Governor of New South Wales (Australia) and in 1811 Rear Admiral.

On the Apollo 8 mission the US astronaut Frank Frederick Borman was one of the first persons to see the unreal landscape of the moon at close range.

Further reading
H. M. S. "Bounty", The Mutiny of the Bounty. Edinburgh 1885
The Voyage of the Bounty Launch, as related in William Bligh's dispatch to the Admiralty and the Journal of John Fryer. London 1934
I. W. Antony, The Saga of the "Bounty". Its strange history related by the participants themselves. New York 1935
G. Mackaness. Life of Vice-Admiral William Bligh. New York 1936
O. Rutter, Turbulent Journey. A life of William Bligh. London 1936
William Bligh/George Hamilton, Meuterei auf der "Bounty". Die Piratenjagd der "Pandora" (1787-1792), ed. H. Homann, reprint, Stuttgart 1983
W. Bligh, Meuterei auf der "Bounty". Hamburg 1992

BORCHGREVINK, CARSTEN EGGEBERG

Norwegian scientist and polar explorer, born 1864 in Oslo, died 1934 in Oslo.

Borchgrevink already participated in long sea travels as a child. In 1888 he went to Australia where he traveled through vast areas of South Australia and gave language lessons at Cooerwell College.

From 1894 to 1895 he devoted his time to the exploration of Antarctica. He attempted to reach the South Pole in 1897; during this expedition he was the first to discover lichen and reached a latitude of 78° 5' S.

Further reading
C. E. Borchgrevink, First to the Antarctic Continent. Being an account of the British Antarctic Expedition 1898-1900. London 1901
–, Naermest Sydpolen Aaret 1900. Kopenhagen and Christiana (Oslo) 1903-1905.
–, Das Festland auf dem Südpol. Breslau 1905

BORMAN, FRANK FREDERIK, II

American astronaut, born 1928 in Gary (Indiana).

Borman was a member of the "Apollo 8" crew and one of the first humans to circle the moon. This mission was his second voyage – in December 1965 he had been the commander of "Gemini 7" capsule and together with James Lovell spent a record 14 days in space. During this mission the first successful rendezvous of two manned space capsules took place: after the start on 4 December, 1965 the two astronauts orbited the Earth for ten days in their spaceship and made preparations for the meeting with "Gemini 6", which after a delay was launched from Cape Kennedy with the astronauts Walter Schirra and Thomas Stafford on board. The rendezvous was initiated during this capsule's second orbit of the Earth. The distance between the two spacecraft was constantly reduced until

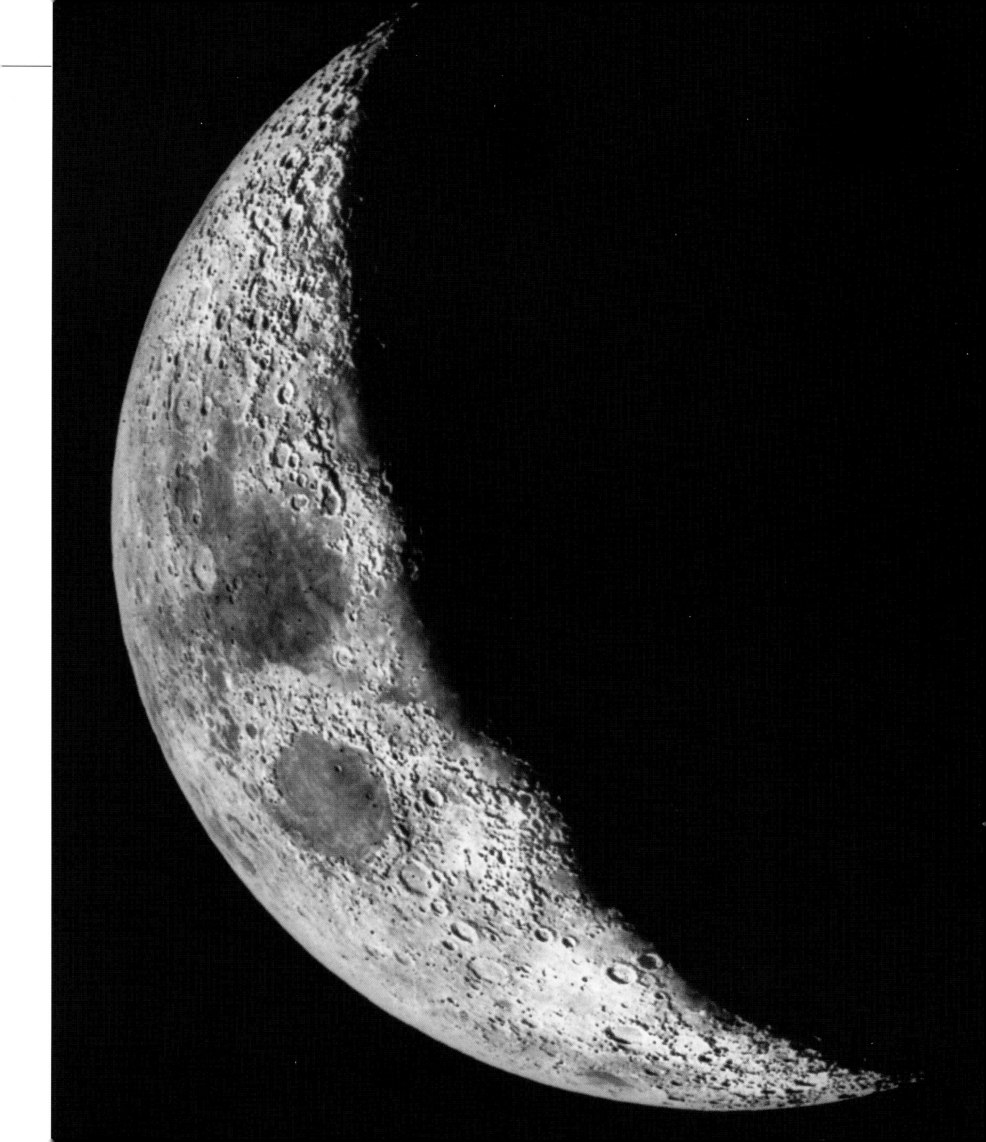

there was less than a meter (three feet) between them. For safety reasons, the two "Gemini" spaceships were not permitted to come into contact. Afterwards the astronauts resumed their space routes and finished the experiment as planned, landing on 16 December (Gemini 6) and 17 December (Gemini 7).

In 1970 Franz Borman left the NASA and became President of an Asian airline company. He later served as President of various American companies.

Further reading
R. Serling, Countdown: An Autobiography.
New York 1989

BOUGAINVILLE, LOUIS ANTOINE DE

French seafarer and explorer, born 1729 in Paris, died 1811 in Paris.

Louis Bougainville was a member of an aristocratic family. At the age of 34 he became Captain in the French navy after having worked as a solicitor, an aide-de-camp general and an embassy secretary. In 1756 he accompanied General Montcalm to Canada, where he distinguished himself during the confrontations at Fort Carillon and Fort St. Sacrement. He learned the sailing trade from the experienced seamen Froger de la Rigaudière, Duclos, Chenard and Guyot.

In 1763 he undertook an expedition to the Falkland Islands, where he founded the first French settlement at his own expense. Three years later he was instructed to undertake a reconnaissance voyage to the Pacific, the aim of which was to spy out the English bases there. Bougainville left France with two ships, the "Boudeuse" and the "Etoile", and reached the Pacific in 1768 via the Magellan Strait, which he took 52 days to navigate. During the continuation of his journey he discovered a group of four small islands that he named "Quatre-Facardins" (today known as Tehai, part of the Poumotou

Group) and dropped anchor at Tahiti, which had been visited in 1606 by the Spaniard Quiroz and a few months before Bougainville's arrival by Wallis, an Englishman. At Tahiti the French were given an especially warm welcome, but due to the inhabitants' passion for stealing this friendship did not last very long.

Sailing on a western course, Bougainville headed for the "Seafarer Islands" (Samoa Group), the "Greater Cyclades" and a group of islands east of New Guinea that he named "Louisiades". In addition he found the passage between the Salomons and the Bismarck Group, explored the northern coast of New Guinea, visited the Dutch settlement Boreo on Borneo and returned around the Cape of Good Hope via Ascension, Cape Verde and Terceira (Azores) to St. Malo on the French channel coast, where he arrived on 16 February, 1769.

Bougainville's circumnavigation of the world had been motivated by scientific as well as political objectives. On the island of Tahiti he established the presence of two races. The members of the one were tall, whereas the other ones were short and had curly hair. The individual groups of inhabitants adhered strictly to their social difference in status, the chiefs were allowed to have several wives, and human sacrifice was practiced. Bougainville described the inhabitants of this Pacific island as the "happiest" people on Earth because in his opinion they did not know any "passions".

Further reading
L. A. de Bougainville, Voyage autour du monde par la frégatte du roi la Boudeuse et la flûte l'Etoile en 1766, 1767, 1768 et 1769. Paris 1772
Ch. de la Roncière, Bougainville. Paris 1842
Les grands hommes de la France: Navigateurs, par E. Goep et G. L. Cordier (Bougainville, d'Entrecasteaux, Dumont d'Urville). Paris 1878
J. S. Martin, Essai sur Bougainville navigateur. La Géographie. Without place of publication 1930
L. A. de Bougainville, Reise um die Welt. Berlin 1972

BOUVET DE LOZIER, JEAN-BAPTISTE CHARLES

French seafarer and explorer, born 1705 in St. Malo, died 1786 in St. Malo.

In 1738, Bouvet de Lozier was instructed by the French India Company to explore the Antarctic waters and make specific hydrographical and geographical studies of the South Sea and Antarctica.

During his venture into the South Atlantic, Bouvet discovered an island which he named "Terre de la Circoncision" (Land of Circumcision, now Bouvet Island) and which he assumed to be part of the Antarctic continent.

When neither Cook in 1775 nor Ross in 1843 succeeded in relocating this island, it was assumed in France that Bouvet de Lozier had been mistaken. But in reality the explorer had merely miscalculated the island's geographic position.

Further reading
Relation de Bouvet de Lozier dans le Journal de Trévoux. Paris 1740
E. Marguet, Histoire générale de la navigation du XVe au XXe siècle. Paris 1931

BRAZZA, PIERRE SAVORGNAN DE

French-Italian Africa explorer, born 1852 in Castel Gandolfo (Italy), died 1905 in Dakar (Senegal).

Pierre Brazza attended the French Naval College in Brest. As an officer he participated in the operations of the French Northern Squadron in the German-French War of 1870/71. At the end of the war he was instructed by the Ministry for Education and Science and by the Parisian Geographical Society to explore the Ogowe River in Gabon, which was almost 1,000 km (600 miles) long. His crew consisted of four white men and twenty Senegalese. When Brazza arrived in the township of Doumé and discovered that the river did not in fact flow in the

Before the invention of photography explorers used to make sketches, which they gave to professional artists on their return to be elaborated. Photography made documentation simpler and allowed one to bring back more striking pictures from distant lands. Here we see a dance by natives in central Africa.

expected direction, he proceeded to the Alima (a right tributary of the Congo) and continued on to the Licona, a river that is also dependent on the water system of the Congo. The hostility of the Apfuru tribe towards Brazza forced the explorer to abandon his work after only three years.

When the Belgian king Leopold II requested Brazza to continue with Henry Stanley's work in Africa, he declined. Instructed by the French minister Gambetta to gain the enlarged "Stanley pool" for France, Brazza set out a second time to central Africa. He made a pact of protection with the powerful black ruler Makoko. In N'Couna (subsequently known as Brazzaville) the explorer left his companions behind and continued on his own. In Vivi his historical meeting with Stanley took place. Due to a shortage in supplies, Brazza was forced to return to Libreville (Gabon).

In the meantime, the French government had taken the view that the Congo basin should remain under Belgian rule. On hearing this, Pierre Brazza inquired in Paris whether he could eventually bring about the foundation of a French Congo state (in addition to a Belgian state). Brazzaville became the capital city of the new Congo colony, which included the region around the rivers Ogowe, Sangha, Alima and Oubangi.

Pierre Savorgnan de Brazza systematically investigated the Ogowe and studied the customs and way of life of the cannibal tribe of the Fans, who were also called "Pahouins". Unlike Stanley, Brazza was in favor of a peaceful exploration of Africa.

Further reading
Général de Chambrun, Brazza. Paris 1930

BREHM, ALFRED EDMUND

German explorer and zoologist, born 1829 in Unterrenthendorf (Triptis), died 1884 in Unterrenthendorf.

In 1847 Alfred Brehm accompanied the German natural scientist J. W. Müller to Egypt. From there he traveled through Sudan and reached Khartoum, the capital of what is now the Republic of Sudan, where he undertook a number of extended safaris.

In 1848, Alfred Brehm explored southeastern Kordofan, a province in central Sudan, and two years later spent some time in the dense forest region on the Blue Nile. In 1851 he returned to Germany with an extensive ornithological collection.

On the commission of the Duke of Saxony, Coburg and Gotha, Alfred Brehm subsequently explored the land of the Bogos (a tribe of the Auga) in Eritrea. The Württemberg scientist T. von Heuglin also spent some time there just a year later.

In the land of the Bogos, Brehm decided to concentrate his research on the habits and customs of the Bogos.

Alfred Edmund Brehm is especially well known for his book "Brehms Tierleben" (Brehm's Animal Life).

Further reading
A. E. Brehm, Reiseskizzen aus Nordostafrika.
3 volumes 1855
–, Ergebnisse einer Reise nach Habesch. 1863
–, Tierleben. 6 volumes. Without place of
publication 1864-1869
H. Arndt (publisher), Brehms Reisen im Sudan
1847-1852. Tübingen 1975
A. E. Brehm, Reisen im Sudan 1847-1852,
ed. H. Arndt. 2nd edition Stuttgart 1983

Alfred Edmund Brehm

BRENDAN

The famous Irish monk, died around 587, often also called Brendanus, is said to have undertaken a legendary ocean voyage. Woodcuts show Brendan with other monks in a small sailboat. In all likelihood, Brendan had not planned his trip on the Atlantic but instead drifted from his intended course. However, Irish monks were in fact quite capable of traveling to distant islands by ship. Legend has it that Brendan discovered an island in the sea – the "Promised Land for Saints." This island was included in maps until the late 16th century.

BRUCE, JAMES

Scottish explorer of Africa, born 1730 in Kinnaird House (Stirlingshire), died 1794 in London.

James Bruce was a descendant of the ancient Scottish royal family. It was not until he inherited a large fortune that he was able to realize his desire to travel to Africa and discover the sources of the Nile.

He was appointed British consul in Algiers, where he studied archaeology and learned the Arabian language. He undertook a major journey through the countries of the Mediterranean, during which he visited Rhodes and the ancient cities of Sidon and Tyre.

From Massaua on the Red Sea, Bruce crossed the Abyssinian highlands. In the old Abyssinian capital of Gondar (2,200 m or 7,200 feet above sea level) Bruce was the guest of Negus, who held court in a palace that had been built by the Portuguese. During his further journey to southern Abyssinia he played a rather dubious role in a civil war. With the help of the warring Gallas, Bruce rediscovered the sources of the Blue Nile ("Bahr-el-Azrak"). His achievement was celebrated enthusiastically back home in Britain, although the fact was overlooked that the Portuguese missionary Pedro Paez had already discovered the sources back in 1615. Bruce returned to London via Gondar.

James Bruce can take more credit for his exploration of the hitherto unknown Abyssinian highlands than for his "discovery" of the sources of the Nile. His comprehensive description of the Negus Empire retained its full validity until the 1930s.

Further reading
J. Bruce, Travels into Abyssinia. 5 volumes.
London 1790
–, Travels to Discover the Source of the Nile in the years of 1768-1772 and 1773. London 1790
–, Zu den Quellen des Blauen Nils. Die Erforschung Äthiopiens 1768-1773, ed. H. Gussenbauer. Stuttgart 1987

BURCKHARDT, JOHANN LUDWIG

Swiss explorer of Africa, born 1784 in Lausanne, died 1817 in Cairo.

Burckhardt was the eighth child of Colonel Johann Rudolf Burckhardt. He received his school education in Basle, then in Neuenburg, before studying at the universities of Leipzig and Göttingen. In 1805 Burckhardt returned to Basle. For personal reasons Burckhardt left Switzerland and moved to England, where he made himself available to the "African Association" in London, whose president at that time was Sir Joseph Banks. In Cambridge Burckhardt studied mineralogy, geology, chemistry and Oriental languages to prepare for his future journeys of discovery to North Africa.

In 1809 Burckhardt left London and headed for North Africa via Malta to explore the Sudan. On reaching North Africa he put on Moslem clothing, converted to Islam and, dressed as an Indian merchant and going by the name of Ibrahim, arrived without incident in Aleppo (Syria). In Damascus he studied the Arabian customs and traditions. In order to intensify his knowledge of Arabic he translated Camper's

The Irish monk Brendan with his brother monks on the legendary Atlantic voyage on which he discovered a mysterious island.

A great empathy for Islam and knowledge of the religion made it possible for the Swiss explorer Johann Ludwig Burckhardt to move around the holy city of Mecca for weeks completely unhindered.

"Robinson Crusoe", transforming the story into the Arabian fairy tale "Dur el Bahr" (Pearl of the Sea).

In 1810 the Swiss explorer and scientist spent some time in the ruined cities of Baalbek and Palmyras. In the course of his further travels he visited the ancient city of Decapolis (East Jordan) before returning to Damascus.

In 1812, dressed in Bedouin clothing, he left the Syrian capital, traveled through the northern part of the Arabian Peninsula and the El Tih desert and reached Cairo on 4 September.

In 1813 Burckhardt undertook a scientific expedition from Assuan to Dar el Mahas on the border of the former Mameluccan town of Dongola, following the eastern bank of the river. During his return journey Burckhardt explored the western banks of the Nile.

Later that same year he traveled through Nubia and in the train of a caravan reached Berber (a town in Sudan also called Barbar) and Chandi (a town in Sudan on the right bank of the Nile). From here he trekked to Suakim on the Red Sea and, via Jiddah, reached the city of Mecca, the holy Islam city. Burckhardt passed the "test" of Moslem orthodoxy before two Ulemas (Turkish scholars), joined the traditional hajj (pilgrimage), was given the complimentary title of "Hajji" and from September to November 1814 was completely free to move around Mecca as he wished – as the first European ever. We are also indebted to Burckhardt for the first accurate description of the Caaba, the holy of holies of the Muslim faith. On his return to Cairo, an outbreak of pestilence forced him to leave the city once more. For a second time he explored the Sinai peninsula, collected a large quantity of old writings and returned to the ancient town of Memphis (Cairo) to evaluate these rarities.

This is where Burckhardt died on 15 October, 1817 in the course of preparing to travel to Timbuktu.

Along with Munzinger, Johann Ludwig Burckhardt is regarded as the greatest Swiss explorer of the African continent. He is mainly credited with exploring the ancient ruins of Egypt and Persia as well as his geographical exploration of the Nile Valley from Assuan to Chandi. Burckhardt bequeathed his 350 volumes of Oriental writings and manuscripts to Cambridge University. After his death, the African Association in London set about assessing his findings. Burckhardt was buried in the Islamic cemetery in Cairo.

Further reading
L. J. Burckhardt's Reisen in Syrien, Palästina und der Gegend des Berges Sinai (From the original English: Travels in Syria and the Holy Land, London 1822). 2 volumes Weimar 1823, 1824
J. L. Burckhardt, Entdeckungen in Nubien 1813-1814, published by H. Arndt. Stuttgart 1981
–, In Mekka und Medina. Der erste Europäer an den heiligen Stätten des Islam, ed. U. v. d. Heyden. Berlin 1994

BURKE, ROBERT O'HARA

Irish explorer of Australia, born 1820 in St. Clearn's, died at Cooper's Creek (Australia) in 1861.

Burke emigrated to Australia in 1853. In 1860 he led an expedition which crossed the Australian continent from south to north – from

Melbourne via Cooper's Creek to the Gulf of Carpentaria. He was the first European to cross the Australian continent in this direction. Burke died of hunger and exhaustion on his return journey.

Further reading
The Burke and Wills exploring expedition.
Melbourne 1861.
A. Moorehead, Treffpunkt Cooper's Creek.
Without place of publication 1966.

BURMEISTER, HERMANN

German South America explorer and natural scientist, born 1807 in Stralsund, died 1892 in Buenos Aires.

After completing his studies in natural science Burmeister turned his attention to active research. In 1837, at the age of 30, he began a scientific exploration of the Río de la Plata region on the South American Atlantic coast between Uruguay and Argentina.

In 1837 he was appointed Professor of Zoology in Halle on the Saale and eleven years later was elected into the Frankfurt National Assembly. From 1850 to 1852 Burmeister carried out his first major journey to South America. He traveled through the two Brazilian provinces of Rio de Janeiro (in southeastern Brazil) and Minas Gerais (in the east). This "mining town" had been developed in the eighteenth century once diamonds had been discovered there. Four years later Burmeister traveled across the as yet unexplored Río de la Plata region of Montevideo, the capital of Uruguay, to reach northern Argentina.

In 1859 he set out on his celebrated "Andes travels". He crossed the Andes and completed his expedition in the Chilean city of Copiapo, the capital of the province of Atacama. By carrying out this expedition Burmeister had opened up a completely route across the Andes. From Copiapo he traveled through Panama to Cuba before returning to Europe.

In 1861 Burmeister moved to Buenos Aires, where he was appointed curator of the Museum of Natural History which was being built at that time. In 1870 Burmeister was also responsible for establishing the Faculty of Natural Sciences in Córdoba (Argentina).

Burmeister is regarded as the original explorer of the Río de la Plata region.

Further reading
H. Burmeister, Reise nach Brasilien. Without place of publication 1853
–, Systematische Übersicht der Tiere Brasiliens. Without place of publication 1854/56
–, Landschaftliche Bilder Brasiliens. Mit Atlas. Without place of publication 1856
–, Reise durch die La-Plata-Staaten. 2 volumes. Without place of publication 1861

BURTON, SIR RICHARD FRANCIS

British Africa explorer and orientalist, born 1841 in Torquay, died 1890 in Bombay.

In 1854 Burton, who had an exceptional gift for languages, visited the Islamic holy cities of Mecca and Medina dressed as a Persian, an action which could have cost him his life at that time had he been unmasked.

In 1855 he undertook a journey of exploration into the empire of Negus accompanied by the Englishman J. H. Speke.

In 1857 Burton was commissioned by the London Geographical Society to explore the large central African body of water, the so-called "Sea of Ujiji". From Zanzibar Burton and Speke proceeded through the territory of Arabian slave traders with their team of 132 men and, after many deprivations, eventually reached Lake Tanganyika in February 1858. In Ujiji the natives informed them that large lakes were located approximately 12 to 15 days' trek from Lake Tanganyika. While Burton, who was racked by fever, was forced to remain in the camp, Speke was able to reach Lake Ukerewe, which he named "Victoria Nyanza". When Speke returned to Bur-

The Irishman Robert O'Hara Burke emigrated to Australia at the age of 33 and then crisscrossed the huge continent in his travels.

The German Hermann Burmeister's main explorations were in South America.

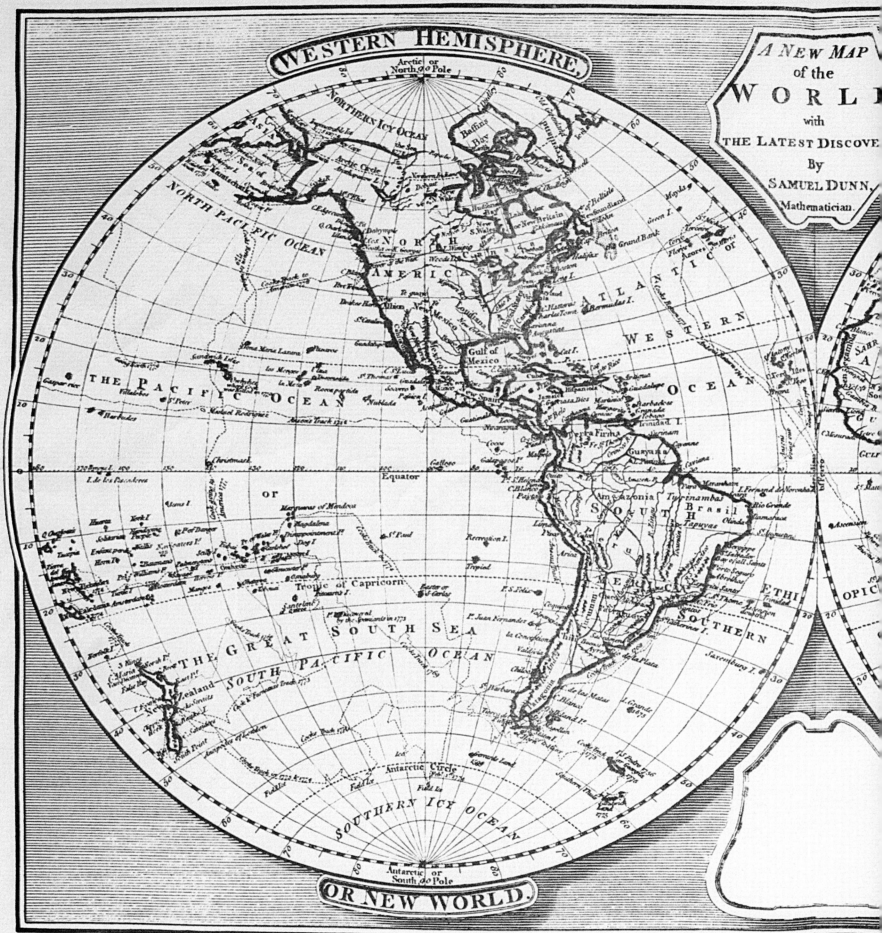

WESTERN HEMISPHERE,

A NEW MAP
of the
WORL
with
THE LATEST DISCOVE
By
SAMUEL DUNN,
Mathematician.

Arctic or
North 90 Pole

NORTHERN ICY OCEAN

Baffins
Bay

Arctic Circle

NORTH PACIFIC OCEAN

NORTH
AMERICA

ATLANTIC

WESTERN

THE PACIFIC OCEAN

Gulf of
Mexico

OCEAN

Equator

or

SOUTH

Brasil

AMERICA

Tropic of Capricorn

THE GREAT SOUTH SEA

SOUTH PACIFIC OCEAN

SOUTHERN

New
Zealand

ETHI

OPIC

Antarctic Circle

SOUTHERN ICY OCEAN

Antarctic or
South 90 Pole

OR NEW WORLD.

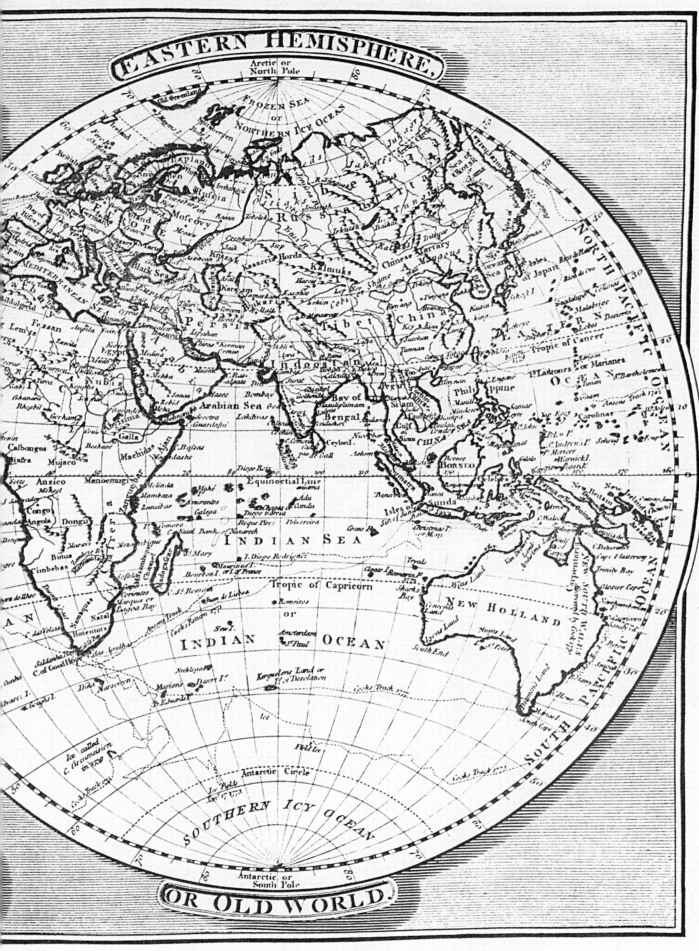

EASTERN HEMISPHERE,

OR OLD WORLD.

OF THE EARTH.

The blank areas on the maps of the world disappeared faster and faster. This map by Samuel Dunn, which shows the western and eastern hemispheres, indicates which parts of the world were already known at the end of the 18th century.

ton and told him of his discovery, no one would believe him. However, Burton later had to admit that Speke was telling the truth.

He undertook two further expeditions to Africa: one to the Gulf of Benin and another to Dahomey. His last expedition took him to Brazil, where he explored the São Francisco River.

Sir Richard Francis Burton spent the latter years of his life in Bombay, where, among other things, he translated the works of the Portuguese national poet Camões.

Further reading
R. F. Burton, Zanzibar, City and Coast. 2 volumes. London 1860
–, The lake regions of Central Africa. 2 volumes. London 1860
K. Andrée, Forschungsreise in Arabien und Ostafrika, nach den Entdeckungen von Burton, Speke, Krapf etc. 2 volumes. Leipzig 1861

BYRD, RICHARD EVELYN

American officer and Arctic explorer, born 1888 in Winchester (Virginia), died 1957 in Boston.

Richard Byrd studied at the Virginia Military Institute, the University of Virginia and the US Naval Academy before becoming a marine pilot. In 1925 he led the "MacMillan Arctic Expedition" to Greenland. In 1926 Byrd, together with his co-pilot Bennett, was the first to fly to the North Pole, setting out from Kingsbay (Spitsbergen) with his three-engined Fokker "J. Ford" (9 May). They required over 15 hours for the 2,200 km (1,370 mile) flight and arrived at the North Pole one day and one night before Amundsen.

Byrd carried out his first Antarctic expedition in 1928 and set up the "Little America I" station (which was followed by two more); a year later,

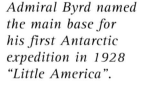

Admiral Byrd named the main base for his first Antarctic expedition in 1928 "Little America".

on 28 November, together with B. Belchen he flew over the South Pole, a feat that brought him the rank of Rear Admiral.

Byrd traveled to Antarctica again from 1933 to 1935, lived alone there for six months and advanced some 200 km (125 miles) into the interior of the continent. During this expedition he made important geographical discoveries such as "Marie Byrd Land", the "Edsel Ford Range" and the "Rockefeller Plateau".

Between 1939 and 1941, he flew over western Antarctica four times as leader of the US Antarctic Service Expedition. From 1946 to 1947 he carried out various research activities within the scope of the "High Jump" operation, and in 1955 he took part in "Operation Deep Freeze" in the Ross Sea.

Richard Byrd flew over both the North and the South Pole. By reason of his geographical research work, he is rightly regarded as one of the most significant polar explorers of the past two centuries.

Further reading
C. Foster, Rear Admiral and the Polar Expeditions. New York 1930
Fr. T. Miller, Byrd's great Adventure. With the complete story of polar expeditions for one thousand years. London 1930
R. E. Byrd, Little America. London 1931

H. Adams, Beyond the Barrier with Byrd. An authentic story of the Antarctic Exploration Expedition. Chicago and New York 1932
R. E. Byrd, Antarctic Discovery. The story of the second Byrd Antarctic Expedition. London 1936
Exploring with Byrd. Episodes from an adventurous life, completed and revised by Rear Admiral R. E. Byrd. New York 1937
R. E. Byrd, Alone. London 1938
–, Allein. 5th edition Wiesbaden 1963

Byrd was the first explorer to reconnoiter the South and North Poles intensively from the air. His first flight together with Floyd Bennet in May 1926 took him from Spitsbergen over the North Pole.

CABOT, JOHN
(GIOVANNI CABOTO)

Italian seafarer in English service, born 1450 in Genoa (?), died 1498 (missing).

In 1484 Cabot settled in the English commercial center of Bristol. He presumably took part in various voyages to the Levant. In front of Columbus, Cabot is said to have expressed the opinion that India and China could be reached via the Northwest Passage, thus breaking the spice monopoly of the Arabs.

After Christopher Columbus' crossing to the New World, Cabot succeeded in convincing the Bristol merchants of the importance of discovering this Northwest Passage. The English king Henry VII gave Cabot permission to undertake a venture into the still unknown American north and to explore all new islands and countries despite the Treaty of Tordesillas, according to which the Portuguese and Spanish had divided the world amongst themselves with the approval of the Pope.

On 2 May, 1497 Cabot left the harbor of Bristol on board the "Matthiew" and reached the North American coast on 24 June, 1497 at Labrador, at Newfoundland or on the Island of Cape Breton (north of Nova Scotia). On his return, Cabot was hailed as the true discoverer of North America and was immediately commissioned with a second expedition. This time he followed the coast in a southerly direction to Cape Hatteras.

Although John Cabot had not succeeded in achieving any material gain on either voyage, he had initiated the search for the Northwest Passage.

Further reading
Barrera Pezzi (C.), Di Giovanni Caboto
rivelatore del settentrionale emisfero
d'America con documenti inediti esistenti
nei R. R. Archevj. di Stato di Milano.
Venice 1881
Sir Charles R. Beazley, John and Sebastian
Cabot, the discovery of North America.
London 1898

CABOT, SEBASTIAN
(SEBASTIANO CABOTO)

Italian seafarer, born before 1485 in Venice (?), died 1557 in London.

Sebastian Cabot participated in the voyages of his father John Cabot between 1497 and 1503 to the North American coast. In 1512 he emigrated to Spain and first served King Ferdinand the Catholic and then Charles I.

Cabot's plan to repeat Fernando Magellan's voyage already came to an abrupt end in the Bay of La Plata (Buenos Aires), where he lost several of his ships. When attempting to travel along the Uruguay, he was attacked by the inhabitants and was forced to retreat. He arrived back in Spain with only one ship left. For alleged abuse of power he was banished to North Africa for some time.

Sebastian Cabot then entered the services of the English King Edward VI, who appointed him director of the Society of Merchant Adventurers for life. From that time onwards, the extension of trade with Russia and the search for the Northeast passage was incumbent on Cabot. He became one of the founders of the British naval power.

Further reading
C. A. P. d'Avezac Macaya, Les navigations terre-neuviennes de Jean et de Sébastien Cabot. Lettre au Révérend Léonard Woods. Paris 1869
Sir C. R. Beazley, John and Sebastian Cabot. The discovery of North America. London 1898

CABRAL, PEDRO ALVAREZ

Portuguese seafarer and explorer, born in 1467 or 1468 in Belmonte, died between 1518 and 1520 in Santarém.

Cabral's historic achievements date back to the year 1500 after the opening of the trade route between Lisbon and Calicut (in East India). He was commissioned by King Manuel the Great to take possession of the entire coast of Malabar (Southwest India) for Portugal and to develop the area economically.

In order to carry out this plan, 1,200 men and a fleet excellently equipped with artillery were placed at Cabral's disposal. Cabral was accompanied by Bartoloměu Diaz, the conqueror of the "Cape of Good Hope", along with six Franciscans under the direction of Father Henrique from Coimbra. With the blessings of the bishop of Viseu, the thirteen caravels set sail on 9 March, 1500. The fleet reached Cape Verde without major incident. It was not long, however, before a terrible storm broke out. One caravel was lost and the others drifted apart. After a thirty-day odyssey on the Atlantic, Cabral landed on a still unknown shore (Porto Seguro), erected a stone cross and named the area "Terra de la Cruz". On an island which today bears the name "Coro Vermelha", the first Mass was spoken, in which a group of natives also participated.

Already during the preparations for departure, Cabral handed a detailed report of the landing on the South American subcontinent to the historian and chronicler Pero Vaz de Cam-inha. It was never conclusively established whether the "detour" to Brazil was deliberate or unintentional. From an economic point of view, the newly discovered region was still uninteresting for the Portuguese, since the only profitable source was the use of the hard woods known as "brazil" (hence the country's name). With a favorable wind behind him, Cabral sailed to the Cape of Good Hope. Not far from this cape a violent storm broke out in the course of which four caravels, amongst them the one with Diaz on board, were lost. Cabral weathered the storm without damage and headed directly for Calicut. The political situation there was complicated. Prior to Cabral's arrival sixty Portuguese had been murdered by fanatical

Pedro Alvarez made his discoveries with a merchant fleet. His greatest achievement was the discovery of Brazil.

In Europe, one was not only interested in the fascinating reports from distant exotic lands, but also in a particular ware which many of the explorers brought back in their ships, especially with the merchant fleets: many different kinds of spices. These were regarded as a great delicacy in Europe. This wood engraving from 1575 shows cinnamon being harvested in the East Indies.

Moslems, and the admiral immediately ordered an attack on the towns of Calicut, Cochin and Cananore by gunfire. The Samurin relented, and the Portuguese ships were filled with the coveted spices.

On the return voyage another caravel was lost not far from Sofala on the coast of eastern Africa; despite this, on 23 July, 1501 Cabral arrived back in Lisbon with six ships. His voyage had finally broken the Arabian monopoly in the spice trade.

Cabral's roundabout route to East India was faster than Vasco da Gama's and soon found general favor.

This engraving from 1673 shows a Portuguese settlement in Brazil. Cotton, tobacco, spices and sugar were taken from here to Europe.

Further reading
C. Pereyra, La conquête des routes océaniques d'Henri le Navigateur à Magellan. Paris 1923
G. de Reparaz, La época de los grandes descubrimientos españoles y portugueses. Barcelona 1931
D. Peres, Historia da expansao portuguesa no mundo. Lisbon 1937-1940
–, Historia dos descubrimientos portugueses. Porto 1943
E. Prestage, Descobridores portugueses. Porto 1943

CA DA MOSTO (CADAMOSTO), ALVISE (OR LUIGI)

Italian seafarer in Portuguese service, born c. 1432 in Venice, died c. 1510 in Rovigo.

Ca da Mosto entered into the service of Henry the Seafarer and on his behalf visited the Cape Verde Islands and Senegal.

In 1456 he discovered the Gold Coast on a voyage of exploration along the coast of Africa. Ca da Mosto was the first (Portuguese) seafarer to reach the equator and supply evidence of his achievement.

Further reading
S. Grynaeus, Novis Orbis. Navigatio ad terras ignotas Aloysii Cadamosti. Basil (Translation: Jost Reichamer: Unbekannte Leute und eine Welt in kurz vergangenen Zeiten erfunden. Nuremburg 1503)
Ca da Mosto's works were also printed in 1519 in Milan.

CAILLIÉ, RENÉ

French Sahara explorer, born 1799 in Mauzé (Deux-Sèvres), died 1838 in La Baderre.

Caillié came from an impoverished family. After reading Daniel Defoe's "Robinson Crusoe" he felt a calling to become a seafarer and explorer.

In 1816 he traveled to West Africa on a troop transporter. Caillié tried in vain to join the expedition of the Englishman Laing in search of the missing Mungo Park. He participated in a French expedition involved in exploring the Senegalese interior, during which he became ill with fever. He returned to France to convalesce. Hardly had he recovered from his illness when he returned to Senegal with the firm intention of revealing the secret of the legendary town of Timbuktu (in present-day Mali). When he presented his plan to the French authorities, asking for financial support, he was turned down as a mere adventurer. As a result he traveled to the English colony of Sierra Leone (West Africa), where the Governor procured a well-paid position for Caillié, who then continued his studies of the Sahara and learned various west African dialects.

In the meantime the Parisian "Société Géographique" had offered a reward of 10,000 francs for the first French explorer to return to France with revealing information about Timbuktu.

Dressed as an Egyptian, Caillié took the risk in April 1827. After a strenuous trek that took almost one year, he arrived in Djenné, a town in the interior delta of the Niger, and several hours later, unhindered but completely exhausted, reached the legendary Timbuktu. Caillié had achieved his life's aim.

The reality of this former commercial metropolis did not correspond to the ideas that people in the Occident had about this place. Caillié searched in vain for the familiar magnificent mosques, the bazaars filled with precious goods and the splendid palaces of the Islamic dignitaries. Even two-story houses were rare. Caillié himself had to spend the night in a shabby inn built from dried mud. After a two-week sojourn the explorer joined a caravan in the direction of Tangier. At the end of July he reached the oasis group of Tafilalet in southern Morocco and on 14 August he arrived at Fez. Via Rabat and Tangier he set out on his journey home and received his well-earned reward in Paris.

The work that René Caillé published ("Journal d'un voyage à Tombouctou et à Djenné dans l'Afrique Centrale"), in three volumes with an atlas, has lost nothing of its scientific value even today.

Under almost inhuman conditions, René Caillié had covered and explored no less than 4,500 km (2,800 miles) of the Sahara without any special equipment and with little financial backing. The German Africa explorer H. Barth described Caillié as the greatest and most commendable Sahara explorer. Almost forgotten, Caillié died at the age of 39.

Further reading
R. Caillié, Journal d'un voyage à Tombouctou et à Djenné dans l'Afrique Centrale. Paris 1830
J. Boulenger, Le voyage de René Caillié à Tombouctou. Paris 1932

CAMERON, VERNEY LOVETT

English Africa traveller and explorer, born 1844 in Radipole (Dorset), died 1894 near Leighton Buzzard, Bedford.

Verney Lovett Cameron was an officer in the British Navy. Originally sent to support David Livingstone, who was in difficulties, Cameron undertook an extensive expedition in 1873 on behalf of the London Geographic Society. His journey took him from Zanzibar into the interior of Central Africa, where he discovered the Lukuga, the outflow of Lake Tanganyika. He proceeded along Lake Kasai, wandered through the headwaters of the Zambezi and Kasai and after an exhausting trek reached Catambela, a small seaport of Benguela (Angola): he was thus the first European to have crossed equatorial Africa.

Cameron is credited with the scientific exploration of central Africa, but also for his campaign against slavery

The Briton Verney Lovett Cameron (left) was a vehement opponent of the slave trade.

The Portuguese Diogo Cão (right) discovered the Congo on his two expeditions. His experiences were the inspiration for a new journey by Bartolomeu Dias de Novaes.

Further reading
V. L. Cameron, Across Africa. 2 volumes.
London 1877.

CÃO, DIEGO

Portuguese seafarer, born 1462, died (missing) 1486.

Diego Cão left Lisbon in 1482 to sail along the coast of western Africa. He eventually reached the mouth of the Congo. King João II of Portugal was highly satisfied with the results of this first expedition and promoted Cão to the rank of Cavalleiro.

In 1485 Cão set out on his second voyage to the Congo, where he succeeded in establishing contact with the native ruler. Cão continued his journey and reached Monte Negro (now known as Cabo Negro). He continued as far as the point that now bears the name of Cape Cross and this is the last time his name is mentioned in the history books. Strangely enough, it is not known whether Diego Cão returned to Lisbon or if he died before reaching the town; nevertheless, because of his lack of success in reaching the southern tip, he was banished from court. Nothing is known about the rest of his life.

CAPELO, HERMENEGILDO CARLOS DE BRITO

Portuguese naval officer and explorer, born 1841 at Palmela Castle (Portugal), died 1917 in Lisbon.

In 1877 Capelo, together with Serpa Pinto and R. Ivens, was commissioned by the Lisbon government to explore the region between Angola and Mozambique and to study the connections between the river systems of the Congo, Quanza, Cumene and Zambezi. The command of this venture was assigned to the Africa explorer Serpa Pinto. While Serpa Pinto discovered the source of the Cubango, Capelo and Ivens, who were suffering from fever, had to return to Luanda. Their aim – the discovery of the outflow of the Quango into the Congo – had come to nothing.

In 1884 Capelo and Ivens undertook a second, successful expedition from Moçamedès (Angola) to Quelimane on the east coast of Africa. During the strenuous 4,500-km (2,800-mile) journey, crossing Africa from east to west, the two explorers made valuable geographic findings about the interior of Africa.

Further reading
Mitteilungen der Gesellschaft für Erdkunde.
Berlin 1877
Mitteilungen der k. u. k. geographischen

Gesellschaft zu Wien. Vienna 1877
Bolletin da Sociedade geographica de Lisboa.
Lisbon 1878
Pello-Hermeneu de Brito Capelo & R. Ivens,
Expedicão scientifica ao interior de Africa.
Observacoes meteorologicas e magneticas.
Lisbon 1879
H. Capelo & R. Ivens. De Angola à contra-costa.
Lisbon 1886

CARPINI, GIOVANNI DE PLANO (PIANO)

Franciscan monk and traveler, born c. 1182 in Umbria, died c. 1255 in Antivari.

In 1245 Giovanni Carpini undertook a diplomatic voyage to the court of the Great Khan Güjük in Karakorum on behalf of the Council of Lyon with another Franciscan monk, Stephen of Bohemia. Traveling from Lyon via Breslau, where they were joined by Benedict of Poland – also a member of the Franciscan order – the three itinerant monks reached Kiev on the Dnepr, where Stephen stayed behind. After a brief rest, Carpini and Benedict wandered through the region of the Golden Horde and were received by Batu, a grandson of Ghengis Khan and ruler of the Golden Horde. They visited Old and New Sarai on the Lower Volga and continued north of Lake Aral along the Syr-Darja River, arriving in Otrar, an important town in the Khanate of Tchaghatai. After spending a long sojourn in Balagasun and crossing the Gobi Desert, they were received by the Great Khan Güjük in Karakorum.

After a four-month stay the travelers set out on their arduous journey home. They arrived back in Europe with a favourable report on the Mongolian ruler's peaceful intentions. Güjük handed Carpini three letters to the Pope; these are still kept in the archives of the Vatican. Folowing his arrival back home (in the winter of 1247/48) Carpini wrote his "Historia Mongolarum".

Apart from specific character studies of the two Mongolian rulers Batu and Güjük (Kuyuk),

we are indebted to Giovanni Carpini for an accurate history of the Mongolian peoples of Asia, rich in both historical and geographical information.

Further reading
P. Bergeron, Voyages faits principalement
en Asie dans les XIIe, XIIIe, XIVe et
XVe siècles par Benjamin de Tudèle, Jean
Plan du Carpini... accompagnés de l'histoire
des Sarrazins et des Tartares et précédés
d'une introduction concernant les voyages
et les nouvelles découvertes des principaux
voyageurs. La Haye 1735
C. Charton, Voyageurs anciens et modernes
ou choix des relations de voyages les plus

intéressantes et les plus instructives.
2 volumes. Paris 1857
Johann de Plano Carpini, Geschichte der Mongolen und Reisebericht. Translated by F. Risch. Leipzig 1930

CARTIER, JACQUES

French seafarer and colonizer, born 1491 in St. Malo (French channel coast), died 1557 in St. Malo

We know nothing of Cartier's family background. However, it can be assumed that from a young age he accompanied Breton fishermen as far as Newfoundland, since he knew of the existence of the Labrador peninsula when he submitted to Admiral Philippe de Chabot and King Frances I his plan of exploring unknown areas in North America and discovering the Northwest Passage in order to reach China.

King Frances I, the colonial antagonist of Spain and Portugal, immediately accepted Cartier's political and military plan. On 20 April, 1543 Cartier left the port of St. Malo with two ships, crossed the North Atlantic, navigated the Belle-Ile Strait, established the island nature of Newfoundland, advanced for several miles up the St. Lawrence River and explored its shoreline. He landed at Cape Gaspé on the Gaspé Peninsula

The French natural scientist Comte de Castelneau explored South America. The photograph shows the Iguacu Falls from the Brazilian side.

and celebrated the first French advance in North America by erecting a ten-meter (32-foot) cross. On 5 September, 1534 he arrived back in St. Malo.

On 19 May, 1535 Jacques Cartier undertook his second North America voyage, this time with three ships. This expedition was not only of a political, but also of an economic nature, since Cartier had been expecting to find large deposits of gold and silver in Canada. On 1 September, the Breton landed on the North American coast. After a thorough exploration of the St. Lawrence River he stayed over winter in the Indian village of Stadacone (later Quebec), founded by Champlain.

With light boats he pushed ahead to a town named "Hochelaga", which became "Ville-Marie", founded in 1642, then "Mont Royal" and eventually Montreal. Not far from Hochelaga, Cartier saw the Ottawa River which, according to claims by the natives from the land of "Saguenay", was rich in gold mines. Cartier arrived back in St. Malo on 16 July, 1536. The adventurous explorer brought back valuable beaver skins, but he had not succeeded in discovering gold.

Despite the protestations of the chief from Stadacone, whom he had brought with him, that "Canada" (the word is derived from the term kanata, meaning village or community in the Huron and Iroquoi languages) was rich in precious metals and even spices, almost another five years were to pass until Frances I equipped a new expedition to North America.

On 23 May, 1541 Jacques Cartier left France with a crew of about four hundred, including farmers, soldiers, merchants and the "Viceroy" of Canada, F. de la Roque de Roberval, this time reaching the waterfalls of La Chine. On 21 October, 1542 Cartier and his crew returned to St. Malo. The rock samples he brought back with him, which he claimed to be gold and diamonds, proved however on closer investigation to be copper and loam.

Cortereal, Cabot and Verrazano had set foot on the Labrador peninsula before Cartier, but Cartier was the first to undertake a systematic colonization in East Canada. However, "Nouvelle-France" or New France was soon forgotten for lack of interest and especially due to the financial malaise of the French king. It was not until half a century later that Champlain developed the French colony in North America.

Further reading
M. Lescarbot, Histoire de la Nouvelle France ... Paris 1609, 1611, 1612, 1617, 1618
Société littéraire et historique de Québec, Voyages de découverte au Canada, entre les années 1534 et 1542, par Jacques Cartier, le Sieur de Roberval, Jean-Alphonse de Xaintoigne ... Quebec 1843
P. Levôt, La Biographie bretonne, article sur Cartier. Without place of publication, 1852

CASTELNEAU, FRANCIS DE LA PORTE, COMTE DE

French naturalist and traveler, born 1812 in London, died 1880 in Melbourne.

With the generous support of the French royal dynasty of Orléans, Castelneau undertook his first expedition to North America as an amateur geologist.

Accompanied by the French mining engineer Orsery and the English botanist Weddell, he traveled to South America in 1843 in order to explore the area between Rio de Janeiro and Lima as well as British and French Guayana. In Brazil the team began the exploration of the Rio Tocantins in north Brazil and the Rio Araguaia, the left tributary of the Rio Tocantins. Castelneau was hindered by the dictator López from exploring Paraguay and instead ventured into the Chaco, a north Argentinean province where he tracked down the daring horsemen tribes of the Guaykurus and Guatos. After crossing the Mato Grosso, he trekked via Santa Cruz de la Sierra into the interior of Bolivia and Peru. His companion Orsery, whom he had sent back to Rio de

In Otto von Kotzebue's account "Voyage of Discovery in the South Seas and to the Bering Strait to Search for a North-East Passage..." there are portraits of the natives of the Marshall Islands. The illustration above shows a native, that below the Chief of the Island of Otdia. The poet Adalbert von Chamisso took part in this voyage.

Janeiro with a valuable collection of exotic plants, was murdered by his porters on the way. On continuing his journey, Castelneau discovered the sources of the Paraguay and navigated the Amazon on his own up to where it flows into the Atlantic.

Extremely ill and almost blind, Francis Castelneau arrived in Paris in 1847 and published fifteen volumes about the flora, fauna and geography of South America between the years 1854 and 1859.

Further reading
Comte de Castelneau, Expéditions dans les parties centrales de l'Amérique du Sud de Rio de Janeiro à Lima au Paraguay pendant les années 1843-1847. Paris 1850

CHAMISSO, ADALBERT VON

Poet and natural scientist, born 1781 in Boncourt Castle (Champagne), died 1838 in Berlin.

In the commotion of the revolution, Adalbert Chamisso's family was forced to flee to Germany. In 1796 he became a page to the King of Prussia and later an officer in the Prussian army. From 1815 to 1818 he took part in a circumnavigation of the world, which he wrote about in wonderful prose in his book "Comments and views during a voyage of discovery." He supplemented the work and in 1836 he published it as "Journey around the world with the Romanzoff expedition of discovery from 1815 to 1818 on the brig Rurik."

Otto von Kotzebue was in charge of this voyage of exploration to the South Sea. It was unusual for a poet to take part in an expedition such as this. In addition to describing the stations of the journey, he vividly recorded life on board the ship.

Adalbert von Chamisso

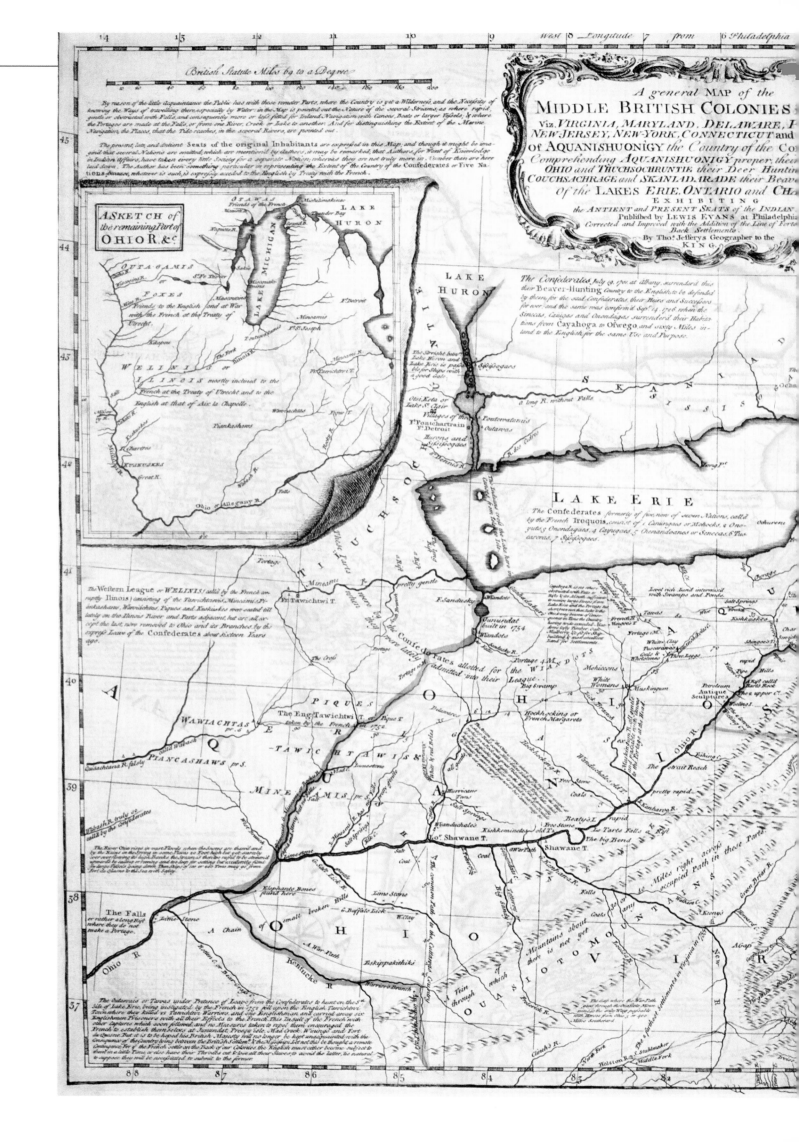

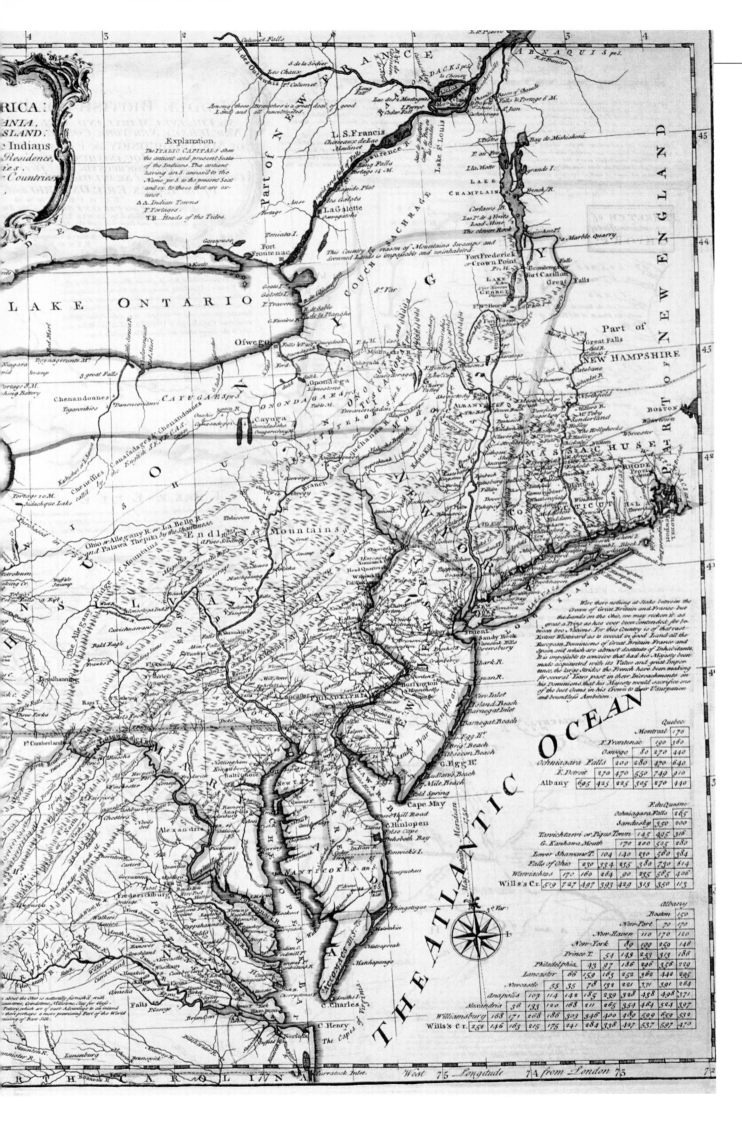

Samuel de Champlain's explorations were concentrated on Canada, which can be seen on this overall map of the middle British colonies in America.

CHAMPLAIN, SAMUEL DE

French-Canadian explorer and geographer, born 1567 in Brouage, died 1635 in Quebec.

Samuel de Champlain was a member of a traditional seafarer family. He participated in the fight against the insurgents ("ligueurs") in Brittany from 1593 to 1598, and once the insurgence had been put down, he traveled to Canada with his merchant friend Du Pont-Gravé from St. Malo. In Canada they visited the former whaling settlement of Tadoussac, navigated the St. Lawrence River up to St. Louis Falls and entered into friendly relations with the Huron, the former inhabitants of Stadacone and Hochelaga.

On his return to France, Champlain wrote in his work "Des Sauvages" (Of the Savages) that the area to the north of the St. Lawrence River was especially suitable for colonization by the French.

In 1604 Champlain sailed to Canada under the command of Vice Admiral Pierre des Monts and accompanied by Du Pont-Gravé and a crew of 120, went ashore on the coast of the present-day New Brunswick and founded two forts and fur trading posts on the "Ile de la Croix" (Island of the Cross) and in Port Royal.

In order to consolidate France's occupation of East Canada, Champlain traveled a third time (1608) to North America and founded Quebec, the oldest town in Canada, on the lower St. Lawrence River. The settlements of St. Anne des Monts, Tadoussac, Trois-Rivières and Montréal were founded.

Samuel de Champlain

Trade with the Canadian natives proved especially difficult in view of the tribal feuds they waged amongst each other. Champlain decided on an alliance with the Algonquins and Huron, who were weaker from a military point of view than the Iroquois and Montagnais. The first beaver, marten, ermine, sable, polecat and otter furs were then shipped to Europe. Nevertheless, it took longer than Champlain had expected for French settlers to arrive in eastern Canada. The English colonizers, by contrast, steadily increased their numbers in this area.

In 1615 Champlain set about exploring this region of French Canada, which was rich in lakes and rivers and was characterized by vast coniferous forests.

Accompanied by a few companions he navigated the Ottawa River in eastern Canada, discovered Lake Nipissing and arrived at Lake Ontario. Champlain was wounded in a battle with the Iroquois.

Only two decades after the foundation of Quebec, the English, who were stronger in numbers, took control of the town after a one-year siege. With the Treaty of Saint-Germain-en-Laye (1632) France was forced to cede the future capital of Canada to the British.

Champlain is considered to be the founder of French Canada.

Further reading
S. Champlain, Des Sauvages, ou voyage de Samuel Champlain, de Brouage fait en la France Nouvelle l'an mil six cent trois. Paris 1603
F. Parkman, Pioneers of France in the New World. Boston 1865
Voyages of Samuel Champlain. Translated from the French by Ch. Pomeroy Otis. With historical illustrations and a memoir by Rev. Ed. F. Slafter. 3 volumes. Boston 1880
H. R. Casgrain, Les origines du Canada. Champlain, sa vie. Without place of publication, 1898
N. E. Dionne, Samuel Champlain, fondateur de Québec. 2 volumes. Quebec 1891-1906
G. Gravier, Vie de Samuel Champlain. Paris 1900
A. H. Gosselin, Le vrai monument de Champlain. Ses œuvres éditées par Laverdière (From the "Mémoires de la Société Royale du Canada, 3e série, 1908-1909, Vol. II, section 1). Société Royale du Canada, Ottawa 1909
R. Finley, Samuel de Champlain. Founder of New France. Toronto 1925
Morris G. Bishop, Champlain. The life of fortitude. London 1949
H.-O. Meissner, Kundschafter am St. Lorenzstrom. Die Abenteuer des Samuel de Champlain. Stuttgart, without year of publication

CHANCELLOR, RICHARD

British seafarer, born ?, died 1556 at sea.

In 1553, on the orders of a group of wealthy London merchants and as captain of the "E. Bonaventure", Chancellor together with Sir H. Willoughby made an attempt to reach India via the Northeast Passage. When they reached the Lofoten Islands a storm drove the ships apart. Chancellor sailed alone around the North Cape, advanced to the White Sea and dropped anchor in Dvina Bay, near what is today known as Archangel. He trekked more than 2,500 km (1,560 miles) overland to Moscow to the court of Ivan the Terrible, where he signed the first British-Russian trade agreement; this was mainly directed against the German Hansa. On his return to London, the Moscow Trading Company was founded and an active exchange of goods between the two countries was established. The search for the Northeast Passage was postponed.

In 1555 Chancellor traveled to Moscow a second time. During his return journey he drowned off the coast of Scotland in 1556.

Further reading
R. Hakluyt, Principall Navigations, Voyages and Discoveries of the English Nation (Description of Chancellor's stay in Moscow). London 1589

Richard Chancellor was the first to establish trading links between England and Moscow. Below we see a contemporary portrait of the Russian metropolis.

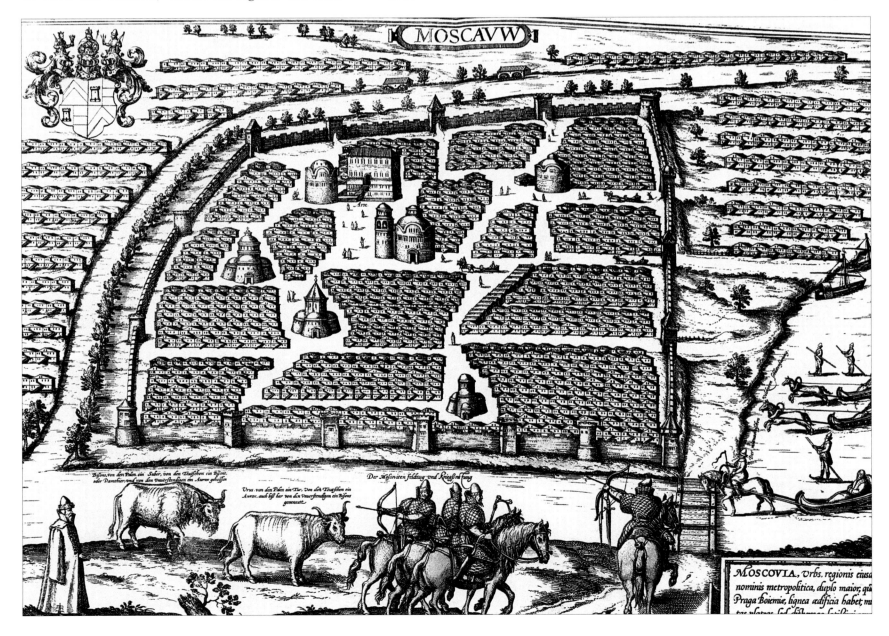

C. Adams, *Anglorum navigatio ad Moscovitas* (*A narrative of the voyage of R. Chancellor*). London 1600
J. V. Hamel, *England and Russia, comprising the voyages of R. Chancellor and others in the White Sea.* London 1854

Near the Lofoten Islands, Richard Chancellor's fleet was scattered by a violent storm, and he had to sail on alone.

CHARCOT, JEAN

French scientist and polar explorer, born 1867 in Neuilly-sur-Seine, died 1936 at sea.

Jean Charcot was the son of the famous physician J. M. Charcot. After studying medicine he turned his attention to the exploration of the Arctic and Antarctica.

In 1904 he was commissioned by the French admiralty to explore the west coast of Graham Land (Antarctica). He set out from Tierra del Fuego and reached the inhospitable Brabant and Antwerp Islands (to the south of the South Shetland Islands). As he continued his journey, Charcot discovered a safe haven (rare in Antarctica) on Viennacke Island, which he named Port Lockroy, and from there explored the Biscoe Islands. He and his team spent the winter on the western side of Graham Land.

In 1905 Charcot attempted another advance in a southerly direction, but was only able to reach a latitude of 67° 30' S. At this point, he disembarked on an island which he named "Terre Loubet" (this was in fact Adelaide Island, which had already been discovered by Biscoe in 1832). Following his scientific exploration of Graham Land, heavy storms forced him to abandon his expedition and return to France.

From 1907 to 1910 Carcot undertook a major Antarctic voyage to Graham Land on the "Pourquoi Pas?", a ship that had been specially constructed for polar waters.

At the conclusion of the First World War, Charcot turned his attention to exploring the Arctic. He concentrated his attention on Greenland, where he carried out hydrographical investigations. In 1934, sailing again on the "Pourquoi Pas?", he undertook a scientific expedition to the east coast of Greenland. There he dropped off the young arctic explorer P. E. Victor in the Bay of Kangerdlugssuag. In 1936 Charcot explored the stretches of Greenland's east coast named after the French hydrographer Blosseville; due to bad weather, however, he was forced to take refuge on Iceland. On 15 September, 1936 he set out once more for Greenland. A terrible storm broke out. Despite the exceptional efforts of the sailors on board, the "Pourquoi Pas?" sank. With the exception of one man, the entire crew perished.

Charcot's death was a serious setback for French polar exploration. An island to the east of King George Sound in Antarctica bears the name of this important explorer.

Further reading
J. B. Charcot, Le Pourquoi-Pas? dans l'Antarctique. Paris 1910
–, La mer du Groenland, croisières du Pourquoi-Pas? Paris 1929

CLAPPERTON, HUGH

Scottish explorer of Africa, born 1788 in Annan (Dumfriesshire), died 1827 near Sokoto (Nigeria).

Hugh Clapperton served with the British Navy from 1806 to 1817 and attained the rank of lieutenant. In 1822, accompanied by Dr. W. Oudney, the British consul of Bornu, and Major Dixon Denham, he set out on an expedition to the Sahara. From Tripoli, the trio eventually reached Kuka, the "capital" of Bornu on Lake Chad, after suffering unbelievable hardship. They were the first Europeans ever to have laid eyes on this freshwater lake in the middle of the desert. While Denham explored Lake Chad, the River Chari and its most important tributary the Logone, Clapperton and Oudney carried on westwards.

When Oudney succumbed to the exertions of the trek, which had lasted several days, Clapperton continued on Cano, one of the major trading posts in the Sahara at that time. The unflinch-

Hugh Clapperton

ing young Scot carried on further, eventually reaching the capital of the seven Haussa states. The sultan there only allowed Clapperton to continue once he had promised to send a medial practitioner, a consul and cartographic material to Sokoto from Britain.

Clapperton had not long returned to his homeland when he received a commission from the "African Association" to set out from the Gulf of Benin and explore the region of Sokoto, Bornu and the upper course of the River Niger. Clapperton was accompanied by R. Lander and three other British explorers, who all succumbed to their exertions not far from Badagri (Nigeria). The Scot and Lander triumphantly reached Sokoto. This was the first time that the region of Africa along the 10° E meridian had ever been explored. As Clapperton was preparing to explore the Sokoto Timbuktu region, he suffered a fatal heart attack on 13 April, not far from Sokoto.

Hugh Clapperton was the first explorer to determine that the River Niger flows in a north-westerly direction before flowing south. He was also the first to undertake a detailed investigation of Lake Chad. Moreover, he provided historians with a great deal of important information on the once mighty empire of Kanem Bornu, which was already in the process of decay at that time.

Further reading
H. Clapperton, Journal of a second expedition into the interior of Africa. London 1828
R. Lander, Records of Clapperton's last expedition to Africa. London 1830
Barrow, Narrative of Travels and Discoveries in northern and central Africa in the years 1822, 1823 and 1824 by Major Denham, Capt. Clapperton and the late Dr. Oudney. London 1862

CLARK, WILLIAM

North American explorer, born 1770 in Virginia, (USA), died 1838 in St. Louis.

Despite a lack of formal education, Clark developed exceptional cartographic skills. In 1803 Meriwether Lewis, another North American scientific explorer, chose Clark to accompany him and advise him on his major Far-West expedition (for details of this expedition, see Lewis).

After returning from this unique historical journey Clark was appointed Brigadier General of the military troops (civil militia) and "Indian Agent"; he held these offices from 1807 to 1813 in St. Louis. From 1813 to 1821 he was Governor of the Mississippi Territory and in 1822 was appointed chief diplomatic representative for "Indian Affairs" in St. Louis.

Clark and Lewis are regarded as the last great explorers of the "Far West".

COLUMBUS, CHRISTOPHER

Genoese seafarer and explorer, born 1451 in Genoa, died 1506 in Valladolid.

Christopher Columbus came from a simple weaver's family and received only elementary schooling. Very little is known about his life in Genoa prior to his 25th birthday. In 1475, on behalf of the Centurione Bank in Genoa, he reached the island of Chios in the Aegean Sea, occasionally accompanied Genoese fishermen on their boats in the Mediterranean Ocean and pursued various activities. His view of the world at that time was formed by the works "Ymago mundi" by Peter of Ailly, the "Historia rerum ubique gestarum" by Pope Pius II, Marco Polo's "Travels" and "Astronomy" by Ptolemaeus.

In 1476 he came to Lisbon, where he married D. Felipa Perestrello y Moñiz in 1478, and settled in Madeira, where his son Diego was born. In 1483 he submitted his ambitious plan to the Portuguese king John II to find the direct sea route to India in a westerly direction, to enter into an alliance with the Great Khan, to encircle the world of Islam and to enter into close trade relations with "Cipango" (Japan), "Cathay" (northern China) and "Mangui" (southern

The coat of arms of Christopher Columbus

China). After thorough examination by a team of mathematicians, theologists and navigators, Columbus' plan was rejected.

In 1485 Columbus went to Spain. He spent some time in La Rabida near Huelva and was received by the Spanish sovereign and his consort in Alcalá de Henares (January 1486) and in Madrid (February). For some time he lived in Cordoba. In 1489 he entered into close relations with the powerful dukes Medinaceli and Medina Sedonia, with Cardinal Mendoza and with the royal treasurer Quintanilla. After the fall of Granada, Columbus was finally able to gain acceptance for his ambitious aim. In Santa Fé he signed the politically most significant contract ever entered into between a private individual and a ruler (the "Capitulations of Santa Fé"). Columbus was promoted to viceroy of the "New World" and to the rank of admiral; he was appointed supreme judge for all disputes between Spain and the future colonies and received the title of "Don" and was granted the right to bear arms.

To finance his enterprise, the Crown contributed one million maravedis (Spanish gold coins). The remaining million was raised by the financially strong Martín Pinzón.

On 3 August, 1492 the three caravels – the "Santa María" (also called "Marie-Galante",

Columbus' egg:
The seafarer impressed
his opponents by
placing an egg on its
"pointed end" in such
a way that it did not
fall over.

Columbus leaves Palos
for America.

Whether Columbus was really welcomed so humbly and showered with presents by the natives on his arrival in the Indies as de Bry depicted the scene in his book is open to question. At any rate, the conquerors were very glad to see themselves in this role.

Short work was made with rebels. Columbus orders them to be hanged from trees as a deterrent for all.

*The landing
of Columbus in
America*

owned by J. de la Cosa), the "Niña" (owned by
Niño) and the "Pinta" (owned by Pinto) – set sail
from Palos before sunrise. The cosmopolitan
crew consisted of Andalusians, Basques, a sailor
from Valencia and several seafarers of unknown
nationality. They were accompanied by a
notary, an interpreter and the seafarers J. de la
Cosa, V. Y. Pinzón, N. Peralonso and S. R. Gama.

On Gomera (Canary Islands), the "Pinta" already had to be repaired. During this forced
sojourn, Columbus explored the islands of Hierro, Fuerteventura and Lanzarote.

On 12 October, Columbus had reached his
goal after a rather dramatic journey: accompanied by M. Pinzón and an armed escort, the
admiral set foot on Central American soil. The
island of "Guanahani" or "Watlin", where they
had landed, they named "San Salvador" in
honor of the Saviour. A notarial act legalised
the occupation of the island by the Spanish
Crown. During the continuation of his journey,
Columbus discovered the islands of "Fernan-
dina" (named in honor of the Spanish king),
where the Spanish saw a hammock ("hamac")
for the first time, "Santa María de la Concepción", Cuba, where Columbus expected to find
rich gold mines and whose inhabitants he assumed to be subjects of the Great Khan, and

Shortly before Columbus left on his third voyage he wrote this letter to his son Diego. The striking handwriting betrays an extremely strong-willed man.

Haiti, which he named "Hispaniola". In the meantime the "Santa María" had been lost and Pinzón had separated from Columbus. On Haiti, a fort named "La Novidad" was built.

Leaving 39 loyal crew members under the command of Diego de Arenas and counting on the support of Kaziken (chief) Guacanagari, Columbus returned to Spain with M. Pinzón, who had joined the admiral again. A hurricane drove the two ships apart. On 18 February, 1493, Columbus landed on the Azores, on 4 March he dropped anchor in the bay of the Tejo, where the Portuguese king paid his respects, and on 15 March he eventually reached the port of Palos. M. Pinzón, who had become an adversary of Columbus, died shortly after his arrival in Spain. In the Spanish court the viceroy was received with great respect; Columbus introduced to the sovereign and his consort the islanders that he had taken with him as subjects of the Great Khan.

Columbus received the immense sum of 335,000 maravedis as well as a pension, which rightly should have gone to the ship's mate Berjemo, since he had been the first to sight land. With a stroke of the pen, the "dominus orbis" – the Pope – declared the overseas possessions legally valid.

While Columbus was enjoying his new position, intensive preparations for a second journey were made. Duke Medina Sedonia financed almost the entire enterprise. The goals of this expedition were systematic settlement, conversion of the islanders to Christianity and the establishment of "diplomatic relations" with the Great Khan.

On 25 September, 1493 the Armada consisting of 17 ships left Cádiz with 1,500 men on board. Twenty farmers were to take care of agriculture in the "New World". On his second journey of discovery, Columbus came across "Dominica" (Sunday). Further islands – "Marie-Galante", "Guadeloupe", "Martinique" (Medina), "Montserrat", "Santa María de la Redonda", "San Martin" and "Santa Cruz" – changed ownership. When Columbus landed on Haiti, he found "La Novidad" destroyed and there was no sign of the crew. A second fort, "Isabella", was erected and Father Boyle was commissioned with the first administration on American soil.

Santo Domingo was established. Since the islanders were not fit for physical exertion, it was necessary to introduce black workers. Columbus thus laid the foundations for slave labor in the "New World", even if only unintentionally. He was blamed for the first serious upheavals amongst the Spanish. To justify himself, he returned to Spain on 10 March, 1496 and received a frosty welcome at the royal court. However, a few weeks later all accusations against Columbus were dropped.

After a two-year sojourn in Spain, Columbus undertook his third expedition to the "New World". Six caravels left the port of Sanlucar de Marrameda on 30 May, 1498; on 31 July, he reached Trinidad on the mouth of the Orinoco. Columbus explored the Gulf of Paria, where he expected to find the sources of the Indus and Ganges. He assumed this area to be a large island and named it "Isla de Gracia". He landed in Santo Domingo, where the administration was in a desolate state. In the meantime a commission under the leadership of Hojeda and Bobadilla had arrived in order to examine the deplorable state of administration on Haiti. Subsequently, Columbus was replaced as viceroy by N. de Ovando and taken to Spain as a prisoner. However, in Granada he was received as a welcome guest by the sovereign and his consort and Bobadilla was removed from office. Despite his rehabilitation, Columbus withdrew to the Zurbia monastery near Granada for the time being and prepared a map of all the islands he had discovered. Unfortunately the original of this map has been lost; a Turkish copy by Piri Reis can be found in Istanbul.

On 9 May, 1502, Columbus began his fourth and last "American journey", for which he received detailed instructions in keeping with the Treaty of Tordesillas. On 15 June he landed on Madinina, then on Santa Lucía and Martinique. He was driven by a storm to the entrance of the present-day Panama Canal, where he searched in vain for representatives of the Great Khan.

However, Columbus' heyday was finally over. On 12 September, 1504 the seafarer, broken and plagued by gout, set off for home; two years later he died in Valladolid.

Columbus is the most controversial figure of all the great adventurers and seafarers. Never before nor after has an explorer given rise to so much dispute among historians and biographers in regard to a just evaluation of his personality as did this proud, presumptuous and self-educated man from Genoa. Roselly de Lorgues, for example, regards Columbus as a "saint", whereas Marius André sees him as an "ignoramus". To this day more than twenty towns, amongst them Nervi, Calvi, Savone, Quinto, claim to be Columbus' place of birth, despite the fact that he wrote "Essendo io nato in Genua" in his will, and historians attribute the Armenian, French, English, Galician and Jewish nationalities to him. Columbus' alleged petitions to the kings of France and England cannot be substantiated historically. If Lisbon had heeded Columbus' petitions, Portugal's influence would not have been restricted to Brazil.

The continent on which Columbus had landed during his fourth journey was named after the seafarer Amerigo Vespucci by the German scholar Waldseemüller. Only the South American republic of Columbia is named after Christopher Columbus.

Further reading
H. Harrisse, Chr. Colomb, son origine, sa vie,
ses voyages, sa famille et ses descendants.
Paris 1884
R. Altamira, Historia de España y de la
civilización española. Barcelona 1910-1911
C. Pereyra, Historia de América. México
1920-1925
H. Vignaud, Le vrai Ch. Colomb et la légende.
Paris 1921
M. André, La véridique aventure de Ch. Colomb.
Paris 1927
J. P. Charcot, Ch. Colomb vu par un marin.
Paris 1928
S. E. Morison, admiral of the Ocean Sea,
a life of Ch. Columbus. Boston 1942

Ballesteros, Cristobal Colón y el descubrimiento de América. 2 volumes. Barcelona 1945

Christoph Columbus, Das Bordbuch 1492. Leben und Fahrten des discoverers der Neuen Welt in Dokumenten und Aufzeichnungen, ed. R. Grün. 3rd edition Tübingen 1974

G. Granzotto, Christoph Kolumbus. Eine Biographie. Hamburg 1988

Das Logbuch des Christoph Kolumbus, ed. R. H. Fuson. Berg.-Gladbach 1989

S. Fischer-Fabian, Um Gott und Gold. Columbus entdeckt die neue Welt. Berg.-Gladbach 1991

U. Bitterli, Die Entdeckung Amerikas von Kolumbus bis Alexander von Humboldt. 4th ed. Munich 1992

J. D. Clare, Christoph Kolumbus – Mutiger seafarer und discoverer der neuen Welt. Nuremberg 1992

G. Faber, Auf den Spuren des Christoph Kolumbus. Reprint. Munich 1992

R. Humble, Die Reisen des Christoph Kolumbus. Nuremberg 1992

S. de Madariaga, Kolumbus. Leben, Taten und Zeit des Mannes, der vor 500 Jahren Amerika entdeckte und damit die Welt veränderte. Munich 1992

P. Marc, Kolumbus entdeckt Amerika. Zurich 1992

F. Niess, Am Anfang war Kolumbus. Die Geschichte einer Unterentwicklung – Lateinamerika 1492 bis heute. 2nd edition Munich 1992

B. Smith, Die erste Fahrt des Christoph Kolumbus 1492. Mödling (Austria) 1992

A. Venzke, Christoph Kolumbus. Reinbek 1992

Ch. Verlinden, Kolumbus. Vision und Ausdauer, ed. D. Junker. Reprint. Göttingen 1992

Christoph Columbus, Das Bordbuch. Leben und Fahrten des Entdeckers der Neues Welt in Dokumenten und Aufzeichnungen – 1492. München 2001

COOK, FREDERICK ALBERT

American conqueror of the North Pole, born 1865 in Callicoon, died 1940 in New Rochelle.

Cook was the youngest of five children born to the German physician Dr. Theodor Koch, who emigrated to the US around 1840. When Cook

Frederick Albert Cook was originally a doctor, and met Peary in the role of a ship's doctor. He is considered to be one of the most prominent experts on the North Pole.

was just five years old his father died; although the family was quite poor, Cook was still able to attend school and university. In 1891 he attained his doctorate and settled in Brooklyn as a physician.

When R. E. Peary was looking for a physician for his planned Greenland expedition, Cook applied for the position and was accepted. Peary and Cook, later to be the two greatest adversaries in the race for the North Pole, were initially good friends. In 1891 Cook gained his first Arctic experience on the journey to northern Greenland with Peary. From 1898 to 1899 Cook, who was obsessed with polar exploration from that time onwards, took part in the South Pole expedition organized by the Belgian Arctic explorer Adrien de Gerlache de Gomery on board the "Belgica". Another celebrated companion was Roald

Amundsen, who was later to conquer the South Pole. The "Belgica" became trapped in ice in the Bellinghausen Sea on 10 March, 1898 at 71° 31' S and 85° 16' W, and Cook spent his first winter in the south polar ice. After this journey the Belgian king Leopold II bestowed a title on Cook for his services to the country. In New York he wrote a book about his experiences.

In 1902 Cook met Peary in Greenland once more as part of a support expedition. After this he concentrated on mountain climbing. His first attempt to climb to the peak of Mount MacKinley, North America's highest pinnacle in the Alaska Range (6,193 m or 20,318 feet), was unsuccessful. In 1906 Cook set out again for MacKinley with a team of ten. After making detailed preparations, during which maps were drawn of more than 3,000 square meters (35,000 square feet) around the foot of the mountain, Cook and Edward Barill, a mine worker from Montana, began their ascent from Ruth Glacier.

On 16 September, 1906 the two men reached the peak. Despite this, Hudson Stuck, who did not ascend to the peak until seven years later, was long regarded as having been the first to conquer Mount MacKinley.

When Cook returned from Alaska he heard that Peary had reached the 87° N parallel during his attempt to reach the North Pole and was thus just a good 330 km (200 miles) short of his goal. But now Cook, who knew the Arctic well and who had familiarized himself with the techniques of the Inuit, also set his sights on reaching the Pole. His plan consisted of advancing straight across Ellesmere Island to Axel Heiberg Island (one of the Sverdrup Islands) and to reach the North Pole directly from there.

On 19 February, 1908 Cook, accompanied by his German friend Rudolf Francke and ten Inuit along with 105 huskies from Annoatok on the Nares Strait (northwestern Greenland), reached Staelworth, the northernmost tip of Axel Heiberg

Frederick Cook's flagship "Resolution" entered Christmas Sound at the end of 1774 and anchored there.

Island, from Ellesmeere Island. Provision camps were set up every 80 km (50 miles). On 18 March Cook set out from Axel Heiberg Island in the direction of the North Pole with four sledges and just four Inuit. After 100 km (60 miles) he sent two Inuit back. With the two remaining Inuit Etukishook and Ahwelah and 26 dogs, Peary's adversary continued his trek to the pole, which he reached on 21 April, 1908 – one year before R. E. Peary.

Frederick Cook had an igloo built, hoisted the US flag, made various scientific observations and wrote a short letter, which he placed in a sealed brass tube. Then they began their strenuous return journey. The ice and weather conditions had greatly deteriorated. They were driven away from their route by a westerly current. Instead of reaching Axel Heiberg Island, where the provision stores were located, they were driven into Crown Prince Gustav Sea and were only able to reach the Jones Sound with a great deal of effort, where they spent the winter near Cape Sparbo. When the sun returned, Cook and his two companions proceeded to Etah on the Nares Strait on northwestern Greenland, where Cook boarded the Danish steamship "Hans Egede" and announced that he had reached the North Pole.

In Copenhagen, Cook was celebrated enthusiastically for this feat. Then the controversy about the North Pole began. Peary's adherents insisted that Cook had not in fact reached the North Pole, as he had not produced any evidence on his return. At the same time, Cook's claim to have reached the summit of Mount MacKinley was thrown into doubt. The argument as to who had in fact been the first to reach the North Pole continued for many years. Cook had no accurate measuring instruments with him and was thus unable to provide definitive proof that he had actually reached the pole. R. E. Peary's assertions are generally given more credibility and he is thus regarded as the true conqueror of the North Pole.

Further reading
F. A. Cook, *Through the First Antarctic Night.* New York 1900
–, *My attainment of the Pole. Without place of publication without year of publication*
–, *Die Erreichung des Nordpols.* Hamburg 1912
E. S. Balch, *Der Nordpol und das Bradleyland.* Hamburg 1914 (in favor of Cook)
M. Lewels, *Dr. Cook und der Nordpol.* School program, Hamburg 1916 (against Cook)
F. Cook, *Zum Mittelpunkt der Arktis.* Braunschweig, Berlin, Hamburg 1928
–, *Wo Norden Süden ist.* Hamburg 1953
A. Freemann, *The Case for Dr. Cook.* New York 1961
Russell W. Gibbons, *An historical evaluation of the Cook-Peary controversy. Without place of publication 1954*
R. Amundsen, *Close calls in my life as an explorer. World's Work, Without place of publication June 1927*

COOK, JAMES

English seafarer and explorer, born 1728 in Marton (Yorkshire), died 1779 on Hawaii.

James Cook came from a modest family background. At the age of eighteen he worked on a coal transport ship and, thanks to his mathematical and hydrographical skills which he had gained through self-instruction, advanced to the position of first officer. In 1755 Cook abandoned his private "career" and joined the Royal Navy as a sailor.

He took part in the siege of Quebec. From 1760 to 1767 the newly qualified "Master" was commissioned to chart the Orleans Channel, the mouth of the Hudson and the coastal regions of Newfoundland, Labrador and Nova Scotia. In 1768 Cook was promoted to the rank of lieutenant and commanding officer of the "Endeavour" and was commissioned to carry out a scientific exploration of the entire Pacific. Cook carried out a total of three extended voyages of discovery in the South Seas.

On 5 August, 1768 the "Endeavour" put out to sea from Plymouth in Devon with a crew of 90 men, including the astronomer Green, the

James Cook, called Captain Cook, found an effective remedy for scurvy, the chronic disease of the early sailors, which led to bleeding of the gums and to teeth falling out. Cook took pickled cabbage on the journey and was thus able to provide his crew with the essential vitamin C.

Cook was very interested in the habits of the natives. This illustration shows him at a feast given in his honor, during a stay on the Hawaii Islands.

Swedish naturalist Solander and the influential Sir J. Banks. Sailing through the "Le Maire Strait" and around Cape Horn, Captain Cook reached Tahiti on 13 April, 1769. There he went on land, set up a fortified camp, established relations with Queen Oberea and, accompanied by the high priest Toupaia, explored the entire group of islands, which he named the "Society Islands".

He continued his journey, reaching New Zealand, where he cast anchor in "Poverty Bay", before circumnavigating the islands. In "Charlotte Bay" Cook climbed a mountain and noticed the strait between the North and South Islands.

On his second circumnavigation he demonstrated that New Zealand consists of two islands. He also made some interesting findings, for instance that the Maoris of New Zealand were disposed to fantasy as well as stealing and fighting and that they indulged in cannibalism, that only the chiefs were permitted to tattoo themselves, that the population nourished itself from a type of bracken root and that a type of flax (phormicum tenax) was grown there.

As Cook was sailing along "Botany Bay" (now Sydney Harbour), his ship ran aground. He was able to continue his journey once the damage had been repaired. He sailed through the "Torres Strait" and explored the coast of New Guinea and the island of Savu Raja. When he reached Batavia, Cook was forced to accept that most of the crew were unfit to work due to the bad swamp prevalent in Indonesia. In mid-March 1771 Cook dropped anchor in Cape Town and on 13 July arrived in Dover, still with a crew of 56.

While Cook had been unable to find the legendary southern continent, "Terra Australis Incognita", and his journey had taken a high toll in regard to human life, the scientific results were quite remarkable: the double island nature of New Zealand had been proven and the "Torres Strait", which from then onwards was named the "Endeavour Strait", had been rediscovered. New South Wales (Australia) now belonged to Britain and the seafarer Cook had become a significant geographer and hydrographer.

In 1772 the admiralty commissioned Cook to carry out a second voyage of exploration in the Pacific. On 13 July, the "Resolution" under Cook's command and the "Adventure" commanded by Furneaux set sail from Plymouth. The two German naturalists Forster (father and son) were also on board. The ships sailed via Funchal, Santiago (Cape Verde Islands) and around the Cape of Good Hope in Cook's search for the southern continent and on 17 January, 1773 Cook crossed the Antarctic Circle and reached a latitude of 67° 15' S. Since it proved impossible to carry on through the ice masses, Cook set a northerly course, discovered the "Pitcairn Islands", sailed through the Paumotu islands, landed on Tahiti, sailed to the island of Tonga-tapu (Nukualofa), landed once more on New Zealand and, on his continued journey, at 71° 10' S reached a point further south than anyone before him.

An insurmountable ice barrier and a dissatisfied crew prevented Cook from carrying on any further. He set a northerly course, first heading towards the Juan Fernández Islands, then the Marquesas Islands and the Easter Islands. The ship again made a stop on Tahiti.

After visiting Tonga and the New Hebrides, Cook, sailing on a westerly course, discovered New Caledonia.

On his return journey through the South Pacific, Cook happened upon New Georgia and the South Sandwich Islands ("Southern Thule"). However, he failed to find "Bouvet Land". On 19 July, 1775 the "Resolution" dropped anchor in Plymouth after three years at sea.

Cook's second circumnavigation of the Earth had cost only a few human lives. His measures against scurvy (he had taken immense quantities of pickled cabbage on board) had proven effective. He was promoted to the rank of captain, admitted to the "Royal Society" and awarded membership as "Fourth captain at the sailors' hospital in Greenwich".

Thirty years before Cook's second world voyage, the British government in London had put up a £20,000 reward for the Briton who discovered the Northwest Passage. Cook, now 48 years old, accepted this challenge.

Cook was killed in a fight between his men and the natives on Hawaii in February, 1779.

On 12 July, 1776 commanding the "Resolution" he left Plymouth harbor accompanied by the naturalists Anderson as well as the future commanding officer of the "Bounty", helmsman William Bligh, and the Swiss painter Weber. Among other things, Cook had been commissioned to set course for New Albion ("Drake Land"), to reach a latitude of at least 65° N and to study the fauna and flora of the Arctic. In Cape Town, Cook was joined by captain Clerke with the "Discovery", and the flotilla set course for the Kerguélen Islands, then for Tasmania and New Holland (Australia). In the Tonga islands Cook charted 61 islands and landed on Tahiti, where the young Dedidi was able to see his homeland once more. On 18 January, 1777 Cook visited the Sandwich Islands, Niihau and Hawaii, then reached the North American coast. He searched in vain for the "Juan de Fuca Strait" (Nootka) and advanced to the "Prince of Wales Cape". After a brief stay with the hospitable Chuktche, he set an easterly course and reached the Beaufort Sea. However, ice masses forced him to turn back. Cook and his crew spent the winter on the Sandwich Islands. A renewed attempt to find Hudson Bay through the Arctic Ocean proved to be unsuccessful.

On 17 January, 1779 Cook landed once more on Owhehee (Hawaii) in the Bay of Karakua, where he was the guest of King Paria and High Priest Koah. An incident – inhabitants of a neighboring island had stolen one of Cook's sloops – triggered an conflict between the British sailors and the inhabitants of the islands, during which Cook was killed on 14 February, 1779.

Under Clerke's command the British ships quickly weighed anchor and landed on Petropavlovsk (Camchatka). Clerke's attempt to reach Hudson Bay via the Arctic Ocean was also unsuccessful. During the return journey this great captain also died. The flotilla sailed through the Sunda Strait and around the Cape of Good Hope, eventually reaching home after an absence of 51 months.

James Cook is not merely the most significant British seafarer and explorer, he is also one of the world's greatest researchers of all time. The length of his scientific voyages on three oceans by far outstripped those of his predecessors, and his ethnographic studies of the peoples of the Pacific islands, New Zealand and Australia provided eighteenth-century Europeans with their first virtually complete insight into this previously more or less unexplored region of the Pacific. Vasco da Gama had conquered the Indian Ocean for Portugal; Cook conquered the Pacific for Britain.

Further reading
A voyage towards the South Pole and round the world performed in H. M. S. "The Resolution" and "Adventure" in the years 1772 to 1775. I/II. London 1777
Des Kapitäns James Cook dritte Entdeckungsreise in das Stille Meer und nach dem Nordpol hinauf der Jahre 1776 bis 1780. Translated from English by G. Forster. Volume I/II. Without place of publication 1787
Captain Cook's journal during his first voyage round the world made in H. M. bark "Endeavour" in the years 1768-1771. London 1893
H. Zimmermann, Die Reise um die Welt mit Kapitän Cook. Mannheim 1781. Edited new edition by H. Franke. Heidelberg 1948
J. W. Vandercook, Great Sailor. A life of the discoverer Captain James Cook. New York 1950
K. Lütgen, Der große Kapitän. Without place of publication 1951
Capt. James Cook, Entdeckungsfahrten im Pazifik. Die Logbücher der Reisen 1768 bis 1779, published by A. Grenfell Price. 2nd reprint Tübingen 1972
Biographie von Kap. Cook in "Cambridge History", Volume VII S. 686. Without place of publication, without year of publication
J. Cook, Entdeckungsfahrten im Pazifik. Die Logbücher der Reisen 1768-1779, ed. A. Grenfell Price. Stuttgart 1983.
G. Forster/G. Ch. Lichtenberg, Cook der Entdecker. Schriften über James Cook, ed. K. G. Popp. Leipzig 1991
P. Marc, Die Reisen des Kapitän Cook. Zurich 1992.
Otto Emersleben, James Cook. Reinbek 1998

CORTEZ, HERNANDO (HERNÁN CORTÉS)

Spanish explorer, seafarer and conquistador, born 1485 in Medellín (Estremadura), died 1547 in Castilleja de la Cuesta (near Seville).

After completing his law studies at the University of Salamanca, this born adventurer set out for Central America. During his stay there H. de Córdoba explored the coast of the Mexican Yucatan peninsula as far as Campeche and J. de Grivalja reached the Panuco River. Both of these explorers brought valuable gold and silver jewelry to Cuba, whereupon the governor in Havana decided to conquer the land of the Aztecs for the Spanish crown. Cortez, Alcalde (chairman of the council) of Santiago de Cuba, was commissioned to carry out this ambitious undertaking.

Cortez' military campaign proved fortuitous right from the outset, as the Aztecs were expecting their banished god Quetzalcoatl (the Plumed Serpent) to return from the east in the year 1519.

On 18 February, 1519 Cortez left the port of Havana with ten ships, 100 sailors, 32 of whom were archers, and 13 arkebusians (sharpshooters), 16 horses, 10 field guns and four falconets (small cannon). Immediately on landing, he founded the city of Vera Cruz and had the assembled "cabildos" (council, senate) bestow unlimited powers upon him.

In order to prevent any attempt at escape, Cortez ordered all the ships to be sunk. He formed an alliance with the Totonacs and the Tlaxcalans (or Tlaxcalteks), who were both subjugated by the Aztecs. Without encountering any resistance the conquistador reached Tenochtitlán, the capital of the Aztec empire, where he took Montezuma prisoner and ruled the empire in his name.

Panfilo de Narvaez, who had been sent by Velasquez to Mexico to check Cortez's authority, was killed in a surprise attack.

During Cortez' absence from Tenochtitlán, his friend P. de Alvarado had caused an uprising amongst the Aztecs through his acts of barbarism and cruelty. Leaving behind his entire artillery, Cortez (who had returned to Tenochtitlán to restore order) was forced to flee the city during the "night of sadness" (noche triste) of 1 July, 1520. Montezuma had died some days beforehand of injuries from a thrown stone. However, near Otombo, Cortez (without artillery) defeated an Aztec army which far outnumbered his own forces, thus giving himself some urgently needed respite.

For the final storming of Tenochtitlán, Cortez had a fleet of brigantines built so that he could seize this lagoon city from the sea via the canal. After 85 days of siege, the tow fell into the hands of the Spaniards and was reduced to rubble.

The complete conquest of the Yucatan peninsula took another two years. While Cortez vanquished the still insubordinate tribes, his comrade-in-arms P. de Alvarado took Guatemala and

In his campaigns of conquest Hernando Cortez was ruthless both with his own men and with the natives. He did not care what means he used to achieve success.

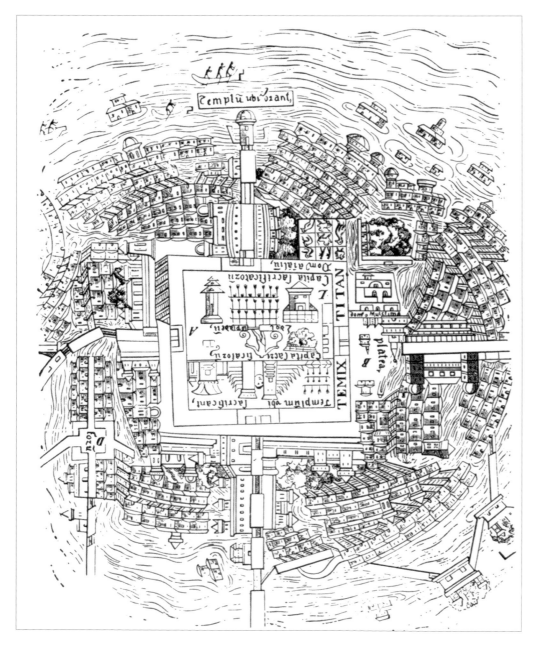

After letters from Cortez to Emperor Charles V, Tenochtitlan, the legendary metropolis of the Aztecs, was rebuilt. The design of the city was an architectural masterpiece.

Montezuma, the ruler of the Aztecs, was treacherously outwitted by Cortez.

supreme court, then to the Viceroy A. de Mendoza. Cortez was finally appointed "Marqués del Valle de Oaxaca" (a Mexican city with rich gold reserves and 28 villages) and from there undertook new expeditions to southern California.

Dissatisfied with having to obey public servants superior to him, Cortez returned to Spain. He died in 1547 on his estate, Castilleja de la Cuesta, without having seen Mexico again.

Besides Francisco Pizarro, Cortez is the most noteworthy figure among the Spanish conquistadors.

Through its conquest of Mexico, Spain became the world's richest nation in the first half of the sixteenth century. Unfortunately, the enormous revenue from the Central American gold and silver mines was wasted in Europe on futile power politics.

The conquest of Mexico was recorded by the Spanish historian Gomera (who did not always adhere to the facts). Bernal Díaz del Castillo, who witnessed the destruction of Tenochtitlán, nar-

C. de Olid conquered the Republic of Honduras. On hearing that Olid had exceeded his authority and intended to conquer a realm for himself, Cortez proceeded through unexplored tropical rainforest towards Honduras. On arriving there, he found that the disobedient Olid had already been killed by Fr. de las Casas.

After three years in Mexico, Cortez decided that it was time to return to his Spanish homeland; however he was only awarded the title of General Captain of New Spain. The administration of the former Aztec Empire was first of all transferred to the audiencia, the officers of the

rated the course of the city's fall in a lively and imaginative manner.

Further reading
W. H. Prescott, History of the conquest of Mexico. 3 volumes. Boston 1843
Díaz del Castillo, Die Eroberung von Mexiko. Translated by H. Seebeck. Gotha 1847
W. H. Prescott, The Spanish Conquistadores. London 1905
C. Pereyra, Historia de América. México 1920-1925
Hernán Cortéz, Testamento de Hernán Cortés. La edición facsimile. Mexico 1930
H. M. Robinson, Stout Cortez. A biography of the Spanish conquest. New York 1931
L. Torres, Hernán Cortés. Saragossa 1939
F. A. Kirkpatrick, The Spanish Conquistadores. 2d Ed. London 1946
K. Klein-Schonnefeld, Cortez und Marina. In: Berliner Hefte für geistiges Leben. 3rd volume, edition 5. Berlin 1948
M. Collins, Cortes and Montezuma. London 1954
J. Descola, Les Conquistadores espagnols. Paris 1957
R. Manzano, Los grandes conquistadores. Barcelona 1958
Fr. R. Majo, Conquistadores españoles del siglo. XVI. Madrid 1963
–, Die Eroberung Mexicos. Eigenhändige Berichte an Kaiser Karl V. 1520-1524. Frankfurt/M. 1979.
H. Cortez, Die Eroberung Mexikos 1520-1524. Auszug aus den Memoiren des Bernal Diaz del Castillo. München 2001
Claudine Hartau, Hernando Cortes. Reinbeck 1994

COUSTEAU, JACQUES YVES

French hydrographer, underwater explorer, documentary film maker, writer and a committed advocate of environmental protection, born 1910 in Saint-André-de-Cubsac, died 1997 in Paris.

On board the specially equipped "Calypso", Jacques Cousteau sailed the oceans for many years, accompanied by a selected team of hydrographers and underwater explorers. His research program ranged from measuring the depth of the oceans to discovering and studying rare marine creatures.

Cousteau was one of the inventors of the aqualung, which allows its wearer to dive to a depth of up to 30 meters (100 feet) without danger, a special underwater camera and a floating island for oceanographical observations. He also made a series of oceanographical films, including "Epaves" (flotsam), "Le monde du silence" (The silent world) and "Le monde sans soleil" (The world without sun). From the 1970s, Cousteau was active in the cause of environmental protection and established the "Cousteau Society", a foundation for the retention of the world's water systems.

Cousteau became known to a wide public through his fascinating underwater films.

Further reading
J. Y. Cousteau, The silent world. London 1953
– and F. Dumas, Le monde du silence. Paris, without year of publication
– Le monde sans soleil. Paris, without year of publication
– and J. Dugan, The living sea. Without place of publication, 1963
– and Ph. Cousteau, Haie. Herrliche Räuber der See. Munich 1971
– and Ph. Diole, Silberschiffe. Tauchen nach versunkenen Schätzen. Munich 1972

– and Ph. Diole, Wale. Gefährdete Riesen der See. Munich 1972
– and Ph. Diole, Kalmare. Wunderwelt der Tintenfische. Munich 1972
– and Ph. Diole, Calypso. Abenteuer eines Forschungsschiffes. Munich without year of publication
– (ed.), Cousteau almanac, Without place of publication 1981ff.

CRIPPEN, ROBERT LAUREL

US American astronaut, born 1937 in Beaumont (Texas).

Robert Crippen is one of the most experienced astronauts of the space shuttle era. In April 1981 he and John Young undertook the first space shuttle flight in the "Columbia", and by October 1984 he had taken part in three further flights. The space shuttle is a carrier system for transporting payloads from the surface of the Earth into orbit and back. In addition, as opposed to launcher rockets, it can be brought back to Earth to be used again; this represented a spectacular innovation in space travel.

On the morning of 12 April, 1981, twenty years to the day after the world's first space flight by the Russian cosmonaut Yuri Gagarin, the astronauts Crippen and Young lifted off from Cap Canaveral in the space shuttle "Columbia". This was the first test flight in the era of shuttle flights. The space tug was the largest and heaviest individual piece of machinery that had ever been put into orbit in one single start. It reached a speed of 28,000 km/h (17,400 mph). During this flight the two astronauts wore pressurized suits and were strapped into ejector seats. The start phase went without incident and the test flight was successfully completed on 14 April, 1981. Several years later the transport system was ready for operation. The number of lift-offs steadily increased. They were now possible at night and in inclement weather, and pressurized suits and ejector seats had become superfluous. The freight holds that were empty during the first flight are now invariably full, and crews of up to six astronauts regularly take part in the space shuttle missions.

In June 1983 besides Crippen and several other astronauts, the first American woman in space, Sally Ride, was a member of the "Challenger's" crew. The astronauts' third flight in October 1984 involved the rescue of a defective satellite; Crippen's fourth mission into space in October 1984, again on board a "Challenger", is remembered for the fact that this was the first time that a shuttle crew had consisted of seven astronauts. During this flight, the astronaut Kathryn Sullivan was the first American woman to walk in space.

Robert Crippen spent a total of 506 hours in space.

Following the "Challenger" disaster of 28 January, 1986, in which all seven crew members lost their lives, Crippen worked in the fact-finding committee, which was set up to discover the causes of this accident. He was subsequently appointed director of the NASA Kennedy Space Center.

CUNNINGHAM, ALLAN

British-Australian scientific explorer, born 1791 in Wimbledon, died 1839 in Sydney.

Cunningham studied jurisprudence before turning his attention to botany. In 1814 he decided to leave Britain to explore Australia. From 1816 to 1827 he traveled extensively throughout Queensland and New South Wales, studying the flora and fauna of these regions of eastern Australia. In 1828 his attempt to reach the sand dunes on Darling River was unsuccessful.

Cunningham was one of the earliest explorers of southeastern Australia.

Further reading
E. Favenc, The history of Australian Exploration. London 1888
J. D. Rogers, A historical geography of the

British dominions. Volume 6, Australasia. Oxford 1923
A. W. José, Histoire de l'Australie depuis sa découverte jusqu'à nos jours. Paris 1930
Australia Dictionary of Biographies. Without place or year of publication
Australian Encyclopaedia. Without place or year of publication

CUNNINGHAM, RONNIE WALTER

US American astronaut, born 1932 in Creston (Iowa).

With the launch of "Apollo 7" on 11 October, 1968, NASA initiated its lunar space program. Along with Ronnie Cunningham, on board this first manned spaceship in the Apollo series were the astronauts Don Eisele and Walter Schirra.

While orbiting the Earth 164 times, they carried out an extensive schedule of experiments and tests until 22 October, including a docking maneuver with the second rocket stage.

These three astronauts were the first to appear in live television transmissions from space. The "Wally, Walt and Don Show" even won a special Emmy Award.

During his one and only flight in space, Ronnie Cunningham spent a total of 263 hours in the capsule. Following his period of activity with NASA, he was on the board of various US companies.

Further reading
R. Cunningham, The All American boys. New York 1977

The Briton Allan Cunningham collected and documented the flora and fauna of Australia.

D

the South American coast as far as Tierro del Fuego and to the Galapagos Islands. Here, for almost a month, Darwin studied the fauna of these islands and on the basis of his findings developed his scientific opus "On the Origin of Species" (1859). Together with Fitzroy he also wrote a three-volume scientific report, which is regarded as a classic among the accounts of exploration and discovery.

Further reading
C. Darwin, Reise um die Welt 1831-36,
ed. G. Giertz. Stuttgart 1981

DAMPIER, WILLIAM

English seafarer and pirate, born 1652 in Somerset, died 1715 in London.

In the course of his many voyages of piracy against the Spanish silver ships, Dampier had returned to England with much important geographical data. As a result, the British Admiralty commissioned him to carry out a voyage of exploration to the South Pacific. In 1699 he sailed in the "Roebuck" around the Cape of Good Hope and continued in the direction of Australia. However, his cartographic drawings were lost when his ship was wrecked near the South Atlantic island of Ascension.

In 1703–07 Dampier took part in a circumnavigation of the world and in 1708 he accompanied Francis Drake on a privateering mission. There years later he returned with booty of 200,000 pounds sterling. William Dampier is regarded as a pioneer of the British rule of Australia. Several islands and regions are named after him.

Charles Robert Darwin

DARWIN, CHARLES ROBERT

British natural scientist, born 1809 in Shrewsbury, died 1882 in Down. Founder of the theory of natural selection (Darwinism).

Charles Robert Darwin took part in a voyage around the world from 1831 to 1836 on board the "Beagle", which sailed under the command of Captain Robert Fitzroy. His journey took him to

G. Zirnstein, Charles Darwin. 5th edition
Leipzig 1985
C. Darwin, Die Abstammung des Menschen.
2nd edition Wiesbaden 1992
–, Über die Entstehung der Arten durch
natürliche Zuchtwahl oder Die Erhaltung
der begünstigten Rassen im Kampfe ums
Dasein, ed. G. H. Müller (Reprint of
9th unabridged edition Stuttgart 1920).
Darmstadt 1992.
–, Mein Leben. Autobiographie. Frankfurt/M.
1993
A. Desmond/J. Moore, Darwin. Reinbek 1994
J. Hemleben, Charles Darwin. Reinbek without
year of publication
E. Mayr, ... und Darwin hat doch recht. Charles
Darwin, seine Lehre und die moderne Evolutions-
theorie. Munich 1994
S. Parker, Charles Darwin und die Evolution.
Triumphe der Wissenschaft. Hanau 1994
A. Sproule, Charles Darwin. Recklinghausen
1994

DAVID-NÉEL, ALEXANDRA

French Asia explorer, born 1868 in St. Mandé,
died 1969 in Digne.

Alexandra David-Néel developed an interest
in Tibet and the Himalayas during her studies
at the "Collège de France". She spent extended
periods in various Lama monasteries, which
gave her an introduction to Lamaism (Tibetan
Buddhism).

At the age of 45 she made the bold decision
to travel to Lhasa, the "city of the holy books".
This undertaking lasted eight months. Dressed as
a beggar woman and accompanied by her adopted son, a young Lama, she nourished herself
solely on "tsampa" (barley flour), a little tea and
butter and reached the Tibetan capital unrecog-
nised. Here she discovered that virtually nothing
had changed since the city was visited by the
Englishman Manning in 1811.

Alexandra David-Néel was the first European
woman ever to have entered Lhasa. She was only
able to reach her goal because she wore even
shabbier clothes than most of the population of
Tibet, a measure that brought her scorn and dis-
dain elsewhere.

Further reading
E. de Margerie, Voyage d'une Parisienne à
Lhasa. Paris 1927
A. David-Néel, My journey to Lhasa. New York
and London 1927
–, Initiations and Initiates in Tibet. London
1931
–, Au pays de brigands gentilhommes (Grand
Tibet). Paris 1933
–, Le Bouddhisme. Paris 1936

*A view of the
fascinating colorful
vegetation of the
Galapagos Islands*

The Galapagos Islands aroused great interest because of their exotic animal life. These gloriously colorful drawings come from the works of William Beebe ("Galapagos, the End of the World"), which appeared in 1926.

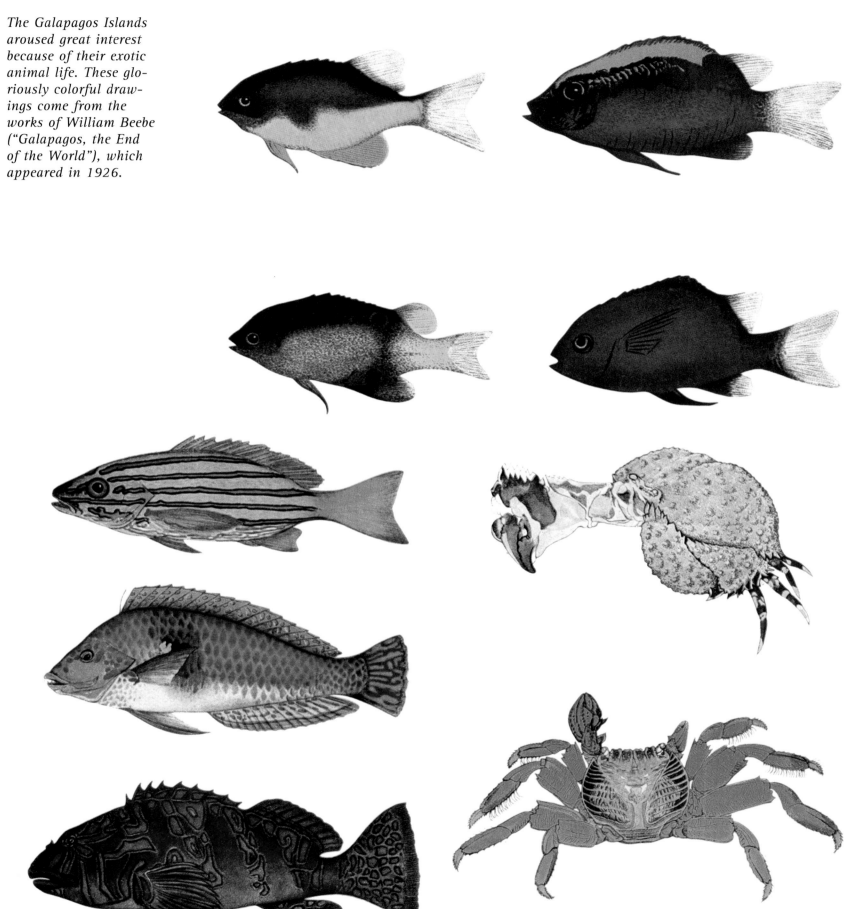

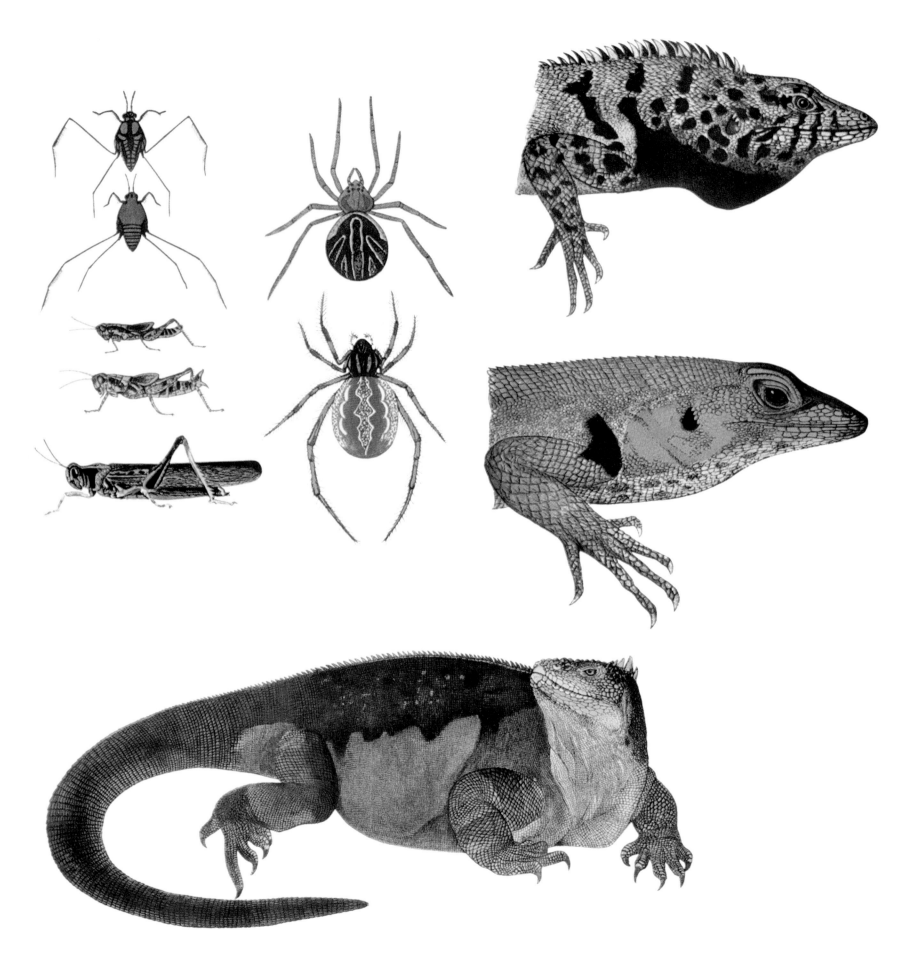

-, *Le vieux Tibet face à la Chine nouvelle.*
Paris 1953
-, *Wanderer mit dem Wind. Reisetagebücher*
in Briefen 1904-1917. Mannheim 1979
-, *Heilige und Hexer. Glaube und Aberglaube*
im Lande des Lamaismus. Reprint of the
3rd edition from 1936, 2nd edition Mannheim
1984
-, *Mein Weg durch Himmel und Höllen. Das*
Abenteuer meines Lebens. Munich 1989
-, *Der Lama der fünf Weisheiten. Basel 1990*
-, *Ralopa. Der Meister geheimer Riten und*
andere unbekannte tibetische Texte. Munich
1991
-, *Liebeszauber und Schwarze Magie. Abenteuer*
in Tibet. 3rd edition Basel 1992
-, *Mein Indien. Die abenteurlichen Reisen einer*
ungewöhnlichen und mutigen Frau. Munich 1992
-, *Leben in Tibet. Kulinarische und andere*
Traditionen aus dem Lande des ewigen Schnees.
4th edition Basle 1994

DAVIS, JOHN

British seafarer and discoverer, born 1550 (?) in Sandridge (Dartmouth), died 1605 near Bintan (Sumatra).

Following meticulous preparations, Davis set out in 1585 to explore the region around the North Pole in an attempt to find the Northwest Passage. He sailed northwards with two ships and rediscovered Greenland (the "Land of Desolation") and circumnavigated the southern tip of this island, which he named "Cape Farvel". He went on land not far from what is today the town of Godthaab (on the west coast of Greenland) and established friendly relations with the local population. Continuing his journey of discovery, he explored Cumberland on Baffin Island, then sailed into the ice-free strait which today bears his name, before returning to England to evaluate his findings.

In 1586 he made a second attempt to advance into the polar region, this time with four ships, two of which were driven in the direction of Iceland. Davis reached Gilbert Sound, but ice masses forced him to abandon his undertaking after crossing the 80° N parallel.

In 1587 Davis was in command of yet another arctic expedition. This time with his three sloops he reached 72° 12' N and sailed into Baffin Bay, where he discovered the high foothills of "Sanderson's Hope", but then turned back due to dangerous pack ice. He then explored the entrance to Hudson Bay before setting out on his return journey.

In 1591 he accompanied the Briton T. Cavendish on a journey to northern waters, and on his own initiative sailed southwards and discovered the "Falkland Islands".

From 1598 to 1600 he took part in a Dutch East Indies expedition and in 1604, as helmsman, sailed on the commission of S. E. Michelbourne to Indonesia, where he was killed near the island of Sumatra in a battle with Japanese pirates. John Davis, the inventor of the "Davis quadrant", was the first European to undertake scientific exploration of the northern Arctic waters.

Further reading
The voyages and works of John Davis the
Navigator. Edited with an introduction and
notes, by Albert Hastings Markham. London
1880
J. Hakluyt, The Principal Navigations,
Voyages, Traffiques and Discoveries of the
English nation. London 1904 (1st printing
1598-1600, numerous editions)

DECKEN, BARON KARL-KLAUS VON DER

German Africa traveler, born 1833, died 1865. Decken abandoned his career in the army and traveled to Africa. He climbed Kilimanjaro to a height of 4,260 meters (14,000 feet), explored the Pangani River (at the foot of Kilimanjaro) and organized a major expedition to explore the Tana, the largest river in Kenya. Decken and many of his companions were killed in a fight with fanatical Somalis.

His geographical and natural scientific findings were evaluated by O. von Kersten.

DEZHNEV, SEMION IVANOVICH

Russian explorer, born around 1605, died 1672 or 1673.

Accompanied by Stadukhin, a Cossack compatriot, Semion Dezhnev took part in an expedition to eastern Siberia in 1645. He reached the Kolyma (a river in eastern Siberia) but was forced to abandon his voyage due to inclement weather conditions. Soon afterwards, Dezhnev made a second attempt to reach the Kolyma. Together with 25 Cossacks and on several "kolchis" (flat boats) he sailed through the East Siberian Sea, sailed around the extreme tip of Siberia (Cape Dezhnev) and reached the mouth of the River Anadyr (1648). Dezhnev had thus discovered the strait between Alaska and Siberia 80 years before Bering and 130 years before James Cook.

In 1650 the unflinching Cossack took part in yet another expedition, this time accompanied by Motora, also a Cossack, to the Anadyr where he explored its banks. Here Motora was murdered by Chukchens.

Dezhnev's travel reports were strongly criticised, especially by the North American historian F. A. Gold. Gold insisted that Dezhnev may well have reached the tip of Asia, but by land, not by sea. The German-Russian historian G. F. Müller brought light to the matter. In 1736 Müller found the travel report written by Dezhnev, addressed to the Voivoden (head) of Jakutsk, containing references to his undertaking in the archives of this town. Unfortunately the Russian governor had not bothered to forward the report to Moscow or St. Petersburg.

Semion Dezhnev, not Bering, was the first person to circumnavigate the easternmost tip of Siberia. A cape bears the name of this great Russian explorer.

Further reading
Y. Semionov, La conquête de la Sibérie du IXe siècle au XIXe siècle. Paris 1938

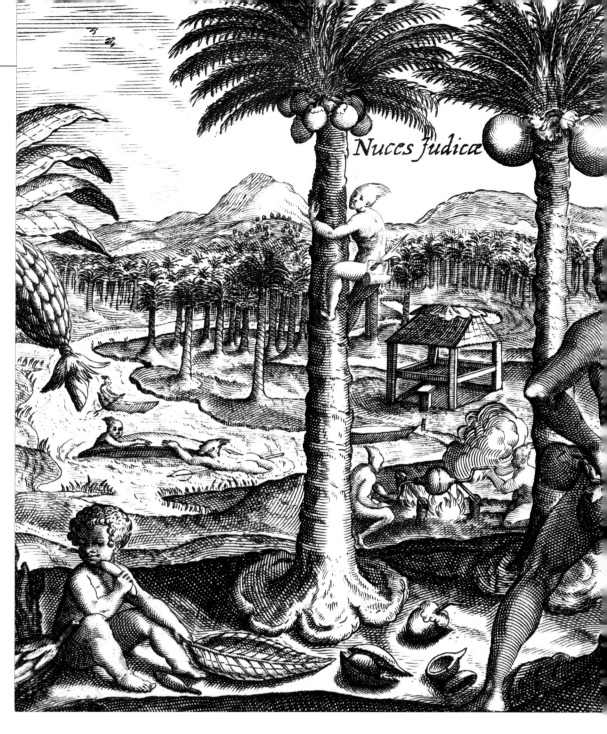

Nuces Judicæ

DIAZ, BARTOLOMËU (DIAS)

Portuguese seafarer and explorer, born c. 1450 on the Algarve, died in 1500 at the Cape of Good Hope.

Diaz was a descendant of the famous seafarer Diniz Diaz, the discoverer of "Cape Verde". In 1481 Diaz took part in a journey organised by Diego de Azambuja to the coast of Guinea. Five years later Diaz, who by that time had amassed a great deal of experience, was commissioned to sail along the coast of West Africa "to its very end". The flotilla which King John II had put at his disposal consisted of two small, but highly manoeuvrable ships especially built for the

The conquerors were so enthusiastic about the riches of nature in the Indies that the depictions that they made of them later took the form of idylls rather than realistic portraits. This engraving by Theodor de Bry (1528–98) shows coconuts being picked.

stormy seas of the South Atlantic: the "São Cristavao" and the "São Pantalea". An additional supply ship was commanded by Pero Diaz, Bartolomëu's brother. Because the mission was carried out in conditions of strict secrecy, there are contradicting reports as to when the expedition actually set out. J. D. Barros, a Portuguese historian (1496–1570), likewise only gives a meagre report of this historically significant journey.

Diaz must have left the Tejo around August 1487. After the ships had rounded the "Black Cape" a violent storm broke out. Icy winds and thick fog made conditions difficult for the crew during the thirteen following days. To ensure that his men came to no harm, Diaz had left the supply ship behind on the coast. When the sea began to calm again on the 14th day, Diaz realised that he had sailed around the southernmost point of Africa, which he named "Cape of Storms" (subsequently altered by the Portuguese king to "Cape of Good Hope"). He sailed northwards and went on land on a shielded part of

the coastline, which the Portuguese gave the name of "Bahia dos Vaqueiros" (now Mosselbaai) because of its large herds of cattle. Although most of his crew were suffering from scurvy and were in poor physical condition, he undertook a three-day journey northwards in the hope of finding the connection between East Africa and the Malabar coast. Diaz advanced to Great Fish River (other sources state Kowie River); however, a threat of mutiny forced him to turn back. On the return journey the crew was able to round the Cape of Storms in peaceful conditions. Several miles to the north they found their supply ship, on which only four seamen were left, dropped anchor on Principe (Gulf of Guinea) and returned to Lisbon after a year and a half at sea. King John was satisfied: he now knew that the lucrative spice trading market was close at hand and that he would be able to force Islam out of India.

In 1500 Diaz took part in Cabral's voyage to Brazil. On route to India from the coast of South America, Diaz's ship sank during a hurricane off the Cape of Good Hope. There are still some mysteries concerning Diaz's death. It is not certain whether Diaz died of grief during this journey over the death of his son or whether he was killed either before or during the storm on the orders of the king (or of Vasco da Gama).

Diaz's bold and successful journey contributed much to the success of Vasco da Gama's undertaking. The Portuguese conquest of the Indian Ocean was now merely a matter of time.

This wood engraving of 1528 shows spice merchants packing their coveted wares. (Ordonnances de la jurisdiction de la prévoste des Marchands de Paris, 1528).

Further reading
C. Pereyra, La conquête des routes océaniques d'Henri le Navigateur à Magellan. Paris 1923
G. de Reparaz, La época de los descubrimientos españoles portugueses. Barcelona 1931
E. Prestage, Descobridores portugueses. Porto 1934
D. Peres, Historia da expansao portuguesa no mundo. Lisbon 1937-1940
–, Historia dos descobrimentos portugueses. Porto 1943

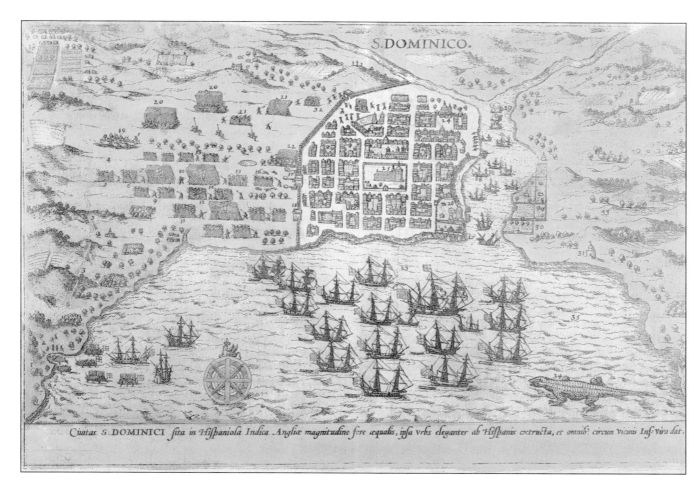

The English fleet under Francis Drake attacks the city of Santo Domino in Haiti.

DJOBEIR, IBN

Spanish-Arabian traveler, born 1145 in Valencia, died 1217 in Alexandria.

After completing his studies of jurisprudence and literature at the universities of Granada and Ceuta, Ibn Djobeir undertook three extended journeys to the Near East. He traveled through Alexandria, sailed to Mecca with a ship full of Moslem pilgrims, reached the towns of Baghdad, Damascus, Accra and Tyrus and recorded his impressions of political and religious conditions and Islamic architecture. His observations and assessments are full of religious comments, although highly reliable from a geographical point of view.

DRAKE, SIR FRANCIS

British seafarer, pirate and circumnavigator of the world, born c. 1540 in Tavistock (Devon), died 1596 off Portobelo (Panama).

Drake came from a poor family. When he was just twelve years old, he entered the services of a coastal shipper who transported cargo from England to France and Holland. On the death of his employer, Drake inherited the ship. History does not record precisely his employment between that time and 1567. In 1565 Drake accompanied Captain John Lovell on a voyage to Mexico, where the latter was involved in the slave trade. On arriving in the town of Río de la Hacha the two seamen were robbed of all their possessions by Spaniards.

In 1567, together with a relative by the name of John Hawkins, Drake set out on an expedition to Mexico. The Flotilla, in which Drake commanded the fourth ship, the "Judith", left Plymouth on 2 October, 1567. The ships took on supplies on the Cape Verde Islands, and two hundred slaves were bought on the coast of Guinea. When Drake and Hawkins wished to sell their human cargo in Río de la Hacha the Spanish

Sir Francis Drake, the famous English seafarer, who was the first ship's captain to survive a circumnavigation of the world.

refused to have any dealings with them. Without hesitation Drake had his ships bombard the town. As the British fleet reached the port of St. John of Ulloa with the intention of dropping anchor, this time it was the Spanish who opened fire, sinking two ships. However, Drake and Hawkins were able to escape the trap laid by the Spanish and reached Plymouth harbour on 25 January, 1568. This incident brought the British hatred of the Spanish to a climax.

In 1570 and 1571 Drake sailed "privately" to the Caribbean archipelago to familiarise himself with this region.

A year later he determined to compete against the great seafarers of Spain and Portugal. On 24 May, 1572 with the Queen's secret approval, Drake set sail from Plymouth for the Gulf of Darien (a bay in the Caribbean Sea) with two ships and landed in Río Francisco. Near the town of Nombre de Díos he was forced back by the Spanish; at Carthage, however, he succeeded in capturing two Spanish treasure ships. Following many armed conflicts in the Gulf of Mexico, Drake returned to England on 9 August, 1573, by which time he had become famous throughout the country.

From 1573 to 1576, he was in the services of Walter Devereux, the Earl of Essex, who put down a revolt in Ulster (Northern Ireland) during this time. After the untimely death of Devereux, Drake was introduced to Queen Elizabeth I by Sir C. Hutton. The monarch gave her blessings to Drake's plan of advancing into the "South Sea" and entering into competition with the Spanish for colonisation. He had the supreme command of five ships (the "Pelican", which was later renamed the "Golden Hind", the "Elizabeth", the "Swan", the "Marygold" and the "Christoph") as well as 164 elite troops. He left Plymouth harbour on 15 November, 1577 and the flotilla sailed to the Cape Verde Islands, where they took provisions on board. From here Drake sailed through the South Atlantic, along the Brazilian and Argentinean coastlines and dropped anchor

in the Bay of Río de la Plata. It took him sixteen days to cross the Magellan Strait, although several days were spent on Horn Island. During his advance along the coast of Chile his men plundered the city of Valparaiso. They continued to the port of Callao, where Drake launched a further attack on Spanish ships anchored in the harbour. Near Cape San Francisco he caught up with the Spanish treasure ship "Cacafuego" and took gold and silver booty to the value of 360,000 pesos. After a brief visit to the small port of Guatulco (Mexico), which he destroyed along with the church that stood there, he set a northerly course and landed in the Bay of San Francisco, which was populated at that time by the Miwok tribe, who gave the British seamen a peaceful welcome. He took possession of the coastal strip in the name of the Queen of England and gave it the name of "New Albion". At the end of July he left North American soil and sailed to the Ladrones Islands (which had been discovered by Magellan). From there he set sail for the Spice Islands, where he exchanged part of his gold booty for spices on Timor. After a brief stopover on Timor, Drake sailed the Indian Ocean, rounded the Cape of Good Hope and, after a short stay in Sierra Leone, returned to Plymouth on 26 September, 1580. In recognition of his lucrative privateering journey as the first British seaman to circumnavigate the world, Drake was knighted by Queen Elizabeth I.

In 1585, as supreme commander, Drake set out with a fleet of twenty-five ships on a large-scale privateering voyage to the Caribbean Sea, and two years later he sank 33 Spanish ships in the port of Cádiz; this attack delayed the planned invasion of England by two years. A campaign against Lisbon was unsuccessful. In 1595 Drake carried out his large-scale attack on the West Indies. After an unsuccessful attempt to take Puerto Rico, Drake set course for the Isthmus of Panama, bombarded the town of Río de la Hacha once more and took the town of Nombre de Dios almost without a fight. Here he contracted

Erich von Drygalski

dysentery on 20 January and died eight days later. The Spanish could breathe a sigh of relief.

The sixteenth century regarded Drake as a national hero. Briton John Corbett compared him to Nelson, thus putting pirates on an equal footing with strategists. The original judgement was in keeping with the spirit of the century; the second bears witness to naïve prepossession. During his "career" Drake remained a broadsword in the Royal Navy, which was still in its infancy. He believed that all means were justified for creating material advantages for his queen, his country and, of course himself, at the expense of Spain.

The strait between the southern tip of America and North Antarctica bears the name of this seafarer and pirate.

Further reading
(Drake left no written documentation of his voyages. The British Museum possesses a few of his letters, which however are of no great historical value.)
Th. Greepe, the true and perfect newes of the worthy and valiant exploits performed by the valiant knight Sir Francis Drake. London 1587
Fr. Petty, The famous voyage of Sir Francis Drake into the south sea and there hence about the whole globe of the earth in the years 1577 and 1580. London 1600 and 1618
F. de Louvencourt, Sieur de Vauchelles, Le voyage de l'illustre seigneur et chevalier François Drake, admiral d'Angleterre, à entour du monde. Paris 1613
S. Clarke, Life and death of the valiant and renown Sir Fr. Drake. London 1681
R. Burton, The English hero or Sir Fr. Drake, London 1687, 1739, 1756
G. L. Browne, Leben des englischen Helden und Ritters F. Drake. Leipzig 1720
J. Barrow, The life, voyages and exploits of Admiral Sir F. Drake. London 1844
K. R. Andrews, Admiral and pirate Francis Drake. London 1967
Francis Drake. Pirat im Dienst der Queen. Berichte, Dokumente und Zeugnisse des Seehelden und seiner Zeitgenossen 1567-1596, ed. J. Hampden. Stuttgaut 1977

DRYGALSKI, ERICH DAGOBERT VON

German polar explorer, geographer and geophysicist, born 1865 in Königsberg, died 1949 in Munich.

From 1891 to 1893 Drygalski explored and researched Greenland's expanses of inland ice, and in 1901 he was commissioned to lead the

Looking at the ships of that time in museums today, one can well ask oneself how it was possible to cross oceans with them, spend months at a time at sea, and survive the most violent storms (ill. following double page). But it is easy to forget that countless ships sank. Courage was accompanied by luck. Every seafarer and explorer was risking his life.

Chronicle of the South Pole expeditions

1774 James Cook reaches 71°10' S.

1820 The British whalers Palmer and Powell undertake the first expeditions to Antarctica.

1821 Englishman Weddell reaches 74°15' S (Weddell Sea).

1899 Norwegian E. Borchgrevink crosses the 78°5' southern parallel.

1909 The Irish polar explorer E. H. Shackleton is the first to reach 88°23' S, but is forced to turn back 178 km before the Pole.

1911 Amundsen is the first man to reach the South Pole on 15 December.

1912 On 17 January, R. F. Scott is the second person to reach the South Pole.

1929 The American Byrd is first to fly over the South Pole on 28 November.

1946 The Byrd expedition undertakes research expeditions to Antarctica.

German expedition to the South Pole. Accompanied by Captain H. Ruser on board the "Gauss" (research ship), Drygalski advanced to the southern Indian Ocean, passed Prince Edward Island, visited the islands of Crozet, Kerguélen and MacDonald and, in 1902, discovered "Kaiser Wilhelm II Land" in eastern Antarctica. While his ship, which had been built according to the design of the "Fram", was enclosed by ice, he and his team undertook extended sledge journeys and a balloon trip into the interior, reaching a volcano free of ice that they named "Mount Gauss". It was not until February 1903 that the "Gauss" was finally released from the clutches of the ice.

A fjord on South Georgia (Scotia Sea) and an island on the eastern coast of Antarctica bear the name of this great German Antarctic explorer.

Further reading
Grönland-Expedition der Gesellschaft für
Erdkunde in Berlin 1891 bis 1893.
Unter der Leitung von E. v. Drygalski.
Gesellschaft für Meereskunde. 2 volumes
Berlin 1897

Iceberg in the Wedell Sea, the Antarctic

Die deutsche Südpolarexpedition auf dem Schiff "Gauss" unter der Leitung von E. v. Drygalski. Friedrich-Wilhelm-Universität. Institut für Meereskunde, Volume 1. Berlin 1902
Allgemeiner Bericht über den Verlauf der deutschen Südpolar- Expedition mit Vorbemerkungen von Fr. v. Richthoven und einem Anhang. Bericht über die Arbeiten der Kerguélen-Station von K. Luyken. Berlin 1903
Die deutsche Südpolarexpedition 1901-1903. Berlin 1905-1931. 20 volumes
E. D. v. Drygalski, Das Deutsche Südpolarwerk. Munich 1932
–, Die Staatsbildungen des arabischen Raumes. Munich 1947
–, Das ostasiatische Gebirgsdreieck und das Chinesische Reich. Munich 1948.

DU CHAILLU, PAUL BELLONI

Franco-American explorer, born 1835 in Paris, died 1903 in St. Petersburg.

At the age of twenty, Du Chaillu left his adopted North American home country and set out for West Africa, where his father owned a trading station at the mouth of the River Gabon. His objective was to explore the Fernando Vaz delta (Gabon) and to open up a northern trading route. During his four-year expedition, he discovered the sources of the River Ogooué and visited the culturally highly developed Pahouins, whose smiths were able to produce better iron than the Europeans and who made a habit of eating the flesh of their deceased. He also discovered gorillas, of which very little had been known in Europe. As evidence he captured two specimens, which however soon died; as a result, many people did not believe his discovery.

Further reading
P. du Chaillu, Voyages et aventures dans l'Afrique équatoriale. Paris 1863

D'Urville's ship, the "Astrolabe", anchoring in a bay of Cocos Island in New Ireland.

DUMONT D'URVILLE, JULES SÉBASTIEN CÉSAR

French circumnavigator of the world and discoverer, born 1790 in Condé-sur-Noireau (Calvados), died 1842 in Meudon. Dumont d'Urville studied ancient and modern languages, physics, botany, astronomy and entomology. In 1819/1820 he took part in a hydrographical expedition in the Mediterranean. On being promoted to frigate captain, he was commissioned by the French government to explore the South Seas and to investigate the mysterious disappearance of the French seafarer La Pérouse. In 1828 he reached the island of Vanikoro to the southeast of the Solomon Islands in the Pacific, where he was able to throw some light on the mystery: La Pérouse's two ships, the "Astrolabe" and the "Boussole", had sunk after colliding with an underwater reef. Some of the crew were able to reach the shore, where most however were killed by natives. Continuing on his journey, Dumont d'Urville visited the Marianas, the Carolinas, Celebes and Batavia (on Java) and returned from

Indonesia to Marseille via St. Helena with a rich collection of botanical and zoological specimens. The almost 900 rock samples and more than 1,500 plant species that d'Urville brought back from his circumnavigation of the world gave European scientists an illuminating insight into the diverse nature of the South Seas. From now on the Pacific archipelago was divided into four major ethnographic groups: the Malaysian Archipelago, Micronesia, Melanesia and Polynesia.

In 1836 d'Urville shared his plan of exploring Antarctica with the French king Louis Philippe I. The following year, he attempted to advance beyond the Antarctic Circle with two corvettes, the "Astrolab" and the "Zélée", and discovered two regions which he named "Joinville Land" and "Louis Philippe Land". Because his crew was suffering badly from scurvy, he was forced to abandon his plans and set sail for Tasmania.

In 1840 he made a further attempt to explore the waters of Antarctica from Hobart (Tasmania). He landed at two locations, which he named "Adélie Land" and "Clarie Coast". The hordes of

D'Urville's ship steering through a dangerous reef on its voyage to Admiralty Bay in 1827. With less luck and an unexpected breeze, the ship would have been wrecked in the shallows.

Caravan in the Sahara

penguins they encountered there were given the name "Adélie penguins".

D'Urville had not been aware that the Briton J. Balleny had visited exactly the same region several months previously on commission of the London-based businessman Enderby. On his return journey, D'Urville encountered the American Wilkes, who was searching for the magnetic South Pole. The French seafarer was killed in a railway accident near Meudon on 8 May, 1842.

Dumont d'Urville's discoveries were confirmed in their entirety in 1911 by the Australian Antarctic explorer Sir D. Mawson.

Further reading
Dumont d'Urville, Voyage au pôle sud et dans l'océanie sur les corvettes de l'Astrolabe et la Zélée. Paris 1846
E. Goep et G. L. Cordier, Les grands hommes de la France, navigateurs (Bougainville, La Pérouse, d'Entrecasteaux, Dumont d'Urville). Paris 1878

E. Marget, Histoire générale de la navigation du XVe au XXe siècle. Paris 1931

DUVEYRIER, HENRI

French Sahara explorer, born 1840 in Paris, died 1892 in Sèvres.

Duveyrier was from a family of the lower aristocracy. He first attended a private school in Bavaria and then a commercial school in Leipzig. He studied the natural sciences as well as the Franconian and medieval German languages, then studied Arabic with the well-known orientalist Fleischer. In 1857 Duveyrier encountered the German explorer Heinrich Barth in London. Barth became Duveyrier's friend and gave him advice on all matters concerning the Sahara. Duveyrier spent a whole year preparing his first Africa expedition, during which time he attended courses in ethnography and linguistics.

Duveyrier's objective was to undertake scientific exploration of the Sahara. In 1859 he set out on his first expedition, aged just nineteen. From Algiers he reached Ghardaia, the largest town in the Oued Mzab, and became the first European to set eyes on El Goléa, 1,000 km (620 miles) south of Algiers. The inhabitants of the region refused to allow the Frenchman and Christian to procure any nourishment; at times he was forced to live on lizards and worms.

In 1860 Duveyrier undertook his second expedition to the Sahara, this time on commission from Napoleon III, in order to explore the region of Constantine (Algeria) and the Tunisian desert.

In the course of this journey Duveyrier was able to make some accurate findings; on its completion he was thus able to set out on his long journey to the Tuaregs of the north. Departing from Ghadamès (Libya), Duveyrier – supported by Ikenuks and Sheik Othman – advanced into the Sahara and was able to reach Rhat (Ghat). Because of the complex situation in this region, he was forced to return to Tripoli, where he begged the Turkish consul to protect him. Despite recurring bouts of fever Duveyrier set out once more. In Rhat, despite protection from the two principal Tuareg leaders, he only narrowly escaped being stoned to death. Nevertheless, he spent a year with the Tuaregs, in order to make detailed studies of these "aristocrats of the desert". He learned their language "Temacheq" and their ancient Libyan alphabet "Tifinar". From Rhat he set out for Mursuk, the capital of Fessan, to explore the southern part of Libya. He searched for traces of the Garamants, who had lived in Phoenicia in the first century AD. In Wadi El Adjal he discovered the Dauda tribe, who fed on worms and lived in strict isolation from other desert tribes. In 1861 Duveyrier returned to Algiers, where he wrote a detailed report of his expedition and prepared a map of the southern Sahara. He was forced to delay his trip home due to a serious nervous disorder.

Duveyrier published his experiences in 1864 in his book "Les Touaregs du Nord" (Tuaregs of the North). These studies provided valuable information about how these tribes lived (some historians believe they are descendants of the Crusaders) and about the geography, hydrology, geology, fauna and flora of the Sahara.

Duveyrier was made a Knight of the Legion of Honour at the age of only 21 and was awarded the Gold Medal by the Geographical Society in Paris. In the course of his journeys to the Sahara he had also established economic relations with the Tuaregs; unfortunately, the French government neglected to derive full benefit from this initiative.

After the French colonel Flatters was murdered by the Tuaregs, Duveyrier was even accused of having portrayed these desert inhabitants in a false light. He therefore set out for Tripoli once more at his own expense, but was unable to resolve the matter.

In 1874 he accompanied a French expedition to the region around Constantine and in 1885 he accompanied the Sultan of Morocco on his journey from Tangier to Meknes. During the course of this journey, he resolved to explore the Rif Mountains and their inhabitants, the Rif Berbers.

By this time Duveyrier's health had greatly deteriorated; after his return to France, life in Paris became more and more unbearable for him. He took his own life in 1892.

Duveyrier is one of the "great" Sahara explorers. Even today he is still held in high international acclaim as a Tuareg specialist. His sincerity and death-defying courage had impressed the Tuaregs. If the French government had utilised the relationships established by Duveyrier, many military undertakings would have been unnecessary.

Further reading
H. Duveyrier, *Exploration du Sahara. Les Touaregs du Nord.* Paris 1864
–, *Journal de route.* Paris 1905
A. Bernard/N. Lacroix, *Historique de la pénétration saharienne.* Algiers 1906

EGEDE, HANS

Norwegian-Danish clergyman and Arctic explorer, born 1686 in Trondenå, died 1758 in Stubbekøbing.

Hans Egede spent fifteen years in Greenland as a missionary and explorer. During this time he founded the township of Godthaab on the southwest coast of Greenland, from where Fridtjof Nansen started his west-to-east crossing of the island in 1888 and explored the entire region of Greenland's west coast.

This scientifically trained missionary gave new impulse to the colonization of the island. His geographical observations provided the first specific information about this country, which was still virtually unknown at the time.

Further reading
H. Egede, Des alten Grönland Neue Perlustration, Oder Eine kurze Beschreibung der Alten Nordischen Colonien. Frankfurt/M. 1730
–, A. Description of Greenland. London 1745
–, Beschreibung und Natur = Geschichte von Grönland. Berlin 1763
–, Die Heiden im Eis. Als Forscher und Missionar in Grönland 1721-1736, ed. H. Barüske. Stuttgart 1986

EHRENREICH, PAUL

German explorer of Brazil, born 1855 in Berlin, died 1914 in Berlin.

Ehrenreich explored the region of the Rio Doce, which had remained unknown for a remarkably long time, and charted the landscape there. In 1884 and 1885 he took part in the Botokuden expedition organized by Maximilian Prinz zu Wied. From 1887 to 1888 Ehrenreich participated in the second Xingu expedition, led by the German physician and ethnologist Karl von den Steinen. Later, Ehrenreich explored the Araguaya River and the eastern Mato Grosso region. His was especially interested in the various Indian tribes, which he closely observed and described in detail.

Unfortunately Ehrenreich did not write any books; he limited himself to short articles in specialist magazines.

EISELE, DONN FULTON

US American astronaut, born 1930 in Columbo (Ohio), died 1987 in Tokyo.

Donn Eisele was the commanding officer of the moon landing capsule on board "Apollo 7", the first manned spaceship of the Apollo program, in October 1968.

The eleven-day mission of astronauts Eisele, Walter Schirra and Ronnie Cunningham confirmed the success of the "Apollo" program. This had been jeopardized after a fire had broken out in the command capsule during a test, killing all three astronauts.

The flight on board the "Apollo 7" was Donn Eisele's only space mission. Following his retirement from the NASA, Eisele established his own consulting company. He opened a space camp for Japanese children in Tokyo. Eisele died on 1 December, 1987 in Tokyo as a result of a heart attack.

ELIAS, NEY

British explorer of central Asia, born 1844, died 1897.

As the son of a foreign trader, Ney Elias was familiar with China from his early childhood. On his first expedition, he studied the lower course of the Hoangho River. He crossed central Asia from east to west and endeavored to compile a documentaion of the height profiles of the old trading routes by taking accurate measurements. In 1880 as a reward for his activities he was appointed British Consul in Ladakh. Later, the government commissioned him to explore the ancient mountain passes on the route to Kashgar. He crossed the Pamir and explored the Amu-Darja region.

Ney Elias published the results of his explorations in specialist journals such as "Petermanns Mitteilungen."

ELLSWERTH, LINCOLN

American polar explorer, born 1880, died 1951.

Lincoln Ellsworth was an engineer who was especially interested in geology. For many years after completing his studies he worked in mining and railway construction.

In 1924 he was commissioned by private sponsors and the Johns Hopkins University to lead an expedition to the Andes.

In the years 1925 and 1926 Ellswerth flew together with Amundsen and later also with the Italian Nobile over the Pole. He was very interested in flying; because of this he crossed the North Pole in a semi-rigid airship and in 1931 he took part in a crossing of the Siberian Arctic Sea coast in the famous airship "Graf Zeppelin".

The Confucius Temple in Jiazhou

This passion almost cost him his life in 1935, when he was surprised by a snowstorm during a flight in a propeller aircraft. In 1939 he set out on an extended flight over Antarctica, with which the USA laid claim to a large region of the Antarctic continent. After 1940 Ellsworth's interest returned to the Andes, where he investigated the Incan culture, especially the mountain forts.

ENGELHARDT, OTTO MORITZ LUDWIG VON

Baltic-German explorer and mineralogist, born 1779 in Wieso (Estonia), died 1842.

After completing his studies at the mining academy at Freiberg in Saxony, Engelhardt set out with K. von Raumer on a mineralogical journey of exploration through Germany and France. In 1811 and 1812 he explored Crimea and Caucasia. From 1815 to 1817 he examined the mineralogy of Estonia and Finland. The Russian csar then sent him on an expedition to Archangel, Perm and Saratov.

Further reading
Otto Moritz Ludwig von Engelhardt and G. Ewers, Beyträge zur Kenntniß Rußlands und seiner Geschichte. Berlin 1816

ENNIN

The Buddhist monk from Japan is regarded as one of the most eccentric explorers of the Middle Ages; born 793, died 864.

In the year 838 Ennin set out on an extended journey through China together with a group of monks and visited the port of Hangchu among other places. He lived in a Korean monastery for some time. In 845 Emperor Wu-Tsung, who was opposed to the Buddhist religion, expelled him from the country, although his return journey took until 848, as he was in the interior of the country at the time. In this way he was able to explore a number of other interesting areas on his way to the coast. In 848 he sailed back to Japan from the coast of the province of Shantung.

Although Ennin's travel reports are missing, many text fragments have been used by other authors; this represents an interesting source of ninth-century Chinese culture.

ERIC THE RED

Norwegian Viking prince, seafarer and discoverer, born c. 940 (950) in Norway, died c. 1007 (1010) in Greenland.

According to Icelandic saga, Eric the Red discovered Greenland; in fact, however, this island had already been discovered unintentionally around 900 AD by the Norwegian Gunnbjörn Ulfson.

Eric arrived on Iceland from Norway around 950, but had to leave again after committing manslaughter; in 982 he discovered the coast of Greenland and gave the island its present name. In 986 Erik the Red founded a settlement on the south of this island, from where his son Leif Eriksson sailed in about 1000 to the coast of North America.

After spending three years on Greenland, Eric the Red returned to Iceland to persuade settlers to join him. The fleet consisting of 35 ships and around 300 settlers, who took with them cattle, agricultural tools and seedlings, encountered a storm half way between Iceland and Greenland. Only some half of the "dragon boats" reached the island. Eric founded two settlements, the "Westbygd" and the "Ostbygd". Cattle breeding, farming and fishing were the main sources of income for the European Greenlanders. Under Eric's rule the first modest house of prayer, called "Thjodhild", was established within the Arctic Circle.

Eric the Red (thus named because of his bright red hair) is closely connected with the history of Greenland. Tools found there prove that the

Remains of a Viking settlement in Greenland founded by Eric the Red in 985

Greenlanders enjoyed quite some prosperity. The problem of the lack of timber was solved by Leif, Eric's son, when he discovered "Markland" (forest land, probably Newfoundland). In the eleventh century Rome established the first Arctic bishopric. Greenland was placed under Norwegian rule in 1261. In 1327 Greenlanders took part in the crusade initiated by Pope John XXII. In 1355 Westbygd ceased to exist, and in 1418 the inhabitants of Ostbygd sent 2,500 walrus tusks to Rome as "Peter's pence". From that time onwards, nothing more was heard from the island.

In 1476 the Dane Jon Skolp unsuccessfully attempted to settle on Greenland, and Rome was also unsuccessful in its attempt to re-establish its northern dioceses by sending the bishops Holar and Skalholt.

In the nineteenth century, Dr. Nordland discovered some skeletons in the churchyard of Herjolfsnes on the southern tip of Greenland, at "Ikigart" (a settlement destroyed by fire). The oldest of these was found at a depth of 140 cm, the most recent at 40 cm. The condition of their teeth indicates that the settlers must have died within a very short period due to a sudden climatic change.

Further reading
J. Fiske, The discovery of America. London 1892
Monographien über Brattalid, Gardar, Herjolfsnes: Dr. P. Nordlund, in: "Meddelelser om Gronland", No. 76, 1930 and No. 88, without place of publication 1934
H. R. Haggard, Eric der Wikinger. Berlin 1986
G. Jones, The Norse Atlantic Saga. 6th edition Oxford 1986

ERIKSSON, LEIF

Norwegian seafarer, born c. 975, died c. 1020.

In around 1000 AD, Leif, the son of Eric the Red, drifted off course while heading for Greenland and ended up on the coast of North America (probably the region around Nova Scotia, Labrador). He named the newly discovered country "Vinland". The Vikings regarded this country as suitable for colonization since it was rich in berries (for making wine), fur-bearing animals and forest land. Vikings returned to this stretch of coastland until well into the twelfth century, and some even settled there. In the course of his many voyages, Leif Eriksson reached the area of present-day Boston and had thus discovered America before Columbus, an event which was, however, of little historical consequence.

EVEREST, SIR GEORGE

British surveyor, born 1790 in Gwernvale (Brocknockshire), died 1866 in London.

Everest served in the British Army. In 1806 he was assigned to the army in India as an artillery officer. Seven years later, the government in London commissioned him to undertake a voyage of exploration to the island of Java. From 1823 to 1843 he was in charge of the trigonometric survey of India. During this time he measured almost the entire Himalayan region to an astounding degree of accuracy.

The world's highest mountain bears his name.

Further reading
An account of the measurement of two sections of the meridional arc of India. Without place of publication 1847

EYRE, EDWARD-JOHN

British explorer of Australia, born 1815 in Hornsea (Yorkshire), died 1901 near Tavistock (Devonshire).

When Eyre failed to be admitted to the military academy, he emigrated to Australia in 1833 and settled in New South Wales. As a cattle drover he was constantly searching for new pastures, and from 1836 he traveled through the as yet unexplored regions of the Darling and Mur-

Chronicle of the settlement of Australia

50,000 BC	Various Asian tribes reach Australia.
From 1500	Seafarers from Spain, Portugal and Holland sail to the "Spice Islands" of Indonesia without knowing that they are close to the legendary southern land.
1606	Willem Jansz is the first European to set foot on northern Australia.
1642	Abel Janszoon Tasman and Ide Holman explore the western coast from north to south and discover an island that they name "Van Diemen's Land" (later Tasmania).
1644	The Dutch are convinced that the country has nothing to offer and decide not to occupy it. They name the continent "New Holland".
1688	Dampier is the first person from Britain to set foot on the northwest coast of Australia.
1770	Captain James Cook is the first European to reach the east coast of Australia. He takes possession for the British Crown and because of the area's mountains and green meadows calls it "New South Wales".
1786	Britain requires a new exile for its convicts and new forests to ensure timber deliveries for shipbuilding. New South Wales, which is rich in forests, is made into a convict colony.
1788	Around 1,400 English convicts land in Australia and found Sydney.
From 1793	The first British settlers arrive in Australia.

ray Rivers as far as Lake Torrens and the lake that today bears his name.

While staying in Adelaide in 1840, he heard reports of luscious pastures in the west of the continent. Accompanied by a white man (Baxter) and three aboriginal load-bearers, he set out in February 1841 on a bold attempt to reach Lake Torrens. The men trekked through arid regions for four weeks. When Baxter was murdered and two of the aborigines fled, Eyre changed his route. Together with his sole remaining companion, Eyre followed the coast of the Great Australian Bight in a westerly direction. By fortunate coincidence, they were provided with fresh water and provisions by a French whaler which had anchored of Cape Research. In early July 1841 they arrived at what is today the town of Albany, having completed the first east-to-west crossing of Australia. Eyre returned to London four years later. In 1864 he was appointed Governor of

Jamaica. The following year a revolt broke out, in the course of which Eyre had 400 islanders put to death; London recalled him from his posting in 1866. The explorer of Australia spent his remaining years in complete seclusion in the English countryside.

E. J. Eyre is the most significant explorer of southern and southwestern Australia.

Further reading
E. Favenc, The history of Australian Explorations. London 1888
A. W. José, Histoire de l'Australie depuis sa découverte jusqu'à nos jours. Paris 1930

FILCHNER, WILHELM

German explorer, born 1877 in Munich, died 1957 in Zurich.

From 1903 to 1905 Filchner undertook a scientific expedition to Tibet, and in 1911/1912 he explored the Weddell Sea in the Arctic and discovered "Prince Regent Luitpold Land" and the "Filchner Shelf Ice" (Edith Ronne Land).

Around twenty years after his first expedition to Asia, Wilhelm Filchner undertook extensive travels through Tibet from 1926 to 1928 and again from 1934 to 1938. The following year, he decided to concentrate his attention on Nepal and did not return from that country until after the Second World War, in 1951. Filchner's last expedition was primarily concerned with geomagnetism.

Further reading
W. Filchner, Ein Ritt über Pamir. Berlin 1903
–, Das Rätsel des Matschu. Meine Tibet-Expedition. Berlin 1907
H. Philipp, Ergebnisse der W. Filchner Vorexpedition nach Spitzbergen. Petermanns Mitteilungen. Gotha 1914
W. Filchner, Zum 6. Erdteil. Zwei deutsche Südpolar-Expeditionen. Berlin 1923
–, Kartenwerk der Erdmagnetischen Forschungsexpedition nach Zentral-Asien, 1926-1928. Petermanns Mitteilungen 215, 231. Gotha 1933
–, Bismillah. Vom Huang-Ho zum Indus. Leipzig 1938
–, A scientist in Tartary: from the Hoang-ho to the Indus. New York 1939

FLINDERS, MATTHEW

British seafarer and explorer, born 1774 in Donington (Lincolnshire), died 1814 in London.

Flinders was more or less self-taught and acquired an extensive knowledge of mathematics and nautical science. In 1795 Flinders traveled to Australia, where he undertook a voyage of exploration in the southern Australian waters in a small schooner by the name of "Tom Thumb", accompanied by G. Bass, a ship's doctor. The two seamen sailed through the channel between the southeast Australian mainland and Tasmania, which they circumnavigated, thus proving its island nature.

This feat saw Flinders promoted to the rank of commanding officer. In 1801 he was commissioned by the British admiralty to explore Australia's coast in the "Investigator". In the course of this extended journey, Flinders explored Spencer Gulf (between Cape Catastrophe and the York Peninsula, southern Australia) and the St. Vincent Gulf (Adelaide). He also sailed along the entire east Australian coast and reached the Gulf of Carpentaria by sailing through the Torres Strait. By the time Flinders landed on the island of Mauritius (after his ship had sprung a leak), he had sailed around the entire coastline of the Australian continent. Flinders was taken prisoner by the French and forced to spend seven years in a cell on the island of Mauritius; he was not able to return home to England until 1810.

Matthew Flinders was the first British seafarer to circumnavigate Australia and provide specific geographical information about the contours of the continent. A river in northern Queensland that flows into the Gulf of Carpentaria, a small island in the Great Australian Bight (southern Indian Ocean) and a town in South Australia bear the name of this significant seafarer and geographer.

Further reading
M. Flinders, Narrative of his Passage in the Schooner Francis. London 1798
A voyage to Australia undertaken for the purpose of completing the discovery of that vast country and prosecuted in the years 1801, 1802 and 1803 in H. M. S. the Investigator and subsequently in the purpose and Cumberland Schooner. 2 volumes London 1814
E. Scott, Life of Captain Matthew Flinders. Sydney 1914
J. Briant, Captain Matthew Flinders. without place of publication 1928
E. Hill, My love must wait. The story of Matthew Flinders. without place of publication 1941
M. Flinders, Die erste Umsegelung Australiens 1801-1876, ed. W. D. Grün. Stuttgart 1984

FORBES, JOAN ROSITA

English explorer and adventurer, born 1893, died 1967.

In 1920, accompanied by Hassanein Bey, an Egyptian Sahara explorer and diplomat, Joan Rosita Forbes reached the Al Kufrah oasis group in the Libyan Desert under the protection of the sultan of the Senussi (an Arab tribe in Cyrenaica).

In 1922/1923 the untiring traveler undertook an extended journey through Asia and stopped off in Yemen and Syria during her return journey. The following year, she wandered through Abyssinia and made topographical studies. Despite being dressed as an Arab she was never permitted to enter Mecca, the city of the prophets.

In 1934 she traveled to Central and South America and flew over vast stretches of the Amazon region.

Joan Rosita Forbes' travels did not provide any significant geographical findings. However, she was the first woman to reach the mysterious Al Kufrah Oasis group.

Further reading
J. R. Forbes, The Secret of the Sahara: Kufora. London 1921 (and 1937)
–, Abessinian Adventures. London 1925
–, Forbidden Road – Kabul to Samarkand. London 1937
–, From Red Sea to Blue Nile. New York 1939
–, Russian Road to India by Kabul and Samarkand. New York 1940

FOUCAULD, CHARLES EUGÈNE VICOMTE DE

French Sahara explorer and missionary, born 1858 in Strasbourg, died 1916 in Tamanrasset (southern Sahara).

In 1876 Foucauld was accepted into the military academy of St. Cyr and in 1878 he attended the cavalry academy of Saumur.

In 1881 he participated in a pacification campaign in Bu Amana (Morocco). From 1883 to 1884 Foucauld undertook his first major expedition through he Moroccan desert. Dressed as a poor Jew, on 20 June, 1883, he set out from Tangier and traveled via Tetuan, Xauan, Tasa and Sefru, before reaching Bou el Djad, from where he advanced into the western Sahara.

On his second journey of exploration, he visited the oases of Laghuat, Ghardaïa, El Goléa and Ouargla, finally reaching Touggourt (southern Algeria). He returned to his starting point via South Tunisia and Gabès (a town in central Tunisia).

Charles Foucauld was ordained as a Catholic priest in 1901. In 1904, together with General Laperrine, another French Sahara explorer, he undertook a political and administrative journey into the region of the Tuaregs. During this expedition Foucauld gathered such a quantity of geographical and ethnographic findings that people in Paris spoke of an "inventory" of the Sahara.

Matthew Flinders

In 1905 Foucauld traveled to the Hoggar (a massif in the Sahara) and settled in Tamanrasset, an oasis in southern Algeria, then in Asekrem, a small town in the Hoggar, where he dedicated his life to the conversion and pastoral care of the people of the desert. In 1916 he was murdered by a fanatical Tuareg in a hermitage in Tamanrasset.

Particular credit is due to Foucauld for his studies of "Temacheq", the language of the Tuaregs, and "Tifinar", their alphabet. The textbook "Grammaire et dictionnaire français-touareg" was published during the course of Foucauld's lifetime.

Further reading
R. Bazin, Charles de Foucauld. Paris 1925
S. E. Howe, Les Héros du Sahara (Le Père de Foucauld, Gén. Laperrine). Paris 1931
A. Goldie, Vie du Père Foucauld. 1858-1916. Paris 1938
P. J. H. Bonnette, L'œuvre des médecins sahariens, collaborateurs du Père de Foucauld au Hoggar. Tours 1938
R. V. C. Bodley, The Warrior Saint (A biography of Ch. de Foucauld). London 1954

FRANKLIN, SIR JOHN

British seafarer and Arctic explorer, born 1786 in Spilsby (Lincolnshire), died 1847 in the Canadian Arctic.

John Franklin joined the Royal Navy at the tender age of fourteen and was praised for his courage in the Battle of Trafalgar and in the wars with the United States of America from 1812 to 1815.

In 1818 Franklin developed an interest in Arctic exploration. On the "Trent", commanded by Buchan, another seafarer and polar explorer, he attempted to find the Northeast Passage. He sailed around Spitsbergen; however, on Buchan's orders he was forced to abandon his planned advance to the West Siberian Arctic Sea.

In 1819 the now experienced Arctic explorer was commissioned by the British admiralty to explore the region around the Great Slave Lake (northern Canada) and the entire course of Coppermine River. Suffering great hardships, he explored the western coast from Coppermine River to Cape Turnagain and returned to Fort Chippewyan (Lake Athabaska) after an absence of sixteen months.

In 1824, again on the commission of the British admiralty, Franklin explored the entire courses of the Mackenzie River and Peel Rivers. He spent the winter of 1825/1826 on Great Bear Lake (northern Canada) and on his subsequent journey reached Point Beechey (Alaska). During this expedition Franklin explored around 4,000 km (2,500 miles) of the northern coasts of Canada and Alaska.

From 1836 to 1843, Franklin was Governor of Tasmania.

In 1845 he was given the difficult task of conquering the Northwest Passage. According to instructions from the British admiralty, Franklin was to sail from Baffin Bay through Lancaster Sound, the Barrow Strait, Melville Sound and the McClure Strait into the Bering Strait, keeping his ship on as straight a course as possible. With two ships, the "Erebus" and the "Terror" (the latter commanded by Captain Crozier), equipped with the most modern measuring instruments available at that time and with supplies for three years, the two ships reached the Lancaster Sound. They were last sighted on 26 July, 1845 by the crew of a Scottish whaling ship; no more was then seen or heard of Franklin and his crew.

Search expeditions led by Richardson (1848), J. Ross (1849), Penny (1850), W. Kennedy (1852) and McClure (1852) failed to provide any information as to the disappearance of the Franklin expedition. It was only subsequent research by Dr. Rae and particularly McClintock which proved that Franklin lost his life on the northwest coast of King William Land.

With Franklin's death the mystery of the Northwest Passage had been revealed, and the most dramatic period of the struggle to conquer the Northwest Passage was over.

Sir John Franklin

Sir John Franklin did not perish when his ship sank, but probably died of food poisoning, together with his entire crew. This contemporary illustration portrays the rescue expedition which searched for Franklin.

An isthmus, a strip of land to the south of the Adelaide Peninsula, a bay in the Gulf of Amundsen and a cape, all located in the Canadian Arctic, bear the name of this great Arctic explorer.

Further reading
J. Franklin, Narrative of a Voyage to the Shores of the Polar-Sea in the years 1819, 1820, 1821 and 1822. London 1823
–, Narrative of a Second Expedition to the Shores of the Polar-Sea in the years 1825, 1826 and 1827. London 1828
Fr. L. McClintock, The Voyage of the "Fox" in the arctic Seas. A Narrative of the Discovery of the Fate of Sir J. Franklin and his companions. Philadelphia 1860
H. D. Traill, The life of Sir John Franklin. London 1896
R. J. Cyriax, Sir J. Franklin's Last Arctic Expedition. London 1939

Life was arduous and dangerous for the explorers. Here Franklin's crew are attempting to get round rapids on land.

FRANZ XAVER (FRANCISCO DE JASSU Y JAVIER)

Spanish theologian and Jesuit priest, saint, born 1506 in Javier Castle (Navarra), died 1552 on the island of Sancian (near Canton). Cofounder of the Jesuit order. In 1541 he traveled to India as a papal legate on the orders of the Portuguese king John III. There, he undertook missionary journeys to such destinations as Ceylon, Malacca and Japan. On 15 August, 1549 he landed in the port of Kagoshima on the southern coast of the Japanese peninsula of Kiushu and is thus regarded as the discoverer of Japan. He wandered through the country for two years. In 1551 Franz Xaver returned to India in order to begin performing missionary work in China from there; however, he died on the island of Sancian off the south Chinese coast before reaching his goal.

A base of the Franklin expedition near Great Bear Lake

FRÉMONT, JOHN CHARLES

North American explorer, born 1813 in Savannah (Georgia), died 1890 in New York.

Although John Frémont refused to attend school, by the time he joined the American navy at the age of seventeen he had gained an extensive knowledge of geometry and algebra. On board the training vessel "Natchez" he introduced the young seamen to mathematics and nautical science.

Frémont intended neither to conquer the southern regions occupied by the Spanish, which were later to become part of the United States, nor to have the native Americans driven from the great plateaus. Instead all he wanted was to scientifically explore the vast areas to the west of the Mississippi.

Accompanied by Nicolets, another natural scientist and explorer, Frémont explored the Allegheny Mountains and sailed down the Mississippi and the Missouri from 1838 to 1840.

It was only through his marriage to the rich senator's daughter Jessie Benton that he was finally able to implement his plan of exploring the as yet almost unknown "Wild West" between 1842 and 1844. Accompanied by his wife, Frémont traveled in a covered wagon through the region that today comprises the sates of Oregon, Idaho, Wyoming, Nevada, Utah and California, gathered geological specimens and made ethnographic observations, studying the customs and habits of the native North Americans.

After his excursion to the Rocky Mountains, he ran for the US Presidency, but he was unsuccessful. Prior to the outbreak of the American Civil War, Frémont was appointed General of the Mississippi Armies and, after the campaign, was elected Governor of Arizona (1878).

Frémont was one of the greatest and last scientific explorers of North America. In the USA he is still regarded today as the "conqueror" of California.

John Charles Frémont

The base camp of John Charles Frémont's expedition

Further reading
J. Ch. Frémont, Narrative of the exploring
expedition to the Rocky Mountains in the year
1842 and to Oregon and North California in the
years 1843-1844. London 1846

FREYCINET, LOUIS-CLAUDE DESAULES DE

French marine officer and circumnavigator of the world, born 1779, died 1842,

As a young officer, Louis-Claude Freycinet participated in the Baudin expedition from 1800 to 1804. During the 1817–29 world circumnavigation in the "Uranie" he had the position of scientific leader. This undertaking above all explored the Marianas. Freycinet also made several forays into the interior of the islands of Guam, Rota and Tinian. However, the expedition also discovered and charted further unknown islands on its continued journey. At the start of 1820 the ship ran aground on a reef and sank. But in a new ship, Freycinet was able to save almost all of his material and return with this to France.

This bold journey was even reflected in literature: The artist and writer Jacques-Etienne Victor Arago wrote an impressive report of this around-the-world voyage in the form of a letter, thus imparting a special atmosphere to this adventure in addition to providing factual information.

FROBISHER, SIR MARTIN

British seafarer and discoverer, born c. 1535 in Normanton (York), died 1594 in Plymouth.

From 1553 to 1554 Frobisher took part in an expedition to the coast of Guinea, and from 1563 to 1573 he was in the services of John Hawkins, another English seafarer and pirate.

In 1576 he undertook a journey to northern waters in search of the Northwest Passage. With two ships, the "Gabriel" and the "Michael", he set sail from the English port of Depford. During his journey he rediscovered the southern tip of Greenland, Cape Farvel, caught a glimpse of the coast of Labrador and sailed into the bay that today bears his name. In his first attempt to conquer the Northwest Passage, Frobisher reached a latitude of 62° 2' N.

In 1577 he made a second attempt to discover the northern Arctic route, this time reaching Hall Island. On his third journey he landed on South Greenland, but still failed to find a passage to the Pacific.

In 1580, Frobisher took part in suppressing a revolt in Ireland and five years later accompanied Francis Drake on his major privateering campaign to the West Indies.

In 1588, Frobisher was knighted for his services in the war against the Spanish Armada. While fighting the ªligueurs´ (rebels) on the commission of the French king Henry IV, he was fatally wounded during the siege of Crozon (Finistère, western France). With his bold advances into Arctic waters, Frobisher initiated the search for the Northwest Passage.

Further reading
A true discourse of the late voyages of discoveries for the finding of a passage to Cathay by the Northwest under the conduct of Martin Frobisher. General: divided into three books. London 1578
J. Campbell, Lives of the Admirals and other eminent British Seamen. London 1750
W. McFee, Sir Martin Frobisher. London 1928
The three voyages of Martin Frobisher in search of a Passage to Cathay and India by the North-West. 2 Bde. London 1938
V. Stefansson, The three voyages of Martin Frobisher. London 1939

FUCHS, SIR VIVIAN ERNEST

British geologist and Antarctic explorer, born 1908 in Freshwater (Isle of Wight), died 1999 in Cambridge.

Sir Vivian Fuchs is best known for his expeditions to Greenland and Africa. As leader of the transantarctic expedition in 1957/1958 he was the first person to cross Antarctica by land – in 99 days.

Freycinet's expeditionary ship "Uranie" in January, 1819, landing at one of the islands which it visited. The circumnavigators of the world were always greeted by the natives immediately, but unfortunately not always in such a friendly fashion as is evidently the case in this scene.

G

GAGARIN, YURI ALEXEYEVITCH

Soviet cosmonaut, born 1934 in Klushino (Smolensk region), died 1968 near Novosyolovo (Vladimir region).

After graduating from secondary school and completing an apprenticeship as a foundryman, Gagarin attended a technical college in Saratov. In 1957 he graduated as a jet pilot in the Soviet Air Force – this was the fulfillment of a childhood dream. He was then enrolled as a candidate in the Soviet cosmonaut training program.

After the Sputnik shock of 1957 the Soviet Union surprised the rest of the world a second

The Soviet cosmonaut Yuri Alexeyevich Gagarin was the first person to orbit the earth.

time on 12 April, 1961. The country announced that Major Gagarin had been the first man to circle the earth in space in the satellite "Vostok 1", a trip that had lasted 89 minutes. He started at 9:07 a.m. Moscow time from Baikonur and circled the planet in an elliptical path that ranged between 175 and 327 km (109 and 203 miles) from the surface of the Earth.

During the course of his flight, Gagarin monitored the board system operations, observed the Earth and outer space through three portholes, noting down his observations or dictating them on tape. Gagarin's health and condition were favorable; his ability to carry out his tasks was not affected in space. During the starting and landing phases his breathing and pulse were slightly elevated; however, when he became weightless both returned to normal. The descent of "Vostok 1" took 30 minutes from the time the braking engine was ignited; in that time alone, Yuri Gagarin covered 8,000 km (5,000 miles). During this landing maneuver the search and rescue groups positioned themselves in the expected landing area. At a height of 7 km (4.4 miles) the pilot's seat was ejected from "Vostok 1", the parachute opened when he reached a height of 4 km (2.5 miles) and Gagarin landed safely at 10:55 a.m. near Smolensk in the Saratov region.

Yuri Gagarin was killed during a test flight on 27 March, 1968.

Further reading
J. Gagarin/ W. Lebedew, Survival in space.
New York 1969
W. Gagarin, My brother Yuri without place of publication 1973
–, 108 minutes and an entire life. Without place of publication 1981
O. Nudenko, Orbits of a life. Without place of publication 1971
W. Stepanow, Gagarin. Without place of publication 1986

A handwritten letter from Vasco da Gama from his time as Governor of India

L'Amirante Don   Vasco de Gama

Vasco da Gama

GAMA, VASCO DA

Portuguese seafarer, born c. 1460 (1469?) in Sines (Alemtejo), died 1524 in Cochin (India).

Vasco da Gama, the son of the governor of Sines, had already attained the rank of captain in the Portuguese navy by the age of twenty. Unlike Columbus, he had an extensive knowledge of mathematics and nautical science. In 1496 his king, Manuel I, proposed the bold plan of advancing from East African shores to the Malabar coast (India), in order to open up a trading route from Lisbon to Calicut. The king commissioned the resourceful da Gama to carry out this significant political undertaking.

Once intensive preparations had been made in secret, the four caravels that had been built especially for this venture set sail from Tejo on 8 July, 1497. The flotilla consisted of the "São Gabriel", da Gama's flagship, the "São Raphael", commanded by Paulo, Vasco da Gama's brother, the "Berrio" and a supply ship. The da Gama brothers were accompanied by N. Coelho and

B. Diaz. The maps they used were supplied by Bishop Ortiz from Tangier and the declination tables were provided by Zarco. B. Diaz was in command of the "Cabo Verde"; his orders were to sail for the El Mina fort on the Guinea coast. Because of thick fog the "São Raphael" lost sight of the rest of the flotilla near "Cabo Bojador"; however, it was able to rejoin it some time later. From that point on Vasco da Gama's squadron sailed for 93 days on the stormy South Atlantic, on some occasions as much as 3,000 km (1,900 miles) from the west African coast, and on 4 November they at last dropped anchor off the island of St. Helena on the west coast of South Africa. After a twelve-day rest the flotilla set sail once more, proceeded around the stormy "Cape of Good Hope" and landed in "Mossel Bay", where a week was to elapse before the natives appeared and allowed the Portuguese to exchange goods. Sailing along the east African coast, da Gama reached Rio do Infante (Great Fish River) on 1 December. On 25 December he reached the coastal strip that he named "Natal" (Christmas). On 10 January, 1498 he reached Laurenco Marques Bay and twelve days later the Quilimane arm of the Zambezi.

On 1 March da Gama landed in Mozambique, the affluent trading town of the Sheik of Quiloa. Once the Arabs realized that the newcomers were not Muslims, open hostility broke out. Da Gama quickly weighed anchor and set sail for the port of Mombassa, where he had to use his artillery to gain some respect. The next and last stage before the crossing was Melinde, where the Portuguese were given a warm welcome, concluded some lucrative business and, to their great surprise, were provided with an experienced pilot by the ruler of the region. Meleno Cana (alias Ahmed ibn Majid) piloted the Portuguese safely to Calicut, where da Gama dropped anchor on 20 May, 1498.

A prisoner brought from Portugal especially for the purpose was the first to set foot on land. By chance he met a Spaniard from Seville who advised him not to do anything that could annoy the "Samurin", the king of Calicut and the Malabar coast. Eventually the Indian potentate granted da Gama an audience in his residence. When da Gama spread out his modest gifts in the samurin's courtyard, the courtiers broke out in derisive laughter. With diplomatic skill, the Portuguese ignored this open insult and, after intensive negotiations, was able to conclude the first Portuguese-Indian trading agreement. The holds of the Portuguese ships were filled with the coveted goods. When da Gama was prevented from returning to his ship by the temperamental Samurin, he was still able to order the crew on board to prepare the ships' artillery for fire, a measure that had an immediate effect.

The flotilla weighed anchor on 29 August, 1498. An Indian squadron dispatched from Cananor was held at bay by some well-placed artillery fire. Because the favorable monsoon wind was over for the season, the return journey was extremely difficult. Thirty men died of scurvy; as a result, the "São Raphael" had to be left behind for lack of sufficient crew members to sail it. The flotilla again stopped at Melinde on the East African coast, before proceeding around the Cape of Good Hope with great difficulty. Vasco da Gama's brother Paulo died on Terceira (Azores). The "Berrio" was the first of the ships to reach Lisbon on 16 July, 1499. On 9 September, 1499 King Manuel received the exhausted, but triumphant da Gama at Restelo in Lisbon.

The goal that had been set by Henry the Seafarer, namely to extend Portugal's power to India, had been achieved. The incursion into the Arabian-Islamic realm had succeeded. Da Gama's journey to India had far-reaching economic consequences. In some places, the price of pepper dropped by half. Many businesses were forced to declare bankruptcy. Venice, Genoa and Pisa were especially affected by the opening of the new trading route: the price of spices were henceforth determined in Lisbon. The wealth of the three

Portugal as a marine and colonial power

1179	Pope Innocence III acknowledges Portugal as a kingdom.
From 1279	Seafaring experiences considerable progress under King Dinis I.
1385	Parliament elects João I as king. The development towards becoming a colonial power begins.
From 1418	Crown Prince Henry the Seafarer promotes voyages of discovery to the Atlantic and Africa.
From 1419	Portuguese seafarers discover and colonize Madeira, the Azores and the Cape Verde Islands.
1471	The seafarer Fernão do Póo is the first European to set foot on the west African coast in the area that is today Guinea and initates exploration of the hinterland, slave trading and Christianization.
1486	Diogo Cão is the first European to land on the coast of what is today known as Namibia.
1488	Bartolomeu Diaz is the first European to sail around the southern tip of Africa.
1494	Portugal and Spain divide their spheres of influence: Around 600 km (370 miles) to the west of the Azores the world is split into two halves from north to south. Spain is given the area to the west of the line, while Portugal takes the eastern part.
1495	Lisbon becomes the hub of global trade under King Manuel I. Settlements are founded in East India, South Africa and Brazil.
1498	Vasco da Gama is the first European to reach what is now Mozambique and eastern India.
1500	Cabral lands on the north coast of Brazil and takes possession of the country for Portugal.
1500	Diego Díaz is the first European to land on Madagascar.
1502	Amerigo Vespucci explores the coast of South America.
1510	Trade settlements in the Far East consolidate Portugal's leading position in the spice trade.
1580	King Philipp II of Spain also becomes King of Portugal as Filipe I.
From 1607	Under Spanish sovereignty, Portugal has to surrender several colonial regions to the Netherlands. Portugal never again achieves its former power.

marine and trading republics gradually began to decline.

Without wishing to play down da Gama's exploits, it must be remembered that B. Diaz had already traced out much of the route to India beforehand. Da Gama only had to overcome the last, although admittedly most difficult hurdle.

In 1502 he sailed to India a second time and founded the trading posts of Cochin and Cananor. Before setting out on his third and last crossing he was awarded the title of Viceroy of India (1524).

The Portuguese national poet Camões extolled da Gama's exploits in his epos "The Lusiads". Da Gama's mortal remains were shipped back to Lisbon (Santa Maria de Belem) from India in 1558.

Further reading
Fr. Hümmerich, Vasco da Gama und die
Entdeckung des Seewegs nach Ostindien.
Munich 1898
C. Pereyra, La conquête des routes océaniques
d'Henri le Navigateur à Magellan. Paris
1923
H. Plischke, Vasco da Gama. Leipzig 1924
Fr. Hümmerich, Vasco da Gama und die
Entdeckung des Seeweges nach Indien. In:
Iberia, Heft 5, 74-82. Without place of pub-
lication 1926
S. W. Bassett, The story of Vasco da Gama.
Philadelphia 1927
P. L. Marini, Vasco da Gama. Turin 1929
E. Prestage, Descobridores portugueses.
Porto 1934
A. Kammerer, Les guerres du poivre, les Por-
tugais dans l'Océan Indien et la Mer Rouge
au XVIe siècle. Le Caire 1935
D. Peres, Historia dos decobriementos portu-
gueses. Porto 1943
Vasco da Gama – Die Entdeckung des
Seewegs nach Indien. Ein Augenzeugenbericht
1497-1499, published by G. Giertz. 2nd ed.
Stuttgart 1986

GESSI, ROMOLO

Italian explorer of Africa, born 1831, died 1881.

In 1876 Gessi was commissioned by Gordon Pascha to explore the as yet unknown region between the White Nile and Lake Albert Nyanza. Accompanied by C. Piaggia, another Italian explorer, he fulfilled his task to Pascha's complete satisfaction. They discovered the catchment area of Lake Albert, traveled around its perimeter and established that the catchment area was not as large as had been charted on Baker's map. At the end of August Gessi and Dr. Junker followed the Sobat (a tributary to the right of the White Nile) to the military station at Nasser. An outbreak of hostilities forced them to abandon their expedition and Gessi was called to arms. During the campaign he followed Suliman Sibér, the son of the discoverer of the Darfur, into the land of the Niam Niam (a tribe in the Congo). Once peace had returned to the region, Gessi explored the Sudan.

Through his scientific exploration of the Sudan, Gessi provided a wealth of new information about this vast country. In the course of his undertakings he was not afraid of publicly condemning the actions of the Arabian slave traders.

Further reading
P. Strobel, La spedizione italiana nell'Africa
equatoriale. Parma 1875
Petermanns Mitteilungen. Gotha 1876
Bulletin de la Société Géographique de Paris
1876
Giornale delle colonie. Without place of
publication 1878
Memorie della societa geografica Italiana.
Without place of publication 1878
P. Matteucci, Spedizione Gessi-Matteucci.
Sudan e Gallas. Milan 1879
R. Gessi, Sette anni nel Sudan Egiziano.
Esplorationi, Caccie e guerre contro i negrieri.
Milan 1891 (revised edition 1930)

GRANDIDIER, ALFRED

French geographer and natural scientist, born 1836 in Paris, died 1921 in Paris.

The name Alfred Grandidier is inseparably associated with the island of Madagascar, which he was the first to explore thoroughly in the

course of his journeys through South America and Asia. From 1865 to 1870 he traveled throughout the island, covering more than 5,000 km (3,000 miles). Grandidier studied Madagascar's flora and fauna and discovered the fossils of an extinct giant ostrich, the legendary rok. He also collected rock samples and made precise measurements. The French scientist published the results of his research in an opus comprising several volumes.

Diego Suarez Bay, Madagascar

H

HANNO

Carthaginian seafarer, c. 500 BC.

Hanno's journey along the west coast of Africa, in the course of which he was able to open up a numnber of new trading posts, is regarded as being one of the most important journeys of ancient times. It appears that the Carthaginian seaman reached the Gulf of Guinea via the mouth of the Senegal. His report has been translated.

Further reading
W. Hörnemann, Hanno zwischen zwei Welten.
Ein abenteuerliches Schicksal. Recklinghausen
1993

HARRER, HEINRICH

Austrian explorer, born 1912 in Kärnten.

Even as a young boy, Heinrich Harrer demonstrated an exceptional passion for adventure. He later took part in the 1936 Olympic Games and became world champion in the downhill skiing event. In 1938, together with A. Heckmair, he was the first to conquer the notorious north face of the Eiger and in 1939 took part in the German Nanga Parbat expedition. When war broke out, he was interned in India but managed to flee to Tibet. After crossing 65 Himalayan passes, he reached the Tibetan capital of Lhasa. From 1944 to 1951 he was an advisor and teacher of the Dalai Lama, the god king and ruler of Tibet.

Isaak Israel Hayes

In 1962 Harrer crossed the tropical island of New Guinea. There, he was the first to climb 32 snow-covered mountains and he also discovered Ja Li Me, a source of stone axes. In 1965 the Austrian president awarded him the title of professor. In 1966 and 1969 Harrer undertook an expedition to the Amazon, in some segments of which he was accompanied by the Belgian king Leopold III, and in 1971 he explored the Sudan and the island of Borneo.

Heinrich Harrer was one of the last great explorers of the twentieth century. His books have been translated into many languages. He produced many film and television series, including some in the USA as from 1967, and owns one of the world's largest collections of Tibetan artifacts. His New Guinea and Amazon collection can be found in the Museum of Ethnology at Zurich University.

Further reading
H. Harrer. Huka-Huka. Bei den Xingu-Indianern
im Amazonas-Gebiet. Berlin 1979
–, Ladakh. Götter und Menschen hinter dem
Himalaya. Berlin 1980
–, Die letzten Fünfhundert. Expedition zu den
Zwergvölkern auf den Andamanen. Berlin 1983
–, Meine Forschungsreisen. Innsbruck 1986
–, Sieben Jahre in Tibet. Mein Leben am Hofe
des Dalai Lama. Berlin 1988
–, Das Buch vom Eiger. 2nd edition Innsbruck
1989
–, Die weiße Spinne. Die Geschichte der Eiger-
Nordwand. Berlin 1989
–, Tibet. Zeitdokumente aus den Jahren
1944-1951. Zurich 1991
–, Erinnerungen an Tibet. Berlin 1993

HAYES, ISAAK ISRAEL

North American Arctic explorer, born 1832, died 1881.

Isaak Hayes originally studied medicine. In 1853 he took part in the second voyage of E. K.

Kanes, another American Arctic explorer, and explored the unknown region around Cape Sabine on Ellesemere Land. The following year he sailed through Smith Sound and Dobbin Bay. In the course of a second winter that he spent there, he explored the Danish outpost of Greenland together with eight companions. Only with extreme effort and the untiring support of the Inuit was he able to reach Kane's ship, the "Advance."

In the meantime Hayes had become convinced that it must be possible to reach the North Pole via an open Arctic sea.

In 1860, generously supported by the American Geographical Society, he set out for Greenland from the port of Boston in the "United States", where he set up a supply base in Foulke Fjord (near Littleton Island) in the region of the Etah Inuit. Despite the inclement weather he reached 81° 35' N. Shortly before this he had explored Grinnell Land.

In 1869 he accompanied the polar explorer W. Bradford to Antarctica for the third time on the "Panther."

Hayes is regarded as a pioneer in the race to the North Pole.

HEARNE, SAMUEL

British-Canadian Arctic explorer, born 1745 in London, died 1792 in England.

Hearne started his career as a naval officer, before becoming an agent and fur trader in the services of the Hudson Bay Company (HBC), for whom he carried out extensive journeys through the Northwest Territories.

In 1769 he was commissioned by Norton, commanding officer of the "Prince of Wales" fort in Churchill Bay, to discover Coppermine River and the Northwest Passage.

Setting out from Fort Churchill (Hudson Bay),

Samuel Hearne, accompanied by some scouts from the Cree and Chippewa tribes, reached the River Kazan after an exhausting trek through the valley of the River Seal; however, he was eventually deserted by the native scouts and forced to turn back.

His second attempt was more successful. Accompanied by a trustworthy scout and friend, the Indian chief Matonabbee, with the chief's wives as porters, and taking advantage of the hatred between the Inuit and the Indians, Hearne was the first European to reach the ice-covered Arctic Ocean and Coppermine River via the Barren Grounds. He returned to Fort Churchill in June 1772.

Samuel Hearne

In his account of his travels Hearne also describes the invention of the snowshoes with which he and his crew were able to move across the snow-covered ground safely.

179

Inuit in a canoe

Sven Hedin

Although Hearne had failed to discover the rich copper deposits that he had hoped to find, the newly discovered areas on the Arctic Circle that were rich in fur-bearing animals were no less important for the HBC than copper ore. Besides, Hearne had discovered a lively fur trade between the Hudson Bay region, the Great Slave Lake and Lake Athabaska. But at the same time fierce competition developed between the two fur trading companies HBC and the Northwest Company, which was not to end until they merged in 1821.

Further reading
A journey from Prince of Wales Fort in Hudson's Bay to the Northern Ocean, undertaken by Samuel Hearne, from the discovery of Coppermines, a North West passage, in the years 1769-1772. London 1795
J. B. Tyrrell, Journals of Samuel Hearne and Philipp Turner. Toronto 1934
S. Hearne, Abenteuer im arktischen Kanada. Auf der Suche nach der Nordwestpassage 1769-1772, ed. V. Matthies. Tübingen 1981.

HEDIN, SVEN ANDERS VON

Swedish Asia explorer, born 1865 in Stockholm, died 1952 in Stockholm.

When he was just twenty-one years old, Sven Hedin participated in an extensive journey throughout much of Asia to gather information about this region, and in 1893 he set out on his first scientific expedition to the 400,000 square kilometer (150,000 square mile) Takla Makan desert.

The following year, he again crossed the inhospitable Takla Makan. Snowstorms, "karabouraus" (sandstorms) and torrential showers of rain were the elements that Hedin constantly had to face. He explored the inner delta of the River Tarim and visited the land of the holy books, Tibet. In the region of the "wild yaks", he charted a large number of salt lakes; he also crossed the Gobi Desert. Hedin discovered the ancient ruins of Loulan, which he then had excavated. The excavation brought a large number of Buddha images, Chinese documents, scripts and numerous painted discs to light. The texts told of the lively exchange of trade between the Chinese and Roman empires. Hedin reached Beijing in 1897.

Hedin's next major journey (1899-1902) was to take him to Lhasa, the religious and cultural center of Tibet. Hedin set out on this adventurous journey dressed as a Mongol and accompanied by a Cossack and a Mendicant monk. Robbers and hostile Lamas (Buddhist priests of Tibet and Mongolia) made life difficult for the small band of travelers. When they reached the route to Lhasa, Hedin's wish to visit the "forbidden city" was dashed: Tibetan warriors expelled him to India.

From 1905 to 1908 Hedin undertook his third major journey to explore the still largely unknown mountain range of the Karakoram and the famous Tashi Lumpo monastery. Bitter cold, attacks by wild yaks and the hostility of Tibetan monks made life difficult for the members of the expedition. Once more, the governor of the province appeared and demanded that Hedin turn back. However, after lengthy negotiations he relented and Hedin was allowed to carry on to Brahmaputra (Tsangpo). After crossing the steep slopes of the Himalayas he reached the town of Shigatse and the legendary Tashi Lumpo monastery. He took part in a Buddhist festivity and visited the Tashi Lama, the representative of

In 1923 Hedin also traveled to the USA. Here he was above all fascinated by the Grand Canyon.

Illustrations from Hedin's account of his travels "Jehol – the Imperial City" of 1940. For ceremonial reasons the streets are decorated with flags. One can see street traders, a Peking barrow, and a coolie who is gathering horse droppings to sell them as fuel.

In the streets of Peking the Emperor's birthday is celebrated with horsemen, elephants, and a ceremonial gate.

the Dalai Lama and the incarnation of the Dyana Buddha.

After spending 47 days here, the explorer had to leave Shigatse. During his return journey he visited several monasteries; in one he found an immense prayer wheel that was kept in operation day and night by two monks. At the foot of the mountain he met an old Mendicant monk who lived in a tiny room in complete darkness. During his Himalayan crossing he was again forced by the Tibetan authorities to change his route. Hedin then decided to advance to the sources of the Brahmaputra. He followed the river in a southwesterly direction and reached a greenish-blue glacier, which fed the Brahmaputra. He then continued on to the holy lake of Manasarova, 4,565 m (14,977 feet) above sea level. The Tibetans believed that sailing on this lake would contaminate it and evoke the anger of the gods. In September Hedin reached the sources of the Indus. He was the first European ever to reach both the sources of the Indus and the Brahmaputra in one journey and he was also the first to chart the Himalayan crossing.

In spite of this extensive undertaking there were still vast areas of central Asia that had not yet been explored or charted. Dressed as a shepherd, Hedin crossed the Himalayas for the seventh time. In 1908 he returned to Sweden.

From 1927 to 1935 Hedin explored and charted more unexplored regions of Mongolia, the Gobi Desert and Chinese Turkestan.

The "Swedish Marco Polo" was the first white man able to scientifically explore the "land of the holy books" that was forbidden to foreigners. As a result of his expeditions many blank areas on the map of central Asia could be filled in, and he also provided Europe with the first specific information on the "roof of the world". Hedin's photographs of Tibet and Lhasa were highly important for Europe's historians and geographers.

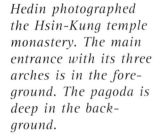

Hedin photographed the Hsin-Kung temple monastery. The main entrance with its three arches is in the foreground. The pagoda is deep in the background.

Further reading
S. Hedin, *Die geographisch-wissenschaftlichen Ergebnisse meiner Reise in Zentralasien 1893-1897. Erg. Heft Petermanns Mitteilungen.* Gotha 1897
–, *Durch Asiens Wüsten. 2 volumes Leipzig 1899*
–, *Im Herzen von Asien. 2 volumes without place of publication 1903*
–, *Scientific Results of a journey in Central Asia. 6 volumes, 2 map volumes. Stockholm and London 1904-1907*
–, *Transhimalaja. 3 volumes, without place of publication 1909-1912*
–, *Zu Land nach Indien. 2 volumes, without place of publication 1910*
–, *Southern Tibet. 9 Bde., 2 Kartenbde. Stockholm and Gotha 1917-1922*
A. Hedin, *Mein Bruder Sven. Leipzig 1925*
Sven Hedin und A. Brockhaus. Eine Freundschaft in Briefen. 2nd edition, without place of publication 1956
R. Essén, *Sven Hedin. Ein großes Leben. Leoni 1959*
W. Hess, *Die Werke Sven Hedins. Stockholm 1962*
E. Wennerholm, *Sven Hedin, without place of publication 1978*
S. Hedin, *Transhimalaya. Entdeckungen und Abenteuer in Tibet. Reprint of 7th edition Mannheim 1985*
D. Brennecke, *Sven Hedin. Mit Selbstzeugnissen und Bilddokumenten. Reinbek 1986*
S. Hedin, *Abenteuer in Tibet. 12th edition Mannheim 1987*

HENRY THE SEAFARER (HENRIQUE O NAVEGADOR)

Portuguese, third son of the Portuguese king John I, born 1394 in Porto, died 1460 in Sagres.

After participating in the storming of the Moorish fort of Ceuta (1415), Henry withdrew from court life and settled on the rocky plateau of Cape São Vicente, Europe's southwesternmost tip, where he had the "Villa Tercanabal" built (also known as the Nautical Academy), in order to develop plans for the future Portuguese empire with several like-minded people.

On his initiative, the seamen T. V. Teixeira and J. G. Zarco repossessed Madeira and Porto

Henry the Seafarer

Santo for Portugal between 1418 and 1420, the Azores were colonized and Cape Bojador was rounded. While the conquest of the Canary Isles in 1425 was unsuccessful, the strategic annexation of the Cape Verde Islands into Portugal's up-and-coming colonial empire succeeded.

However, Henry's main goal was a concerted campaign with the ruler of Ethiopia against Islam. But a plan such required a permanent land connection with the Negus. As such contact right across Central Africa was impossible in the 1430s, it had to be created via the sea. This in turn meant advancing beyond the equator.

In 1441 the Portuguese began their so-called "cape jumping" on the west African coast. In 1442 N. Tristão was the first to venture past Cape Blanco to Arguin Bay, and Diniz Diaz rounded Cape Verde and landed on the island of Bezeguiche (1444). In a renewed attempt Tristão sailed into the mouth of the Rio Grande (1446). The following year, the Portuguese reached Guinea, and in 1448 the first settlement was established in the Bay of Arguin. Two years before Henry's death, San Jorge da Mina on the Gulf of Guinea was the most important transshipment center for gold, wheat and black slaves. Portugal bought 700 to 800 slaves each year from Arabian slave traders. Although Henry formally forbade all raids between Cape Verde and Cape Blanco, slave trading yielded enormous profits for both sides.

When Henry, known as the "Seafarer" although he never went to sea, died in 1460, the foundation stone of the Portuguese colonial empire had been laid, and this opened up the direct sea route to India. The seafarers Bartolomëu Diaz and Vasco da Gama completed the work that Henry had began.

Heyerdahl's bizarre raft the "Kon-Tiki", seen here before the voyage in the port of Callao. It is a copy of the historic Indian rafts of the Pacific Ocean.

Further reading
E. Engel, Heinrich der Seefahrer. In: O Comercio do Porto. Porto 1894
C. Pereira, La conquête des routes océaniques d'Henri le Navigateur à Magellan. Paris 1923
E. Prestage, Descobridores portugueses. Porto 1934
D. Peres, Historia dos descobrimentos. Porto 1943
Heinrich der Seefahrer oder Die Suche nach Indien. Eine Dokumentation mit Alvise da Ca Da Mostos erstem Bericht über Westafrika und den Chroniken Zuaras und Barros über den Infanten, ed. R. Kroboth/G. Pögl. Stuttgart 1989

HEYERDAHL, THOR

Norwegian ethnologist, zoologist, geographer and scientific explorer, born 1914 in Larvik.

From an early age Heyerdahl was interested in the anthropology of Polynesia; his studies were considerably simplified by the fact that he had access to the Kroepelian Library, the largest private collection of Polynesian literature. He specialized in zoology and geography at Oslo University.

In 1937, on Kroepelian's recommendation Heyerdahl and his young wife received an invitation from the Grand Chief of Tahiti, Tiriiero, to visit the South Seas. They stayed for a year on the island of Fatuhiva (Marquesas group), where they studied the customs and lifestyle of the island inhabitants. In 1938 Heyerdahl left the South Seas and headed for the United Kingdom, the USA and Canada to study the museums of those countries and try to discover the origins of the Polynesian race and culture. During his research work in the Museum of British Columbia, he published his theory (New York, 1941) that Polynesia had been populated during two migration flows, one from Peru and the other from British Columbia.

To prove his theories, which were met with resistance and criticism even amongst his closest friends, Heyerdahl set out in 1947 on his celebrated "Kon-Tiki" expedition (named in honor of the legendary pre-Incan ruler Kon Tiki, who sailed from Callao to the 8,000 km (5,000 miles) distant Raroia Atoll of the Tuamotu group in 101 days). Heyerdahl proved that it was possible to sail from the west coast of South America to reach Polynesia in a balsa boat ("balsa" = Spanish: raft, a water craft constructed from bundles of bulrushes, as used on the west coast of South America). At the same time he proved the seaworthiness of this type of vessel.

In 1952 Heyerdahl organized and led the explorers of the Norwegian archaeological expedition to the Galapagos Islands, some 1,000 km (600 miles) from Peru. In the course of their extensive excavations, professional archaeologists from Norway and the USA discovered 130 miniature clay ships that were identified by the Smithsonian Institute in Washington as pre-Columbian ceramics from Ecuador and northern Peru.

Between 1955 and 1956 Heyerdahl undertook a largely archaeological expedition accompanied by 23 experts, including four world famous archaeologists, from the USA and Norway to Easter Island. Research work showed that the island had been populated around a thousand years earlier than scholars had previously assumed. Heyerdahl also made interesting findings concerning the island's colossal stone figures. In the course of further excavations the fortified village of Morongo Uta (on Rapa Iti) was uncovered. The results of this major research expedition were discussed and their accuracy confirmed at the 10th Pacific Scientific Congress in Honolulu (1961) at many archaeological, geographical and ethnographic meetings.

From 1969 to 1970 Heyerdahl undertook his famous "Ra I expedition". On a 15 meter (50 foot) Egyptian boat constructed of papyrus, made according to designs from the time of the Pharaohs, he sailed, accompanied by an international team of experts, from the ancient Phoenician port of Safi (on the west coast of Morocco) in the direction of Central America. After travel-

ing for around 5,000 km (3,000 miles) on an eight-week journey of adventure (with storms and a broken rudder) Heyerdahl was forced to abandon his undertaking not far from the island of Barbados in the British Antilles.

Ten months later Heyerdahl repeated the journey. With the 12-meter (40-foot) "Ra II", built by four Aymara Indians (a tribe from southern Peru, bearers of the Tiahuanaco culture), he sailed from Safi across the Atlantic in 57 days and, at the end of a 6,100-km (3,800-mile) journey, landed on the island of Barbados.

In 1977-78 in the reed boat "Tigris", which had been built according to Sumerian designs, Heyerdahl set out from Basra and sailed through the Persian Gulf to the town of Djibouti.

In 1983 the Norwegian discovered the ruins of a highly developed ancient culture on the Maldives.

He was able to prove theorists wrong and demonstrated that it would indeed have been possible to reach the Central American archipelago from West Africa even in light and simple, but strong boats and for major cultures to come into contact with one another. Heyerdahl had also proved that the oceans had not been a hindrance for cultural exchange between different peoples.

Further reading
T. Heyerdahl, Paa jakt efter Paradiset. Oslo 1938
–, American Indians in the Pacific. The Theory behind the Kon-Tiki Expedition. Stockholm, London, Chicago 1952
–, Archaeological Evidence of Pre-Spanish Visits to the Galapagos Islands. Memoir of the Soc. for American Archaeology, No. 12. Salt Lake City 1956
–, Reports of the Norwegian Archaeological Expedition to Easter Islands and the East Pacific. 2 vols. Santa Fé, London, Chicago, Oslo 1961
–, Vanished Civilizations. London 1963
–, Indianer und Alt-Asiaten im Pazifik, Vienna 1965
–, Sea Routes to Polynesia. London, Chicago 1967

–, The Ra Expedition. Oslo 1970
–, Die Kunst der Osterinsel. Munich 1975
–, Zwischen den Kontinenten. Archäologische Abenteuer. Munich 1975
–, Kon-Tiki. Berlin 1976
–, Kon-Tiki. Ein Floß treibt über den Pazifik. Berlin 1980.
–, Tigris. Auf der Suche nach unserem Ursprung. Neuaufl. Munich 1990
–, Wege übers Meer. Völkerwanderungen in der Frühzeit. Neuaufl. Munich 1990
–, Fua Maluku. Reise zu den vergessenen Kulturen der Malediven. Reprint. Vienna 1991
–, Fatu Hiva. Zurück zur Natur. Reprint. Vienna 1993

HILLARY, SIR EDMUND

New Zealand mountaineer and researcher, born 1919 in Auckland.

On 29 May, 1953 on his second attempt the New Zealand beekeeper Hillary, together with the Nepalese Sherpa Tensing Norgay, was the first man to climb Mount Everest (8,848 meters or 29,029 feet).

Further reading
E. Hillary, Ich stand auf dem Everest. Meine Erstbesteigung mit Scherpa Tensing. 5th edition Mannheim 1974

HOLUB, EMIL

Czech explorer of Africa, born 1847, died 1902.

In 1872 the young physician set out for the diamond mining fields on the River Vaal. In addition to practicing his profession, he busied himself intensively with geography and ethnography and undertook some extensive journeys in the region of Potchefstroom (a town in southwestern Transvaal), where he investigated the ethnographic and geographical conditions of Griqualand. In the course of his further travels Holub visited extensive regions of the eastern Transvaal state.

He explored the Zambezi between 1874 and 1876. From Potchefstroom he crossed the Limpopo, and in August he reached the upper

View of the imposing Mount Everest

The highest mountains

1. Mount Everest, Himalaya, 8,848 m (29,029 ft)
2. K2, Karakorum, 8,611 m (28,251 ft)
3. Kangchenjunga, Himalaya, 8,579 m (28,146 ft)
4. Lhotse, Himalaya, 8,501 m (27,890 ft)
5. Makalu I, Himalaya, 8,475 m (27,805 ft)
6. Lhotse Shar, Himalaya, 8,383 m (27,503 ft)
7. Dhaulagiri, Himalaya, 8,172 m (26,811 ft)
8. Manaslu, Himalaya, 8,156 m (26,759 ft)

course of this vast east African river and thoroughly explored 100 km (60 miles) of its banks. In April 1876 Holub reached Kimberley (northern Cape province) armed with a map of the Victoria Falls and a rich ethnographic collection.

Holub's third journey to Africa took place from 1883 to 1887. This time he explored the central course of the Zambezi, traveled through the Barotse Flood Plain (today a province in the west of Zambia) and the land of the Mushukalambwe (a Bantu tribe on the central Kafue, Zambia).

Dr. Holub acquired a great deal of geographical and ethnographic knowledge about the landscape on Lake Bangweolo and Lake Nyassa and about the Zambezi.

Further reading
Mitteilungen der k. k. geographischen Gesellschaft in Wien. Vienna 1875 and 1877
Petermanns Mitteilungen. Gotha 1876 and 1877
E. Holub, Few words on the native question. Kimberley 1877
–, The Victoria Falls. Grahamstown 1879
–, Eine Kulturskizze des Marutse-Mambunda-Reiches in Südafrika. Vienna 1879
–, Sieben Jahre Südafrika. Vienna 1880
–, Von Kapstadt ins Land der Maschkulumbe. 2 volumes. Vienna 1889-1890

Caravans in the Libyan Desert

HORNEMANN, FRIEDRICH KONRAD

German explorer of Africa, born 1772 in Hildesheim, died 1801 in Bokane (Nigeria).

On the recommendation of Professor Blumenbach, Hornemann traveled to Egypt on the commission of the London African Association; this country was to serve as his point of departure for his exploration of the Sudan and the Niger.

He set out from Cairo, accompanied by the German traveler J. Fremdenburgh, who had converted to Islam, and reached the Siwa and Audchila oases (the largest of the Jalu oases) in the Libyan desert; on 17 November, 1798 he reached Mursuk in Fessan. He then returned to Tripoli and prepared a second Sudan expedition.

In 1799 Hornemann set out from Tripoli for Mursuk, where he joined a caravan heading southwest towards Bornu in January 1800. His intention was to explore the land of the Haussa (a people in central Sudan with colonies in areas such as northern Nigeria). Hornemann died during this journey.

It has never been ascertained whether Hornemann actually reached the Niger on his last expedition. In any case, he was the first European to send specific news of Bornu to Europe and the second (after the Italian Malfante) to explore the Sudan.

Further reading
F. Hornemanns Tagebuch seiner Reise von Kairo nach Mursuk in den Jahren 1797-1798, bearbeitet von C. König. Weimar 1802
F. Pahde, Der erste deutsche Afrikaforscher F. K. Hornemann, geb. 1772, gest. 1801. Without place of publication 1895

HUDSON, HENRY

British seafarer and Arctic explorer, born c. 1550, died 1611, probably on the west coast of Hudson Bay.

The origins and age of this important English seafarer are uncertain. The earliest mention of

him was in 1607 when he was commissioned by the Muscovite trading company to reach India via the North Passage. He left London on 23 April, 1607, sailed from the Shetland Islands to the east coast of Greenland to a latitude of 73° N, followed the glacial boundary in a north-easterly direction and landed on Spitsbergen. On the eastern side of this group of islands he was prevented by pack ice from traveling any further. After five months' absence he arrived back in London.

In late April 1608 he made another attempt to conquer the Northeast Passage. This time he followed the traces of the English explorers Pet, Willoughby and Burrough. However, the masses of ice of Novaya Zemlya thwarted his plan once more.

He started his third Arctic voyage in March 1609 on a ship of the Dutch Company, in the employment of the Netherlands. His reasons for this change are not known. This time he followed the route that had already been taken by the Dutchmen Heemskerck and Barents. Hudson again failed to conquer the masses of ice around Novaya Zemlya or to enter the dreaded Kara Sea. He changed course, sailing past the southern tip of Greenland, reached the North American coast at Nova Scotia, from where he endeavored to reach India via the Northwest Passage. When he saw a wide strait in the vicinity of the 41st degree of latitude, he believed that he had discovered the entrance to the passage. In fact, however, he had discovered the mouth of the river now named after him, where the Dutchman Peter Minuit 1626 built the seaport of New Amsterdam, later renamed New York. On his further travels through the Davis Strait, he was forced by mutineers to turn back.

Shortly after his return to England, three English merchants equipped a further expedition to find the Northwest Passage and handed over the helm to Hudson. From London (17 April, 1610) he reached Frobisher Bay via the Faroe Islands, Iceland, sailed around Cape Farvel (the southern tip of Greenland), discovered the "Hudson Strait" (also named after him) near what is now known as Resolution Island. The Hudson Strait is a body of water that stretches both to the south and to the north. Hudson believed it to be the "South Sea" and was convinced that he had solved the problem of the Northwest Passage. Traveling further south, he went ashore in what is now called James Bay and stayed there over winter. The sailors' forced inactivity together with the unusual cold and lack of food gave rise to an open mutiny in June 1611, while Hudson was preparing to continue his journey. The captain, his son and seven of his loyal crew were marooned in a sloop and left to their fate; they were never seen again. Only a small part of the remaining crew reached England, where all were sent to prison despite their accounts of Hudson's severity towards them.

During his four ventures into the Arctic, Hudson had developed a keen exploratory spirit. His logbooks contain a wealth of precise scientific notes which proved invaluable to his successors.

Hudson Bay, Hudson Strait and the Hudson River were known prior to Hudson's voyages to North America, but were named after this important seafarer.

Further reading
H. R. Cleveland, Life of Henry Hudson. In: Library of American Biography T. 10, without place of publication 1834
G. M. Asher (ed. by Hakluyt Society), Henry Hudson, the Navigator. The original documents in which his career is recorded, partly translated and annotated, with an introduction. London 1860
John M. Jr. A. Read, A Historical Inquiry concerning Henry Hudson. New York 1909
L. Powys, Henry Hudson. London and New York 1928
C. H. L. Ewen, The North-West Passage. Light on the murder of Henry Hudson. London 1938
L. J. Burpee, The fate of Henry Hudson. Reprinted from the Canadian Historical Review, without place of publication 1940
–, The discovery of Canada. Toronto 1944

HUMBOLDT, ALEXANDER FREIHERR VON

German natural scientist and world traveler, born 1769 in Berlin, died 1859 in Berlin.

Alexander Freiherr von Humboldt came from a family of major landowners in Prussia. He attended the universities in Frankfurt/Oder, Göttingen and Freiberg (Saxony) and complimented his theoretical knowledge through extensive travels to France, England and the Netherlands. In Germany he was an acquaintance of Goethe, Schiller, Fichte and Schelling. Despite his aristocratic background, Humboldt held a certain admiration for the French revolution. He chose not to practice a technical profession, sold his lands and went to Paris in 1797. There he made the acquaintance of well-known Frenchmen such as Saint-Hilaire, Laplace and Monge. In the French metropolis he set his sights on either accompanying Napoleon on his campaign to Egypt or participating in the world voyage of seafarer N. Baudin, which was currently under preparation.

In Marseille, Humboldt and his friend, the French botanist Aimé Bonpland, waited for a boat to take them to Algiers. But because the departure was delayed excessively, Humboldt and Bonpland traveled to Spain where eventually, after long negotiations, they received permission from the government in Madrid to explore the Spanish region of South America.

On 5 June, 1799, the two scientists left Tenerife and went ashore in Cumaná (east of the mouth of the Río Manzanares, then New Andalusia) on 17 July. Equipped with state-of-the-art measuring equipment and actively supported by the Spanish authorities, they proceeded inland and reached – via the Río Apure (left tributary of the Orinoco) – the Orinoco, which they then explored almost to its source in the Sierra Parima on the Brazilian border. Their plan to explore Brazil afterwards was thwarted by the Portuguese governor. When they arrived back in Cumaná, the two men had explored almost the entire region of the Orinoco, South America's third-largest river, and had made the most extensive findings to date about the geography and zoology of the Llanos, about the rainforest Indians and about the production of Curare, a plant-based poison. In November 1800 they sailed via Guayana to Havana on Cuba and from there onwards to Carthagena (northern Columbia), where they explored the Río Magdalena, Columbia's largest river. Riding a mule, the explorers reached Bogotá, 2,460 m (8,070 feet) above sea level, where they were given a warm welcome by José C. Mutis, a celebrated Spanish botanist and cleric. A week later, in January 1802, they arrived in Quito, the capital of Ecuador. They then climbed the Chimborazo (6297 m), an extinct volcano in the Andes, although they did not reach its peak. In Ciudad de los Reyes (Lima) they rested for a while, and on their subsequent trek through Mexico they visited the ruins of the ancient Aztec Empire and investigated its history. Via Havana and New York they returned to Bordeaux in 1804.

Humboldt lecturing to the Academy

Alexander von Humboldt in his library, 1856. Color lithography after a watercolour painting by Hildebrandt

Over the next twenty years, Humboldt, who had now acquired world fame, devoted his time to scientific travel reports; these were published in 36 volumes in 1834. In 1827 and 1928 Humboldt gave lectures on physical cosmography at Berlin University, which initiated a new heyday of natural sciences in Germany.

On the recommendation of the czar, he traveled to Russia in 1829 and undertook an extensive expedition to Siberia with the natural

scientist Ehrenberg, the chemist G. Rose and the engineer Menchenine. From Petersburg via Moscow, Nishni-Novgorod, Kasan, through the land of the Kirgizes and across the Ural Mountains, they reached Tobolsk, went round the Altai Mountains and proceeded to Dsungaria. Crossing the Russian Turkestan, the explorers returned via Astrakhan on the Caspian Sea through the Don region to St. Petersburg.

From 1845 to 1862 Humboldt worked on his famous "Kosmos" (five volumes), a synthesis of his complete scientific findings.

The Spanish and Portuguese explorers had been sent out to South America to conquer large Indian empires. Humboldt had traveled to the South American subcontinent in order to open it up for science. He is one of the founders of climatology, oceanography, meteorology and glaciology.

Further reading
A. v. Humboldt, Versuch über den politischen Zustand des Königreiches Neu-Spanien, enthaltend Untersuchungen über die Geographie des Landes, über seinen Flächeninhalt. 4 volumes, Tübingen 1809-1813
–, Voyages aux régions équinoxiares du Nouveau Continent, fait en 1799-1804. 30 volumes, Paris 1814-1826
–, L'examen critique de l'histoire de la Géographie du Nouveau Continent. 5 volumes, Paris 1836-1839
–, Reise nach dem Ural, dem Altai und dem Kaspischen Meer auf Befehl seiner Majestät des Kaisers von Rußland im Jahr 1829, ausgeführt von A. v. Humboldt, G. Ehrenberg und G. Rose. 2 volumes, Berlin 1837-1842
–, Reisen in Amerika und Asien. 4 volumes, Berlin 1842
–, Asie centrale. Recherches sur les chaînes de Montagnes et la climatologie comparée. 3 volumes, Paris 1843
–, Lettres américaines (1798-1807). Paris 1906
H. Beck, Alexander von Humboldts Reise durchs Baltikum nach Rußland und Sibirien 1829. 2nd, revised edition Stuttgart 1984
K. Schleucher, Alexander von Humboldt. Der Mensch. Der Forscher. Der Schriftsteller. Darmstadt 1984
H. Beck, Alexander von Humboldts Amerikanische Reise. Stuttgart 1985
A. v. Humboldt, Ansichten der Natur. 2nd ed. Frankfurt/M. 1987
A. Gebauer, Alexander von Humboldt. Forschungsreisender Geograph Naturforscher. Ein großer Sohn Berlins. Berlin 1987

This suspension bridge over the Chambo River in Peru near Penipé in Peru looks very fragile. The painter P. A. Marchais created this travel document after a sketch by Humboldt. This method was usual practice at that time.

W. Rübe, Alexander von Humboldt. Anatomie eines Ruhms. Munich/Berlin 1988
A. v. Humboldt, Aus meinem Leben. Autobiographische Bekenntnisse. 2nd edition Munich 1989
–, Reise in die Äquinoktial-Gegenden des Neuen Kontinents, ed. O. Ette. 2 volumes Frankfurt/M. 1990
Alexander von Humboldt. Weltbild und Wirkung auf die Wissenschaften, ed. U. Lindgren. Cologne 1990
K. R. Biermann, Alexander von Humboldt. 4th edition Leipzig 1990

A. Meyer-Abich, Alexander von Humboldt. Reinbek, without year of publication
A. v. Humboldt, Die Wiederentdeckung der neuen Welt. Munich 1992
Alexander von Humboldt und das neue Geschichtsbild von Lateinamerika, ed. M. Zeuske/B. Schröter. Leipzig 1992
Alexander von Humboldt – Die andere Entdeckung Amerikas, ed. W. Greive, Loccum 1993
A. v. Humboldt, Briefe aus Amerika 1799-1804, ed. U. Moheit, Berlin 1993
–, Die Reise nach Südamerika. 3rd edition Göttingen 1993

Julius Schrader painted Humboldt as an old man in oil in 1859.

JÄHN, SIGMUND

German cosmonaut, born 1937 in Rautenkranz.

Sigmund Jähn grew up and lived in the former German Democratic Republic. In 1955 he joined the army, where he served as a pilot and commander. In 1976 he was chosen by the former USSR to undertake training as a cosmonaut and on 26 August, 1978 he flew into space together with cosmonaut Valery Bykovsky as the first German on board the space capsule "Soyuz 31". In the course of this flight, which lasted eight days, they visited the cosmonauts Vladimir Kovalenok and Alexandr Ivanchenkov on board "Salyut 6". After this mission he returned to the GDR and was promoted to the rank of Major-General.

Since the German unification, Jähn has been working as a consultant at the German Research and Experimental Institute for Aeronautics and Astronautics in Cologne-Porz.

Sources and further reading
S. Jähn, Experiencing space, without place of publication 1983

JERMAK, TIMOFEYEVICH (YERMAK, TIMOFEYEVICH)

Cossack leader (Atamen), born between 1520 and 1530, died 1584 on the Irtysh (Siberia).

Few details of Jermak's life have been definitively established to date. For some time, he fought against the Livland knights and Swedes on the Livland border, where he was commander of a Cossack battalion. Once peace was restored, this champion of freedom moved to the Volga, where he lived both as a fisherman and river pirate. When the troops of the czar started to clear this region of insubordinate subjects, Jermak moved, accompanied by Koltsos, another leader of the Cossacks, into the high north of the country where he entered the services of the Stroganovs, a family of Russian pioneers who commissioned him with conquering the regions around the Tobol and Irtysh Rivers. However, the main objective of this campaign was the control of the trade routes from the Ural Mountains to Mangaseia (land of the Samoyeds), which were in the hands of the Siberian Khan Kukum.

On the Tura River (a tributary of the Tobol) the Ostiak and Vogul tribes were forced to pay tribute. In 1582, Jermak reached the Tobol River with his troops, who were armed with guns and cannons. After Jermak's victory over Kukum, the latter's son Mahmetkul rounded up all available forces and inflicted a severe defeat on the Ataman. However, during a third confrontation, Mahmetkul's hordes were again defeated. Jermak and his troops stayed over winter near Isker, Kukum's camp, and gained a third victory over the Tartars. The path for systematic colonization of the region between Ob and Yenissei was open, but the Siberian rulers still refused to become dependent on Moscow. As Jermak was preparing to set out for the town of Bukhara (in Russian Turkestan) in order to initiate trade relationships with this powerful metropolis on behalf of the Stroganovs, he was attacked and killed by Kukum in his camp on the Upper Irtysh on 5 August, 1584.

Jermak initiated the systematic colonization of Siberia. It was not until a quarter of a centu-

The conqueror of Siberia, Timofeyevich Jermak. The oil painting is by an unknown Russian master of the first half of the 18th century.

Illustration on next double page: Siberia, where Timofeyevich Yermak was born, had always been regarded as a very inhospitable area. Contemporary illustrations such as this painting by Vasiliy Ivan Surikoch show this very vividly.

ry after his death that Siberia as far as the Yenissei was firmly under Moscow's control with the establishment of the towns of Surgut (1594), Tobolsk (1587), Tara (1594) and Tomsk (1604).

Sources and further reading
A. F. Golder, *Russian Expansion on the Pacific, 1641-1850.* Cleveland 1914
Y. Semionov, *La conquête de la Sibérie du IXe siècle au XIXe siècle.* Paris 1938

JOLLIET, LOUIS

Franco-Canadian explorer, born c. 1645 near Quebec, died 1700 near Quebec.

Jolliet studied at the Jesuit school in Quebec and entered the Jesuit order in 1662. Five years later he left the order and went to France, but returned to Canada the following year. In the year 1670, Jolliet undertook his first extended journey through western Canada. In 1672 Talon, the Governor of Nouvelle-France, the area settled by the French in eastern Canada, commissioned Joillet, the "coureur de bois" (woodsman), to discover the "Ocean of the South" and the mouth of the Mississippi, which was thought to be on the Pacific Ocean. (For a description of the course of this journey see Marquette, Jacques.)

After this historically significant expedition to the Mississippi, Jolliet proceeded to Quebec from Sault-Sainte-Marie. In 1676, he requested of the French minister Colbert permission to establish a French colony in Illinois. When the minister declined Jolliet's application, the explorer went to the lower St. Lawrence River. In 1679 he received the fief of Sept Iles Minqan, and in the middle of that year Jolliet undertook an expedition through eastern Canada, accompanied by eight Franco-Canadians. He traveled on the Sagenay River from Tadoussac, a whaling settlement, to Lake Saint-Jean. It is not certain whether he reached Lake Mistassini via the Ashwapmuchuan or the Washimeska River, nor whether he also explored the Marten River to its tributary, the Rupert River (approximately 25 km or 16 miles from lake Nemiskau) in the course of this journey. On 25 October, Jolliet was back in Quebec.

For the geographical findings that he made during this exploration he was granted Anticosti Island in the mouth of the St. Lawrence River as a fief. During his next expedition, Jolliet prepared a map of the St. Lawrence River up to its mouth and charted the west coast of Newfoundland.

During his last expedition in 1694 he circumnavigated Cape Saint-Charles (Belle-Ile Strait) and sailed north along the coast of Labrador up to East Zoar.

There is still some uncertainty surrounding the death of this famous woodsman. In mid-1700 he left Quebec, probably in the direction of his Anticosti estate, and presumably died somewhere on this journey.

By their courageous venture, Louis Jolliet and Jacques Marquette had solved the geographical enigma of the Mississippi. They initiated the great expedition of the French Mississippi explorer Cavelier de la Salle, who traveled down the river to its mouth.

Inhabitants of Sumatra from Willem Lodewijcksz' account of his travels of 1598

Sources and further reading
A. Hamy, Au Mississippi, La première ex-
ploration 1673. Le père Jacques Marquette de
Laon 1637-1675 et Louis Jolliet, d'après
M. E. Gagnon. Paris 1878
Fr. B. Steck, The Jolliet-Marquette-Expedition,
rev. ed. Quincy (Ill., USA) 1928
J. Delanglez, The life and voyages of Louis
Jolliet. Chicago 1948

JUNGHUHN, FRANZ WILHELM

German explorer of Southeast Asia, born 1812 in Mansfeld, died 1864.

Junghuhn only entered the field of research after a rather adventurous life. He studied medicine, botany and geology in Halle and Berlin. He reached the rank of company surgeon in the Prussian army. However, after a duel he was sentenced to a long prison term. But he fled after a short time and saved himself in the Foreign Legion, where he worked as a medical officer. He was eventually made health oficer in Batavia. In this way he gradually took up research activities that led him to the islands of Java and Sumatra.

A serious illness forced Junghuhn to remain in Holland between 1849 and 1855. However, he eventually returned to Indonesia, where he continued his research of the two islands.

Franz Wilhelm Junghuhn is regarded as one of the most interesting explorers of Java and Sumatra.

JUNKER, WILHELM

German-Russian Africa explorer, born 1840 in Moscow, died 1892 in St. Petersburg.

In 1874, Junker traveled through Tunisia and Egypt. Three years later, accompanied by Gessi and Russel, he undertook a scientific expedition into the region of the Blue Nile in order to complete the existing maps of this area. During this expedition he explored the system of the Blue Nile and its tributaries. In 1880, Junker explored the area of the White Nile and proceeded as far as Lake Albert. Between 1880 and 1885 this untiring explorer discovered the Nepoko, the headstream of the Aruwimi (right tributary of the Congo) and explored the headwaters of the Uëlle, which he however mistook for the headwaters of the Chari.

In 1886 Franz Junghuhn traveled from Lado (on the Upper Nile) via Unyorozum to Lake Victoria, visited Tabora, the center of the Arabian slave trade, and reached Bogamoyo north of Dar es Salaam.

Sources and further reading
W. Junker, Reisen in Afrika 1875 bis 1886.
3 volumes. Vienna 1889-1891
Petermanns Mitteilungen, Gotha 1876-1879

The jungle in the Congo.

KAEMPFER, ENGELBERT

German explorer, born 1651 in Lemgo, died 1716 in Lemgo.

Kaempfer studied medicine and natural sciences in Gdansk, Krakov and Königsberg before migrating to Sweden. From Uppsala, he traveled with a Swedish trade mission to Russia and Persia. Accompanied by a Dutch trade mission, he went to Batavia (Java) and then Japan (1690), where he undertook scientific exploratory work for two years. His image of Japan remained universally valid in Europe until well into the nineteenth century. He returned to Europe in 1694.

Kaempfer is regarded as the "Humboldt of the seventeenth century".

Further reading
E. Kaempfer, Amoenitatum exoticarum. Without place of publication 1712 (the only one of Kaempfer's works published during his lifetime)
Sir H. Sloane, The history of Japan. Without place of publication 1727
E. Kaempfer, Geschichte und Beschreibung von Japan. Lemgo 1777-1779
–, Geschichte und Beschreibung von Japan. 2 volumes. Reprint of the edition of 1777-1779. Mannheim 1964

–, *Am Hofe des persischen Großkönigs 1684-1685*, ed. W. Hinz. Stuttgart 1977
–, *Phoenix persicus. Die Geschichte der Dattelpalme. Marburg 1987*

The Far North: Explorations in the Arctic Regions. Edinburgh 1865
Arctic Exploration in search of Sir J. Franklin. London 1903

KANE, ELISHA KENT

American Arctic explorer, born 1820 in Philadelphia, died 1857 in Havana (Cuba).

Kane studied medicine and was employed as a ship's doctor. After his exploration of the Philippines, Dr. Kane devoted himself to the study of the Arctic. He planned to reach the North Pole on the open waterway between Ellesmere Land and western Greenland, the Smith Sound, the "Kane Basin" (named after him), the Kennedy and Robeson Canals. In 1850 this explorer took part in the Grinnell expedition which set out in search of J. Franklin, who had been missing since 1845.

In 1853 the generous support of Grinnell allowed Elisha Kane to put his plan into action. Accompanied by Dr. J. J. Hayes, another Arctic explorer, and a small crew he sailed through the Smith Sound, stayed over winter in a bay on the west coast of Greenland (Inglefield Land) and explored the "Kane Basin". In June 1854, a sailor sent out by Kane reached a latitude of 80° 35' N. The crew had to abandon Kane's ship, the "Advance", when it became enclosed by ice, but with the aid of the Etah Inuit they managed to reach Upernavik on the west coast of Greenland in three small lifeboats after an extremely difficult journey.

In 1857 Kane died on Cuba as a result of his taxing journey to Greenland.

Further reading
The US-Grinnell Expedition in search of Sir J. Franklin: a personal narrative by E. K. Kane. New York 1854
Arctic voyages and discovery. The exploring voyages of Dr. Kane. London 1860

KERGUÉLEN DE TRÉMAREC, YVES JOSEPH DE

French seafarer and discoverer, born 1734 in Quimper, died 1797 in Paris.

Already as a young man, Kerguélen sailed in the Nordic waters to Greenland.

In 1772 he prepared a major expedition on the "Ile de France" (Mauritius) to explore Antarctica. With two ships, the "Fortune" and the "Gros-Ventre", he penetrated into the South Sea and on 12 February discovered an island (one of the later so-called Kerguélen island group) which he circumnavigated.

After his return, King Louis XV instructed Kerguélen to colonize the island and gave him command over a flotilla once more.

In the year 1774, Kerguélen de Trémarec set out from France with the "Roland", a warship, the "Dauphine" and the "Oiseau" and sailed in a southwesterly direction. In addition to a number of fellow Frenchmen, the flotilla had several domestic animals, seeds and agricultural equipment on board, since this time the group of islands was to be colonized systematically. When Kerguélen went ashore on Mauritius, the governor of that island absolutely refused to believe the existence of this group of islands in the South Atlantic. Despite these unfavorable conditions, Kerguélen continued his journey, sighted the island group on 14 December, but could not land because of violent storms and returned to Brest via Madagascar. Nevertheless, the commanding officer of the "Oiseau" risked a landing in a sheltered haven which he subsequently named "Baie de l'Oiseau" (Bay of the Bird).

At the end of December, 1685 Kaempfer arrived with his caravan in Bandar Abbas on the Persian Gulf. After a period of rest because of the tropical heat, the journey was continued to India (ill. following double page).

Because of his failure, Kerguélen was tried by court martial in France, spent five years imprisoned in the fortress of Saumur (Loire) and wrote a report of his travels. James Cook confirmed Kerguélen's discovery in 1776. A group of islands in the south of the Indian Ocean bears the name of this French seafarer.

Further reading
Kerguélen de Trémarec, Relation de deux voyages dans les mers australes et les Indes faits en 1771, 1772, 1773 et 1774. Paris 1782
E. Marguet, Histoire générale de la navigation du XVe au XXe siècles. Paris 1931

KOZLOV, PETER KUSMICH

Russian explorer of Asia, geographer, topographer and natural scientist, born 1863 near Smolensk, died 1935 in Peterhof.

Peter Kozlov studied geography, topography and natural sciences. As an assistant of the "Second Przevalski Expedition" in 1883 he explored the Humboldt Chain, the southern Kuku-nor Mountains, the valleys of the Yellow and the Blue River, the Burkhan-Buddha Mountains, Lake Djarin and Lake Orin and reached Lake Lob-nor, where the expedition camped for fifty days. Via Khotan, Kozlov crossed the Takla Makan Desert with a small group and reached Lake Kara-karul (Tajikistan), where the expedition broke up. From 1888 to 1890 he undertook another journey to East Asia under the direction of General Pevtsov, and between 1893 and 1895 he partook in the expedition of Raborovski as a scientific advisor. During this venture he explored the Nan-chan Mountains (north of Lake Kuku-nor) and the Tien-chan mountains (Sinkiang) to the Amnyermachin massif, where Raborovski fell ill; Kozlov then took charge of the expedition.

In 1899 he led a scientific expedition for the first time, from Altayskaya (Kazakhstan) to the Altai Mountains where he studied the topography, reached Kharaussu, crossed the Gobi desert and reached Lake Tsaidamnor (in the southern Altai Mountains). After crossing the Burkhan-Buddha Mountains in June 1900 he reached the Yellow River where it flows into Lake Orin at a height of 4,900 m (16,100 feet) above sea level. He then explored the northern Mekong delta before returning to Russia.

The meteorological and ethnographic observations made by Kozlov's during this expedition, which lasted for almost three years, contributed to his reputation as a scientist.

On his fourth journey he proceeded from Kiachta (in the south of Transbaikalia) in the direction of Urga (today's Ulan Bator), crossed the Gobi Desert from north to south and reached Khara-khoto, the capital of the ancient kingdom of Si-Hia, where he found hundreds of Buddha statues, paintings and a valuable library with books and manuscripts written in the Si-hia or Tangutic language. Continuing on his journey through the Nanchan Mountains, he reached Sining (east of Lake Kuku-nor), visited the important Gumbum monastery, where he was received by the Dalai Lama, sailed across Lake Kuku-nor, visited the Labrang monastery and finally returned to Kiachta after a two-year absence.

Between 1923 and 1926 Kozlov undertook his last journey to northern Mongolia, where he discovered several graves of important Hun leaders in Noin-ula, about 100 km (60 miles) north of Urga.

Apart from Przevalski and Potanin, Kozlov was the most important Russian Asian explorer and archaeologist of the nineteenth and twentieth centuries.

Further reading
Rapport préliminaire sur un voyage de trois ans dans l'Asie centrale accompli par V. I. Raborovski et P. K. Kozlov. St. Petersburg 1897
Mongolie et Kam, travaux de l'expédition de la Société Impériale russe de géographie en 1899-1901 sous la direction de P. K. Kozlov. St. Petersburg 1905

KRAPF, JOHANN LUDWIG

German Protestant missionary and explorer of Africa, born 1810 in Derendingen, died 1881 in Korntal.

Krapf was trained as a missionary by the Protestant Mission Society at Basle. On behalf of the London mission, Krapf was sent from Egypt to Abyssinia in order to carry out his work as a missionary. He fled to Mombassa in eastern Africa, established the missionary station of New Rabai (Rabai Mpya) together with J. Rebmann, another missionary, and studied the dialects of central Africa.

Accompanied by J. Rebmann, he explored northern Kenya and today's Tanzania in 1847, and in 1848 the two explorers discovered the Kilimanjaro, the highest massif in Africa, and Mount Kenya, Africa's second-highest mountain. The following year, Krapf and Rebmann wandered through the area where the city of Nairobi is situated today and the region of the Kikuyu, a northeastern Bantu tribe in central Kenya. With the aid of missionary J. Erhardt, they established the existence of large lakes in the African interior.

In 1867, Krapf accompanied Lord Napier as an interpreter to Ethiopia.

Further reading
J. L. Krapf, Vocabulary of the Galla language.
London 1842
–, Vocabulary of Six East African languages.
Tübingen 1850

View of Kilimanjaro, the highest mountain in Africa. The German missionary Krapf discovered it in 1848. The mountain was not climbed until 1889, by Hans Meyer and L. Purtscheller.

The illustrations on the preceding double pages show stages of the journeys round the world made by Adam Johann von Krusenstern. Left: Krusenstern's ship off the island of St. George. Right: A Spanish settlement near St. Francisco. In his book Krusenstern also showed products made by the natives, for example handmade articles from Alaska (ill. right).

–, *Outline of the elements of the Kishuali language, with special reference to the Kinika dialect. Tübingen 1850*
–, *Reisen in Ostafrika, ausgeführt in den Jahren 1837 bis 1853. 2 volumes, Korntal and Stuttgart 1858*
–, *Reisen in Ostafrika ausgeführt in den Jahren 1837-1855, ed. W. Raupp. (reprint of the 1858 edition, Stuttgart). Münster 1994*

KRUSENSTERN, ADAM JOHANN VON

Russian seafarer, born 1770 in Hagudi (Estonia), died 1846 in Ass (Reval).

In 1803, on behalf of the imperial Russian admiralty, Krusenstern undertook a circumnavigation of the Earth, whose principal aim, however, was to establish extensive trade relations with Japan.

With two ships – the "Neva" and the "Nadiejeda" – he left Kronstadt, rounded Cape Hoorn (South America), visited and explored Nuku-Hiwa (Marquesas) and headed for the Japanese empire. When his diplomatic mission came to nothing, he explored the Kamchatka peninsula, the most remote Russian province whose "capital" St. Peter and Paul greatly disappointed him because of its poverty. In the north of Sakhalin Island he came across not Aïnus, the native inhabitants, but scruffy Tartars. After visiting Canton and Macao and having made inquiries about the Chinese secret societies, Krusenstern set off on his home journey. He sailed through the Sunda Strait, around the Cape of Good Hope and arrived back in Kronstadt after a three-year absence.

Krusenstern was the first Russian to sail around the world and to cross the equator with Russian ships.

Further reading
A. J. v. Krusenstern, Reise um die Welt in den Jahren 1803, 1804, 1805 und 1806. 3 volumes. St. Petersburg 1810, 1811 and 1814
–, Recueil de mémoires hydrographiques pour servir d'analyse et d'explication à l'Atlas de l'Océan Pacifique. St. Petersburg 1824

L

LA CONDAMINE, CHARLES MARIE DE

French mathematician and scientific explorer, born 1701 in Paris, died 1774 Paris.

La Condamine studied physics and mathematics. He was a member of the "Académie des Sciences", which in 1735 commissioned La Condamine and the scholars Godin and Bouguer to determine the shape of the Earth at the equator, the deviation of the magnetic needle from the astronomical meridian and the expansion of metals in South America.

In May 1735 he sailed to Carthagena (Columbia) and from there continued on to Panama and Ecuador. At Río Esmeraldas he was the first European to find rubber and he also discovered the noble metal platinum. He then carried out his most important measurements to the northeast of the Incan city of Quito and recognized that the Earth indeed was round (as did an expedition that had been sent to Lapland at the same time).

After completing his scientific experiments in March 1743, the scholar turned his attention to geographical and ethnographic studies. For his return journey La Condamine chose the hazardous route through the Amazon rainforest, which Orellana, Pizarro's comrade-at-arms, had taken before him at the start of the sixteenth century. From what is today known as Cuenca, the capital of the Province of Azuay (Ecuador), La Condamine and his companions sailed the Chincipe on a raft until they reached Marañon, then sailed down the Amazon to its mouth. Most of the river inhabitants treated the scientist in a friendly manner, so that La Condamine was generally able to make his valuable ethnographic observations without much difficulty. One of the tribes he examined deformed their children's skulls up to the age of six in such a way as to resemble plates, while another tribe, the Albans, made holes in their cheeks and ear lobes with parrot feathers. In spring 1745 La Condamine returned to Paris.

La Condamine's geographical and ethnographic travel reports have lost nothing of their validity to the present day.

Further reading
Ch. M. de La Condamine, Relation abrégée
d'un voyage fait dans l'intérieur de l'Amérique
méridional. Paris 1791

LAING, ALEXANDER GORDON

Scottish explorer of Africa, born 1793 in Edinburgh, died 1826 near Timbuktu.

Aged just 17 Laing joined the British Colonial Army where he reached the ranks of lieutenant and then major. In 1822 he traveled to Sierra Leone (western Africa), entered the service of the governor as general adjutant and was commissioned mainly with developing trade relations between the British and the local population. During this period, Laing undertook extended journeys to the Timannee, Kooranko and Soolima tribes from the west African coast. When he attempted to explore the sources of the Niger on the eastern slopes of the Loma Mountains, his plans were thwarted by the hostility of the natives.

After spending a period of time in England, Alexander Laing returned to Africa in the year 1825, this time to Tripoli. From there the major was able to reach the legendary city of Timbuktu via Gadames (oasis in Libya) and In-Salah (an oasis town in the center of the Algerian Sahara Desert), where he remained from 18 August to 22 September. Laing was murdered by Arabs near Arauan, north of Timbuktu, in the course of his return journey to Tripoli.

Laing can be particularly credited with exploring the hitherto unknown landscapes of Timannee, Kooranko and Soolima. His claim to have discovered the sources of the Niger was met with a great deal of doubt and mistrust by the geographers of his time. Laing was the first European to stay in Timbuktu.

Further reading
G. Laing, Travels in Timannee, Kooranko and Soolima, countries in Western Africa. London 1855

LANDER, JOHN

English explorer of Africa, born 1807, died 1839.

From 1830 to 1831 John Lander accompanied his brother Richard on an expedition on the Niger, where they established that the Niger flows into the Gulf of Benin. They subsequently discovered the Benue, the most important tributary of the Niger.

After this strenuous undertaking, the Lander brothers led several trading missions in the Niger region organized by the Liverpool businessman McGregor Laird.

John Lander died aged just 32 as the result of a wound that he had incurred while sailing on the Niger. The British government described him as one of the most daring pioneers of the British colonial empire.

Further reading
J. Lander, Journal of an expedition to explore the course and termination of the Niger, 3 volumes. London 1832

J. and R. Lander, Narratives of the adventures and sufferings of John and Richard Lander on their journey to discover the termination of the Niger, 2 volumes. London 1833

LANDER, RICHARD LEMON

English explorer of Africa, born 1804 in Truro (Cornwall), died 1834 on the island of Fernando Póo (Gulf of Guinea).

In the year 1825, Richard Lander accompanied H. Clapperton, a British explorer of Africa, on his expedition of discovery to the region of the Niger. Soon after the two explorers had reached Sokoto (in the northwest Niger region), however, Clapperton died; Lander subsequently returned to England, where he wrote reports of his travels.

A group of Africans from Rwanda in Duke Adolf Friedrich von Mecklenburg's account of his travels, 1907-1908. Illustrations of travel descriptions were usually made by painters afterwards at home, on the basis of preliminary sketches by the explorers. Their authenticity is thus somewhat questionable.

continue Clapperton's work. After an extremely strenuous trek the two brothers were able to determine that the Niger, the third-largest river in Africa, flows into the Gulf of Benin. During this expedition they also discovered the Benue, the largest tributary of the Niger. Two years later, Richard Lander took part in McGregor Laird's exploratory expedition on the Niger. However, Lander died as the result of an injury without having made any significant geographical discoveries.

Further reading
R. Lander, Records of Captain Clapperton's
Last Expedition to Africa with the subsequent
Adventures of the author, 3 volumes. London
1830
–, Journal of an expedition to explore the course
and termination of the Niger. London 1832
R. and J. Lander, Narratives of the adventures
and sufferings of John and Richard Lander
on their journeys to discover the termination of
the Niger, 2 volumes. London 1833
McGregor Laird/R. A. K. Oldfield, Narrative
of an expedition into interior Africa by the river
Niger in steam-vessels in 1832-1834. London
1837

LA PÉROUSE, JEAN FRANÇOIS GALAUP, COMTE DE

French seafarer and discoverer, born 1741 in La Gua (Albi), died 1788 near the Pacific island of Vanikoro.

When King Louis XVI commissioned La Pérouse with a major scientific circumnavigation of the world in early 1785, the latter had already demonstrated his marine skills during the French-English battles off the coast of North America. The purposes of this circumnavigation were to examine Spanish, British and Russian trade in the Pacific, to gather definitive information concerning the "Friendly Isles" (Tonga group), the Louisiade archipelago, the Awacha or Bering Islands, the Kurile Islands, the Riu-Riu Islands, Formosa, the Marianas, the Carolinas, the Moluccas, Ile de France (Mauritius) and Cape

Jungle scene in central Africa

In 1830 Richard Lander and his brother John were commissioned by the British government to

Bouvet. In addition, the Gulf of Carpentaria (northern Australia) and New Zealand were to be explored.

Besides La Pérouse, who commanded the "Astrolabe", and the commanding officer of the "Boussole", Langle, several other important scientists took part in this expedition, including the mathematician Monge (who had to leave the ship in Madeira as a result of sea sickness) and the astronomer Dagelet.

The ships set sail from Brest on 1 August, 1785. The journey took them via Madeira and around Cape Horn to Easter Island. After a brief visit to the Sandwich Islands, Jean La Pérouse took a northerly course and sighted Mount St. Elias (5,486 m or 18,000 feet) in Alaska. On continuing his journey he discovered "Necker Island" to the north of the Sandwich Islands. He then sailed across the Pacific and took on supplies in the Portuguese base of Macao (in early 1787). Once the ships were stocked with supplies they continued on to Formosa, the Riu-Riu Islands and Korea, where they discovered the La Pérouse Strait between the Russian island of Sakhalin and the Japanese island of Hokkaido. Sailing in a northerly direction, La Pérouse dropped anchor in the port of Petropavlovsk on the Kamchatka peninsula, from where B. de Lesseps, the son of a French consul, was sent to France with the first reports of the expedition. Because of a strong westerly wind, they were unable to reach the Kurile Islands. La Pérouse subsequently set course for the island of Manua (Samoa), where captain Langle and ten crew members were killed by natives while fetching water.

The next stage on La Pérouse's journey was Botany Bay on the east coast of Australia, from where he sent a letter back to France that he would be setting out for New Caledonia and Santa Cruz de Mendaña. La Pérouse's ships were lost not far from the island of Vanikoro (Santa Cruz group, Melanesia). The reason for this calamity has never been fully clarified. Forty years later the French seafarer Dumont d'Urville found some remains of the "Astrolabe", the captain's flagship.

Despite the disaster, the scientific results of this undertaking were remarkable. La Pérouse was able to correct many cartographic faults made by the Dutch in the Pacific, prove the island character of Sakhalin and send a comprehensive report about Easter Island back to France. The strait between the islands of Sakhalin and Hokkaido bears the name of this seafarer.

Further reading
La Pérouse, Voyage autour du monde, publié conformément au décret du 22 avril 1791, et rédigé par L. A. Milet-Mureau, 4 volumes. Paris 1797
Fragments du dernier voyage de La Pérouse. Quimper 1797
B. de Lesseps, Voyage de La Pérouse rédigé d'après ses manuscripts originaux. Paris 1831
E. Goep et G. L. Cordier, Les grands hommes de la France, Navigateurs. Paris 1878
Centenaire de La Pérouse. Bulletin de la Société de Géographie. Without place of publication 1888
A. Bellessort, La Pérouse. Paris 1926
G. Chinard, Le voyage de La Pérouse sur les côtes de l'Alaska et de la Californie. Baltimore 1937
J. F. de La Pérouse, Zu den Klippen von Vanikoro. Weltreise im Auftrag Ludwigs XVI. 1785-1788, published by Fischer. Stuttgart 1987

LA SALLE, RENÉ ROBERT CAVELIER, SIEUR DE

French discoverer and explorer, born 1643 in Rouen, died 1687 in Texas.

La Salle came from a family of wealthy cloth merchants. He joined the Jesuit order when he was 15 years old, and taught at several high schools before emigrating to Canada in 1666. In 1669 La Salle sold his La Chine property (near Quebec) and was given permission by Governor De Courcelles to carry out his plan of exploring the "sea of the south" (Gulf of Mexico) from the heart of North America. Two Sulpicians, Dollier de Casson and Breham de Gallimé, both topogra-

René Robert Cavelier La Salle

phers by trade, accompanied La Salle for part of the journey before returning north to carry out missionary work among the natives. La Salle explored the Ohio as far as the "St. Louis Falls" on his own. It has never been irrefutably proven whether he actually reached the Mississippi during his second exploratory expedition.

La Salle established friendly relations with the new governor Frontenac, and set up Fort Frontenac at the entrance to Lake Ontario, for which he was elevated to nobility.

In 1678 King Louis XIV commissioned La Salle to construct a series of fortifications in "New France" (the eastern part of Canada) to consolidate the French rule there.

After making detailed preparations for three years, on 4 January, 1682 La Salle set out on his Mississippi journey accompanied by 23 Frenchmen, 18 Mohegan and Chuan Indians, ten Indian squaws and three children. On 9 April, 1682 he reached the mouth of the great river, took possession of the delta region for France and named it "Louisiana" in honor of the French king.

On La Salle's return to France the king appointed him supreme commander of Louisiana and, in 1684, commissioned him to sail up the Mississippi with a hundred soldiers to force back the Spanish. The flotilla reached the Gulf of Mexico without incident but was unable to find the mouth of the river and landed around 650 km (400 miles) to the west of the delta. When La Salle attempted to reach the river by land he was murdered by one of his fellow countrymen in 1687 after entering the region occupied by the Ceni tribe.

La Salle was the first European to sail and explore the entire length of the Mississippi from the Great Lakes.

Further reading
H. Joutel, Journal historique du dernier voyage que Monsieur de la Salle fit dans le Golfe de Méxique. Paris 1713
La Salle and the discovery of the Great West. London 1899

L. Lemonnier, Cavalier de la Salle explorateur du Mississippi. Paris 1942
Ch. de la Roncière, Cavelier de la Salle explorateur de la Nouvelle France à Louisianne. Tours 1943
H.-O. Meissner, Louisiana für meinen König. Die Abenteuer des Robert de La Salle. Stuttgart 1966

LEICHHARDT, FRIEDRICH WILHELM LUDWIG

German explorer of Australia, born 1813 in Trebatsch, died 1848 in central Australia.

Leichhardt studied medicine in Berlin and London. In 1841 he traveled to Australia and settled in Port Jackson (Sydney). The following year, he set out on his own on a botanical expedition from Newcastle (on the east coast of Australia) to Moreton Bay (Brisbane), subsequently exploring the Brisbane River.

From 1843 to 1844 Leichhardt explored Wide Bay (east coast of Australia) and traveled through the hills around the Darling River. During a renewed expedition from Brisbane (1844-45) in a northerly direction he reached the Gulf of Carpentaria (Arnhem Land). In 1846 the London Royal Geographical Society awarded him a gold medal.

Two years later Leichhardt set out from the east coast of Australia, intending to reach the west coast of the continent via Lake Eyre. He went missing during this east-west crossing. In 1851 a search expedition found several of his personal belongings.

Leichhardt was one of the first scientific explorers of Australia, especially of Queensland (in the northeast). A river in Queensland, a town near Sydney and a mountain bear his name.

Further reading
F. W. L. Leichhardt, Journal of an Overland Expedition in Australia from Moreton Bay to Port Essington. London 1847
D. Bunce, Twenty-three Years' Wanderings including travels with Dr. Leichhardt in North and Tropical Australia. Geelong 1857

Dr. G. Neumayer, Dr. L. Leichhardt. Briefe an seine Angehörigen. Hg. v. Dr. G. Neumayer und O. Leichhardt als Naturforscher und Entdeckungsreisende. Hamburg 1881
F. von Müller, The Fate of Dr. Leichhardt. Melbourne 1885
J. F. Mann, Eight months with Dr. Leichhardt in the years 1846-1847. Sydney 1888
W. Beard, Journey Triumphant. The story of Leichhardt's famous expedition from the Darling Downs to Port Essington. Lewes 1955

LE MAIRE, JAKOB

Dutch seafarer, born 1585 in Antwerp, died 1616 at sea.

On 14 June, 1515 Jakob Le Maire left the Netherlands, sailing from Texel with two ships to southern South America in order to find the passage to the Pacific. The following year, together with W. C. Schouten he discovered "Le Maire Strait", which is named after him, between the southern tip of Terra del Fuego and Estados Island. Le Maire rounded the cape, which was named "Cape Horn" after Schouten's place of birth. Until the opening of the Panama Canal in the early twentieth century Cape Horn was a well traveled trading route as an alternative to the Magellan Strait, which was hazardous and subject to the monopoly of the East Indian Company.

Further reading
O. Le Maire, L'origine anversoise des célèbres navigateurs Isaac et Jacques Le Maire. Extrait des communications de l'Académie de Marine de Belgique. Anvers 1950
Bibliographie von Le Maire in "Biographie nationale" (pp. 760-769). Bibliothèque Nationale de Bruxelles. Brussels, without year of publication

LENZ, OSKAR

German explorer of Africa and geographer, born 1848 in Leipzig, died 1925 in Sooss near Baden (Austria).

Jakob Le Maire

Lenz was an assistant at the Geological Society in Vienna. At the age of 26 Oskar Lenz undertook his first expedition to Gabon (western Africa). After studying the geological substructure of Corisco Bay, he sailed up the Muni (Corisco Bay in the Gulf of Guinea), visited the waterfalls at N'Tambuni, made ethnographic observations of the Fans and explored the Munda and Gabon Rivers. In January 1875 Lenz sailed the Ogowe to the mouth of the Ngunié (a tributary of the Ogowe) and reached the Schebe, a tributary of the Ogowe in the northeast.

In 1879 the German African Society commissioned him to explore the Moroccan section of

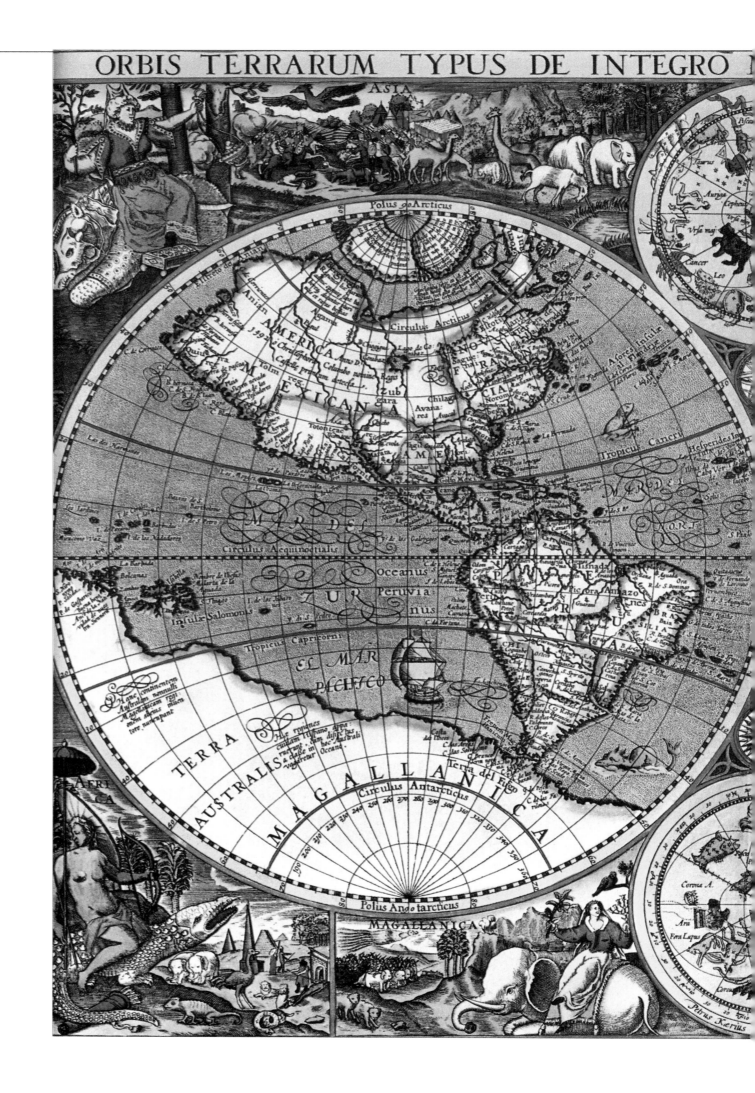

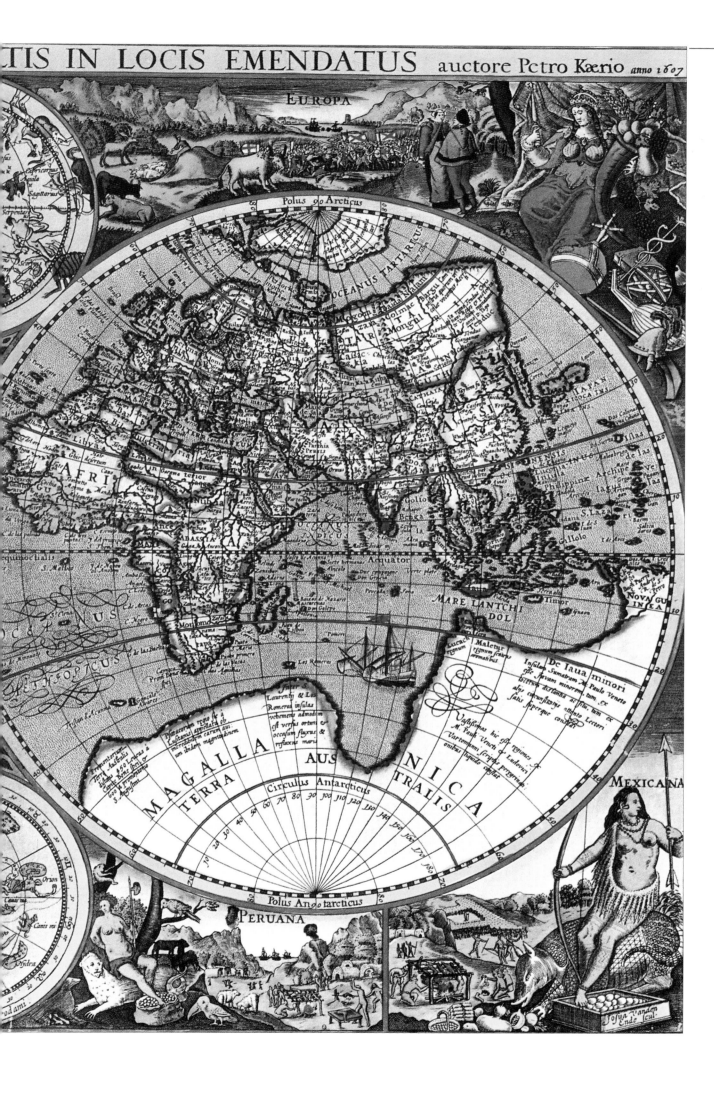

TIS IN LOCIS EMENDATUS auctore Petro Kærio anno 1607

EUROPA

This was the picture of the world in the 16th century, when Jakob Le Maire sailed to South America.

The Soviet cosmonaut Alexei Arkhipovich Leonov

exploring the Hoggar massif; he set out instead for Senegal, where he was given a cordial welcome by the French authorities. Lenz returned to Europe with many new geographical and ethnographic findings.

From 1885 to 1887 Lenz undertook a further expedition to equatorial Africa, where he explored the Stanley Falls, sailed up the Congo to Kasongo (in the eastern part of the Congo), reached Lake Tanganyika and Lake Nyassa, and carried on to the Zambezi.

Lenz's geological and geographical findings concerning the High Atlas and Gabon are of significant scientific value.

Further reading
Zeitschrift der Gesellschaft für Erdkunde zu Berlin. Without place of publication 1875
Petermanns Mitteilungen. Gotha 1875-1878
Deutsche Geographische Blätter. Without place of publication 1877 and 1878
Mitteilungen der k. u. k. geographischen Gesellschaft zu Wien. Without place of publication 1877 and 1878
O. Lenz, Skizzen aus Westafrika. Berlin 1878
Österreichische Monatsschrift für den Orient. Without place of publication 1879
O. Lenz, Timbuktu. Reise durch Marokko, die Sahara und den Sudan, 2 volumes. Leipzig 1882

LEONOV, ALEXEI ARKHIPOVICH

Soviet cosmonaut, born 1934 in Listuyanka (Siberia).

Leonov, the youngest of the first 20 Soviet cosmonauts who began their training in March 1960, was the first person to leave a space capsule in orbit.

With the launch of the spaceship "Voshkod 2" with cosmonauts Leonov and Pavel Belyayev on board, the USSR initiated a spectacular space experiment in March 1965. At the beginning of the second orbit of the Earth, Alexei Leonov left the inner space vessel through an air lock, wearing a newly designed space suit with its own life support system. He remained in the opened air lock

the Atlas Mountains and study the geological substructure. Setting out from Tangier, Oskar Lenz, accompanied by the Arab leader and interpreter Butabel and the Spaniard C. Benitez, crossed the High Atlas and was the first European to set eyes on the oasis of Tindouf (western Sahara) on 10 May, 1880. With the assistance of the local sultan, the German explorer was able to reach Timbuktu on 1 July without incident. Shortage of money prevented him from

for ten minutes and then floated in space for a further ten minutes, connected to the mother ship by nothing more than a safety line which contained cables for voice transmission and medical and telemetric data. By carrying out this experiment scientists were able for the first time to examine the cosmonaut's health, ability to work and coordination in space outside the capsule. Lenov's ECG rate and breathing were not unduly raised, nor did he lose his sense of orientation in relation to the space ship's axes. It was thus proven that humans could survive outside the space capsule, whether on expeditions to the moon or when carrying out repairs to the exterior of space stations. Leonov refuted the fear that humans could lose their sanity after spending time in space. In this respect, Leonov's experiment can be regarded as one of the great pioneering events in space travel.

The ship's return to Earth was eventful. The automatic landing system broke down due to a malfunction in the bearing regulation system. The ship was thus forced to circle the Earth once more, during which time a decision was made to initiate the landing manually for the first time. After 26 hours and 17 orbits of the Earth, the cabin containing the two cosmonauts landed in a snow-covered forest in the Ural Mountains. The search party was only able to find Leonov and Belyajyev after several hours in this desolate, isolated region.

In 1968 Leonov underwent training to circle the moon in a "Soyuz" capsule; however, this project had to be abandoned because of technical difficulties. He prepared himself until the end of 1969 for a possible moon landing, but this mission was also postponed. On 15 July, 1975 he and V. Kubassov set out on a new space mission on board the "Soyuz 19". This was followed a short time later by the American space capsule "Apollo" with astronauts T. Stafford, D. K. Slayton and V. Brand. The goal of these two flights was the first joint US-Soviet space mission. Using a newly developed connector system the two space capsules were joined on 17 July and remained together for almost 48 hours; an air lock chamber enabled the occupants to move freely between the two spacecraft. This mission was brought to a successful conclusion on 21 July (Soyuz 19) and 24 July (Apollo) when the two space ships landed safely.

Until his retirement in October 1991 Leonov occupied various positions in the Russian space program. Among other things, he was deputy head of the cosmonaut training scheme.

Further reading
A. Leonov, Wait for us, stars. Without place of publication 1967
–, Stellar roads. Without place of publication 1977
–, Life among the stars. Without place of publication 1981
–, Man and universe. Without place of publication 1984

LEWIS, MERIWETHER

North American explorer, born 1774 in Albermale (USA), died 1809 in Nashville.

From an early age Lewis was interested in zoology and botany and undertook extended hunting expeditions to the North American wilderness. He studied mathematics and Latin. Then, as a member of the military, he took part in the battles against the Indians in Ohio. In 1801 he was appointed private secretary to President Jefferson. Two years later his employer commissioned him to carry out a major "Far West Expedition". The main objective of this undertaking was to explore the Mississippi and the Missouri and their tributaries, as well as to expand domestic trade in North America. During the second half of 1803 the future participants in this expedition took part in a special training course.

On 14 May, 1804 Lewis and his companion W. Clark, another experienced North America explorer, set out on their expedition with 45 men. They sailed the Mississippi and reached

Missouri. By the end of October the expedition had reached the settlements of the Mandan Indians, in today's North Dakota, where they were given a friendly welcome. The explorers were fortunate to meet the French Canadian fur trader Toussaint Charbonneau, who offered his services as an interpreter, and his wife Sacajawea, an Indian squaw from the Shoshone tribe who had been kidnapped as a young girl; this couple lived in the Rocky Mountains. In the spring of 1805 the expedition set out once more, and after three weeks reached the mouth of Yellowstone River.

On 12 August, they reached the sources of the Missouri arm, named Jefferson Fork, and continued to the sources of Columbia River. While camping in this climatically pleasant area, Sacajawea saw her parents for the first time in many years. Thanks to the assistance of the Cochoni, who provided the expedition with horses and boats, Lewis and Clark continued on their journey in the direction of the Pacific. After crossing the Bitter Root Mountains, they came upon Clearwater River, where they entrusted their horses to the Nez Percés tribe.

Sailing down Snake River, they reached Columbia River and on 7 November they were very close to the Pacific. They set up Clatsop Fort at the mouth of Columbia River and spent the winter on the northern Pacific coast. This forced sojourn was especially hard and monotonous for the members of the expedition. Notwithstanding a shortage of food and the bitter cold, Lewis and Clark undertook a number of extended journeys along the coast, making geographical and ethnographical findings. On 23 March, 1806 the expedition set out on its return journey and on 23 September reached St. Louis.

Lewis and Clark had almost completely clarified the geographical conditions of the US west. In addition, the expedition brought back many new zoological and botanical findings from the region to the west of the Mississippi. Meriwether Lewis, who was nominated as governor of Louisiana in 1809, died that same year of unexplained causes. Clark occupied several high government positions and died in 1838 as a well-respected citizen of St. Louis.

Lewis and Clark are regarded as the last great explorers of the "Far West".

Further reading
O. D. Wheeler, The Trail of Lewis and Clark
1804-1806. A story of the great exploration
across the Continent in 1804-1806, 2 volumes.
New York and London 1806
P. Gass, Voyage des Capitaines Lewis et Clark
depuis l'embouchure du Missouri jusqu'à l'entrée
de la Columbia-River dans l'Océan Pacifique, fait
1804, 1805 et 1806 par ordre du Gouvernement
des Etats-Unis. Pittsbourgh 1807, Philadelphia
1812
C. Smyth, Builders of America (Vol. 9: Lewis and
Clark. Pioneers in America's westward movement). New York and London 1931

*With his daring at-
tempts Otto Lilienthal
showed that man can
imitate birds and soar
into the air.*

LILIENTHAL, OTTO

German engineer and aviation pioneer, born 1848 in Anklam, died 1933 in Berlin.

Otto Lilienthal carried out intensive studies on the flight of birds and soon recognized the aerodynamic advantages of a curved wing structure. From 1891 he flew his homemade gliders more than 2,000 times from high points, achieving distances of up to 3,000 meters (almost 2 miles). His endeavors provided the first secured knowledge of the dynamics of flying – much of the Wright brothers' work was in fact based on Lilienthal's findings.

Further reading
W. Schwipps, Otto Lilienthal und die Amerikaner. München 1985
–, Lilienthal. Die Biographie des ersten Fliegers. 2nd revised ed. Planegg 1986
–, Der Mensch fliegt. Lilienthals Flugversuche in historischen Aufnahmen. Bonn 1988
O. Lilienthal, Der Vogelflug als Grundlage der Fliegekunst. Ein Beitrag zur Systematik der Flugtechnik (1889 version). 3rd ed. Dortmund 1992

LINDBERGH, CHARLES AUGUSTUS

American pilot, born 1902 in Detroit, died 1974 on Maui (Hawaii).

On 21 May, 1927 Lindbergh was the first person to fly solo across the Atlantic, in the "Spirit of St. Louis". He set out from New York and reached Paris after 33 hours. With no radio and equipped only with a compass and a map he flew approximately 6,000 km (3,700 miles).

LIVINGSTONE, DAVID

Scottish doctor, missionary and explorer of Africa, born 1813 in Blantyre near Glasgow, died 1873 in Chitambo (Zambia).

As a young boy, Livingstone worked as a wire weaver in the Blantyre factory. With the exception of novels, he read everything that he could lay his hands on, but especially old travel reports. At evening classes he learnt Latin. As a spinner in the factory he had the financial means to study medicine and theology on reaching the age of 18. He completed his studies with a degree, but his plan to work as a doctor and missionary in the Far East was thwarted by the opium wars.

In 1841 he traveled to South Africa as a missionary; nine years later he began work as a researcher. Accompanied by Murray and Oswald, two Englishmen, he discovered Lake Ngami (Bechuanaland) on 1 August, 1849. The following year he reached the Zambezi near Sesheke. In 1852 he asked his family to join him in Africa. With the help of the Makololos, a South African tribe, Livingstone planned to explore the whole of southern Africa as far as Angola. The missionary had become an important explorer. As the first European, he traveled on the Zambezi to Kazembe in a pirogue, a fast water vessel made from a tree trunk. In order to escape from the slave traders of Portuguese Africa, Livingstone traveled via Cassange and Bihé to Luanda, a Portuguese port and the capital of Angola, where he arrived completely exhausted on 31 May, 1854.

As soon as he had recovered from his fever, he undertook a trek to Lake Dilolo, discovered the source of the Kasai, a left tributary of the Congo, and arrived in Linyanti, the capital of the Makololos. In the course of the major Zambezi expedition that followed he discovered the Victoria Falls, the falls of the middle Zambezi, in 1855. He set out on his home journey via Tete and Quelimane.

Livingstone received an enthusiastic welcome and was given the title of Consul General of the African East Coast. While in Britain, he left the London Missionary Society.

Between 1858 and 1864 he undertook his second major expedition to central Africa. In the course of a further Zambezi expedition he explored the Shire River, penetrated as far as the

Charles Lindbergh with his wife Anne Morrow Lindberg before a joint flight from New York via Alaska to Tokyo. Lindbergh became world-famous through his spectacular flight across the Atlantic Ocean from New York to Paris over a distance of approximately 6,000 km (3,700 miles) in 33 hours.

The above drawing was made by Henry Morton Stanley: Livingstone sitting and reading in a hut.
The engraving on the right shows Livingstone as the frontispiece of the first edition of Stanley's book "How I Found Livingstone".

A picture which went around the world: Stanley greets Livingstone, whom he has just traced.

Livingstone and Stanley explore togther. At the mouth of the Ruzizi they collect animals from the water with nets.

Livingstone has himself paddled along the Kassai in a canoe by natives.

Livingstone died in this little hut in the village of Chichambo, having contracted dysentery.

Murchison Falls, discovered Lake Chirous and Lake Nyassa in 1859. In order to be better equipped to combat the slave trade on Lake Nyassa – with 20,000 slaves transported on this lake every year and sold to Kilwa – he had a boat sent from England that could be dismantled. A tragic event in which the English bishop Mackenzie died during a confrontation with the black population brought discredit upon the explorer, and the London government refused to provide any further financial aid. Livingstone gave up and returned to Britain.

In 1866 he undertook a scientific expedition to central Africa on behalf of the English government. He traveled upstream on the Rovuma River, went around Lake Nyassa and proceeded in the direction of the southern tip of Lake Tanganyika. In November 1867 he discovered Lake Meru and in April 1868 Lake Bangweolo.

At the same time, two Englishmen, Speke and Grant, were exploring Lake Victoria-Nyanza. The source of the Nile had already been discovered, but there was still uncertainty about the maze of lakes and tributaries in the region of the source of the Nile. From that time onwards David Livingstone's aim was to solve this geographical enigma. In 1871 the missionary and explorer was believed missing.

H. M. Stanley, a journalist and adventurer, traveled to central Africa with a large entourage in search of Livingstone. On 28 October, the historical meeting between these two Africa explorers took place in Udjidji on the northeast bank of Lake Tanganyika.

Despite being ill with fever, Livingstone set out in 1873 to thoroughly explore the Zambezi and to sail on Lake Bangweolo. In the village of Chitambo on Lake Bangweolo, death put an end to his plans. His body was taken to Zanzibar and transported to London, where he was buried in Westminster Abbey.

Livingstone spent almost a quarter of a century in deepest Africa. He not only discovered Lakes Ngami, Nyassa, Meru, Shirwa and Bang-

weolo but also explored the mighty Zambezi and Lualaba Rivers.

As a philanthropist and true friend of the black population, he confronted the mighty slave traders without fear. Livingstone was convinced that only the occupation of the whole of central Africa by the English would be able to put an end to slavery. This theory of course met with the wholehearted approval of the English government.

Livingstone's travel reports were translated into practically all major languages. A town in Zambia, 32 waterfalls on the Lower Congo (Livingstone Falls) and a mountain range (Livingstone Mountains) in Tanzania are named after this great explorer.

Livingstone crosses the Makata River with his native bearers.

Further reading
D. Livingstone, Missionary travels and researches in South Africa, including a sketch of sixteen years' residence in the interior of Africa and a journey from the Cape of Good Hope to Loanda on the West Coast. London 1857
–, Narrative of an expedition to the Zambezi. London 1865

The last journals of David Livingstone in Central Africa from 1865 to his death, 2 volumes. London 1874
H. v. Barth, David Livingstone. Without place of publication 1882
The life and travels of D. Livingstone with a biographical note by G. S. Maxwell. London 1927
W. C. W. Kamp, Livingstone in donker Afrika. Pretoria 1936
H. Beck, Große Reisende. Without place of publication 1971
H. Wotte, David Livingstone. Das Leben eines Africa explorers, 4th ed. Leipzig 1988
P. Marc, Mit Livingstone durch Afrika. Zurich 1993

LOVELL, JAMES ARTHUR, JR.

US astronaut, born 1928 in Cleveland (Ohio).

James Lovell, a former navy pilot, was the first astronaut to travel into space four times. As the pilot of "Gemini 7" he spent two weeks in space in December 1965, which was a record at the time. In November 1966 he was commander of "Gemini 12", the last mission of this kind. As commander of the moon landing unit he took part in the first orbit of the moon in December 1968 on board "Apollo 8". In April 1970 he was a crew member on board the "Apollo 13" lunar mission. Shortly after take-off an oxygen tank exploded in the service unit, so that most of the spaceship's systems were put out of action. Nevertheless, the astronauts were able to return to Earth safely. James Lovell spent a total of 30 days in space.

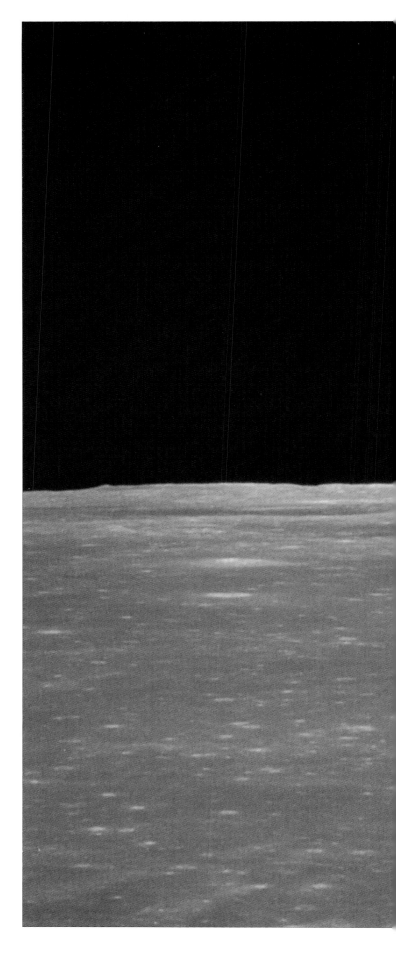

A fantastic perspective: This is how the astronauts saw the earth from the moon.

MACKENZIE, SIR ALEXANDER

Scottish explorer and furrier, born 1755 in Inverness (1764 in Stornoway?), died 1820 in Mulnain.

As a furrier working on behalf of an English trading company, Alexander Mackenzie spent a number of years in the Canadian forests. His extensive forays awakened in him the calling to be an explorer.

In June 1789 he undertook his first major expedition into the far north from the trading post and fort Chipewyan on Lake Athabaska, accompanied by four male and two female Franco-Canadians. The small group reached the Great Slave Lake via the Slave River, and after an exhausting trek Mackenzie reached the Beaufort Sea (Arctic Sea), sailing on the river which today bears his name. He was disappointed to find that he had arrived at the Arctic Sea. On 12 September, 1789, Mackenzie arrived back in Chipewyan, having covered and charted approximately 4,000 km (2,500 miles) of the Canadian wilderness.

His second expedition, of October 1792, took him to the Pacific Ocean. After intensive preparations and using the most modern equipment available, he left from Chipewyan, accompanied by six "coureurs de bois" (woodsmen), his deputy Mackay and two Indians, conquered the Rocky Mountains, explored the Fraser and Bella Coola Rivers and reached the Pacific Ocean on 22 July, 1793, not far from Prince of Wales Island, where he left a small commemorative plaque with the inscription "A. Mackenzie, arrived from Canada via the overland route. 22 July, 1793."

Alexander Mackenzie was the first European to travel overland across the continent, charted hundreds of square kilometers of Canadian forest and exploited new and profitable fur grounds. In 1802 he was made a peer.

Further reading
Mackenzie's Voyage to the Pacific Ocean in 1793. Historical Introduction and footnotes by Milo Milton Quaite. Chicago 1931
Voyages d'Alexandre Mackenzie dans l'intérieur de l'Amérique septentrionale faits en 1789, 1792 et 1793. Paris, without year of publication
H.-O. Meissner, Immer noch 10.000 Meilen zum Pazifik. Die Abenteuer des Alexander Mackenzie. Stuttgart 1966

MAGELLAN, FERNANDO (FERNÃO DE MAGALHÃES)

Portuguese seafarer and discoverer, first circumnavigator of the world, born around 1480 near Sabrosa, died 1521 on Mactán (Philippines).

In 1505, Magellan entered the services of the Portuguese navy. He took part in the conquest of Goa on the Malabar Coast. He was instructed by Albuquerque to set out in search of the "Islas Especieirias" (Spice Islands) and sailed on the Pacific Ocean, covering a distance of almost 1,000 km (600 miles), discovered various islands. He fell out with Albuquerque, left the India Army and returned to Portugal.

Magellan was wounded while storming the Moorish citadel of Azamur. After a dispute with King Manuel I in 1517 he went as a "transfuga" (refugee) to Seville, where he publicly revoked his Portuguese citizenship, took on Spanish nationality and married the daughter of Diego Barbosa, a rich Portuguese. He began relations with "Domus Indica" and befriended the Dutch ship owner C. de Haro.

In 1518, Fernando Magellan put forward a plan to the Spanish king Charles I (later the German emperor Charles V) to sail around South America and to claim the Pacific Ocean with its many island bases for Spain. The monarch agreed under the condition that Magellan discover at least six islands rich in raw materials. As a reward he could expect the title of governor, the right to carry weapons in public, a twentieth of the profits of the endeavor, a fifth of the income of two island and a fifth of the sale price of the shipload (Treaty of Valladolid, 22 March, 1518). When the enterprise was made public, not only the Portuguese envoy to the Spanish court protested, but also many influential Spanish had reservations about the decision to commission a "foreigner" with such an important expedition.

The five ships that were provided to Magellan by Charles I had to be thoroughly overhauled beforehand. On 20 September, 1519, the flotilla consisting of the "Trinidad" (Magellan's flagship), the "San Antonio" (under the command of J. de Cartagena), the "Concepción" (commanded by Quesada), the "Victoria" (commanded by L. de Mendoza) and the "Santiago" (steered by J. Serrano) put to sea at San Lúcar. The Italian nobleman and historian Antonio Pigafetta was on board, and posterity can thank him for a highly picturesque account of this first circumnavigation of the Earth.

By the end of November the squadron had reached the height of Pernambuco (eastern Brazil), on 13 December the bay of Rio de Janeiro, on 24 February, 1520 the Gulf of St. Matthew and on 31 March the Bay of St. Julian, where Magellan ordered that food rations be drastically reduced, a measure that led to open rebellion.

There and then Magellan disposed of the two ringleaders Mendoza and Quesada. J. d. Cartagena, the third person involved, was marooned on the inhospitable coast together with a French crew member.

When in the second half of October the "Concepción" and the "San Antonio", which had sailed in advance to find out what lay ahead, discovered a seemingly endless bay, Magellan on hearing this news began with his daredevil endeavor. Within 27 days he had conquered the "paseo" and discovered the connection between the Atlantic and the Pacific Ocean. This was named "Magellan Strait" and the land to the south of it "Tierra del Fuego".

The distance of approximately 5,000 km (3,000 miles) that now followed through "El Pacífico" (the peaceful ocean) from the southern tip of the Americas to the Philippines was to prove a veritable hell for the Spanish. Sailing past the luscious Phoenix, Gilbert and Marshall

Fernando Magellan was the first man to circumnavigate the earth.

Theodor Bry made
this copper engraving,
which is supposed to
portray the Strait of
Magellan, the passage
that Magellan discov-
ered. Magellan died in
a fight with natives on
the Island of Macatán,
which he tried to
Christianize by force.

Magellan made the first circumnavigation of the world in this ship.

Islands, Magellan only headed for two islands, "St. Paul Island" (Poumotou) and "Shark Island" (Manihiki). After a laborious journey he dropped anchor at the "Ladrones Islands" (Isles of Thieves). On 18 March, 1521, the "St. Lazarus Islands" (Philippines) came into view. After a brief sojourn on the islands of Malhon and Limassova, Magellan landed on Cebu. He started an extensive campaign of Christianization, during which idols were destroyed and mass baptisms performed. Even the king and his entourage had themselves baptized. When the small neighboring island Mactán resisted colonization, Magellan called for a punitive campaign. On 27 April, Fernando Magellan was killed in battle against the Mactán warriors.

Under the command of Del Canos (also known as Delcano or Elcano) the two remaining ships, the "Victoria" and the "Trinidad", weighed anchor. When the "Trinidad" set out to return to Spain in an easterly direction via the Magellan

Strait, she was captured by the Portuguese not far from the Moluccan island of Ternate. On the island of Tidor, Del Cano was able to buy a shipment of pepper; this covered the full costs of the world circumnavigation despite the loss of four ships.

On 6 September, 1522, the "Victoria" arrived back in Spain as the only one of five caravels.

Magellan's world circumnavigation had demonstrated the spherical nature of the Earth. The Pacific Ocean was no longer a "mare incognitum". For some Portuguese, especially for the king, the journey of the rejected seafarer was a national humiliation. Magellan had disproved the claim of the Portuguese that the waters of the Moluccas were too shallow and therefore dangerous for sea journeys. On the other hand, it was largely due to Magellan that the contentious problem of the affiliation of the Spice Islands had been resolved in favor of Portugal (Treaty of Saragossa). Del Cano enjoyed the material advantage of the first world circumnavigation. He was given the coat of arms with the proud inscription "Primus circum dedisti me" by Charles I.

Further reading:
Magellan. Aus dem Logbuch einer Weltumseglung. Essen 1991
R. Humble, Die Reise des Magellan. Nürnberg 1991
St. Zweig, Magellan. Der Mann und seine Tat. 12th ed. Frankfurt/M. 1994

MAGYAR, AMERIGO LADISLAUS

Hungarian explorer of Africa, born 1817, died 1864.

On hearing of the first important discoveries in central Africa, Amerigo Magyar gave up an officer's career in the Argentinean navy and went to Benguela, Angola, in 1847. There he married the daughter of an African prince from Bihé in the mountainous region of central Western Angola and undertook extensive expeditions into central Africa, helped by the slaves of his wife. In 1848 he traveled on the Congo to the cataracts of Faro-Songa and in 1849 roamed through the highlands of Bihé, which he also explored thoroughly. From 1851 to 1854 he visited the Lower Congo, the Kasai and the Upper Zambezi. He subsequently carried out some research into the Lowale tribe in Angola. Between 1860 and 1864 the untiring Hungarian traveled along the coast from Benguela to Moçamedes. Magyar died at the age of 47 after a short term of service in the Portuguese administration in Benguela.

Magyar's expeditions complemented Livingstone's scientific explorations. Since he undertook his travels without the help of measuring instruments, however, many of his geographical entries were not entirely accurate.

Further reading
J. Hunfalvy, Magyar Lazlo Del-afrikai levelei es naplokivonatai. Pest 1857

L. Magyar, Del-afrikai utazasai. Without place or year of publication
1849-1856 evekben. I. Pest 1859
Mitteilungen der k. u. k. geographischen Gesellschaft. Without place of publication 1860
Petermanns Mitteilungen. Gotha 1857
(Colley's comments on Magyar's travels)

MALFANTE, ANTONIO

Genoese explorer of Africa, born in the fifteenth century; year of death unknown. His nationality is disputed.

Antonio Malfante was the first European to travel through the Sahara Desert, on commission from the Genoese Centurione Bank in 1447. The aim of this journey was the exploration of gold deposits, since the usage of gold had been steadily increasing in Genoa; the major objective in particular was to pre-empt the Portuguese, who at that time had been making quite some progress in exploring the west coast of Africa and the outskirts of the Sahara Desert. We only know of Malfante's journey through a letter which was discovered in Paris around 1918 by the French historian Charles de la Roncière.

Malfante probably was a merchant, since he wrote in his letter that "merchants traveled in complete safety here" (in the Sahara desert). His document is a picturesque geographical and ethnographic description and should be treated with caution in regard to its scientific content. Be that as it may, Malfante was the first European to give an account of the sleeping sickness and to press on as far as Tamentit (on the River Niger), i.e. Tuat, via Oran or Constantine (trade routes led from these two commercial centers into the center of the Sahara). There, Malfante discovered that the gold came from Sudan and was exchanged for salt in Tuat. During his stay, he was taken care of by chief Sidi-Yahia ben Sadir. Malfante did not proceed any further than the Tuat oasis, since he thought that the River Niger was the upper course of the Nile. Malfante

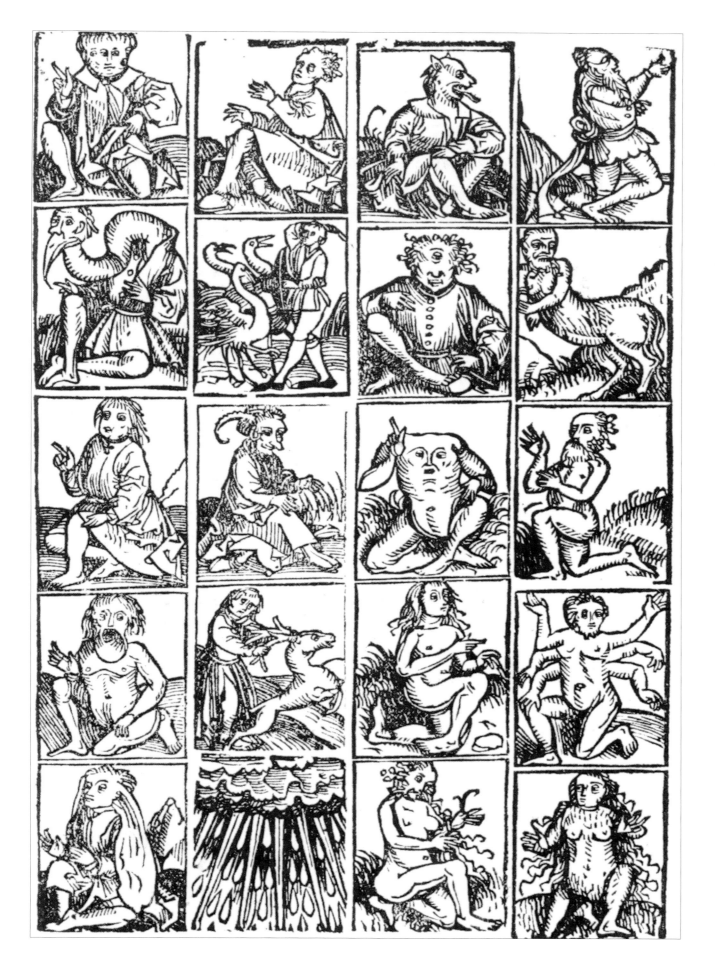

People have always been keenly interested in knowing what the living creatures in other lands looked like. The earliest accounts already contained reports of fabulous creatures and monsters. The imagination was given free rein. It was not until the 19th century that one began to portray exotic worlds objectively and scientifically, and to banish myths of shadow feet, breast faces and one-eyed creatures.

was never troubled by Muslims, who allegedly had hostile feelings towards Christians.

Antonio Malfante was the first explorer to bring specific detailed information regarding the gold and salt trade from central Africa to Europe.

Further reading
Mungo Park, Travels in the Interior of Africa. London 1799
Pompilio Schiarini, Antonio Malfante, mercante genovese della prima metà del Secolo XV e Viaggiatore nell'interno del Continente africano, in: Bollettino della R. Società Geografica Italiana. Without place of publication 1921, pp. 441ff.
Letter of the Genuese Antonio Malfante to the Genuese Giovanni Marino, ed. Charles de la Roncière in: La découverte de l'Afrique au moyen-âge. Le Caire 1929, pp, 145ff.

MANAROV, MUSA KHIRAMANOVICH

Soviet cosmonaut, born 1951 in Baku (Azerbaijan).

Musa Manarov is the world's most experienced space traveler. During his two sojourns on board the space station "Mir" he spent a total of 541 days in space.

In December 1987, the space capsule "Soyuz TM-4" – in which Manarov was accompanied by the cosmonaut Vladimir Titov – docked with the space station "Mir".

Prior to its planned re-entry into the atmosphere and disintegration in March 2001, "Mir" circled the Earth at a height of approximately 350 km (220 miles). It consisted of three cylindrical modules two to four meters (6 to 13 feet) in diameter, had an overall length of 13.5 meters (44 feet) and weighed 21 tons. Its volume of approximately 100 cubic meters (3,500 cubic feet) offered room for a much improved interior with individual cabins and a shower. "Mir" constituted the principal unit of a large orbiting station. Six connection modules were available, for the docking of both manned Soyuz transporters and unmanned maintenance craft.

During their record sojourn in space of 366 days and 19 hours – the first stay that lasted longer than a year – Manarov and Titov undertook scientific studies, experiments and three space walks, during two of which they repaired an X-ray laboratory which was also docked to the space station.

In the course of their space travels, Manarov and Titov were visited by two international cosmonaut crews. During the last third of their mission a doctor found them in good physical condition, although they had a serious argument before he left. The two cosmonauts did not speak to each other for three days.

On 21 December, 1988 they returned to earth and completed their mission successfully. Manarov and Titov were able to walk over fairly long distances unaided only two days after their return; their movements were coordinated and once again well adapted to the conditions of gravity – proof of the fact that humans can better cope with such conditions than had been previously assumed.

MARCHAND, ETIENNE

French seafarer and explorer, born 1755 on the island of Grenada, died 1793 on the "Ile de France" (Mauritius).

In 1790 Marchand was commissioned by the Marseille trading company to sail to the north coast of North America to handle lucrative fur transactions. As commander of a 300 ton sailing ship, Marchand took the opportunity to circumnavigate the world. He crossed the Atlantic, sailed round Cape Horn, headed for the Marquesas Islands, discovered the islands of Fatu-Hiwa, Motane and Hiwoa, which he collectively named "Islands of the Revolution" (today Marquesas), visited the island of Madre de Dios (Vaitahu), headed for Alaska and explored Queen Charlotte Island. During a foray into this island he ex-

For many years the space station "Mir" operated as a scientific laboratory in space. In March 2001 it was abandoned and a controlled crash induced, in order to prevent damage on the Earth.

changed worn out clothing and old household effects for expensive furs, of whose value the local hunters were not aware. South of Queen Charlotte Island, Marchand explored Nootka Island and then sailed on to the Sandwich Islands, where he landed on Hawaii. In Macao, a Portuguese base in China and his next destination, Marchand sold his valuable freight of furs and returned to Marseille in 1792 via Bourbon Island (La Réunion) and St. Helena. A few months after his return he was drawn again to Bourbon Island, where he died in 1793.

Marchand's travel report, recounted by the second officer of the "Solide", Captain Marchal, and written down by Roblet, the ship's surgeon, is almost as valuable as La Pérouse's scientific report in terms of content.

Further reading
Voyage autour du monde pendant les années 1790, 1791, 1792 et 1793 par Etienne Marchand, précédé d'une introduction historique, auquel on a joint des recherches sur les terres australes de Drake et un examen critique du voyage de Roggeveen, par P. Claret Fleuriau. Vols. VI and VIII. Paris, without year of publication

MARQUETTE, JACQUES

Franco-Canadian explorer and missionary, born 1637 in Laon (France), died 1675 on Lake Michigan.

After his studies at the Jesuit School in Nancy (Lorraine), Marquette joined the Jesuit Order and settled in Quebec in 1666. In the town of Trois-Rivières he learned the language of the Algonquians. He spent some time in Sault-Sainte-Marie, at the missionary outpost of La Pointe du Saint-Esprit and in Chequamegon Bay on the westernmost tip of the Upper Lake to preach the Gospel to the Canadian Indians. Repeated attacks by the Huron and Ottawa forced Marquette to abandon his plans to convert these people.

In 1671 he went to Michilimackinac, Michigan, where he and Jolliet, a Franco-Canadian "coureur de bois" (woodsman), were instructed to explore the Mississippi. The aim of this large-scale expedition was to reach the "Southern Ocean", since it was still thought that the Mississippi flowed not into the Gulf of Mexico, but into the Gulf of California.

Accompanied by five companions, Marquette and Jolliet left Michilimackinac in 1673 in two boats. They followed the west Coast of "Green Bay" (Lake Michigan) to the missionary outpost of Saint-François-Xavier and traveled up the Fox River to the village of Mascoutens. On 15 July they reached the Wisconsin River, a tributary of the Mississippi, near Prairie du Chien. This was the point of departure for the historical journey on the immense river, which was named "Mississippi" by the original American inhabitants. The first Indians they encountered were the Peorias, an Illinois tribe, whose principal settlement was located where the Iowa River flows into the Mississippi. At the confluence of the Missouri and the Mississippi the explorers saw giant rock drawings depicting Indian deities. In mid-July the small group had reached Quapaw, the southernmost village on the Arkansas River (34° 5' N). Marquette now knew that the Mississippi did not flow into the Pacific Ocean but into the Gulf of Mexico. Since forging further ahead could have proved dangerous to the other five participants, Marquette and Jolliet decided to turn back. They were approximately 1,100 km (700 miles) from the Gulf of Mexico. Without any great difficulty they reached the site of present-day Memphis, Tennessee, where the two explorers handed over a report of their expedition to the Mosopolea Indians, who then conveyed it to Colonel Bird in Virginia. Where the Illinois River flows into the Mississippi, the explorers left the latter and followed its tributary to the village of Kaskaskia. At the end of September 1673 they arrived in Chicago, from where they proceeded along the west bank of Lake Michigan to "Stur-

On his travels, Jacques Marquette was particularly interested in the various Indian tribes and their way of life.

geon Bay", then to "Green Bay" and from there to the missionary outpost of Saint-François-Xavier. Here, the two pioneers went their separate ways after having covered and explored a stretch of approximately 4,350 km (2,700 miles).

In October 1674 Marquette undertook a journey accompanied by P. Morteret and J. Largilier, two Franco-Canadian explorers, to establish a missionary outpost in the village of Kaskaskia. The expedition had to be interrupted in Chicago because Marquette had fallen ill. After having spent the winter there, the three explorers and missionaries reached Kaskaskia at the end of March 1675. Since Marquette's state of health was deteriorating daily there was no question of penetrating into the Mississippi region. The group started back in the direction of Michilimackinac. It is not known whether the travelers reached the Saint Joseph River via Chicago and then along the south bank of Lake Michigan or via Kankakee and South Bend in Indiana. From the mouth of the Saint Joseph River they proceeded north, until Marquette died at a place now known as Ludington on the northeast bank of Lake Michigan.

With their courageous journeys, Marquette and Jolliet solved the geographical enigma of the Mississippi. They ushered in the great expedition of the French Mississippi explorer Cavelier de la Salle, who traveled on the river to where it flows into the sea.

A town on the south bank of the Upper Lake is named after the explorer and missionary Jacques Marquette.

Further reading
J. Sparks, Life of Father Marquette (Library of American Biography Vol. 10). Without place of publication 1838

*Récit des Voyages et des Découvertes du Père
Marquette (with a translation of the same).
Unfinished letter of Father Marquette to Father
C. Dablon, containing a journal of his last
visit to the Illinois. Historical Collection of
Louisiana. Without place of publication 1846
H. H. Hurlbut, Father Marquette at Mackinaw
and Chicago. A paper read before the Chicago
Historical Society. Chicago 1878
A. Hamy, Au Mississippi. La première ex-
ploration 1673 de Père Jacques Marquette de
Laon 1637-1675 et de Louis Jolliet, d'après
M. E. Gagnon. Paris 1878
Reuben G. Thwaites, The Jesuit Relations
and Allied Documents. Vol. 59. Cleveland
1900
Fr. B. Steck, The Jolliet-Marquette Expedition.
Rev. edition. Quincy (Ill., USA) 1928*

MAUCH, KARL

German explorer of Africa, born 1837 in Stetten,
died 1875 in Stuttgart.

Karl Mauch was the son of a master carpenter
and became an elementary school teacher. Even
as a young man his desire to explore lured him
to South Africa. Since he had spent his meager
savings within a short time, he had to earn his
crossing as a sailor.

Through the intervention of the geographer
August Petermann, the founder of "Petermanns
Geographische Mitteilungen" (Petermann's Geographical Reports) and German polar researchers, Mauch received the necessary means
for procuring the appropriate equipment. In the
course of numerous expeditions he explored
the Transvaal and the region between the two
African rivers Limpopo and Zambezi. The result
of his travels was the charting of Transvaal and
the discovery of rich goldfields (the Tati gold-
field in southern Rhodesia and the gold veins
of the Matabele and Marchona land in eastern
Rhodesia, now Zimbabwe).

Karl Mauch's most significant achievement
was the discovery of the mighty stone palace of
Great Zimbabwe south of Lake Kyle, during his
last journey in 1871. He was the first to recognize the archaeological importance of this find.

This old African royal residence was probably
erected by the Shona people between the
eleventh and the fifteenth centuries. Although
hardly anything was left of the nearby gold-
mines by the time Mauch arrived, Zimbabwe's
wealth and its political significance must have
been due to its gold.

Even though the German Africa traveler
Adam Renders had discovered the ruins four
years before Mauch, it was Mauch who drew the
archaeologists' attention to Zimbabwe.

Despite this archaeologically and historically
important discovery, Kaul Mauch was soon forgotten. He died tragically after falling out of a
window.

*Further reading
Petermanns Mitteilungen: Ergänzungsheft 37.
Gotha 1874
Karl M. Mager, Karl Mauch. Without place
of publication 1895
Karl Mauch. In: Kurt Hassert, Die Erforschung
Afrikas. Leipzig 1941*

Above: Natives work on tree bark in order to extract juice from it. Below: A native village.

MAWSON, SIR DOUGLAS

English-Australian explorer, born 1882 in Bradford, died 1958 in Adelaide.

Douglas Mawson studied geology and mineralogy at the University of Sydney. In the year 1903, he undertook a scientific expedition to the New Hebrides in the southwest Pacific to study the geological foundation of the island group. Three years later he accompanied the British polar explorer S. E. Shackleton on his journey of exploration to the South Pole, in the course of which he climbed the active volcano Mount Erebus in Antarctica.

From 1911 to 1914 he was head of the Australian Antarctic expedition and made important geographical discoveries, for which he was made a peer and received the "Founders' Medal of the Royal Geographical Society".

From 1929 to 1931 he was head of the British-Australian and the New Zealand Antarctic expeditions.

During his 34-year term of office as a professor of geology and mineralogy, he made an invaluable contribution to the study of Antarctic geography.

Further reading
D. Mawson, The Home of Blizzard, being the story of the Australian Antarctic Expedition, 1911-1914. 2 volumes. London 1915 (2nd ed. London 1930)
C. F. Lascron, South with Mawson. Reminiscences of the Australian Antarctic Expedition, 1911-1914. London and Sydney 1947

McCLINTOCK, SIR FRANCIS LEOPOLD

British polar explorer, born 1819 in Dundalk (Ireland), died 1907 in London.

Francis McClintock joined the British Royal Navy as a young man and was promoted to the rank of acting Sub-Lieutenant in 1831, Captain in 1843, Vice-Admiral in 1877 and finally Admiral in 1884.

In 1848 Francis McClintok accompanied Sir J. C. Ross as second lieutenant of the "Enterprise" on Ross' search for the John Franklin expedition and two years later he participated in the Austin expedition as first officer of the "Assistance". In the course of the Belcher expedition he explored 2,270 km (1,408 miles) of the Arctic alone on a sledge in 105 days, proceeded into Prince Patrick Land and discovered Emerald Island, north of Melville Island.

In 1857, Lady Franklin commissioned the world-famous sleigh-rider to solve the mysterious disappearance of her husband once and for all. Francis McClintock cruised the arctic waters of Canada in the "Fox", a 177-ton steamship, explored Somerset and Prince of Wales Islands, the Boothia peninsula and King William Land, where McClintock's Lieutenant Hobson discovered the Franklin expedition's logbooks on the north coast near Point Victory on 5 May, 1859; skeletons and a lifeboat were also discovered. The route taken by the Franklin expedition could thus be largely reconstructed.

McClintock was knighted on his return to England in September 1859.

The passage between Victoria Island and Prince of Wales Island was named after this important explorer.

Further reading
The Voyage of the "Fox" in the Arctic Seas. (Report on the search for Franklin). Without place of publication 1859
J. Brown, The north-west Passage and the plans for the search for Sir John Franklin. London 1860
Die Franklin-Expedition und ihr Ausgang. Auffindung der Überreste von Sir Franklins Expedition durch Sir L. McClintock. Feierstunden, Malerische Feierstunden. Amerika, volume. 2. Without place of publication 1874
F. G. Jackson, A thousand Days in the Arctic. With preface by Admiral Sir L. McClintock. 2 Vols. London 1899
Sir C. R. Markham, Life of Admiral Sir Leopold McClintock. Cambridge 1909

McCLURE, SIR ROBERT JOHN MESURIER

British polar explorer, born 1807 in Wexford (Ireland), died 1873 in London.

In 1836, McClure accompanied the polar explorer G. Back on his expedition from Repulse Bay to the mouth of Big Fish River; twelve years later he took part in a search expedition for John Franklin.

In the year 1850, Robert McClure undertook a further polar expedition, which set out to reach the Arctic from the west via a detour past South America and through the Pacific Ocean. He was commander of the "Investigator" and was accompanied by Sir Robert Collinson, commander of the "Enterprise". On this journey McClure discovered the Prince of Wales Strait, located between Banks Land in the north, Bering Land in the south and Prince Albert Land. On a sleigh, McClure arrived at the point in the Barrow Strait that had already been reached by ships from the east. The Northwest Passage to the far north of Canada was thus almost conquered. Almost two years after McClure's success, his ship was still enclosed by ice. His crew, which had already been reported missing in England, was miraculously saved by Lieutenant Pim of the "Resolute" and arrived back in England in September 1854.

On his return in London, McClure received the long-standing reward of 10,000 pounds and a knighthood.

Further reading
A. Taylor, Geographical Discovery and Exploration in the Queen Elisabeth Islands.
Ottawa 1955

MENDAÑA DE NEYRA, ALVARO DE

Spanish seafarer and explorer, born 1541 in Spain, died 1595 on the Santa Cruz Islands.

In 1566 Mendaña was commissioned to rediscover the "Isles of Fortune" in the Pacific, which were said to have been originally discovered by the Inca Tupac Yupanqui.

With two ships, the "Dos Reyes" and the "Todos los Santos", Mendaña sailed from Callao (the port of Lima, Peru) in the direction of Australia and in 1567 discovered a group of islands which he named "Solomon". The Spaniards did not take a particular liking to these islands and continued their journey. On 15 January, 1568 Mendaña sighted a small island which he called "Jesús" and two larger islands which were given the name "Santa Isabella". In view of the hostile nature of the inhabitants, who practiced cannibalism, Mendaña abandoned his plans to advance further into the western Pacific and returned to Peru.

In 1595 he undertook a second journey to the Pacific and this time discovered a group of islands that he named "Marquesas de Mendoza" in honor of the governor of Peru, Marqués de Mendoza. Another island was named "Santa Cruz"; Mendaña and his wife chose this island as the site of a Spanish colony. Mendaña's sudden death and the romantic adventures of the Spanish with the women of the island, which invoked the anger of the male population, placed the settlers in a difficult situation. Mendaña's wife and her lover Francisco de Castro decided to take command and sailed to Manila to call for reinforcements. However, their pleas were rejected; Castro and Isabel Mendaña, whom he had married in the meantime, did not return to the "Marquesas de Mendoza", but instead traveled to Mexico (Acapulco), leaving the remaining settlers to their fate.

Further reading
E. Charton, Relation de voyage que fit A. de Mendaña à la recherche de la Nouvelle-Guinée. Second voyage, Vol. 4. Paris 1854
G. A. Marcel, Mendaña et la découverte des Iles Marquises. Paris 1898
W. A. T. Amherst. The discovery of the Salomon Island by Alvaro de Mendaña in 1568. London 1901

Sir Robert John Mesurier McClure

Mendaña de Neyra launched his expeditions from the port of Peru. This map from the first half of the 16th century shows South America as it was known then. The starting point of Peru, which was so important for the Spanish, was portrayed in a separate stylized map of the city (left).

MERBOLD, ULF DIETRICH

German astronaut, born 1941 in Greiz (former German Democratic Republic).

Ulf Merbold spent his childhood in the former GDR, but managed to flee to West Germany at the age of nineteen. In 1977, as a scientist working at the Max Planck Institute, he was chosen as a payload specialist to accompany "Spacelab 1" as part of the STS-9 space mission. Although the Americans were unwilling to accept foreigners in the group of astronauts in Houston, in return for developing the Spacelab the ESA was offered a coveted place on board the space shuttle "Columbia".

Merbold was thus the first non-American in the crew of an American space shuttle.

The "Columbia" lifted off on 28 November, 1983 and returned to Earth on 8 December, 1983. From 22 to 30 January, 1992 Ulf Merbold was again on board an American space shuttle as a payload specialist; this time it was the "Discovery". In October 1994 he took part in the "Euromir" space mission. The flight lasted four weeks and was carried out in cooperation with Russian cosmonauts.

After his first flight in space Merbold was appointed head of the astronauts' office of the German Aerospace Research and Test Institute in Cologne-Porz. However, he gave up this position to prepare for his second NASA flight. Ulf Merbold now works with the European Astronaut Center in Cologne.

Further reading
U. Merbold, Flug ins All: Von Spacelab 1 bis zur D1-Mission: Der persönliche Bericht des ersten Astronauten der Bundesrepublik. Bergisch-Gladbach 1986

MESSNER, REINHOLD

Italian mountain climber, author and filmmaker, born 1944 in Brixen.

Reinhold Messner climbed Mount Everest (8,848 meters or 29,029 feet) together with Peter Haberer and the Nanga Parbat, without the use of high-altitude breathing apparatus.

In 1979, together with Michael Dacher, he climbed K 2 (Mount Goodwin Austin in the Karakoram Mountains) and in 1980 he climbed Mount Everest again, this time alone. In 1984 he carried out his first "double eight-thousand" climb (the G I and G II summits in the Karakoram Mountains). By 1986 Reinhold Messner had become the first person ever to climb all 14 eight-thousand meter mountains on Earth without the aid of high-altitude breathing apparatus. In 1990, he crossed Antarctica on foot together with Arved Fuchs.

Ulf Merbold in his spacesuit at the Gagarin Training Camp near Moscow in August, 1994.

Reinhold Messner pulls a high-tech sled which was specially constructed for him by Opel (in December, 1999). Two of these sleds can be connected by a cross-country ski to form a catamaran, so that the equipment can also be used on water. Messner planned to use this vehicle on a future polar expedition.

Messner has written numerous books on his expeditions and mountain climbing and the scripts of several television films.

Further reading
R. Messner, Wettlauf zum Gipfel. Strategie und Taktik meiner Höchstleistungen. Munich 1986
–, Die schönsten Gipfel der Welt. Künzelsau 1989
–, Die Freiheit, aufzubrechen, wohin ich will. Ein Bergsteigerleben. Munich 1991
–, Überlebt. Alle 14 Achttausender. 5th ed. Munich 1991
–, Grenzbereich Todeszone. Cologne 1992
–, Antarktis. Himmel und Hölle zugleich. Munich 1993
–, Alle meine Gipfel. Das alpine Lebenswerk. Reprint. Munich 1993
–, Berge versetzen. Das Credo eines Grenz-gängers. Munich 1993
–, Bis ans Ende der Welt. Alpine Heraus-forderungen im Himalaya und Karakoram. 3rd, revised edition. Munich 1994
–, Dreizehn Spiegel meiner Seele. Munich 1994

MEYER, HANS

German explorer of Africa and geographer, born 1856 in Hildburghausen, died 1929 in Leipzig.

Hans Meyer studied in Berlin and Strasbourg. Between 1881 and 1883 he traveled to various regions around the world, visiting the Near East, India and the Philippines, where at Virchov's suggestion he carried out his first anthropo-logical research into the Igorrats, who were headhunters. A year after his return, Dr. phil. Meyer was appointed head of the Bibliographi-cal Institute.

In 1887 he began his research activities in Africa. He crossed South Africa, Mozambique and Zanzibar and carried out an expedition to Kilimanjaro, which he climbed together with Eberstein, although he alone managed to reach a height of 5,450 m (17,880 feet).

In 1888 Meyer set out on his second journey of exploration. While crossing the Usambara

The "green hell" at Kilimanjaro, which was explored by the German Africa expert Hans Meyer.

mountain range (in the northeast of Tanzania) he was taken prisoner by Arabs and held to ransom; he was eventually released once the payment was made.

In 1889 Hans Meyer, accompanied by L. Purtscheller from Salzburg, led a third expedition to Snow Mountain, which he climbed as high as Kaiser Wilhelm Peak (today Uhuru Point) on 6 October, so that he could explore the interior of the crater. He then made several attempts to climb the Mawenzi, the second-highest peak of Kilimanjaro. He reached a height of 5,250 m (17,225 feet) and also explored the Pare Ugueno Mountains.

Ten years later in 1898, accompanied by E. Platz, Hans Meyer circled the entire Kilimanjaro from Marangu (today the point of departure for climbing this mountain). He again undertook a geological investigation of the crater and made Ice Age findings.

In 1911 Meyer carried out a further expedition to Rwanda, during which he carried out geological research on the Virunga volcanoes (north of Lake Kivu), climbed the Karisimbi (extinct volcano in the northwest of Rwanda) and the Niragongo. His return journey took him through North Burundi to Tabora.

In 1929 the untiring Africa explorer died in Leipzig of a dysentery infection – in the meantime he had been awarded an honorary Chair of Colonial Geography at Leipzig University.

Hans Meyer's most significant achievements were his accurate geographical and geomorphological research of Kilimanjaro, his politico-economic analysis of the former German field of interest and his anthropological research of the Guanche (native population of the Canary Isles).

Further reading
H. Meyer, Kilimandscharo. Berlin 1900

MITCHELL, SIR THOMAS LIVINGSTONE

Australian explorer, born 1792, died 1855.

In 1831 Mitchell undertook a scientific exploration to the Australian interior, to find proof for the escaped convict G. Clarke's claim of the existence of a large continental lake. In the course of this expedition Mitchell discovered Lake Macintyre.

In 1835, accompanied by A. Cunningham, another Australian explorer, Mitchell explored the Darling River. During this journey Cunningham was murdered by aborigines.

The following year, he explored the region of the Murray River, charted its tributary system and in 1845 explored large areas of New South Wales.

Mitchell is regarded as one of the greatest pioneers and explorers of southeastern Australia.

Further reading
The Australian Encyclopaedia
The Australian Dictionary of Biography
E. Favenc, The history of Australian
Explorations. London 1888
A. W. José, Histoire de l'Australie depuis
sa découverte jusqu'à nos jours. Paris
1930

MUNK, JENS

Norwegian-Danish seafarer and polar explorer, born 1579 in Norway, died 1628 in Copenhagen.

After an eventful youth in which he proved himself to be a bold seafarer on many occasions, Jens Munk was commissioned at the age of forty by the Danish king Christian IV in 1619 to investigate the coast of east Greenland and to find the sea route to China and India via the Arctic Sea.

Munk, who was convinced of the success of this undertaking, left the port of Elseneur in May with two ships and set course for Greenland. In June he rounded Cape Farvel, Greenland's southernmost tip, and then sailed into Hudson Bay, reaching a latitude of 63° 20' N.

The unfavorable weather conditions forced Munk and his crew to spend the winter in the Canadian Arctic ("Munk Vinterhavn"). This winter in the far north proved to be a disaster for Munk's crew. When most of the members of the expedition had died of scurvy and Munk himself had written his will, the captain decided to abandon his plans and return home.

After a long, stormy crossing Munk landed first in Norway, then in Denmark. The Danish king was naturally pleased to see Munk return home, since in Denmark this expedition had been reported missing. However, Munk had difficulties in coming to terms with the failure of his plan, in which he had placed so much hope of success for his king.

Regardless of the failure, which was above all due to the lack of suitable equipment, Munk's undertaking represents a considerable achievement along the arduous road to the conquest of the Arctic. On the other hand, his geographical sketches of Hudson Bay (discovered by H. Hudson in 1610) are of little scientific value.

Further reading
J. Munk, Navigatio Septentrionalis det er
Realtion eller Beskrivelse om Seiglads
og Reyse paa denne Norvestiske Passage.
Copenhagen 1623
The Expedition of J. Munk to Hudson's
Bay in search of North-West-Passage in
1619-1620. Translated from Munk's
Navigation Septentrionalis. Copenhagen 1624
A. & J. Churchill, The Expedition of Jens
Munk to Hudson's Bay in search of the
Hudson's Straits in order to discover a passage
betwixt Greenland and America to the West
Indies. A Collection of Voyages. Vol. 1.
London 1744
C. P. Rothe, Den Danske Admiral J. Munk's
Livs og Levnets Beskri-velse. Copenhagen
1747-1750
The Hakluyt Society, Danish Arctic Expedition.
Book 2. London 1897
J. Munk, Über den Nordpol nach China?
Auf der Suche nach der Nordwestpassage.
Eine Seefahrertragödie des 17. Jahrhunderts,
ed. T. Hansen. Tübingen 1974

*Norway, the land
of fjords and home
of Jens Munk*

MUNZINGER PASHA, WERNER

Swiss explorer of Africa, born 1832 in Olten, died 1875 in Aussa (Ethiopia).

Munzinger grew up in Bern. At that city's university he studied geography, history and modern languages; he also studied Oriental languages at Munich and Paris Universities.

In 1852 he traveled to Cairo, and the following year he spent time in Massaua (a port on the Red Sea), where he concentrated on the study of

traveled extensively throughout this region from 1855 to 1861. In the west of the country he reached Kassala (a town in eastern Sudan) on the Gash and Gos Redjeh on the Atbara (right tributary of the Nile). In the east of Bogoland, Munzinger reached the coast of the Red Sea. In the meantime the Swiss explorer had attained a reputation as a reliable geographer and ethnographer. Munzinger took part in an expedition to the sultanate of Wadai, to search for the missing Dr. Vogel under the leadership of the Austrian Vice Consul of Khartoum, T. von Heuglin. Accompanied by Kinzelbach, another member of the expedition, Munzinger explored the land of the Barea (a tribe of northern Ethiopia) and, traveling via Kassala and Khartoum, reached the town of Al Obeid in Kordofan. He returned to Switzerland via Keren and Massaua.

In 1863 Munzinger again spent time in eastern Africa. On commission from a Swiss company from Alexandria, he undertook extensive business trips to the Red Sea. He subsequently assumed the position of vice consul for both the British and French governments in Massaua. In the service of the British government, he explored all the passes in the Ethiopian highlands, thus providing the government with valuable strategic services. It is thanks to Munzinger that the British Abyssinian war, commanded by Lord Napier, was over very quickly. However, Munzinger's exploratory tours aroused the hostility of the Ethiopians. In 1869 he only narrowly escaped being murdered in the land of the Bogos.

In 1871, accompanied by the British captain S. W. Miles, Munzinger traveled to the northeast of the Abyssinian highlands. That same year the Viceroy of Egypt appointed him governor of Massaua and in 1872 governor general of the province of Suakim (Red Sea). He was finally awarded the coveted title of "pasha" and appointed Governor-General of East Sudan.

However, relations between the rulers of the Tigre (tribe in North Ethiopia) and Egypt had since deteriorated so that war seemed inevitable.

Semitic languages. From there he undertook his first scientific expedition to Keren (mountainous region in Ethiopia) and the land of the Bogos (Agau tribe in Eritrea), a region that was previously only known to missionaries. Munzinger

Menelik, King of the Shoa (a tribe of the Galla) and Emperor of Abyssinia, offered to mediate. Munzinger was commissioned to lead the negotiations. Accompanied by his wife and Haggenmachers, another Swiss Africa explorer, along with 350 soldiers, Munzinger set out from the town of Massaua and first explored the region around Tejura (southern Eritrea). From there he proceeded inland and, after a strenuous journey, reached Lake Assale (northern Ethiopia, north of Makale). Menelik's negotiator Ras Buru also arrived on the scene. A week after Munzinger's arrival in late October, Galla warriors forced their way into his camp. Munzinger and his wife were murdered. Haggenmacher and Ras Buru only just escaped the massacre, but died of exhaustion on their return journey.

Along with Burckhardt, Munzinger is regarded as the greatest Swiss explorer of Africa. His geographical and ethnographic findings, particularly relating to the land of the Bogos, earned him great respect as a scientist even during his lifetime.

Further reading
W. Munzinger, Sitten und Rechte der Bogos.
Winterthur 1859
–, Ostafrikanische Studien. Schaffhausen und
Leipzig 1864
J. V. Keller-Zschokke, Werner Munzinger
Pascha. Leben und Wirken. Aarau 1891

MYLIUS-ERICHSEN, LUDWIG

Danish Arctic explorer, born 1872 in Vyborg, died 1907 in Greenland.

From 1902 to 1907 Mylius-Erichsen led a "literary" expedition to Greenland in order to study the dialects and customs of the Inuit.

During his second expedition together with the cartographer and lieutenant Höj Hagen and the Inuit J. Brönland, he charted a large part of the west coast of Greenland. The undertaking ended with the tragic death of the three-man expedition.

A search party found a letter signed by Mylius-Erichsen and dated 8 August, 1907, which stated that he and his companions had met the Greenland expedition from Koch, had reached the outermost tip of Peary Land on 1 June and discovered that the presumed "Peary Channel" in fact did not exist.

The tongue of land between Independence and Denmark Fjord in the north of Greenland bears the name of this Arctic explorer.

Further reading
Rapporter fra L. Mylius-Erichsen og Alf Trolle
om Danmark-Ekspedition til Grønlands
Nordøstkyst 1906-1908. Jørgen Brønlund's
Dagborg i Tidsrummet fra 1. Maj-19. Okt.
1907. Den Danmarks Havn i Foraaret 1908
foreløbigt udar bejdede Overseattlse Danmark-
Ekspeditionens Deltagere. Copenhagen 1934

*Inuit with sled in the
Arctic today*

NACHTIGAL, GUSTAV

German explorer of Africa, born 1834 in Eichstedt, died 1885 near Cape Palmas.

Nachtigal studied medicine and became a military physician in the Prussian Army (1858). He was forced to give up his profession because of tuberculosis and traveled to northern Africa in 1861 to recuperate. Nachtigal prescribed himself exploration of Africa as a cure. He learned Arabic and studied the customs of the desert-dwellers.

In 1863 he entered the service of the Bey of Tunisia as a physician and soon became his closest advisor. In Tunisia he met the German Africa explorer Rohlfs, who had been commissioned by the King of Prussia to transport gifts to the Sultan of Bornu for his friendly support of the German Africa explorers. Gustav Nachtigal persuaded Rohlfs to allow him to carry out this mission.

In order to reach Kuka, the residence of the Sultan of Bornu, Nachtigal, who had practically no experience in desert travel, had to cross the Libyan Desert. On 17 February, 1869 he set out from Tripoli, accompanied by a local guide, three servants and ten camels, and reached Mursuk without incident, where he met the Dutch traveler A. Tinné. Because putting together a caravan was taking too long for Nachtigal's liking, he decided to make an excursion to the still unexplored massif. Accompanied by a guide, Nachtigal explored the "roof" of the Sahara and its in-

Gustav Nachtigal

habitants, the "Tedas" (men of the rocks). This people of just 25,000 regarded the Tibesti Mountains as its personal property. The men were extremely robust and could travel 800 to 1,000 km (500 to 600 miles) through the desert with very little water. They killed their quarry from a great distance with throwing knives. On his return to Mursuk, Nachtigal had to spend the whole winter recovering from his strenuous journey. In 1870 Nachtigal traveled to Kuka and the following year reached Kanem-Bornu.

Instead of taking the usual route back to Tripoli, in 1872 Nachtigal traveled to Bagirmi (the former Sudan empire) and explored the Chari, the main tributary of Lake Chad. In 1873 he traveled to the Sultanate of Wadai, where he searched for traces of the German Africa explorer E. Vogel, who had been murdered there, and in 1874 he journeyed through Darfur (region in the midwest of Sudan), Kordofan (province in the center of the Republic of Sudan) and reached Khartoum, the capital of Sudan.

After six years of absence Nachtigal returned to Europe in 1875 with a rich collection of geographical specimens. He was elected chairman of the Geographical Society in Berlin. In 1882 Bismarck appointed him Consul General in Tunisia, and two years later the meritorious researcher was made imperial representative for Togo and Cameroon.

On 18 April, 1885 Nachtigal died of tuberculosis on board a ship. In keeping with his wishes he was buried in Cameroon.

Gustav Nachtigal's principal achievement was his geographical and ethnographic exploration of the Tibesti massif. Even today, his findings are still regarded as the most precise from a scientific point of view. Nachtigal also provided posterity with a highly accurate description of Borku, at the southeastern edge of the Tibesti massif.

Gustav Nachtigall in a victory pose, with his native bearers and a young lion.

Further reading
Petermanns Mitteilungen. Gotha 1869,
1871, 1873-1875
D. Berlin, Erinnerungen an Gustav
Nachtigal. Berlin 1887
J. Wiese, Gustav Nachtigal. Berlin 1914
E. Banse, Große Forschungsreisende
(incl. Nachtigal). Munich 1933
–, Unsere großen Afrikaner (incl. Nachtigal).
Munich 1940
G. Nachtigal, Sahara und Sudan. Erlebnisse
sechsjähriger Reisen in Afrika. 3 volumes.
(unaltered reprint of the Berlin and Leipzig
edition from 1879-1889). Graz 1967

Fridtjof Nansen

Nansen and his crew leave the "Fram" on March 14, 1895 to reconnoitre the wilderness of ice.

NANSEN, FRIDTJOF

Norwegian zoologist and Arctic explorer, born 1861 at Hof Mellon-Frøen (near Oslo), died 1930 in Lysaker.

At the age of only 21, Nansen took part in a journey to Jan Mayen Island (Greenland Sea) on board a whaling vessel. In 1888, together with O. Sverdrup, he was the first person to cross the 3,000 m (10,000 foot) Greenland ice massif from east to west on skis and with sledges on runners. After carefully studying the North Polar journeys of the Austrian O. Lenz and the North American De Long, Nansen came up with the plan of drifting along with the ice to the vicinity of the North Pole in a specially constructed ship and then covering the rest of the journey on foot. However, he was unable to determine the optimal route. Many of his fellow countrymen and well-known scientists believed Nansen's plan was too dangerous or, in fact, impossible.

Convinced of the success of his undertaking, Nansen had the government pay for a ship to be specially constructed for the northern waters by shipbuilder C. Archer. The ship was named "Fram" (forward).

On 24 July, 1893 after months of careful preparation, Nansen left the port of Christiana (Oslo). Eight lifeboats followed his ship so that they would be able to provide immediate assistance in the event of a shipwreck. On the Kara Sea he had floating supplies attached to the ship. Sailing past the North Cape, and after crossing the Barents and Kara Seas, the "Fram" reached Cape Jelyuskin; just a few miles to the east of these Siberian foothills, the ship was enclosed by the ice masses on 25 September, 1893.

This was the start of the actual "drift": The ice masses carried the ship onwards. Once they had reached the latitude of Franz Joseph Land Nansen was able to disembark (14 March, 1895). With almost 600 kilograms (1,300 pounds) of equipment, three sledges, 28 Samoyed dogs, two kayaks and food for three months, the explorer and lieutenant Johansen left the ship and set out

The crew of explorers of the Nansen expedition pose for the camera on skis and with their dogs.

In March, 1895 the crew strenuously dig Nansen's "Fram" clear.

Nansen observes an
eclipse of the sun on
April 6, 1894 and
records the data.

These little tents served
the Polar explorers as
a meagre protection
against the icy winds
when they were recon-
noitring outside of the
ship.

in the direction of the North Pole. In spite of incredible hardships and exertion they reached a latitude of "only" 86° 12' N, further north than anyone before them, before having to turn back. With great exertion, they reached Cape Flora and Alexander Land. In Hammerfest, Nansen received the news that the "Fram" had reached 85° 57' N and was now resting safely in the port of Tromsö. On 9 September, 1896 the two Arctic explorers arrived in the Norwegian capital in good health. With Otto Sverdrup as captain, the "Fram" also arrived in Oslo having sailed via Spitsbergen.

Through their achievement Nansen and his companion Johansen had provided an unparalleled demonstration of physical endurance, courage and cooperation. The fact that they did not manage to conquer the Pole in no way detracted from their achievement. Nansen had proven that the North Pole could be reached via the frozen, constantly moving sea with the appropriate equipment.

Nansen never again set out into the Arctic Sea after this adventure; he dedicated his life to assisting prisoners of war and refugees during the First World War ("Nansen Passport"). He was awarded the Nobel Peace Prize in 1922.

Further reading
F. Nansen, Auf Schneeschuhen durch Grönland. 2 vols. 1891
–, In Nacht und Eis. 3 vols. Without place of publication 1897/98
–, The Norwegian North Polar Expedition – Scientific results. 6 vols. Oslo 1906
F. Nansen, Gjennem Sibirien. 1914
–, Sibirien, ein Zukunftsland. Without place of publication 1914
–, Unter Robben und Eisbären. Without place of publication 1926
–, Durch den Kaukasus zur Wolga. Without place of publication 1930
W. Bauer, Fridtjof Nansen. Humanität als Abenteuer. Munich 1956
F. Nansen, In Nacht und Eis. Die norwegische Polarexpedition 1893-1896. 4th unrevised ed. Mannheim 1985
D. Brennecke, Fridtjof Nansen. Reinbek 1990

NEARCHOS

Greek fleet commander and friend of Alexander the Great, fourth century BC.

Nearchos accompanied Alexander the Great on his Indian campaign to the mouth of the Indus. From what is today Karachi, he set out with 150 ships to explore the marine route to the Persian Gulf, while Alexander returned home overland. Nearchos reached the mouth of the Tigris via Hormuz at the entrance to the Persian Gulf.

NIEBUHR, CARSTEN

German explorer, born 1733 in Lüdingworth, died 1815 in Meldorf.

Carsten Niebuhr came from a farming family. At the age of 20 he moved to Hamburg, where he studied theology and mathematics. He spent some time in Göttingen. In 1761 Niebuhr was commissioned by King Fredrick V of Denmark to undertake an exploratory expedition to the Arabian peninsula, accompanied by F. von Haven, a professor of Oriental languages, P. Forskål, a natural scientist, C. C. Cramer, physician and G. W. Baurenfeind, a painter and copper engraver.

From Copenhagen, Carsten Niebuhr's expedition traveled to Marseille and reached Smyrna via the island of Malta. From there Niebuhr continued to Constantinople, visited Alexandria, Cairo, the ports of Jeddah and Loheia on the Red Sea and eventually reached Mecca. The expedition explored the entire southern Arabian Peninsula, especially Yemen and its legendary capital Sana.

In Mecca, Niebuhr boarded a ship and sailed to Bombay, a city which especially impressed the explorer. In the course of his return journey Niebuhr visited Maskat, Basra, Persepolis (where he made some records of ancient Persian writings), Baghdad and Mossul before returning to Copenhagen in 1767 via Krakow, Dresden and Hamburg.

MAKOU

The explorers' ships before the harbour of Macao, Hong Kong's neighbouring island.

Niebuhr is especially credited with his geographical research and description of Yemen, which was still virtually unknown at the time, and the Red Sea.

Further reading
C. Niebuhr, Beschreibung von Arabien. *Copenhagen 1772*
C. Niebuhrs Reisebeschreibungen nach Arabien und anderen umliegenden Ländern (Reise durch Syrien and Palästina). Copenhagen 1774

C. Niebuhr, Reisebeschreibung nach Arabien und den umliegenden Ländern. Einschließlich: Reisen durch Syrien und Palästina. 3 vols. Unrevised reprint of the editions from Copenhagen 1774-1778 and Hamburg 1837. Graz 1960
–, Beschreibung von Arabien. Unrevised reprint of the edition from Copenhagen 1772. Graz 1969
–, Entdeckungen im Orient, ed. R. and E. Grün. Tübingen 1973
–, Reisebeschreibung nach Arabien und anderen Ländern. 2nd ed. Zurich 1993

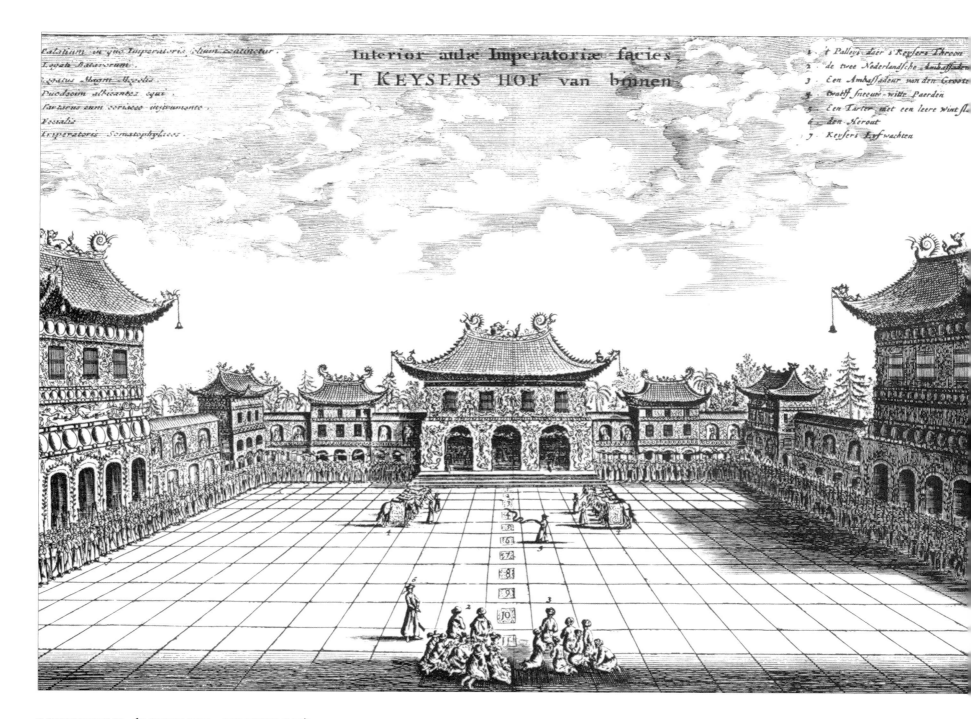

NIEUHOF (NIJHOF, NEUHOF), JOAN

Dutch steward and copper engraver, born 1618 in Uelzen, died 1672 on the north coast of Madagascar.

After spending some time in Brazil, Nieuhof set out in 1653 on his first voyage to East India. He first landed on the island of Java, where he was appointed first steward of the Dutch trade delegation that was to travel to China to establish new relations between the Netherlands and China. During his journey through Canton, the Pojang Sea and the Kaiser Channel to Peking, Nieuhof made many detailed copper engravings of the cities and landscape which gave a friendly, peaceful impression of the Middle Kingdom when they were published in Europe (after Nieuhof's death).

Two years after his return to the Netherlands, Joan Nieuhof again traveled to India in 1659 and in 1661 he was appointed commander-in-chief of the Coylan citadel on the Malabar coast.

The portrait of the Imperial Court from Joan Nieuhof's account of his travels, "Pictures from China".

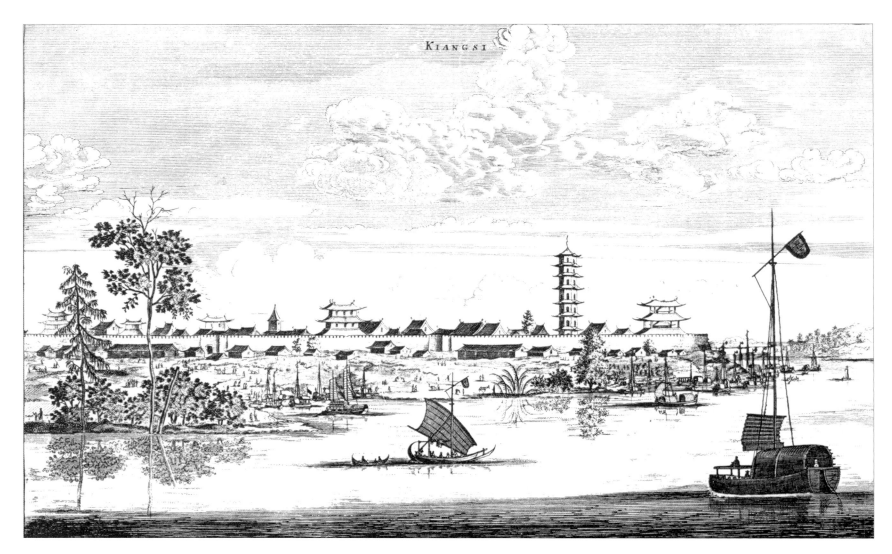

KIANGSI

The Europeans were greatly fascinated by Nieuhof's accounts of his travels and illustrations such as these. They showed a hitherto unknown picture of the Empire, without frightening mythical creatures.

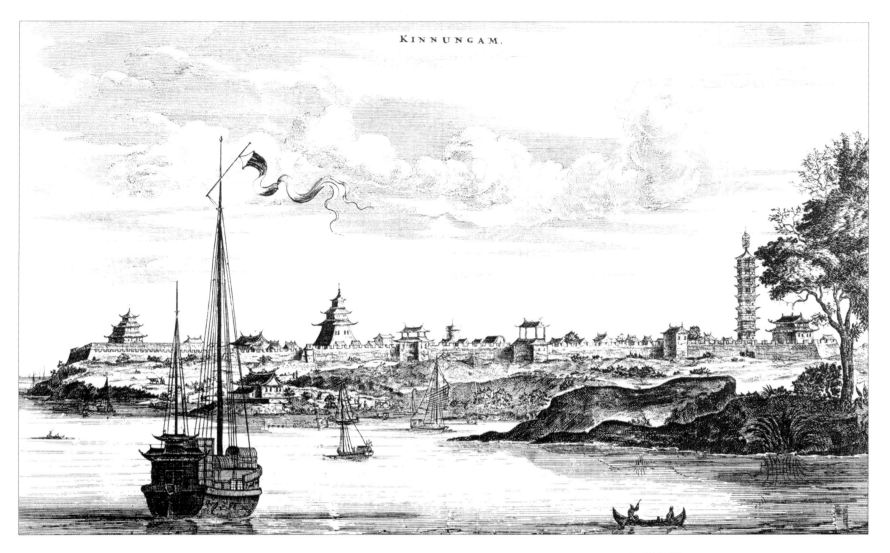

KINNUNGAM.

Many illustrations from Nieuhof's book show the explorers' ships off the coasts which they are approaching. Sometimes it is a city on the coast, sometimes imposing ranges of mountains.

Joan Nieuhof

After 1666 he retired from service for a number of years and investigated the flora and fauna of the Batavia region. The pictures that he made during this time were published in a book in 1682.

After spending some more time in the Netherlands in 1671, Joan Nieuhof traveled to India for a third time. Along with several sailors and the helmsman, Nieuhof lost his life during a sojourn off the coast of Madagascar to stock up the ship's supplies.

NOBILE, UMBERTO

Italian general, aeronautical engineer and Arctic explorer, born 1885 in Lauro, died 1978 in Rome.

From a very young age Nobile showed interest in airships and Arctic exploration. In 1926 he accompanied the Norwegian Arctic explorer R. Amundsen and the American Arctic aviator A. Ellsworth on their successful North Polar flight as helmsman on the airship "Norge", which set out from Spitsbergen.

In 1928, accompanied by an exclusively Italian crew, Nobile attempted to repeat the flight from 1926 in the airship "Italia". During a snowstorm, the airship lost height and crashed to the ground. One crew member was killed; Nobile and eight others were injured. It was not until 15 days later that news of the disaster reached Europe. In the course of a large-scale search campaign, the two French aviators Guilbaud and de Cuverville and the celebrated Arctic explorer R. Amundsen were killed in an accident. On 20 June, 1928 an Italian search plane found the remains of the airship and three days later Nobile was rescued by a Swedish freighter. His companions were salvaged by a Russian icebreaker on 13 July. On his return to Italy, Nobile was found responsible for the accident by the Italian aviation authorities and was discharged from the army.

In 1932 he went to Moscow, where he worked as an aeronautical advisor to the Russian government. Four years later Mussolini called him back to Italy; after the war he was a Communist member of parliament for several years.

Further reading
Die Vorbereitungen und die wissenschaftlichen Ergebnisse der Polarexpedition der "Italia", ed. U. Nobile. Petermanns Mitteilungen. Gotha 1928
M. Gallian, I Segreti di Umberto Nobile. Rome 1928
E. Lundborg, The Arctic Rescue. How Nobile was saved (translated by A. L. Olson). New York 1929
U. Nobile, Im Luftschiff zum Nordpol. Without place of publication 1930
W. Meyer, Der Kampf um Nobiles Versuch einer objektiven Darstellung und Wertung der Leistungen des italienischen Luftschiffers. Berlin 1931
E. Dithmer, The truth about Nobile (Including a preface to Nobile's book "In volo alla conquista des segreto polare" (translated from the Danish). London 1933
U. Nobile, Posso dire la verità. Storia inedita della spedizione polare dell'"Italia". Verona 1944
H. Straub, Nobile, der Pol-Pionier. Zurich 1985

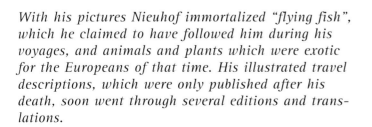

With his pictures Nieuhof immortalized "flying fish", which he claimed to have followed him during his voyages, and animals and plants which were exotic for the Europeans of that time. His illustrated travel descriptions, which were only published after his death, soon went through several editions and translations.

Umberto Nobile (left) und Nils Adolf Nordenskiöld (right)

NORDENSKIÖLD, NILS ADOLF ERIK

Swedish Arctic explorer and natural scientist, born 1832 in Helsinki, died 1901 in Dalbö, Lund.

Nordenskiøld studied natural sciences, but he was forced to leave Finland for political reasons and moved to Stockholm, where he turned to Arctic research. In 1858 the young scholar took part in the Torrell Spitsbergen expedition, in 1861 he discovered hitherto unknown islands in the Northeastland group. In 1868, he reached the northernmost latitude ever attained by an Arctic explorer in his ship "Sofia" and in 1872 he explored extensive areas of the Greenland interior ice on a reindeer sleigh. Three years later he explored the mouth of the Dvina.

Nordenskiøld's plan to cross Lake Kara and the Laptev Sea as well as the East Siberian Sea and to explore the almost 6,000 km (3,730 mile) North Siberian coastline interested both Russian merchants and the Swedish Royal Family.

After months of intensive preparation, on 18 July, 1878 the ice-resistant "Vega" set sail from Tromsø under the command of captain Palander, along with the "Lena" and two supply ships. The undertaking was financed by the Swedish king, by Baron Dickson and by the Russian merchant Sibirikovn. In addition to Swedish engineers, scientists and seal hunters, the Russian lieutenant Nordqvist, the Italian officer Bove and lieutenant Hovgaard from the Danish Navy took part in this trip.

By the end of July Nordenskiøld had reached Yugor Strait and by 6 August, Dicksonhafen, where Sibirikov's ships, the "Express" and the "Fraser", sailed up the Yenissei, passing Cape Chelyuskin through the Laptev Sea. The "Vega" reached the mouth of the Lena without incident, where the "Lena" explored the river of the same name. 200 km (120 miles) short of the Bering Strait, Nordenskiøld's bold journey was stopped by ice masses. The "Vega" was enclosed by ice in Koljucinskaya Bay from 28 September, 1878 until 18 July, 1879. Nordenskiøld used this time to study the customs and habits of the Chutches and the Samoyeds as well as the flora and fauna of eastern Siberia. When the ship was freed from the ice, Nordenskiøld reached Bering's target of Serdezh Kamen and two days later rounded the Asian North Cape.

On the coast of the Bering Strait the crew witnessed the gruesome killing of 12,000 seals, and

Inuit sledge

from Port Clarence (North American coast) the scientist set course for home via Japan, Ceylon and around the Cape of Good Hope. The crew reached the Swedish capital in good health on 24 July, 1880. That same year, Nordenskiøld was raised to nobility and the Laptev Sea was renamed "Nordenskiøld Sea".

Nils Adolf Erk Nordenskiøld opened up the first north polar trading route and proved that with the right equipment and detailed preparations, it was possible to conquer the arduous Northeast Passage without damage. His geographical, ethnographic and hydrographic research work gave him his well-deserved scientific reputation.

Further reading
A. E. Nordenskiöld, Vegas förd kring Asien och Europa. 2 Vols. Without place of publication 1880-1881

Nordenskiöld's "Vega".

–, Die Umseglung Asiens und Europas auf der Vega. Without place of publication 1882
Lt. Hovgaard, Nordenskiölds voyage around Asia and Europe. London 1882
S. Hedin, Adolf Erik Nordenskiöld. Without place of publication 1926
A. E. Nordenskiöld, Nordostwärts. Die erste Umsegelung Asiens und Europas 1878-1880, ed. H. J. Aubert. Stuttgart 1987

ORBIGNY, ALCIDE DESSALINE D'

French researcher and botanist, born 1802 in Couëron, died 1857 in Pierrefitte-sur-Seine.

Alcide D'Orbigny studied the natural sciences. In 1826 he was commissioned to carry out an exploratory expedition to South America despite the limited nature of funds available for this undertaking. For eight years he traveled through Peru, Chile, Bolivia, Argentina and the south of Brazil. During these extended journeys he identified 6,900 animal and 1,500 plant species and sketched a precise map of the mountain region.

On his return to France he published his most important work "L'Homme Américain" in 1839, in which he described the Indian tribes of Peru and Brazil and demonstrated that climate and altitude have effects on the human species.

Besides Humbolt, D'Orbigny is one of the great scientific explorers of South America. Making a personal fortune through precious metal finds was not in the botanist's interests. He spoke

Argentina, in this case Patagonia, was one of D'Orbigny's main areas of research.

out for the emancipation of the native peoples from the white dictators, lived for some time among the legendary "Gauchos", gathered enlightening information about the Aymaras, the former upholders of the Tiahuanaca culture, and about the Quechuas, from whom the Incas are said to have descended. D'Orbigny is regarded as the founder of "scientific Americanistics".

Further reading
A. d'Orbigny, Voyage dans l'Amérique
méridionale, le Brésil, la République
argentine, la Patagonie, la République
du Chili, la République du Pérou
exécuté dans le cours des années 1826,
1827, 828, 1830, 1831, 1832 et 1833.
Paris 1835

ORELLANA, FRANCISCO DE

Spanish conquistador, born c. 1500 in Trujillo (Spain), died c. 1546 in the Amazon region.

Orellana took part in the conquest of Peru under the Pizarros. He then turned to Gonzalo Pizarro, who devised the plan of conquering "all the land to the east of the Andes". The Spanish expected to find rich gold mines (Eldorado) in this vast rainforest region.

In 1539 Orellana took part in the historically significant and unparalleled campaign of Gonzalo Pizarro, who initiated the conquest of the Amazon region. Accompanied by several hundred Indian soldiers, Orellana and Pizarro set out from Quito across the "Cordillera de los Andes" (Spanish name for the Andes) into the Brazilian

Orellana claimed to have encountered these mythical figures on his journey by raft through the Amazon region – the Amazons, who eventually gave the river its name.

The Amazon winds its way through the green hell of the jungle.

heartland, and after unspeakable exertion they reached the valley of Río Napo (left tributary of the Amazon). On their journey to this valley the two conquistadors had lost virtually all of the highland Indians, who were unable to cope with the different climatic conditions. They built a raft and sailed across the Río Napo to the point where the Aguarico flows into the Napo.

When Gonzalo Pizarro heard from the natives of the existence of a fertile stretch of land on the mouth of the Curaray, he sent Orellana to carry out the necessary exploratory work. During this time Pizarro set up a fortified camp in the middle of the rainforest. When Orellana had not returned to the camp after several weeks, Pizarro organized an exploratory and search expedition which covered almost 500 km (300 miles); however he was forced to abandon the search and only reached Quito with extreme effort in June 1542.

However, Orellana was the first European to sail the entire river, which he named "Amazon" (in honor of the female warriors of the region), and on 24 August, 1542, after a strenuous journey down the river lasting eight months, he reached the open Atlantic.

When he returned to Spain, Charles V granted Orellana permission to set up a colony in the newly discovered land. In 1544 the conquistador returned to "New Spain". While attempting to repeat his remarkable journey in the opposite direction he died of exhaustion not far from what is today the town of Manaus (on the left bank of the Río Negro).

Orellana is regarded as the pioneer of exploration along the world's largest river and of the conquest of Brazil.

Further reading
R. Müller, Orellana's Discovery of the Amazon River. Guyaquil 1937
E. Jos, Centenario del Amazonas: La expedición de Orellana y sus problemas históricos (Revista de Indias, year 3, No. 10, year 4, No. 11 and 12). Without place of publication 1942
L. Benites Vinueza, Argonautas de la Selva (An account of the exploration an conquests of F. de Orellana). Mexiko 1945

OVERWEG, ADOLF

German explorer of Africa, born 1822 in Hamburg, died 1852 in Maduari (Lake Chad).

In 1850 the British government commissioned Dr. Overweg to accompany the Englishman James Richardson and the German Africa explorers Heinrich Barth on an expedition to Sudan. Setting out from Tripoli, they traveled via Mursuk, Ghat and Agadès, reaching Sudan in early January 1851. They separated in the village of Taghelel, intending to join up again at the start of April in Kuka on Lake Chad.

Richardson died en route to Zinder (traveling in a southeasterly direction) in late February 1851. Barth and Overweg proceeded southwest and separated after a few days. Overweg crossed the region to the west of Bornu to Tessaua (today on the Niamey-Zinder highway) and then concentrated on exploring Lake Chad, on which he was the first European to sail. In September 1851 Overweg and Barth took part in a foray of the Uelad-Sliman Arabs to Kanem-Bornu before returning to Kuka. After wandering across the Bauchi plateau (mountainous region of Nigeria) Overweg undertook an expedition to the region of Kuka. Suffering from fever, he reached Kuka, but died in Maduari on Lake Chad aged only 30.

Overweg's chief accomplishments are his geographical research of Lake Chad and his ethnological findings about the Budumas, a tribe living on the islands in Lake Chad.

Further reading
C. Ritter, Über Dr. H. Barths und Dr. Overwegs Begleitung der J. Richardsonschen Reiseexpedition zum Tschadsee und in das innere Afrika (with map). Berlin 1850
J. Hogg, Norice of recent discoveries in Central Africa by Dr. Barth and Dr. Overweg. London 1852
K. v. Schleucher, Frühe Wege zum Herzen Afrikas. Without place of publication 1969

P

PALLAS, PETER-SIMON

German-Russian explorer of Asia, born 1741 in Berlin, died 1811 in Berlin.

Pallas studied medicine, natural sciences and foreign languages in Halle, Göttingen and Leiden. He spent several extended periods in London and The Hague. He also published numerous discourses on zoology and botany.

In 1768 Pallas traveled to St. Petersburg on the invitation of the Academy of Russian Sciences, where he was commissioned by Catherine II to discover and to describe the "riches" of Siberia. For six long years Pallas traveled throughout the vast czarist realm as a scholar, observer, politician and scientist.

Setting out from Moscow, he traveled to the land of the Mordvins. He was the first to describe the ruins of Bolgar (the ancient capital of the Bulgarian kingdom on the Volga), spent the winter in Simbirskiy, researched the ruins of Saraychik, crossed the land of the Bashkir and spent a second winter in Ufa (on the Belaya). He continued through the entire Ural region, visited Yekaterinburg and Tobolsk, followed the course of the Irtysch near Omsk, sighted Krasnoyarsk (Yenissei) and Irkutsk (Lena), sailed on the world's deepest lake, Lake Baikal, and advanced to the upper course of the Amur. On 30 July, 1774 he arrived back in St. Petersburg. His geological, geographical, ethnological and historical research exceeded all expectations of the scientific committee of the St. Petersburg Academy.

In 1783, accompanied by his wife and daughter, the aging explorer undertook an expedition to the Volga region. They visited Astrakhan on the Caspian Sea, wandered through Tauria (now Crimea), returned to St. Petersburg after almost two years and settled in Crimea.

Plagued with homesickness, the almost seventy-year-old left the peninsula and returned to Berlin, where he died on 8 September, 1811.

Pallas's geographical, ethnological and above all his economic studies did not merely represent a significant advance in these disciplines; they also contributed to Russia's rapid conquest of Siberia.

Further reading
P. S. Pallas, Reise durch verschiedene Provinzen des Russischen Reiches in einem ausführlichen Auszuge. Frankfurt and Leipzig 1776-1778
–, Voyage en Sibérie. Bern 1791 (?)
–, Physikalisch-topographisches Gemälde von Taurien. St. Petersburg 1796
–, Bemerkungen auf einer Reise in die südlichen Statthalterschaften des Russischen Reiches, in den Jahren 1773 und 1794. Leipzig 1799-1801
J. Trusler, The Habitable World described. Or the present state of the people in all the parts of the globe collected from the earliest and latest accounts of historians and travellers of all nations. Vol. 2. Dublin 1788

PAPANIN, IVAN DIMITRIYEVITCH

Soviet Arctic explorer, born 1894 in Sevastopol, died 1986.

Following the unheavals of the Russian revolution, Papanin committed his life to the exploration of the Arctic. From 1932 to 1933 he was in charge of the Arctic stations at Spitsbergen and from 1934 to 1935 at Cape Chelyuskin, on the Taymyr Peninsula, the northernmost point on the Asian mainland. He was then appointed head of the drifting Arctic station "North Pole 1".

Under the leadership of Professor O. J. Schmidt, the four participants – the hydrobiologist P. P. Shirshov, the geophysicist E. K. Fyodorov, the radio operator Krenkel and Papanin – were flown with their heavy equipment to a position of 89° 25' N and 78° 40' W with four large aircraft on 21 May, 1937. The team was only a few kilometers from the North Pole.

Before landing, the aircraft tossed heavy weights on to the ice to ensure that it could bear their weight. They then landed on an ice floe 1.5 km (1 mile) long and almost 3 m (10 feet) thick. After setting up the accommodation, observation and stock tents, the aircraft left the polar station on 6 June, 1937. The triangular ice floe, with sides 3 to 4 km (3 miles) in length, drifted in the direction of the Atlantic at varying speeds. On 19 February, 1938 the immense floe reached the southeast coast of Greenland. Papanin and his men had taken 274 days to cover 2,000 km (1,200 miles); they were then picked up by the icebreakers "Murman" and "Taymir". During this journey they had explored and researched hitherto uncharted waters and carried

out 150 astronomical determinations of their geographical position. Papanin had continued and supplemented Nansen's invaluable observations of the ice drifts and ocean depths and currents. Life was also discovered in the vicinity of the North Pole.

After returning from the Arctic, Papanin headed the administration of the Northeast Passage. On the basis of Papanin's "North Pole 1 Station" an entire series of observation stations were established after 1950.

Further reading
O. J. Schmidt, Die Arbeiten der Station Nordpol. Russian edition. Without place of publication 1940
I. Papanin, Das Leben auf der Eisscholle. Ein Tagebuch. Without place of publication 1947

PARK, MUNGO

Scottish surgeon and explorer of Africa, born 1771 in Fowlshields, died 1806 in Bussa on the Niger (western Africa).

Mungo Park

Chronicle of the North Pole expeditions before Papanin

1553 Briton Hugh Willoughby attempts to find the Northeast Passage, but dies while spending the winter on Kola.

1594 Dutchman Willem Barents is unable to find the Northwest Passage on any of his three voyages.

1616 Briton William Baffin advances further into the Arctic than anyone before him.

1725 Dane Vitus Bering discovers Alaska and explores the Siberian coast.

1819 John Franklin explores coastal sections of the Northwest Passage.

1831 James Clarke Ross determines the position of the North Magnetic Pole.

1878 Adolf Nordenskiöld is the first person to sail the Northeast Passage.

1888 Fridtjof Nansen is the first man to cross Greenland's ice sheet on skis.

1903 Roald Amundsen is the first person to sail the entire Northwest Passage.

1926 Amundsen, Nobile and Ellsworth are the first to fly over the North Pole in an airship.

The explorer's life was full of tribulations: Mungo Park and his crew can be seen here crossing the Black River on a rickety wooden bridge.

Park studied medicine. In 1793 he took part in a voyage to Sumatra, from which he returned with many hitherto unknown, exotic fish species.

On the commission of the London African Association in 1795, he undertook his first scientific exploratory expedition to the Niger. He learned the Mandingu language. Arabian slave traders took him captive; however, he was able to escape. With a high fever he reached the town of Silla, around 500 km (300 miles) from the legendary city of Timbuktu. There, he attempted in vain to obtain more information concerning the further course of the Niger. In the trail of a caravan, he reached Pisania, the starting point of his journey in June. Two years later Park published an account of his western African experiences in London.

In 1805, despite numerous warnings, Park undertook his second journey to the Niger. Accompanied by his brother-in-law and thirty soldiers, he set out from Pisania (Nigeria) in the direction of Senegambia. By the time they arrived in Ségou, a town in the Bambarra region, Park's team had been reduced to just eight men. On 16 November he sailed the longest Niger meander on a pirogue. Amadi, his native guide, left him after just several days. In his last letter to reach London, he wrote that the Niger did not flow into Lake Chad as had been assumed, but in fact flowed to the south. Nothing more was then heard from the explorer.

Five years after Park had disappeared without a trace, an expedition sent out by the African Association was only able to establish that the explorer and his few remaining companions had been ambushed and killed. Whether Park was killed by the riverside inhabitants or by his own companions or whether he drowned in the rapids near Bussa Falls has never been determined.

Mungo Park was the first European to explore the Niger further than the city of Timbuktu and to recognize that the Niger is an independent river system. He thus disproved the theory that the Niger flowed into Lake Chad in inner Africa.

Further reading
M. Park, Travels in the interior of districts of Africa. London 1799.
F. de Lenoye, Le Niger et les explorations de l'Afrique Centrale depuis Mungo Park jusqu'au Docteur Barth. Paris 1858

*M. Park, Reisen ins Innerste Afrika 1795-1806. Newly published by H. Pleticha. Tübingen 1976
K. Lupton, Mungo Park. Wiesbaden 1980*

PARRY, SIR WILLIAM EDWARD

English seafarer, discoverer and Arctic explorer, born 1790 in Bath, died 1855 in Bad Ems.

In 1803 Parry joined the Royal Navy and five years later, as second officer, accompanied the polar explorer Sir John Ross on his journey to the Arctic waters.

In 1819 he was commissioned by the British Admiralty to find the Northwest Passage. With two ships, the "Hecla" and the "Griper" (commanded by Liddon), Parry sailed through the Davis Strait on 4 July and reached Cape Byam Martin in the south of Lancaster Bay without incident. Here he discovered that Lancaster Bay was in fact a strait between North Devon Land and Baffin Land, which he named "Barrow Strait", and formed the southern arm of the Prince Regent Strait. As the compass no longer functioned reliably as they sailed into Lancaster Bay, the explorer realized that he was not far from the North Magnetic Pole. On 5 August Parry discovered the Leopold Islands, and a short time later he landed on the small island of Beechey. Continuing on his journey, he discovered the entrance to the Wellington Channel, the islands of Cornwallis, Bathurst and Melville, which he named the "Georgian Islands" (in honor of King George III) and which were called the "Parry Islands" by geographers. The further north Parry sailed into Baffin Bay, the larger the pack ice became and the smaller the icebergs. He spent the winter in Port Winter on Melville Island, which he explored in June 1820 with a small team. In July, Parry decided to continue his journey, reaching 74° 26' N and 113° 47' W before having to turn back.

In 1821 Parry made a renewed attempt to find the Northwest Passage. With the "Hecla" and the "Fury" (commanded by Lyon) he reached Hecla Bay on Southampton Island. He spent the winter there and studied the customs of the Arctic inhabitants.

On his third trip to the North American Arctic in 1824 he lost the "Fury" near Somerset Island.

In 1827 Parry attempted to reach the North Pole from Svalbard (Spitsbergen) and ventured as far as 82° 45' N, around 800 km (500 miles) from the North Pole.

Although Parry did not sail through the Northwest Passage or discover the North Pole, his Arctic journeys brought some clarity to the many islands of North Canadian waters. His geographical discoveries, his scientific studies of the Arctic inhabitants and his new techniques for surviving the winter in polar waters (strict discipline in the camp, practical activities, effective measures against scurvy) put him among the ranks of the great geographers, ethnographers and Arctic specialists.

*Further reading
Sir W. E. Parry, Journal of a Voyage of Discovery to the Arctic Regions 1818. London 1820*

Sir William Edward Parry

For protection against the wind, the Inuit built shelters of snow. This way, they could sit and fish for hours on end.

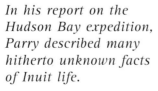

In his report on the Hudson Bay expedition, Parry described many hitherto unknown facts of Inuit life.

–, Journal of a Second Voyage to the Discovery of a North-West Passage from the Atlantic to Pacific, performed in the years of 1821, 1822, 1823 in H. M. S. "Fury" and "Hecla". London 1824-1825
–, Journal of a third Voyage to the Discovery of a North-West Passage from the Atlantic to Pacific performed in the years of 1824 and 1825 in H. M. S. "Fury" and "Hecla". London 1826
–, Narrative of an Attempt to reach the North Pole in Boats. London 1828
S. M. Schmucker, Arctic Explorations and Discoveries during the nineteenth century, being accounts of the expeditions to the North Seas. Conducted by Ross, Parry, Back, Franklin, McClure and others. New York and Auburn 1857

PAVIE, AUGUSTE

French explorer of Asia, born 1847 in Dinan, died 1925 in Thourie (Ile-et-Vilaine).

For a long time Pavie worked as a telegraph officer in small military posts of Kâmpôt in the southwest of Cambodia, before being commissioned by the French government to carry out several missions, including an expedition to the Gulf of Siam and Lake Tonlé-Sap as well as terrain studies for the construction of a telegraph line from Phnom Penh to Bangkok. At the same time, Pavie was to chart the whole of Cambodia. During these extended expeditions, in addition to making a large number of geographical and ethnographic findings, he persuaded the Cambodians to work together with the French authorities.

In 1886 he was appointed Vice Consul in Louangphrabang (northern Laos). Through his skilled negotiations, he persuaded the Laotian aristocracy to recognize French sovereignty over the Meos and Thai mountain peoples. In 1887 he successfully negotiated with Siam, which signed over the left bank of the Mekong to France.

By the time Pavie was called back to France in 1895, he had explored the whole of Indochina (Vietnam, Laos and Cambodia). Pavie's cartographic works of Indochina are of significant scientific value. He is regarded as the "peaceful conqueror" of Indochina and did great service to secure peace in this area.

Further reading
E. Grenard, Mission Pavie. Paris 1879-1895
P. P. Curet, Voyages en Laos, Indochine, par
A. Pavie (Mission Pavie, Géographie et Voyages).
Without place of publication 1900
P. Lefèvre-Pontalis, Voyages dans le Haut-Laos.
Introduction par A. Pavie. Paris 1902
E. Diguet, Les Montagnards du Tonkin. Paris
1908
A. Pavie, La conquête des cœurs. Le pays des
millions d'éléphants et du parasol blanc. Paris
1921
–, Eine friedliche Eroberung. Indochina 1888.
Tübingen 1967

PAYER, JULIUS RITTER VON

Austrian Arctic explorer, born 1841 in Teplitz-Schönau, died 1915 in Veldes.

From 1857 to 1859, Julius Payer attended the Theresian Military Academy in Vienna. In the years 1859 and 1867, he took part in the battles of Solferino and Custozza. Before turning his attention to Arctic research, he undertook extensive mountain expeditions to the Adamella, Presanella and Ortler Alps.

In 1869-70 he was a member of the second German Arctic expedition to Greenland and in

Julius Ritter von Payer

1871 (together with Karl Weyprecht) he participated in the "Isbjörn expedition". On 14 July, 1872 Payer and Weyprecht left the Norwegian port of Tromsø in the direction of the North Pole (see Weyprecht).

After this historically significant journey to the North Pole, Payer turned his attention to painting.

Parry also observed the Arctic fauna. The engraving from his book shows the mighty walrus.

A dramatic situation on Peary's expedition to Franz Joseph Land: A dogsled has plunged into an ice crevasse.

Further reading
J. v. Payer, Die Österreichisch-Ungarische Nordpol-Expedition der Jahre 1872-1874. Vienna 1876

PEARY, ROBERT EDWIN

American naval officer and discoverer of the North Pole, born 1856 in Cresson, died 1920 in Washington D. C.

In 1881 Peary joined the Navy as a marine engineer. He spent several years in Nicaragua and Panama. Peary's studies of scientific discourses about the interior ice fields of Greenland awakened in him the urge to explore the Arctic region.

In 1886 he sailed to Greenland in the "Eagle" and, accompanied by a Dane who lived on the island, traveled far into the interior of the country.

Five years later he undertook his first scientific expedition to Greenland together with his wife. As he advanced into the "Inglefield Gulf" (on the northwest coast of Greenland) his ship, the "Kite", became enclosed in pack ice and was unable to continue. Together with his Norwegian companion E. Astrup, Robert Peary then crossed northern Greenland from west to east and back, thus proving that Greenland was, in fact, an island.

Between 1893 and 1906 Peary explored the Arctic region and waters, studied the customs and lifestyle of the inhabitants of the area and advanced increasingly further towards the North Pole. The US government became interested in Peary's plan and provided him with the "Theodore Roosevelt", a 1,500 ton motor boat especially constructed for Arctic waters, in which he left New York in July 1908.

When Peary had sailed through the Robeson Channel on his way to the North Pole and the ice became increasingly hazardous, he decided to spend the winter on Cape Columbia (Ellesmere Land), 640 km (400 miles) from the North Pole. On 1 March, 1909 he started out on his trek to the Pole. One month later he had covered more than 160 km (100 miles) and was just 260 km (160 miles) from his goal. On 6 April Peary and his five companions, four of whom were Inuit, finally reached the North Pole. Whether he really reached the pole at that time is still a matter of controversy to the present day. New photogrammetric examination of pictures taken at his destination suggest that he did actually reach his goal. F. A. Cook claims to have conquered the North Pole on 21 April, 1908.

After his promotion to rear admiral in 1911 Peary retired from public life.

Peary's success was mainly due to his detailed preparations and his conviction that he would be able to reach the North Pole with the help of experienced local Inuit, who knew the terrain. His cartographic sketches of the east coast of Greenland do not invariably correspond to the actual

Left: Robert E. Peary in his Arctic outfit.
Right: The triumphant Peary hoists the US flag at the North Pole.

coastline and have given rise to some justified criticism over the years.

Further reading
R. E. Peary, Northward over the "Great Ice" in the years 1886 and 1891-1897, 2 Vols. New York 1898
-, Nearest the Pole 1905-1906. New York 1907
-, The discovery of the North Pole. Without place of publication 1910
-, Secrets of Polar Travel. New York 1917
W. H. Hobbs, Peary (Biographie). New York 1936

D. Rawlins, Peary at the North Pole. Washington 1973
R. E. Peary, Die Entdeckung des Nordpols 1908-1909. Stuttgart 1981

PELLIOT, PAUL

French researcher and sinologist, born 1878 in Paris, died 1945 in Paris.

Pelliot was Professor of Sinology at the "Ecole Française d'Extrême Orient". From 1906 to 1908, accompanied by the cartographer Dr. Vaillant, he

Carl Peters and his companions make their way through the African jungle.

Kuchar oasis. There, Pelliot found ancient manuscripts, early Chinese coins and funerary caskets, while Dr. Vaillant charted the oasis. In October 1907 the expedition reached the capital of the province Urumqi (Ti-hua), where Pelliot was greeted very cordially due to his knowledge of the Chinese and Turkish languages. In December the group reached Touen-huang, in the far west of Kansu.

Around 20 km (12 miles) from this town, by sheer chance Pelliot discovered the "Thousand Buddhas" grottos. In these caves he found around 15,000 ancient Chinese manuscripts from the time prior to the great Mongolian invasion (1035) and several paintings on silk and hemp, which are today exhibited in the Louvre in Paris. Paul Pelliot's significant findings now enabled the sinologists to work with original material and many unsettled points in Chinese history were able to be clarified; and it is thanks to Dr. Vaillant's cartographic records that last blank spots on the map of Chinese Turkestan were filled in.

Further reading
P. Pelliot, Mission en Asie centrale.
Paris 1920-1921

PETERS, CARL

German Africa explorer, born 1856 in Neuhaus on the Elbe, died 1918 in Bad Harzburg.

Carl Peters studied history and geography at the Universities of Göttingen, Tübingen and Berlin. He was a pupil of Georg Waitz and grew up in the Chauvinistic atmosphere of the German unification. He gained his degree in 1879; nevertheless, he did not apply for a position as a university lecturer. For some time he lived a rather withdrawn life, teaching at a private girls' school in Hanover and awaiting his "fate", which he was convinced would be something out of the ordinary.

In 1881 he went to London, where he came into contact with an open and politicized socie-

undertook a scientific journey to Chinese Turkestan, from Kaschgar to Kansu. Setting out from Tashkent (Siberia) and traveling via Osh, within nine days the expedition had passed the Pamir Mountains. They reached Kaschgar, the first major town in Chinese Turkestan, 28 days later. The next stage of their journey was the

ty – as opposed to that which he had left behind him in the Hohenzollern dynasty. On his return to Hanover he published his philosophical work "Willenswelt und Weltwille" (World of volition and volition of the world).

In 1882 he traveled to London a second time to attend his uncle's funeral. During the year he spent in the English capital he became acquainted with the British author Stacey, who told him of the gold reserves in Mashonaland (East Rhodesia). In 1884 he made a proposal to the German Foreign Office to colonize Mashonaland. However, in July Chancellor Bismarck informed him that the German Reich recognized the region to the south of the River Zambezi as British territory.

When Peters then made the same proposal to the president of the Colonial Society, Prince von Hohenlohe, he received the reply that the society did not practice colonization. Eventually Count Behr-Bandelin responded to Peters' proposal to found a "Society for German Colonization". Around 30 members were invited to join this exclusive club. Its so-called "four-point program" was to pursue a dynamic colonial policy; to expedite German colonization in order to prevent other nations accessing the few remaining "free" regions in Africa; for the German government to take practical steps to show the German people the direction of colonial expansion; and to convince the members of the necessity of the society.

According to Peters, a dynamic colonial policy would compensate for the "negligence" of the last two centuries in regard to colonization.

However, in the meantime Peters had tired of the government's indecision. Accompanied by Dr. C. Jühlke, Count Pfeil and his fellow countryman A. Otto, Peters traveled to the east African coast, from where he traveled to the interior of the continent with an escort of 36 armed porters, five servants and an interpreter and concluded no less than a dozen contracts with the local potentates.

Peters' expedition had immediate political consequences: Bismarck had warships sail to the coast of Zanzibar. East Africa was split into two: The British were given Kenya and Uganda, while the Germans took German East Africa.

In 1887 Peters took part in an expedition to liberate Emin Pasha. In 1891 he was appointed Imperial Commissioner for the Kilimanjaro region. From 1899 to 1901 he explored the region between the Zambezi and the Sabi (a river in former Rhodesia, today Zimbabwe).

Peters is regarded as the founder of German East Africa.

Further reading
C. Peters, Willenswelt und Weltwille. Leipzig 1883
–, Deutsch-National. Berlin 1887
–, Die deutsche Emin-Pascha-Expedition. Munich, Leipzig 1891
–, New Light on Dark Africa. London 1891
–, Äquatorial- und Südafrika nach einer Darstellung von 1719. Without place of publication 1895
–, Im Goldlande des Altertums. Forschungen zwischen Zambezi und Sabi. Munich 1902

PICCARD, AUGUSTE

Swiss physicist, born 1884 in Basle, died 1962 in Lausanne.

In 1931 Auguste Piccard and his assistant F. Kipfer carried out the first stratospheric flight in a hot-air balloon. Starting from Augsburg in southern Germany, they reached a height of 15,781 meters (51,775 feet). In a later flight from Zurich in 1932 his balloon reached a maximum height of 16,940 meters or 55,577 feet (acknowledged by the FAI as 16,201 meters or 53,135 feet). In 1934 his twin brother Jean Félix Piccard reached a height of almost 17,500 meters (57,400 feet) in a balloon.

From 1947 Auguste Piccard carried out deep sea experiments and in 1953 he reached a depth of 3,150 m (10,335 feet) in the deep sea diving device "Bathyscaphe" (the first of its type).

Deep-sea exploration before Piccard

1521 During his circumnavigation of the Earth, Fernando Magellan attaches an iron ball to a 700 m (2,300 ft) rope and finds that it does not touch the ocean floor.

1818 In the North Atlantic, species of worms and jellyfish are brought to the surface from a depth of 1,800 m (5,900 ft).

1857 The first transatlantic telegraph cable is laid between Ireland and Newfoundland.

1875 A depth of 8,341 m (27,365 ft) is sounded near the Antilles, and 9,427 m (30,928 ft) in the Pacific.

1898 Under the leadership of Karl Chun, a steamship sets out across the Atlantic and the Indian Ocean and brings back rocks and marine animals. It took until 1940 for all the finds to be analysed.

1925 A comprehensive picture of the bed of the Atlantic is made for the first time with the help of the sonic depth finder developed by Alexander Behm.

1934 William Beebe and Otis Barton have themselves lowered to a depth of 800 m (2,620 ft) below the ocean surface in a steel sphere.

1938 In South Africa, a lungfish presumed extinct for 65 million years is drawn out of the water.

1947 Jacques Cousteau brings the undersea world to television with his first recordings.

PICCARD, JACQUES

Swiss ocean researcher, son of Auguste Piccard, born 1922 in Brussels.

In 1960 in the diving boat "Trieste" Jacques Piccard reached a depth of 10,912 m (35,801 feet) in the Mariana Trench and brought back proof that it is possible for higher life forms to exist even in the deepest parts of the ocean. With Jacques Piccard's assistance, deep sea diving boats were constructed for tourist purposes in 1964.

Further reading
Prominente in der Umweltdiskussion. Beiträge
zum III. Internationalen WWF-Kongreß.
Berlin 1974
J. Piccard, Logbuch aus der Meerestiefe.
Stuttgart 1975

PINTO, ALEXANDER ALBERTO DA ROCHA SERPA

Portuguese Africa explorer, born 1846 in Tendais (Cinfaes), died 1900 in Lisbon.

Pinto studied in Lisbon and joined the Portuguese Army in 1864. From 1877 to 1879 he traveled through Mozambique and the region around the upper Zambezi. Setting out from Bihé (mountainous region in Angola) in May he undertook his extensive east-to-west crossing of South Africa. During this unparalleled research expedition, he explored the region around the sources of the Cuanza and the Cubango, explored the banks of the Uhengo to the point where it flows into the Zambezi, sailed down the Zambezi, overcame numerous cataracts, undertook an additional excursion to the Kalahari Desert and advanced as far as the Victoria Falls. He spent some time at the Shoshong missionary station and returned via Pretoria.

In 1889 Alexander Pinto was appointed Governor-General of Mozambique. That same year he explored the Chire, the main tributary of the Zambezi. When as Governor General he suggested uniting Angola with Mozambique, the

British government asked for Lisbon to call him home as they believed such a plan posed a serious threat of interrupting the continuous "Cairo–Cape" line.

This scientifically trained officer and explorer almost completely clarified the geographical conditions of central Africa. His astronomical observations were extraordinarily accurate.

PINZÓN, VICENTE YÁNEZ

Spanish seafarer, born c. 1460, died after 1520.

As captain of the "Niña", Pinzón accompanied Columbus in 1492 on his first journey to the New World, and on 6 June, 1499 he was commissioned to carry out a exploratory voyage of his own; however, he was not permitted to hinder either the Portuguese or Columbus. In November 1499 he set sail from Palos (Spain) and was the first Spaniard to cross the equator. On 26 January, 1500 he set foot on the South American coast at Cape Augustine. He can thus legitimately be regarded as the discoverer of Brazil, as the Portuguese Pedro A. Cabral did not arrive there until three months later. Pinzón took possession of the country for Spain and then sailed northwards. He discovered the mouth of the Amazon and returned to Spain via Hispaniola (Haiti), arriving home in September 1500.

In 1508 and 1509 Pinzón and Juan Díaz de Solís led another expedition to central America, where they were commissioned to find the passage to India. Traveling along the coast from Honduras and Yucatán they probably reached the Mexican town of Tampico, but they were unable to find a direct sea route to the Pacific.

PIZARRO, FRANCISCO

Spanish conquistador, born 1475 in Trujillo, died 1541 in Lima. Pizarro came from an aristocratic family. He had no formal education and traveled to Central America at the age of 30 and took part in the expeditions of Ojeda (1509) and

N. de Balboa (1513). After trying his hand at cattle-breeding for some time in Panama, he came up with the bold plan of conquering Peru, a country rich in precious metals. Diego de Almagro and the clergyman F. de Luque financed this undertaking. The inhospitable Peruvian coastline caused the expedition a great deal of difficulty. In 1524 the small group had only covered one-third of the overall journey and two years later reached the San-Juan River. Once he had landed on the island of Gallo, Pizarro was ordered to abandon his mission immediately. However, he chose to ignore this order. With thirteen volunteers he continued on his journey and reached the large, rich city of Tumbes (in northwestern Peru). The Spaniards' shining armor and dashing appearance amazed

The proud conquistador Francisco Pizarro

Facing page: Jacques Piccard presents his miniature submarine on Lake Geneva.

In the year 1528 Pizzaro proudly stands before the Council of India, asking for permission to acquire Peru and to keep it under his control.

the local population. As Pizarro's action still made no impression on the governor, he returned to Spain and presented himself to the king. In 1529, the king gave him permission to conquer Peru for the Spanish crown and to give it the name of "New Castilia".

On 13 May, 1531 Pizarro and his four brothers and half-brothers landed in Tumbes, where they founded the Spanish colony of San Miguel de Piura. At this time the Inca city was in the midst of a dynasty crisis, something which Pizarro put to his advantage. Atahualpa, the son of Huayna Capa and a concubine, had defeated the legal heir to the throne Huascar, the son of Huayna Capa and his legitimate wife, in the battle of Ambato (north of Quito) and taken him captive. He thus had unrestricted control over the united Inca empire. When Pizarro arrived, Atahualpa was visiting the hot sulfur springs of Cajamarca (380 km or 240 miles from Lima). He

believed the Spaniards to be returning gods, since according to legend the god of creation Tici Viracocha, who had once abandoned the people because he was dissatisfied with them, would return at some unspecified time. On the advice of his astrologers, the Inca emperor invited the conquistador into his palace. Pizarro trekked to Cajamarca with 106 soldiers and 62 riders along lavishly designed roads and suspension bridges, where he faced an army of 40,000 warriors. In this awkward situation, the Spaniard had to negotiate very quickly. He led the Inca leader into an ambush and had his bodyguard killed before personally taking the god-king captive on 16 November, 1532. The fall of their leader deprived the Incas of their will to fight. Pizarro promised the Inca leader that he would be released on payment of a large ransom. However, when the local population collected the money and brought it to Pizarro he had the Inca leader sen-

This engraving by Theodor de Bry documents the memorable meeting between Pizzaro, Diego de Almagro and Hernando de Luque in 1526 in Panama, where they decided to establish a "compaña".

tenced to death in an unjust trial. Atahualpa was strangled to death on 29 August, 1533.

By 1535 Peru was completely under the control of the Spanish. That year Pizarro founded the city of Ciudad de los Reyes (Lima), thus giving the "Gobernación de Nueva Castilla" (the government of New Castillia) a capital. He ruled the northern part of the conquered country, while his comrade-at-arms Almagro ruled the southern half. This distribution led to open military confrontation between the two rivals. Pizarro took Almagro prisoner and had him put to death. On 26 June, 1541 Pizarro was killed by Almagro's followers in Lima. The confrontation between the two parties did not end until the Spanish monarch had Peru placed under the direct control of the crown and appointed a viceroy to administer the country.

Francisco Pizarro takes a unique position among the Spanish conquistadors. This unedu-cated, callous and much-maligned adventurer did not merely conquer this enormous area for the Spanish colonial empire, he also saved the Spanish state treasury from imminent bankrupt-cy through the rich flow of silver and gold from Peru. However, Spain's power politics in Europe used up a large part of the South American revenue. Pizarro failed as a governor, as he had absolutely no idea of administrative technique. But his skills lay in the firmly disciplined way he ran his army and in his military strategy. He created the core of a flexible colonial army that was able to handle all that was put in its way, which secured Spain's rule on the South American continent for hundreds of years. In the city of Tumbes, the Spaniards became familiar for the first time with a culture not inferior to their own. The Incas, the "sons of the heavens" (aris-tocracy), had forced a type of agricultural com-munism on the Quechua and Aymara tribes. All

This engraving from 1673 shows a view of the mighty Peruvian city of Cuzco after its defeat by Pizzaro.

Atahualpa, king of the Incas, is taken prisoner.

The king of the Incas was brutally murdered by Pizzaro's men.

details of public and private life were regulated. Quechua was the official spoken language, while the official "written" language was Quipu, a system of knots practiced by the Quipucamayocs (civil servants). This highly educated people fell into political and cultural inactivity within only a few years of the Spanish invasion.

Further reading
Ternaux-Compans, Voyages, relations, mémoires originaux pour servir à la conquête de l'Amérique, 20 Vols. Paris 1837-1841
W. H. Prescott, History of the conquest of Peru, 3 Vols. Boston 1847
Fr. de Xeres, Verdadera Relación de la conquista del Perú. Libros, I. Madrid 1853
R. Altamira, Historia de España y la civilización española. Barcelona 1910-1911
C. Pereyra, Historia de América. Mexico 1920-1925
P. Pizarro, Relation of the discovery and Conquest of the Kingdoms of Peru. Translated and published by P. A. Means. 2 Vols. New York 1921
H. B. Bonte, Franzisco Pizarro. Der Sturz des Inkareiches. Leipzig 1925
H. Cunow, Geschichte und Kultur des Inkareiches. Amsterdam 1927
L. Baudin, Vie de François Pizarro. Paris 1930
F. A. Kirkpatrick, The Spanish Conquistadores. 2nd Ed. London 1946
J. Descola, Les conquistadors espagnols. Paris 1957

Das ist der edel Ritter · Marcho polo von Venedig der groſt landtfarer · der uns beſchreibt die groſſen wunder der welt die er ſelber geſehen hat · Von am auffgang biß zu dem nydergāg der ſunnē · der gleychē vor nicht mere gehort ſeyn

R. Manzano, *Los grandes conquistadores españoles*. Barcelona 1958

Fr. R. Majo, *Conquistadores españoles del siglo XVI*. Madrid 1963

Die Eroberung von Peru. Die Augenzeugenberichte von Celso Gargia, Gaspar de Carvajal, Samuel Fritz. Published by R. and E. Grün. Tübingen 1973

POLO, MARCO

Venetian merchant and globetrotter, born 1254 in Venice, died 1324 in Venice.

Marco Polo came from a family of merchants. His father Nicolò Polo and his uncle Matteo Polo had spent several years in the land of the Ilkhane (Iran and Iraq), the Golden and White Hordes and conducted lucrative business in the Muslim khanates of Chiva, Buchara and Kokand. The two Venetians had favorable relationships with Hülägü, a nephew of Genghis Khan, and the Great Khan Qubilai. Marco's "career" was thus more or less a matter of course.

The route which Marco Polo took on his voyage to the Far East is difficult to reconstruct, since in his travel diaries he frequently wrote of countries that he had never seen; his reports are thus based in part on mere assumptions.

In 1271, Marco Polo set out from Venice on board a ship (accompanying his father and uncle) to the port of Lajazzo (Armenia Minor), traveled through the south of the Rum Seljuk empire (southern Turkey), followed the course of the Tigris, visited Mossul and Baghdad, joined another ship in the Persian Gulf and finally landed in Hormuz. From this harbor town, Polo proceeded to Kerman, a trading town in the land of the Ilkhan, and then carried on to Balch (Afghan-Turkestan) and Kashgar (the khanate of Chaghatai). Traveling via Khotan and Hsiliang, he reached Khanbalik (Beijing), the capital of the Great Khan Qubilai (Khubilai), the founder of the Mongolian Yüan dynasty which ruled China up to 1368. Marco Polo spent 17 years in China. He learned the Mongolian language, but not Chinese. Placed in charge of several diplomatic missions, Marco Polo undertook extensive journeys to Burma, Tonkin and Annam.

His return journey via land and sea routes took him from Khanbalik through Kathai (northern China) to the port of Zaitun (today Chuan Chafu). He spent a short time on the island of Java. Traveling from Hormuz via Calicut (Malabar coast) and Somnath (Gudcherat, Gulf of Cambay) Marco Polo reached Trapezunt on the Black Sea by land. After almost quarter of a century, he arrived back in Venice in 1295, only to find that the celebrated travelers had been forgotten.

Facing page: Marco Polo as seen by a contemporary artist.
Above: Marco Polo's dwelling in Venice

In the course of the Genoese Venetian war Marco Polo ended up in prison. He used the time to dictate his travel reports to his fellow prisoner Rusticus von Pisa (1298-99).

Polo's Asian adventure, which was committed to paper in his "Travels", contained so many astounding reports that his contemporaries believed many of his tales to be mere fabrication. However, subsequent scientific research (by Yule and Pauthier) has shown that Polo's stories were in fact based on the truth.

The Venetian's travel tales were much read and discussed during the fourteenth, fifteenth and sixteenth centuries.

Of the three great medieval globetrotters (W. v. Rubruk, Carpini, Marco Polo), Marco Polo visited most countries of the Great Khan, covered the most distance, spent the longest time in Asia and brought to Europe the first specific historical and geographical reports about the Far East.

Further reading
M. Polo, Marco Polo Veneziano delle Maraviglie del Mondo da lui vedute. Genua 1298
Marshden, The travels of Marco Polo. London 1818
Pl. Zurla, Di Marco Polo e degli alteri viaggiatori piu illustri con appendice sulle antiche mappe idro-geografiche lavorate in Venezia. Venice 1818-1819
A. Bürck, Reisen des Marco Polo, with supplements by Neumann. Leipzig 1855
E. Charton, Voyageurs anciens et modernes ou choix des relations de voyages les plus intéressantes et les plus instructives. Vol 2. Paris 1857
Bianconi, Degli scritti di Marco Polo. Bologne 1862
Pauthier, Le livre de Marco Polo par Rusticien de Pise. Paris 1865
H. Yule, The book of Sir Marco Polo. London 1903
M. Polo, Von Venedig nach China. Die größte Reise des 13. Jahrhunderts, 9th Ed. Stuttgart 1986
H. Schreiber, Marco Polo. Karawanen nach Peking, 9th ed. Vienna/Heidelberg 1990
P. Marc, Marco Polos wunderbare Reisen. Zurich 1992
Marco Polo. Das Buch der Wunder. 84 Miniaturen. Lucerne 1995

Juan Ponce de Leon

PONCE DE LEON, JUAN

Spanish conquistador, born 1460, died 1521.

Ponce de Leon presumably took part in Columbus' second voyage. In 1502 he was on Hispaniola (Haiti) and belonged to the entourage of the local governor, until he was replaced by Diego, son of Columbus. In the year 1513 he set out on a new journey and reached Florida. Puerto Rico's second-largest city, Ponce, was named after him.

PORDENONE, ODERICH OF

Franciscan monk and globetrotter, born 1286 in Pordenone (Friaul), died 1330 in Udine.

In 1313 Oderich of Pordenone was commissioned by his monastic order to convert the unbelievers of the orient. Setting out from Padua,

The itinerant monk Pordenone explored the coast of Java.

the monk traveled by land to Hormuz on the Persian Gulf, visited the entire Malabar coast, the islands of Ceylon, Sumatra, Java, Borneo and spent three years in the Chinese towns of Canton, Peking and Nanking.

In the course of his return journey, Oderich of Pordenone crossed Tibet and Afghanistan, spent quite some time in the Afghan capital of Kabul, wandered through northern Persia and eventually arrived in Avignon to present his report to the Pope after an absence of almost sixteen years in all.

While preparing for a second journey to the orient, Oderich of Pordenone died as a result of the exertion of his first journey. Shortly before his death he dictated his travel report to William of Solagna.

Oderich is regarded as the most reliable reporter on the Far East after Marco Polo. He recorded many details that had escaped the Venetian's attention.

Further reading
Odoricus (Matthiussi), Itinerarium fratris
Odorici de mirabilibus orientalium Tartarorum.
In Hakluyt: The principal Navigations, vol 2.
London 1598
The Travels of Friar Odoric of Pordenone,
1316-1330, by Sir H. Yule, Hakluyt Society,
London, without year of publication

PRZEVALSKI, NIKOLAI MICHAILOVICH

Russian explorer of East Asia, born 1839 in Kimborowo (Smolensk), died 1888 in Karakol (Przevalsk).

Nikolai Przevalski studied in Smolensk and at the military academy in St. Petersburg. During his voluntary stay in Siberia from 1867 to 1869 he undertook his first exploratory expedition to the Ussuri (a tributary of the Amur). In 1870 he set out on his second trip to Asia, accompanied by Lieutenant Pilzov and two

Nikolai Michailovich Przevalski

In 1879 he made a renewed attempt to reach the Tibetan capital. Traveling via Hami, through the Gobi Desert and the rugged mountainous landscape of Tang-la, he proceeded in the direction of Lhasa. Around 200 km (120 miles) before reaching the sacred city of Buddhism, Przhevalski's expedition was stopped by the Tibetan authorities. During his return journey he again explored Kuku-nor Lake, spent some time in the Cheibsen monastery, crossed the Gobi Desert and reached Russia again via Urga.

In 1883 he decided to make one more attempt to reach Lhasa. This trip, known as the "second Tibet journey", is both the longest and most significant trip carried out by Przevalski. From Kyachta he set out to reach the cultural center of Tibet by taking the shortest route through Turkestan. Crossing the Burkhan Buddha Mountains and passing Jarin and Orin lakes, he reached the Blue River at an altitude of 4,000 meters (13,000 feet), which he was however unable to cross because his equipment was unsuitable for such an undertaking. He then decided to travel to the Yellow River, which he was unable to explore because he was attacked by bandits. He continued his journey to Gas Lake (200 km or 120 miles from the Lob-nor Lake). After a brief stop in the town of Khotan, the small group crossed the northern part of the Takla-makan Desert and reached Karakul, where the expedition split up. Although Przevalski was never permitted to visit Lhasa, the result of his exploratory expedition was nevertheless satisfactory. The explorer took two years to evaluate the material he brought home with him.

On his third journey he died in Karakol on the east bank of Lake Issyk-Kul, which was subsequently named Przhevalsk in his honor.

Przevalski was the most important explorer of central Mongolia, the Dzungarskiy, the Karakoram Mountains and northern Tibet. His studies of the wild camels and horses (the Przevalski's horse named for him) are very informative. Almost all explorers of Asia in the nineteenth and

Cossacks. Traveling from Kyachta they journeyed via Peking, Dolonnor, Ordos, Alachan and the celebrated monastery of Cheibsen (approximately 65 km or 40 miles from Sining) to the southern Kuku-nor Mountains and explored the lake of the same name. Since they ran out of money, they had to abandon their goal of reaching Lhasa. They crossed the Gobi Desert and returned to Russia via Urga (Ulan Bator), which they reached on 5 September, 1873. During his three-year journey through central Asia, Nikolai Przevalski had covered vast areas of country which at that time had not been seen by any European with the exception of Père Huc.

Three years later Przevalski undertook his second scientific expedition to east Asia. Accompanied by just four companions he explored the courses of the rivers Ili and Tarim, the southern part of Lob-nor Lake (in the province of Sinkiang) and then returned to Russia to evaluate his geographical findings.

In his accounts of his expeditions to China, Przevalski wrote about the peculiar charm of the inhabitants and landscape.

twentieth centuries followed in his tracks. His research work was continued by the Russian travelers Pievzov, Potanin and the Grum-Grchimailo brothers.

Further reading
N. M. Przewalski, Reisen in die Mongolei, im Gebiet der Tanguten und in den Wüsten Nordtibets 1870-1873. 2 Vols, Russian edition. Without place of publication 1873-1876
–, Reise an den Lop-nor und Altyntagh. In: Erg. Heft Petermanns Mitteilungen. Gotha 1878
–, Von Saissan über Hami nach Tibet. Russische Ausgabe Without place of publication 1883
–, Reisen in Tibet und am oberen Lauf des Gelben Flusses 1878-1880, Russian edition. Without place of publication 1883
D. Rayfield, Lhasa war sein Traum. Die Entdeckungsreisen von N. Prschewalskij in Zentralasien. Wiesbaden 1977

PYTHEAS OF MASSALIA

Greek geographer, astronomer and mathematician, fourth century BC.

We are indebted to Pytheas for the first information about the northwest of Europe. Around 330 BC he traveled from Massalia (Marseille) via Cádiz to the British Isles and to Thule, to the German Bight and the Baltic Sea. He carried out measurements of the altitude of the sun, established the exact position of the celestial North Pole and made the first accurate statements concerning the tides.

RALEIGH, SIR WALTER

British seafarer, pirate and writer, born c. 1552 in Hayes Barton (Devonshire), died 1618 in London.

Raleigh attended Oriel College in Oxford. He was involved in the Huguenot wars in France under Admiral Coligny (1569).

After spending a period of five years in France, Raleigh joined his half-brother Sir Humphrey Gilbert in voyages of piracy in the Spanish West Indies. He thereby became a protagonist of the British marine supremacy against the Spanish in the New World. From 1580 to 1581 he spent time in Ireland and won the favor of Queen Elizabeth I, who knighted him in 1584. The following year, he was appointed Vice-Admiral and from 1585 to 1586 was the Member of Parliament for Devon. From 1584 to 1587 he sent several expeditions to Virginia (USA) in order to colonize the region. However, the Queen forbade Raleigh from personally taking part in these undertakings.

In 1595 Raleigh was involved in his first expedition to Guyana (South America), where he explored the Orinoco, but did not find the so-called "Eldorado" (land of gold). A year later, he participated in the conquest of Cadiz (Spain), together with Essex, Howard and Lord Thomas. In 1598 he was elected Member of Parliament for Dorset and in 1600 was made governor of the Channel Island of Jersey.

After the death of Queen Elizabeth I (1603) Raleigh's fall from grace began with the arrival of the new king James I, king of Scotland and England. James had Raleigh incarcerated in the Tower of London for alleged high treason, where he remained for 13 years. During this time he wrote the "History of the World". In 1617 Raleigh was pardoned. He undertook a second journey to Guyana; on his return Raleigh was taken to the Tower once more and, on the instigation of Spain, he was sentenced to death. He was hanged in "Old Palace Yard" on 7 November, 1618. His grave is located in St. Margaret's Church in Westminster. Raleigh's literary output – a mixture of nonsense and tall tales – is very extensive. There have also been numerous biographies written about his life.

Further reading
Sir Walter Raleigh, History of the World (written in the Tower between 1603 and 1616). London, without year of publication
Biographies: W. Oldys (1736), T. Birch (1751), A. Cayley (1805), P. Fraser-Tytler (1833), E. Edwards (1868), J. A. St. John (1868) and W. Stebbing (1891)
G. M. Towl, Sir Walter Raleigh. His exploits and voyages. Without place of publication 1891
G. Trease, Fortune, My Foe: The Story of Sir Walter Raleigh. Without place of publication 1949
W. Raleigh, Beschreibung des goldreichen Königs Guianae zu America (Anno 1603), die Fahrten Sir W. Raleighs. Vienna, without year of publication
W. Raleigh, Gold aus Guyana. Die Suche nach El Dorado 1595, published by E. Larsen. Stuttgart 1988

RASMUSSEN, KNUD JOHAN VICTOR

Danish Arctic explorer and ethnologist, born 1879 in Jakobshavn (Greenland), died 1933 in Copenhagen. Rasmussen's father was Danish; his mother came from Greenland. While still relatively young, he undertook extended journeys to

Sir Walter Raleigh

Sir Walter Raleigh (at the right in this illustration) in confident pose in a conversation with the chief of a friendly tribe. Raleigh's bodyguards are positioned close to the tent.

In 1921 Rasmussen set out on the greatest ethnographic expedition ever to be undertaken by a scientist, to study all the Inuit tribes of northern Greenland as far as the Bering Strait. On 7 September Rasmussen set out together with the cartographer Freuchen, the archaeologist Therkel Mathiassen, the ethnographer Kaj Birket-Smith and several Inuit. They traveled across Baffin Land and spent the winter on Hudson Bay, where the scientist met the Caribou Inuit, whose life was regulated by the migration of reindeer, for the first time.

After another expedition the scientists separated. Freuchen and Mathiassen explored Baffin Land, Birket-Smith studied the Caribou Inuit, while Rasmussen, together with Qavigarssuaq, an Inuit from Thule, and his wife undertook a 3,000 km (1,900 mile) journey of exploration of Hudson Bay as far as Kotzebue Sound on the Bering Strait. This strenuous, but successful ethnographic exploration took eighteen months; it was the longest and most significant journey that any scientist had ever undertook to study the inhabitants of the Arctic. Rasmussen explored eastern Greenland once more from 1931 to 1933. Rasmussen's ethnographic studies of the Greenland and Canadian Inuit are of considerable scientific value.

various Inuit tribes and studied their customs and habits. In order to assist the Inuit in bartering their natural wares for European ready-made products, Rasmussen founded the Thule trading post (today an important US air force base) in 1910 in North Bay (a region in the northwest of Greenland where the Etah Inuit live).

In 1912, together with cartographer Peter Freuchen and two Inuit, Rasmussen explored the interior ice fields to the west and east of Parry Land. During this successful expedition, Rasmussen and his companions traveled 1,230 km (765 miles); on average they covered 65 km (40 miles) each day.

From 1916 to 1918 Rasmussen explored northern Greenland (the "Second Thule Expedition") together with the Danish Arctic explorer L. Koch, the Swedish botanist T. Wulff and four Inuit. In 1919 he studied the folklore of the Inuit of Angmagsalik, which provided material for his book "Myter og Sagn fra Grønland".

Further reading
K. J. V. Rasmussen, Min Rejsedagbog.
Skildringer fra den første. Thule-Ekspedition.
Copenhagen and Christiana (Oslo) 1915
–, Fra Grønland til Stillehavet. Rejser og
Mennesker fra 5. Thule-Ekspedition 1921-
1924. Copenhagen 1925-1926
–, Across Arctic America. Narrative of the
Fifth Thule-Expedition. London 1927, New York
1927
–, Mindeudgave. Udgivet af Peter Freuchen,
Therkel Mathiassen, Kaj Birket-Smith. 3 vols.
Copenhagen 1934
E. Wieder, Knud Rasmussens letzte Grönland-
fahrt. Salzburg 1936
M. Hausmann, Da wußte ich, daß Frühling war.
Songs of the Inuit, compiled by K. Rasmussen.
Zurich 1984

K. Rasmussen, Die Gabe des Adlers. Eskimomythen aus Alaska, 2nd ed. Berlin 1988

RICE, ALEXANDER HAMILTON

North American explorer of the Amazon, born 1875 in Boston, died 1956 in Newport.

While still studying, Alexanderb Rice undertook extended journeys in the Rocky Mountains and to Hudson Bay. In 1901 he traveled to Egypt, Greece and Turkey, then set out for Australia and South America, where he crossed the Andes in Ecuador on foot.

In 1906 Dr. Rice began his Amazon scientific activities in earnest. Setting out from Caracas he crossed the inhospitable Llanos del Orinoco (Orinoco basin) and finally reached Bogotá. From there, he crossed the Andes for a second time to explore the sources of the Uaupès (a river in Brazil and Columbia). After a strenuous

"The Childhood of Sir Walter Raleigh," painting by Sir John Everett Millais, 1870.

Entertaining Prince Kung

650 km (400 mile) trek he finally reached the influx of the Uaupès into the Rio Negro at Santo-Joaquin. The scientist remained in this unhealthy region for nine months, during which time he sailed the entire Uaupès and charted the course of the river from its source to its mouth. He then explored the Rio Iniriada (a right tributary of the Rio Guaviare) before returning to New York in 1908.

In 1911 Rice traveled to Columbia to explore the Caquetá region (between the Caquetá River and its left tributary, the Rio Ajaju) and the Amazon Basin. Setting out from Bogotá, he traveled to the Mesa de Iguaje and crossed the region of Rio Hilla to Rio Ajaju and the tributaries of the Rio Caquetá. He sailed the Rio Iniriada, the Rio Papunau (southern tributary of the Rio Iniriada) and the Rio Negro.

In 1919, Alexander Rice explored the Rio Negro once more, followed by the Rio Casiquare (a river in southern Venezuela), the upper Orinoco region, the Brazilian section of the Amazon and the area of Guyana bordering on Venezuela. In the course of his attempt to reach the sources of the Orinoco, Rice was attacked by Guahatibos (so-called white Indians). He subsequently returned to North America to evaluate his findings. In the year 1923 Rice traveled to Bolivia, Chile, Argentina, Uruguay and southern Brazil for the last time. Alexander Hamilton Rice is regarded as the most significant explorer of the Amazon in the first half of the twentieth century.

Further reading
Dr. A. H. Rice, From Quito to Iquitos via the River Napo. Geographic Journal Without place of publication 1903 (April)
–, The Rio Negro, Amazonas Map. Geographical Journal. Without place of publication 1918 (October)
–, The Rio Negro, Casiquiare Canal and Upper Orinoco Map. Geographical Journal. Without place of publication 1921 (November)
C. E. Key, Les expolorations du XXe siècle. Paris 1937

RICHARDSON, JAMES

British missionary and explorer of Africa, born 1806 in Boston (Lincolnshire), died 1851 in Bornu (Sudan).

In 1840 Richardson traveled to the Sultanate of Morocco as a correspondent for a British magazine. Five years later the former missionary was commissioned by the British government and the Society for the Abolition of Slavery to open up new trading routes from Tripoli to the Ghat Oasis around 1,000 km (600 miles) to the south and to take action against slave trading. Although the Tuaregs were friendly towards Richardson, he was only able to advance as far as Mursuk.

On his return to England, Richardson persuaded the government to send a well-equipped expedition to Sudan, in order to establish trading agreements with the local Moslem rulers and to put an end to slavery. Two German Africa explorers, Heinrich Barth and Adolf Overweg, took part in this important undertaking. Traveling via Mursuk, Ghat and Agadès, they reached the small town of Taghelel in Sudan. There, they separated on 10 January, 1851 with the intention of meeting again in April in Kuka on Lake Chad. Richardson set out in the direction of Zinder and from there headed towards Kuka. During this journey he died of exhaustion in the small village of Nguruta.

Further reading
J. Richardson, Touarick Alphabet with corresponding Arabic and English letters. London 1847
–, Travels in the great desert of Sahara in the years 1845-1846. 2 Vols. London 1848
–, Dialogues in Bornu and English. Grammar of the Bornu and Kanuri Language. London 1853
–, Narrative of a Mission to Central Africa performed in the years 1850-1851. 2 Vols. London 1853
–, Travels in Marocco. London 1859

RICHTHOFEN, FERDINAND VON

German researcher, born 1833 in Carlsruhe (Silesia), died 1905 in Berlin.

Facing page: Ferdinand von Richthofen in conversation with Prince Kung, a drawing by Richthofen himself, c. 1870 (Travels to China and Japan, 1868–72).

Preceding pages: This copperplate engraving from 1797 by Godefroy depicts natives and Europeans in picturesque poses by the legendary statues on the Easter Islands. Roggeveen had discovered the islands at Easter 1722.

Richthofen studied at Breslau and Berlin Universities, and then remained for some time In Austria to analyze the geology of Tyrol.

When the "Middle Kingdom" was reopened to Europeans following the opium war (1840 to 1842), Ferdinand von Richthofen took part in a German expedition to China. For twelve years (1860-1872), he traveled through twelve of China's provinces, Siam, the Sunda Islands, Japan, the Philippines, Formosa and the US states of California and Nevada.

Richthofen is regarded as being the leading China researcher of the second half of the nineteenth century as well as a pioneer of modern geography and geomorphology.

Further reading
F. v. Richthofen, China, Ergebnisse eigener Reisen und darauf gegründete Studien (1877-1885). Berlin and Leipzig 1877-1912
E. Tiessen (ed.) Ferdinand von Richthofens Tagebücher aus China. Berlin 1907
F. v. Richthofen, China. Ergebnisse eigener Reisen und darauf gegründeter Studien.
Vol. 1 (reprint of the Berlin 1877 edition). Graz 1971

A typical native hut in the Sahara Desert

ROGGEVEEN, JAKOB

Dutch seafarer, born 1659 in Middelburg, died 1729 in Middelburg.

With a commission to explore the legendary southern land in the South Pacific, Jakob Roggeveen set sail for the East India Company in January 1722. Via Cape Horn, he reached the Pacific, where at Easter 1722 he discovered an island which he named Easter Island. Strong currents prevented Roggeveen and his crew from landing on the island, but they did however establish contact with the local population and were able to admire the large tufa statues of the inhabitants' ancestors; even today, the origin and function of these giant statues have yet to be satisfactorily explained. Roggeveen did not succeed in his quest to discover the great southern land.

ROHLFS, GERHARD

German explorer of Africa, born 1831 in Vegesack, died 1896 in Rüngsdorf.

Gerhard Rohlfs was the fourth of seven children. When he was a young boy his health was so poor that doctors gave him little hope of survival. The sickly child absolutely refused to attend school. He was expelled from high school at the age of sixteen and joined the small army of Bremen, where he was promoted to the rank of Lieutenant during the Schleswig War. After he was demobilized he attempted to study medicine at various universities; however, he was not fond of the campus life. He then joined the Foreign Legion and took part in a campaign against the rebellious Kabyles (a Berber tribe in the mountains of Algeria and Morocco). He achieved the rank of Sergeant and was awarded the coveted "Légion d'Honneur". During the campaign in North Africa, Rohlfs learned to speak Arabic and studied the customs and habits of the North Africans. He especially acclimatized himself to the harsh conditions of the Atlas countries.

Rohlfs (seated at the center) and his companions and aides in northeast Africa, 1868.

In 1861 Rohlfs left the Foreign Legion and set out for Tangier. He spent a year preparing for his journey to Timbuktu, which he hoped to reach from Algiers. The insurrection of the Sheik of Monts Ouled-Nail (mountain range in northern Algeria) prevented Rohlfs from carrying out his plan. He then decided to undertake a tour of Morocco, which he traveled through disguised as an orthodox Moslem doctor. He visited the oasis of Tafilalet (in southeastern Morocco), which he thoroughly investigated. Traveling to Tuat, via Igli, Beni-Abès and Adrar, after a strenuous trek he reached the In-Salah oasis, the largest of the Tidikelt oases, on 17 September, 1864. Rohlfs was the second European (after the British Major Laing), to set foot on this oasis. He carried out some geographical and topographical research of the oasis, but because of a shortage of money and time he missed joining a caravan to Timbuktu. Rohlfs was forced to postpone his plan of reaching the legendary city. He returned to Tripoli via Ghadamès.

Hardly he had set foot in Europe before he began planning his next journey to Africa. This time he planned to advance from Tripoli to the as yet unexplored Hoggar massif. In 1865 he arrived in Ghadamès, where he attempted in vain to join a caravan heading in the direction of the Hoggar. The hostilities of the Tuaregs further prevented him carrying out his plan. Rohlfs therefore changed the direction of his journey and reached Lake Chad via Kauar and Kuka. He was greeted in a friendly manner by the Sultan of Bornu. He continued on to the Bauchi Plateau (mountainous region of central Nigeria), to the Benue, which he sailed to its mouth, and to the Niger. Traveling via the towns of Ilorin and Ibadan (Nigeria), he reached Lagos, the former capital of Nigeria. Gerhard Rohlfs was the first person to cross Africa from the Mediterranean to the Gulf of Benin. From that time onwards his international reputation as a Sahara specialist was assured.

In 1868 the British government commissioned him to take part in Lord Napier's campaign against Theodoros, the emperor of Ethiopia. After this he bade farewell to Britain and traveled through large parts of Abyssinia.

In 1869 Rohlfs undertook a major journey of exploration to the oases of Audshila, the largest of the Jalu oases (in northwestern Libya), and Siva (northwestern Egypt). He attempted in vain to reach the Kufra Oases with three other German scientists. Sand dunes reaching heights of up to 150 meters (500 feet) forced them to abandon the expedition and make the return journey.

On 18 December, 1878 Rohlfs made a renewed attempt to reach the Kufra oases, once the imperial gifts had arrived from Germany for the Sultan of Wadai. Among other things, Rohlfs was to explore the ground properties of the Libyan Desert on commission from the Khedive of Egypt. Rohlfs' nephew A. Strecker, the Austrian photographer L. von Csillagh, the master locksmith F. Eckardt from Saxony-Weimar and the watchmaker K. Hübner from Graz accompanied the untiring explorer. From Bir-Milrha they traveled to Sokna, the principal town of the Jofra oasis. There the expedition rested for a month. In mid-July they reached the Aujila oasis. On 1 September, 1879 after a strenuous trek Rohlfs was the first white man ever to reach Taiserbo, one of the Kufra oases. During its return journey the expedition was attacked and all their equipment was stolen. Rohlfs' diary was lost, but not the map of the Kufra oases. On 29 October, the members of the expedition, with the exception of L. von Csillagh, who died while traveling through the Fessan in Rhat, arrived in Benghasis, with no money but in relatively good health.

It was not until 35 years later that an Italian prisoner of war unwillingly set foot in the Kufra oases again.

At last Europe had accurate information concerning the Kufra oases. With Rohlfs' expedition, almost the entire Libyan Desert had been explored. From then on the traveler concentrated on committing his travels to paper.

During his almost twenty years of research and exploration in northern Africa, Gerhard Rohlfs performed invaluable services in studying the geography of the Sahara. The accuracy of his topographical and geographical measurements earned him high esteem as a scientist even during his lifetime. Alongside the two Frenchmen Caillié and Duveyrier, Rohlfs is the third great explorer of the Sahara.

Further reading
G. Rohlfs, Reisen durch Marokko. Bremen 1869
–, Im Auftrage seiner Majestät, des Königs von Preußen mit dem englischen Expeditionscorps nach Abessinien. Bremen 1869
–, Von Tripolis nach Alexandrien. 2 vols. Bremen 1871
–, Mein erster Aufenthalt in Marokko. Bremen 1873
–, Quer durch Afrika. 2 vols. Leipzig 1874, 1875
–, Drei Monate in der Libyschen Wüste. Kassel 1875
W. Jordan, Die geographischen Resultate der von G. Rohlfs geführten Expeditionen in die Libysche Wüste. Sammlung gemeinverständlicher Vorträge von Virchow und Holtzendorff, Nr. 218. Berlin 1875

G. Rohlfs, Kufra. Leipzig 1881
–, Meine Mission nach Abessinien im Winter 1880/81. Leipzig 1883
K. Guenther, Gerhard Rohlfs. Freiburg. 1912
E. Banse, Unsere großen Afrikaner (including Rohlfs). Berlin 1940

Sir John Ross discovered the North Magnetic Pole on 1 June, 1831 (woodcut after a drawing by Paul Bender, 1896).

H.-O. Meissner, Durch die sengende Glut der Sahara. Die Abenteuer des Gerhard Rohlfs. Stuttgart 1968

G. Rohlfs, Quer durch Afrika. Die Erstdurchquerung der Sahara vom Mittelmeer zum Golf von Guinea 1865-1867, ed. H. Gussenbauer. Stuttgart 1984

ROSS, SIR JAMES CLARK

British polar explorer and discoverer, born 1800 in London, died 1862 in Aylesbury.

Ross joined the Royal Navy aged just 12. In 1818 he accompanied his uncle John Ross and from 1819 to 1827 he accompanied Parry on

First encounter with the natives of "Booth-ia", 1829/30, after a sketch by Sir John Ross

their Arctic journeys in an attempt to find the Northwest Passage. From 1829 to 1833 Ross took part in two large-scale Arctic expeditions organized by John Ross, in the course of which the Boothia Peninsula, King William Land and the North Magnetic Pole were discovered. Two years later he explored Baffin Bay.

His next expeditions took him to Antarctica. Sailing from the port of Hobart (Tasmania), where he had heard of the discovery of Balleny Island, Adélie Land and the Côte de Clarie, Ross advanced into Antarctic waters with two ships, the "Erebus" and the "Terror". He gave the name "Victoria Land" to a region of Antarctica south of Australia which he explored; he also named two mountains "Mount Erebus" and "Mount Terror" (for the two ships). In 1843, Ross was the first person to reach a latitude of 79° 10' S.

His last journey was to search for signs of the lost J. Franklin expedition. Sailing with the

"Enterprise" and the "Investigator", he explored the coasts of Baffin Bay, questioned every Inuit that he met, reached Barrow Strait and spent the winter on Leopold Island. When he had still not discovered a trace of Franklin by spring 1849, he returned to England in disappointment.

James Clark Ross was the first explorer to cross the 79th southern parallel, thus pointing the way for modern Antarctic explorers such as Scott, Shackleton and Amundsen. "Ross Island", the "Ross Sea" and shelf ice in southern Antarctica are named for this brave explorer.

Further reading
Sir J. M. D. Richardson and J. E. Gray, Zoology of the voyage of H. M. S. Erebus and Terror under the command of Sir J. C. Ross. London 1844-1875
Sir James C. Ross, A Voyage of Discovery and Research in Southern and Antarctic Regions during the Years 1839-1843, 2 Vols. London 1847

Encounter with Inuit people on Sir John Ross' second expedition, after a sketch by himself

ROSS, SIR JOHN

British seafarer and polar explorer, born 1777 in Inch (Scotland), died 1856 in London.

Ross took part in various naval battles during the French-English conflict under Napoleon I. He was promoted to the rank of lieutenant.

In 1818 John Ross was commissioned by the British admiralty to explore north Canadian waters and to find the Northwest Passage through Baffin Bay.

With two ships, the "Isabel" (his flagship) and the "Alexander" (commanded by Parry), Ross sailed through the Davis Strait into Baffin Bay, he explored the east coast of Greenland, established contact with the Inuit, reached Smith Sound without any difficulty, but was not able to proceed any further than 76° 46' N. Because Parry accused him of falsifying a report, the British government refused to provide John Ross with any further financial assistance for a second journey to the Arctic.

Sponsored by the wealthy businessman Felix Booth, in 1829 Ross set out once more for Arctic waters in the "Victory", where he discovered a peninsula which he named for his sponsor "Boothia". He also discovered King William Island and the North Magnetic Pole.

On 26 August, 1833 Ross and his crew were found by whalers and brought back to England. After receiving a rapturous welcome, John Ross was knighted by Queen Victoria and was appointed rear admiral.

Further reading
W. H. Bishop, The Voyages and Expeditions of Cpt. Ross, Parry and Franklin in Search of a Northwest Passage. London (1834?)
R. Huish, the last Voyage of Cpt. Sir J. Ross to the Arctic Regions. London 1835
Sir J. Ross, Memoir of Admiral A. J. Krusenstern, translated from the German by C. Bernardi and edited by S. J. Ross. Without place of publication 1856
S. M. Schmucker, Arctic Explorations and Discoveries during the nineteenth century, being accounts of the expeditions to the North Seas.

Conducted by Ross, Parry, Back, Franklin, McClure and others. New York and Auburn 1857
J. Ross, Zum Magnetpol in der Arktis. Bericht über die Expedition von 1829 bis 1833, ed. G. Grümmer. Rostock 1991

RUBRUK (RUYSBROEK), WILHELM VON

Flemish Franciscan monk and explorer of Asia, born c. 1210 in Rubrouck, died after 1290, probably on Mount Athos (a monastic republic in northeastern Greece).

In 1253 Rubruk was commissioned by the French king Louis the Pious to travel to the court of the Great Khan Mangu to negotiate conditions for a possible alliance against Islam and to initiate missionary work in the Far East.

Traveling from Akra (Kingdom of Jerusalem) via Constantinople, the monk reached the Kuman region, traveling by foot and ox cart (Khanate of the Golden Horde), where he visited the towns of Old Sarai and New Sarai on the lower Volga. He then proceeded to the north of The Caspian Sea and north of the Aral Sea to Balagasun (Khanate of Chaghatai), crossed the Irtysch and reached the realm of the Great Khan. He spent two months in the "capital" Karakoram as the guest of the Khan. Without having gained any definitive information Rubruk returned, this time north of the Lake Balqash, through the Khanate of the White Horde. On reaching Old Sarai, he turned south, traveled through Georgia, the realm of the Rum-Seljuks, and reached Akra again via Cyprus in 1255.

Rubruk's journey (1253-55) across Asia was a remarkable physical achievement. His travel report provided the first specific information about the customs and habits of the Mongolian peoples under the rule of the Great Khan.

Further reading
P. Bergeron, Voyages faits principalement en Asie dans les XIIe, XIIIe, XIVe et XVe siècles par

Benjamin de Tudèle, Jean Plan du Carpini,
N. Ascelin, Guillaume de Rubruquis... accom-
pagnés de l'histoire des Sarrazins et des Tartares
et précédés d'une introduction concernant les
voyages et les nouvelles découvertes des prin-
cipaux voyageurs. La Haye 1735
L. de Backer, Guillaume de Rubruk, ambassadeur
de Saint Louis en Orient, récit de son voyage
traduit de l'original latin. Paris 1877
H. Herbst, Der Bericht des Franziskaners Wil-
helm von Rubruk über seine Reise. Leipzig 1925
W. v. Rubruk, Reisen zum Großkhan der
Mongolen. Von Konstantinopel nach Kara-
korum 1253-1255, published by H. Leicht.
Stuttgart 1984

RUGENDAS, JOHANN MORITZ

German traveler, painter and drawer, born 1802, died 1858.

The Augsburg artist Rugendas achieved acclaim as a result of his travels to South America. From 1821 to 1825 he spent time in Brazil and traveled from 1831 to 1847 through Mexico, Peru, Chile, Bolivia and once more to Brazil.

Particularly Humboldt, with whom Rugendas had made acquaintance in Paris in 1825, was highly enthusiastic about the artist's masterly drawings, which accurately reflected the South American tropical world.

This romantic illustration from Rugendas' work "Voyage pittoresque dans le Brésil" from the year 1827 depicts a liana bridge.

SAINT-HILAIRE, AUGUSTIN FRANÇOIS CÉCAR PROUVENSAL DE

French explorer of South America, born 1779 in Orléans, died 1853 in Orléans.

Saint-Hilaire studied zoology, botany and entomology. In 1816, he was instructed by the Paris Academy of Sciences to undertake a large-scale expedition to Brazil. For almost six years, the scientist explored large areas in the interior of Brazil, Paraguay and Uruguay.

From Rio de Janeiro Saint-Hilaire, popularly referred to as the "French Humboldt", traveled for fifteen months throughout the province of Minas Gerais, reached the Rio Jequitinhonha, where he carried out research on the Botokudes, an Indian tribe of warriors. He returned to Rio de Janeiro via the Rio San Francisco. From there he sent a consignment to the museum in Paris comprising 200 different birds and 800 insects, 200 packets of seeds of exotic plants and two papers on the flora of Minas Gerais.

During a second expedition he visited the province of Espíritu Santo. He explored the unhealthy region of the Rio Doce and visited the towns of Campos on the Rio Paraiba and Vitoria, the capital of Espíritu Santo. Back in Rio de Janeiro he sent a further collection of exotic plants to Paris.

His third expedition took Hilaire to the provinces of Minas Gerais, Goias and São Paulo. When he lost his only reliable companion in São João del Rei, he decided to continue his journey on his own. He reached the source of the Rio Francisco, explored the sulfurous source of the Araxa and traveled on to the "diamond province" of Paracatu. From there, Hilaire reached the province of Goias and its capital Vila-Boa, the abject poverty of which disappointed him. On reaching the border of the province of Mato Grosso, he was refused entry by the Portuguese authorities.

Via Vila Boa and Meia Ponte he arrived back in São Paulo in December 1819. During a stay that lasted several weeks he sorted his collection and visited the nearby towns of Itu, Porto-Feliz and Sorocaba. Then he changed the direction of his journey and reached Curitiba (now the capital of Paraná state) via Itararé. After exploring the "Serra" of Paranagua and visiting the towns of Porte Alegre, Rio Grande and São Francisco de Paulo, a place famous for its dried meat, he crossed the border in October 1820 and reached the Spanish settlements of Montevideo. Continuing his journey, he explored the Rio Negro and for several weeks lived in a desert area inhabited only by jaguars and ostriches. Sampling a small amount of wild honey almost cost Hilaire his life. After visiting the ruined missionary outposts of the Jesuits in Paraguay, he returned to Brazil and arrived back in Rio de Janeiro towards the end of 1821.

During his fourth and last journey through Brazil he again visited the region of São Paulo and explored the Serra of Mantiqueira, a mountain range in the northeast of the country.

In June 1822 Saint-Hilaire arrived back in Paris, in a state of complete exhaustion and almost blind.

The outcome of Augustin Hilaire's research activities over a period of six years was overwhelming. He explored Brazil from the source of the Rio Tocantins to the mouth of the Rio Prata.

In the course of this 12,000 km (7,460 mile) journey he classified and described 48 mammals, 450 birds, 35 reptiles and 48 fish, approximately 16,000 insects, beetles and butterflies, many of which had been unknown. The rock samples that he returned to Europe gave important indications to the geologists concerning the reserves of ore in Brazil. Auguste Hilaire also studied the way of life of the "Paulistas" (town-dwellers) and of the "Mineiros" (inhabitants of Minas Gerais).

Further reading
A. de Saint-Hilaire, Voyages dans les provinces de Rio et de Minas Gerais. Paris 1830
–, Voyages dans le district des diamants et sur le littoral du Brésil. Paris 1833
–, Voyages aux sources du Rio de S. Francisco et dans la province de Goyaz. Paris 1847
–, Voyages dans les provinces de Saint-Paul et de Sainte-Cathèrine. Paris 1851
–, Voyages à Rio Grande do Sul. Paris 1887

SCHILTBERGER, HANS

German Orient traveler, born 1380 near Freising, died c. 1440.

In 1394, Schiltberger fought as a shield-bearer against the Turks and was taken prisoner near Nikropolis in Bulgaria by the Turks in 1396 and later by the Mongolians. His odyssey through the Middle and Far East lasted thirty years. He became familiar with Isphahan, Samarkand, Erivan, Astrakhan, the Ural Mountains, Siberia and southern Russia. On the Black Sea, he was eventually able to flee together with four other Christian prisoners. In 1427 he arrived back in Bavaria. Hans Schiltberger's report, "Journey to the Heathens", posthumously published in Ulm in 1473, elevates him to the status of the first German world traveler.

Further reading
J. Schiltberger, Als Sklave im Osmanischen Reich und bei den Tataren (1394-1427), ed. U. Schlemmer. Stuttgart 1983

Chronicle of Brazil to the 19th century

1000 BC	Approximately 3.6 million people from various tribes live in the area of present-day Brazil.
Since 1499	The Spaniard Vincente Yáñez Pinzón is the first person to sail along the east coast of Brazil.
1500	The Portuguese seafarer Pedro Álvarez Cabral lands on the northeast coast of Brazil, takes possession of the country for Portugal and founds the port of Bahia, present-day Salvador.
1515	The Portuguese begin the exploration and colonization of Brazil.
1541	Portugal declares Bahia (Salvador) the capital of Brazil.
1554	São Paulo is founded.
1565	Rio de Janeiro is founded.
1600	After the extinction of the Charrúa Indians, the Portuguese occupy the north and the Spaniards the south of present-day Uruguay.
1621	Portugal separates the Brazilian colony into two partly autonomous general governments.
1696	Gold is found for the first time in the mountains north of Rio de Janeiro and soon after this other metal ores, diamonds and semi-precious stones.
1763	Rio de Janeiro takes over from Bahia (Salvador) as capital of Brazil.
1822	The Portuguese crown prince declares Brazil a constitutional monarchy independent of its mother country and has himself crowned Emperor Pedro I.

SCHIRRA, WALTER MARTY, JR.

US astronaut, born 1923 in Hackensack (New Jersey).

Walter Schirra, a former navy pilot, is the only one of the first seven astronauts to travel into space on board the three space capsules "Mercury", "Gemini" and "Apollo". During his second journey in December 1965, on "Gemini 6", he and Thomas Stafford managed to approach the "Gemini 7" spaceship, manned by the astronauts Frank Borman and James Lovell, to within a distance of 30 centimeters (one foot). Schirra was also a crew member of "Apollo 7", the first manned Apollo mission in October 1968. He spent a total of 12½ days in space during his three trips. In 1969 he left NASA to work in business; he founded his own consulting company in 1978.

Further reading
R. N. Billings, Schirra's space. Boston 1988

SCHMIDT, OTTO JULYEVICH

Russian mathematician and Arctic explorer, born 1891 in Mogilyov, died 1956 in Moscow.

From 1929 to 1933 Schmidt undertook several scientific expeditions into the Russian Arctic and carried out hydrographical research in the Barents and Kara Seas. From 1932 to 1939 he was the head of the main administration for the Russian north route; in this position he was head of the entire Soviet Arctic exploration. After the Second World War he turned his attention to writing the monumental "Bolshaya Sovetskaya Enzyklopediya". In order to explore the Arctic better from a scientific point of view, Otto Schmidt developed the principle of stationing scientists near the Pole for one year's duration before relieving them by aircraft. The Russian pilot Vodopyanov successfully implemented Schmidt's plan for the first time in 1936. Otto Schmidt was undoubtedly one of the greatest Arctic explorers of the twentieth century.

SCHNITZER, EDUARD (EMIN PASCHA)

German Africa explorer and adventurer, born 1840 in Oppeln, died 1892 in Kanema (central Africa).

Eduard Schnitzer studied medicine. From 1865 to 1875 he was a surgeon in the Turkish Army, after which he went to Egypt. In 1876 he was made Chief Medical Officer by Gordon, a British officer who was killed by the Mahdi during the capture of Khartoum in 1885, and the following year governor of the Upper Nile region. During the invasion by the Mahdi (the "well-guided" in Arabic, here referring to Muhammad Ahmad Abd Allah) Schnitzer was cut off from all access routes. In 1888 he was met by Stanley's expedition, but Schnitzer refused to join it. A mutiny forced Schnitzer to flee to the east African coast; in 1889 he returned to Germany, where he became a member of the German East Africa Society. Accompanied by Dr. Stuhlmann, another physician, Dr. Emin Pasha undertook a further expedition to central Africa. While traveling to the Uëlle, a river in northern Congo, Emin Pasha was murdered by an Arab.

Overestimated as an administrator but unsuited as a geographer, Eduard Schnitzer earned particular merit as an ethnographer and naturalist.

Further reading
Emin Pascha. Eine Sammlung von Reisebriefen und Berichten Dr. Emin Paschas aus den ehemaligen ägyptischen Äquatorial-Provinzen und den Grenzländern, published by Dr. G. Schweinfurt, Dr. Ratzel, R. W. Felkin and G. Hartlaub. Leipzig 1888
Tagebücher, published by F. Stuhlmann. 4 vols. Without place of publication 1915-1927
H.-O. Meissner, An den Quellen des Nils. Die Abenteuer des Emin Pascha. Stuttgart, without year of publication
Emin Pascha. Gefahrvolle Entdeckungsreisen in Zentralafrika 1877-1892, ed. H. Schiffers. Stuttgart 1983

SCHWEINFURTH, GEORG AUGUST

German explorer of Africa, born 1836 in Riga, died 1925 in Berlin.

Schweinfurth studied botany in Heidelberg, Munich and Berlin. In Berlin, he met the famous Africa explorer Heinrich Barth. This acquaintance and the preoccupation with a large collection of plants from the estate of the deceased Baron of Barnim aroused the young botanist's interest in African flora.

From 1864 to 1866 he undertook an extensive preparatory journey to the Red Sea and the Nile region.

In 1868, Schweinfurth was commissioned by the Humboldt Foundation to carry out botanical research in the area of Bahr el-Ghasal, a left tributary of the White Nile. After thorough preparations and taking into account the experiences of the expedition of A. Tinné, Steudner and Heuglin, he started out on 5 January, 1869 from Khartoum into the area of Bahr el-Ghasal and researched the native peoples of the Mangbetu (a tribe in the area of the middle Uëlle and middle Bomokandi Rivers), the Nuer (a semi-nomadic tribe in southern Sudan) and the Aka (a Pygmy tribe).

Schweinfurth was the first European to succeed in carrying out ethnographic research into the Niam-Niam, a tribe of cannibals. Via Khartoum, the researcher returned to Egypt in 1871, albeit empty-handed: His extensive collection of exotic plants had fallen victim to a fire.

In 1872-73 Schweinfurth explored the oases of the eastern Libyan desert together with the geologist K. Zittel, the surveyor Dr. Jordan, the botanist P. Ascherson and the photographer Remelé, and in 1875-76 – this time accompanied by Dr. Güssfeldt – he explored the area between the Nile and the Red Sea.

In Cairo he founded the Egyptian Institute and the Geographical Society on behalf of the Khedive. For several years he was director of the museums of the Egyptian capital.

Georg August Schweinfurth

Georg Schweinfurth's ethnographic, cultural and historical investigations of the area of Bahr el-Ghasal and its inhabitants number among the most significant of all African research undertakings.

Further reading
Petermanns Mitteilungen. Gotha 1863-1865, 1867-1874
Dr. G. Schweinfurth, Linguistische Ergebnisse der Reise nach Zentral-Afrika. Berlin 1873 (supplement to Zeitschrift für Ethnologie 1872)
–, Im Herzen von Afrika. Leipzig 1874
Georg Schweinfurth. Lebensbild eines Africa explorers. Letters from 1857-1925, ed. K. Guenther. Stuttgart 1954
G. Schweinfurth, Im Herzen von Afrika, ed. H. Gussenbauer. Stuttgart 1984

SCORESBY, WILLIAM

British seafarer, whaler and Arctic explorer, born 1789 in Whitby, died 1857 in Torquay.

After studying natural sciences at Edinburgh University, Scoresby devoted himself to the exploration of the Arctic. This scientifically trained seafarer and whaler undertook a total of seventeen journeys into the Nordic seas between Greenland and Spitzbergen. In 1822 he succeeded in reaching the east coast of Greenland, which even in summer is usually surrounded by an extensive layer of thick ice.

Scoresby is considered as the founding father of modern Arctic exploration. His accurate scientific travel reports provided a basis for almost all major Arctic explorers during the nineteenth century. He drew up the first precise map of the east coast of Greenland between the latitudes of 69° 30' and 75° N.

"Scoresby Sound", a fiord in the east of Greenland, bears the name of William Scoresby's father; "Scoresby Land" is named after the British seafarer.

Further reading
W. Scoresby, Journal of a Voyage to the Northern Whale-Fishery; including Researches and Discoveries on the Eastern coast of West Greenland, made in the Summer of 1822, in the Ship Baffin of Liverpool. Edinburgh 1823

Robert Falcon Scott

SCOTT, ROBERT FALCON

British Antarctic explorer, born 1868 in Devonport (today part of Plymouth), died 1912 in Antarctica.

Scott joined the Royal Navy and in 1886 served as a torpedo specialist in the West Indian Squadron.

When in 1902 an international congress decided to explore Antarctica from several directions, Great Britain claimed the area known as the "Ross Dependency" and commissioned Captain Scott with a large-scale expedition. On board the "Discovery" he first explored the Ross Barrier and then went ashore in Whale Bay (also known as Balloon Bay). In the eastern part of the frozen wasteland he discovered an area which he named "King Edward VII Land" and then stayed over winter near Mount Erebus, a volcano on Ross Island. While most members of the expedition worked on specific Antarctic projects, Robert Scott penetrated far into the interior of the continent and reached a latitude of 82° 17' S after an extremely difficult trek through the mountain range of South Victoria Land. The following year, he climbed several immense mountains of ice in Victoria Land, which reached heights of up to 3,000 meters (9,850 feet).

In 1911 he started his final advance to the South Pole. From New Zealand he traveled to Antarctica and established a base on Cape Evans, 50 km (30 miles) north of Hut Point. At the same time his rival Amundsen had set up his quarters in Whale Bay.

On 1 November, Scott started the race with 12 companions, two motorized snow vehicles, and ten sledges which were drawn by ponies from Mongolia and only a few huskies. On 10 December, Scott arrived at Beardmore Glacier, and by 3 January, 1912 he had reached a latitude of only 87° 32'. The journey from this glacier to the Pole was extremely arduous: Since all the ponies had died, Scott and his companions had to pull the sledges themselves, and despite their special clothing they suffered frostbite to their limbs. On 17 January, Scott had finally achieved his goal. However, he was immensely disappointed to find that Amundsen had already reached the South Pole a month beforehand. Norway, not Great Britain, was the winner of this race. On his return journey, two of his companions – Wilson and Bauwers – died, and Scott himself succumbed on 29 March. On 30 October, a search team found the camp with the frozen explorers. Scott had kept his diary up to his final hour.

Scott's Arctic ship "Terra Nova" is seen at the horizon in the midst of pack ice.

Scott and his companions outside Amundsen's tent.

Scott's body was found by a search party; this picture shows his burial.

SELER, EDUARD GEORG

German ethnologist and researcher of America, born 1849 in Crossen (Oder), died 1922 in Berlin.

On completion of his scientific studies, Seler carried out research for the Ethnological Museum in Berlin. In 1899 he was appointed professor.

From 1887 to 1911 Eduard Seler undertook an expedition to Mexico, where he investigated the pre-Columbian cultures; he was particularly interested in the Maya.

SHACKLETON, SIR ERNEST HENRY

Irish-British Antarctic explorer, born 1874 in Kilkee (Ireland), died 1922 at sea (South Georgia).

Shackleton was educated at Dulwich College and joined the British Merchant Navy. From 1901 to 1904 he accompanied Scott on board the "Discovery" for the National Arctic Expedition.

In 1907 he decided on the audacious plan of conquering the South Pole. On board the "Nimrod" Earnest Shackleton first of all attempted to anchor in Whale Bay (also called Balloon Bay) and go ashore, but he was prevented by the insurmountable masses of ice. His attempt to call at King Edward II Land was also thwarted. Eventually the explorer managed to establish a camp on Ross Island. There, one group climbed Mount Erebus and another proceeded in the direction of the South Magnetic Pole, which it reached on 16 January, 1909. In the meantime, Shackleton prepared himself for his advance to the Pole.

On 19 October, 1908, he set out with Adams, Marshall and Wild along with four Manchurian ponies and provisions for three months. On 26 November the group reached 82° 17' S and had thus broken Scott's record. In the meantime, however, Shackleton had lost all his ponies, and each member of the expedition had to carry 100 kg (220 pounds) of luggage. Beardmore Glacier

There two main reasons for the fact that Scott was beaten by Amundsen in the race to reach the South Pole: Scott's approach was far more difficult than Amundsen's, and he had made the serious mistake of using ponies rather than huskies to draw the sledges. Scott's was the final endeavor in the dramatic period of Antarctic exploration.

Further reading
R. F. Scott, The Voyage of the "Discovery".
2 vols. London 1905
–, Narrative of a Journey to the Shores of the
Polar Sea. London 1910
Scott's last Expedition. The personal journals
of Captain Scott. London 1923
St. L. Gwynn, Captain Scott. A Biography.
London 1929
Ch. H. Avery, No Surrender. The story of
Captain Scott's journey to the South Pole.
London 1933
W. Holwood, The true Book about Captain Scott.
London 1954
P. Brent, Captain Scott – Die Tragödie in der
Antarktis. Mannheim 1977
K. Holt, Scott-Amundsen. Wettlauf zum Pol.
Neuausg. Vienna 1979
R. Huntford, Scott & Amundsen. London 1979
R. F. Scott, Letzte Fahrt. Scotts Tagebuch.
10th ed. Mannheim 1981
P. Marc, Amundsen und Scott am Südpol.
Zurich 1992

Eduard Georg Seler

proved especially arduous for the explorers. On 20 December, the small group reached the King Edward VII ice plateau (2,200 m or 7,220 feet above sea level), and on 9 January, 1909, Shackleton had reached 88° 23' S, a distance of 178 km (111 miles) from the South Pole. Heavy storms forced him to abandon his plans, and on 27 February he and his companions arrived back at the base camp.

In 1914, Shackleton led an expedition to the Weddell Sea and stayed over winter in Prince Regent Luitpold Land, which had been discovered by Filchner in 1912. When his ship, the "Endurance", was crushed by heavy pack ice, he undertook an almost 1,200 km (750 mile) drift journey with his 22-strong crew in the direction of South Georgia. After five months, the shipwrecked crew was saved by a Chilean warship. In 1921, Shackleton prepared another expedition on South Georgia, but died of a heart condition on his Antarctic voyage.

Shackleton's failure can mainly be put down to his use of ponies instead of huskies and the fact that he was prevented from taking the shortest route from Whale Bay to the Pole. Nevertheless, his attempt to reach the South Pole can be regarded as a unique physical achievement.

Further reading
–, The Heart of the Antarctic, 2 vols. Philadelphia 1909
J. R. E. Wild, Shackleton's last voyage. London 1923
H. R. Mill, The life of Sir E. Shackleton. London 1924
E. J. B. Watson, Shackleton in the Antarctic. London 1943
Mit der Endurance in die Antarktis. Shackleton's Südpol-Expedition 1914-1917. Die legendären Fotos von Frank Hurley. Cologne 2001

Eduard Seler investigated the pyramid of Xochialco near Cuernavaca.

*Philipp Franz
von Siebold*

*Franz von Siebold 1796-1866. Leipzig 1943
Philipp Franz von Siebold (1796-1866). Ein
Bayer als Mittler zwischen Japan und Europa,
published by M. Henker. Munich 1993*

SOTO, HERNANDO DE

Spanish conquistador, born 1486 in Barcarrota
(Badajoz), died 1542 on the Mississippi.

De Soto accompanied the two Spanish explorers P. A. Davila and Pizarro on their expeditions
in Central and South America.

In 1532, de Soto came up with the ambitious
plan of acquiring Florida. The Spanish suspected
that this as yet unexplored North American
peninsula was rich in gold and silver mines,
which could compensate for the reduced production of the Mexican and Peruvian mines.

In 1539, de Soto sailed with a flotilla from
Cuba to Florida and disembarked at the site of
today's city of Tampa. Over the next three years,
he explored the present-day state of Alabama
under enormous difficulties, reached the Appalachian Mountains, finally reached the Mississippi
and died there of exhaustion. From the mouth of
the Mississippi, his lieutenant, Luis de Moscoso,
reached the present-day city of Tampa by the sea
route in improvised boats.

Even though de Soto did not succeed in finding precious metals during his campaign of conquest through the south of the North American
continent, his expedition nevertheless represented an important advancement for the geography,
hydrography and ethnography of Florida to the
Mississippi.

*Further reading
Histoire de la conquête de la Floride par les
Espagnols sous Ferdinand de Soto, écrite par un
gentilhomme de la ville d'Elvas. Paris 1699
W. Lowery, The Spanish settlements within the
present limits of the United States 1513 to 1561.
New York 1901
E. G. Bourne, Spain in America. London 1906
H.-O. Meissner, Der Kaiser schenkt mir Florida.
Die Abenteuer des Hernando de Soto. Stuttgart
1967*

SIEBOLD, PHILIPP FRANZ BALTHASAR JONKHEER VON

German explorer of Africa, born 1796 in
Würzburg, died 1866 in Munich.

After studying medicine, Siebold joined the
services of the Dutch East India Company as a
physician.

From 1823 to 1830 and from 1859 to 1862,
Siebold explored the whole of Japan. Due to his
extensive research work he was regarded as the
most important authority on Japan in the nineteenth century.

*Further reading
Ph. Fr. B. Siebold, Nippon. Archiv zur Be-
schreibung von Japan und dessen Neben- und
Schutzländern, 20 Vols. Leiden 1832-1834
Werner Siebold, Ein Deutscher gewinnt Japans
Herz. Lebensroman des Japanforschers Philipp*

SPEKE, JOHN HANNING

British Africa explorer and discoverer, born 1827 in Jordans (Somerset), died 1864 in Nerton Park (near Bath).

In 1858, Speke undertook an expedition to central Africa together with the Africa explorer Burton. Without encountering any special difficulties, they discovered the eastern shore of Lake Tanganyika. According to Arabic reports and the map of J. Erhardt, a missionary, a large lake existed to the east of Zanzibar which was called "Ukerewe" by the Arabs and "Nyanza" by the natives. On their return journey, Speke's friend Burton fell ill with fever and had to stay behind in Tabora. Traveling alone, Speke reached Lake Ukerewe (in the headwaters of the River Nile) and in honor of the British queen named it "Victoria-Nyanza". Speke was convinced that this lake was the source of the River Nile.

On his return to London he was commissioned by the Royal Geographical Society in London in 1860 to determine once and for all whether Lake Victoria was in fact the source of the Nile. Together with Captain Grant, Speke discovered the Kagara River, the actual headstream of the River Nile (30 km or 20 miles from Lake Tanganyika), reached the Nile on 21 July, 1862 and continued to the Rippon Falls. From Khartoum he telegraphed a message to Khartoum: "The Nile is settled."

The year after his return from Africa, the explorer died as the result of a hunting accident.

Further reading
J. H. Speke, Journal of the discovery of the source of the Nile, 2 vols. London 1863

SPIX, JOHANN BAPTIST VON

Zoologist and traveler, born 1781, died 1826.

After completing his theology studies, Spix became involved with medicine and zoology. Together with his traveling companion, the botanist Carl Friedrich Philipp von Martius, he explored Brazil from 1817 to 1820 on commission from the king of Bavaria and collected a

Spix in the Amazonian forest. Nine men were not enough to span this immense tree trunk with a circumference of 25 meters (over 80 feet).

A waterfall in the
tropical rainforest

wealth of geological and ethnographical findings, including observations of more than 3,300 animals. One of his main areas of research was the Amazon.

Six years after returning from Brazil. Spix died from the after-effects of tropical fever. He left behind many descriptions of South American fauna, which however he had not been able to complete himself. His three-volume work was completed in 1831 by Martius.

STANLEY, SIR HENRY MORTON (BORN AS JOHN ROWLANDS)

British Africa explorer, born 1841 in Denbigh (Wales), died 1904 in London.

Early in life Stanley was orphaned, ran away from the poorhouse and managed to go to North America, working as a cabin boy. In New Orleans he was welcomed into the house of an American named Stanley, whose name he adopted (his original name was in fact John Rowlands). From 1861 to 1865 he served both the Northern and Southern states in the North American Civil War. Together with Lord Napier, he then traveled to Abyssinia as a newspaper correspondent.

The last that had been heard from the Scottish missionary and explorer David Livingstone was on 7 July, 1868 at Lake Bangweolo; he was since assumed missing. In England a search expedition was about to set out when the British consul telegraphed from Zanzibar that Livingstone was alive but in difficulties on Lake Tanganyika.

On receiving this news, M. B. G. Bennett, the son of one of the directors of the "New York Herald", instructed the journalist Stanley to go to the missionary's assistance.

In March 1871 a well-equipped 192-strong private army set out from Bagamoyo, north of Daressalam, in the direction of Lake Tangan-

Two portraits of Stanley: at left as a young man, and at right as an experienced explorer

yika. Stanley was accompanied by only two Englishmen, Farquhar and Shaw. After encountering various difficulties Stanley eventually reached the eastern shore of Lake Tanganyika on 10 November, where the historical encounter between the two unlike explorers took place in the small village of Ujiji. Together they traveled on the still relatively unknown vast African "inland sea".

As a journalist, Stanley took part in a punitive campaign carried out by the British army against the Ashanti, an African tribe in the south of Ghana. When Livingstone died later the same year, Stanley resolved to continue the work of this great Scotsman.

Stanley's great expedition was announced by two major newspapers, the "New York Herald" and the "Daily Telegraph".

An impressive 356-strong private group reached Lake Victoria after an arduous trek, and the lake was explored in its full length. Accompanied by an armed escort of the black prince Mtésa, ruler of Uganda, Stanley explored the area of Lake Albert. On board the "Lady Alice", a river boat, he traveled on the Congo River and reached the "Stanley Falls" northeast of the Congo despite the persistent hostility of the inhabitants of the shoreline. At the confluence of

the Congo and Aruwimi Rivers he had to disperse a flotilla of fifty pirogues with automatic firearms. By the time the explorer reached the "Stanley Pool" he had cleared 32 cataracts. In early August, his private army had dwindled to such an extent that he was dependent on help. On 9 August, 1877 he arrived in Boma on the mouth of the Congo River.

Henry Morton Stanley's ventures were unique in the history of African exploration. Nevertheless, when he proposed the British government to include the whole of the Congo region into its colonial empire, the government in London declined. The British Cabinet regarded Stanley as a mere adventurer and sensationalist journalist.

In disappointment, Stanley left Great Britain and turned to the "Association internationale africaine", founded by the Belgian King Leopold II. In 1879 he traveled a second time on the Congo River, this time on behalf of the Belgian government. In 1880, the French explorer Brazza pre-empted him on the right bank of the Congo River. Seven years later he was again serving the British government and in 1888 he helped Emin Pasha, ruler of Egyptian Sudan and a friend of the British, to ascend the throne once more. During this expedition he explored Lake

Native war canoe

Young Africans by the fireside

Edward and the Semliki River, which connects Lake Edward and Lake Albert. In 1899, Stanley was knighted. As a member of the British parliament he devoted himself to the study of colonial issues.

Stanley is the most celebrated British explorer of central Africa apart from Livingstone. Unlike the latter, who was a philanthropist, Stanley never hesitated to accept help from the notorious slave traders to realize his goals. All of Stanley's expeditions were realized at great expense. Through skillful contracts with the black potentates he procured an African empire for King Leopold II which was eighty times larger than the Belgian mother country. Opposite the French town of Brazzaville, Stanley founded the town of Leopoldville.

Stanley Falls (seven waterfalls of the Lualaba River, which is called Congo from this point onwards), Stanley Pool (the lake-like widening of the Congo River before the Lower Guinea) and the town of Stanleyville (today Kisangani) are named for this explorer of Africa.

Further reading
H. M. Stanley, How I found Livingstone, travels, adventures and discoveries in Central Africa, including a month's residence with Dr. Livingstone. London 1872
–, Through the dark continent or the sources of the Nile around the great lakes of equatorial Africa and down the Livingstone River to the Atlantic-Ocean. London 1878
Lettres de H. M. Stanley. Paris 1879
H. M. Stanley, In darkest Africa. 2 vols. London 1890
W. G. Brattelot, Stanleys Nachhut in Jambuya unter Major Edm. M. Brattelot. Hamburg 1891
P. Reichard, Stanley. Berlin 1897
D. Stanley, Mein Leben. 2 Vols. Munich 1911
"Autobiographie" von H. M. Stanley, Paris 1911
J. Wassermann, Das Leben Stanleys. Zurich 1949
H. M. Stanley, Wie ich Livingstone fand 1871. 2nd ed. Stuttgart 1986
–, Wie ich Livingstone fand. Tatsachenbericht. Berlin 1988

STARK, DAME FREYA MADELINE

French traveler, born 1893 in Paris, died 1993 in Asolo (Italy).

After reading the book "A Thousand and One Nights", the then nine-year-old girl was inspired to undertake exploratory journeys later in her life.

During her extensive scientific ventures she went to Luristan in the south of Kurdistan (Persia), an area inhabited only by the Lurde nomads, whose main occupations were smuggling and thieving. Despite these dangers the explorer managed to make important archaeological findings about the ancient sites of Larti and Hindimini. She also visited the "Valley of the Assassins" (Arabic for hashish-smokers), the place of residence of this secret sect which was founded in 1090 by the Persian Hasan ibn al-Sabbah. The members of this fanatical and violent political and religious community had the habit of intoxicating themselves with hashish and then killing their opponents.

Following her exploration of Persia, Freya Stark devoted herself to studying the Arabic peninsula, where she explored the southern part of Hadramaut. Her numerous travel books convey a fascinating picture of her expeditions and are rich in historical and topographical information. Freya Stark was the first adventurer to explore both the wild region of Luristan and Arabia.

Further reading
F. Stark, the Valleys of the Assassins and other Persian Travels. London 1934
–, The Southern Gates of Arabia. A Journey in the Hadramaut. London 1936
–, Seen in the Hadramaut. London 1938
–, A Winter in Arabia. London 1940
–, Letters from Syria. London 1942
–, The coast of Incense. London 1953
L. Moorehead (Hg.), Letters, 8 Vols. Without place of publication 1974-1982.
F. M. Stark, Im Tal der Mörder. Eine Europäerin im Persien der dreißiger Jahre. Stuttgart 1991
–, Der Osten und der Westen. Ansichten über Arabien. Dortmund 1992
–, Im Tal der Mörder. Munich 1993
–, Pässe, Schluchten und Ruinen. Die abenteuerliche Reise einer Frau auf den Spuren Alexander des Großen in Kleinasien. Stuttgart 1993
–, Die Südtore Arabiens. Munich 1994
–, Wilde Frauen reisen anders. Berlin 1994
F. M. Stark, Pässe, Schluchten und Ruinen. Munich 1995

Henry Morton Stanley's handwriting

STEFANSSON, VILHJALMUR

Canadian Arctic explorer and ethnologist, born 1879 in Arnes (Manitoba), died 1962 in Hanover (New Hampshire).

In 1904-05, Stefansson undertook an archaeological journey to Iceland on behalf of Harvard University. In 1906 he joined an Arctic expedition in his capacity as an ethnologist and lived alone amongst Inuit in the winter of 1906-07. In 1910, in the course of extensive excursions on Coronation Gulf, he discovered an almost unknown tribe of "white" Inuit, possibly the descendants of migrant Vikings. During the time he spent with the Inuit, Stefansson adapted to their way of life, confirmed John Rae's theory of Arc-

Facing page, top: African farmstead with clay pots and calabashes

Facing page, bottom: Market stall with fabrics and food and a small tailor's shop, c. 1900

Sir Aurel Stein undertook extended trips to the deserts of the Asian interior.

tic survival and made important anthropological findings about the inhabitants of the Arctic.

From 1913 to 1918 he was head of the Canadian Arctic Expedition financed by the Canadian government. The aim of this venture was to explore the Beaufort Sea and the Canadian islands. Stefansson discovered the Brock-Borden and the Meighen Islands, studied the hydrographical nature of the Beaufort Sea and explored Banks Land.

After the successful realization of this expedition, he retired from public life and began to write his travel reports. From 1932 to 1945 he was a scientific advisor to Pan American Airways for the Arctic flights.

Vilhjalmur Stefansson's scientific work on the Canadian Arctic was without doubt the most important of the twentieth century. He put Dr. John Rae's theory into practice and especially underlined the economic importance of the Arctic. His findings on the geographical and mete-

orological conditions of the Arctic proved invaluable to civil airlines for their flights over this region.

Further reading
V. Stefansson, My life with the Eskimos. London 1913
–, Das Geheimnis der Eskimos. Without place of publication 1925
–, The friendly Arctic. The story of five years in Polar Region. New York 1921
–, Länder der Zukunft. 2 Bde. Without place of publication 1923
–, Unsolved Mysteries of the Arctic. London 1939
–, Ultima Thule. London and New York 1940 and 1942

STEIN, SIR (MARK) AUREL

British explorer of Asia and archaeologist, born 1862 in Budapest, died 1943 in Kabul.

After studying the archaeology of Persia and India at Tübingen and Oxford Universities, he went to England in 1884 and then traveled to northwestern India in 1888.

From 1900 to 1901, 1906 to 1908 and 1913 to 1916 Stein undertook extensive archaeological expeditions through the deserts of inner Asia and the Chinese part of Turkestan. In addition he explored the scientific importance of the old trade routes between Indian and China, especially of the former Silk Road from Sian via Ansi, Keria, Khotan, Kaschgar to Balch and its auxiliary route to Samarkand. He also explored the province of Beluchistan.

From 1927 to 1936 he set out several times to the northwestern frontier of India, into the province of Beluchistan and into Iran. In the course of these archaeological expeditions Stein found a close prehistoric relationship between the valley of the Indus and Iran.

Stein's principal achievement was the discovery and excavation of ancient sites in the deserts of the interior of Asia. He pointed out the importance of the early civilizations of Chinese Turkestan's oases and found that paper documents could survive conservation in the dry desert sand for centuries without damage. The importance of his discovery of ancient Chinese manuscripts in the valley of the grottoes of the "Thousand Buddhas" ranks in importance with the discovery by the Frenchman P. Pelliot. Part of this unique documentary treasure is kept at the British Museum in London.

In 1904, Aurel Stein became a British citizen and in 1912 he was knighted for his services to science.

Further reading
A. Stein, Ancient Khotan. 2 vols. Oxford 1907
–, Marco Polo's Account of a Mongol Inroad into Kashmir. London 1919 (from the Geographical Journal, August 1919)
–, The Thousand Buddhas. London 1921
–, Innermost India. 4 vols. Oxford 1928
–, On Alexander's Track to the Indus. London 1929

–, Archaeological Reconnaissances in North-Western India and South-Eastern Iran. London 1937
–, Old Routes of Western Iran. London 1940

STUART, JOHN McDOUALL

Scottish explorer of Australia, born 1815 in Dysart (Fife), died 1866 in Nottingham Hill.

After two unsuccessful attempts to cross Australia from south to north, Stuart succeeded in conquering the continent from Adelaide on the south coast via Alice Springs in the center of the continent to Darwin on the north coast in 1862. A telegraph line was later erected along the route taken by Stuart; this served as orientation for subsequent explorers of Australia such as P. E. Warburton and J. Forrest.

Stuart is regarded as one of the most important explorers of Australia.

Further reading
Explorations in Australia. The journals of J. M. D. Stuart during 1858, 1859, 1860, 1861 and 1862, when he fixed the centre of the continent and successfully crossed it from sea to sea. Edited from Mr. Stuart's manuscript by W. Hardmann. London 1864

STURT, CHARLES

British explorer of Australia, born 1795 in India, died 1869 in Cheltenham (England).

From 1813, Sturt served as a soldier in British India. In 1827 his regiment was transferred to Australia, where the following year Sturt investigated the Macquarie River as head of an expedition and, accompanied by the explorers Wellington and H. Hume, discovered the Darling River and explored more than 100 km (60 miles) of its banks.

On his second expedition he discovered the Murray River together with Fraser and Maclay, explored its tributaries and arrived back in Sydney in a state of starvation and almost blind.

In 1844, Sturt undertook his last great expedition from Adelaide in the direction of Lake

John McDouall Stuart, Scottish explorer of Australia

Torres. The 12-strong expedition, which had been intending to reach the Gulf of Carpentaria, proceeded as far north as 24° 40' S before being forced back by a terrible drought. When Sturt subsequently explored Cooper's Creek, he discovered luxuriant expanses of greenery. This finding put an end to the claim that western Queensland consisted only of infertile soil. After a journey full of privation during which several members of the expedition died of exhaustion and scurvy, the group arrived back at its starting point in Adelaide.

Sturt was one of the first and most important explorers of the interior of Australia and is regarded as the "father of Australian exploration".

Further reading
C. Sturt, Narrative of an Expedition into Central Australia, performed during the years 1844, 1845 and 1846, together with a notice of the Province of South-Australia in 1847, 2 vols. London 1849

Ayers Rock, the largest monolith on Earth, is an important sacred site of the Australian aborigines.

T

TARDY, DE MONTRAVEL LOUIS FERDINAND DE

Admiral and circumnavigator of the world, born 1811, died 1864.

After taking part in a journey of exploration with Dumont d'Urville in the year 1837 Tardy turned his attention to studying the coast of South America. His geographical work contains significant information about the mouths of the Orinoco, the Amazon and the La Plate, about the coast of Japan and the Sea of Okhotsk. In 1854 Tardy took possession of New Caledonia for France.

Valentina Vladimirovna Tereshkova

TASMAN, ABEL JANSZOON

Dutch seafarer and explorer, born 1603 in Lutjegast (Groningen), died 1659 in Batavia.

In 1642 Van Diemen, the Dutch governor general of Dutch India (Indonesia) in Batavia, commissioned Tasman to carry out an exploratory voyage to the Great Australian Bight to determine the contours of the continent. Prior to Tasman, other Dutch seafarers such as Janszoon, Hartogzoon and Houtman had already carried out voyages of exploration to the southern Australian waters.

Tasman set sail from Mauritius, took a southern course and discovered the island of Tasmania, which he named "Van Diemen's Land" in honor of his governor and superior. Continuing on his journey he discovered land again in 1643 (New Zealand), which he named "State Land" and assumed that it was part of Australia. Tasman unwittingly sailed through what was later to be named Cook Strait (between the North and South Islands of New Zealand) and reached the Tonga Islands. From there, he took a westerly course, passed the Fiji Islands and sighted New Ireland (Bismarck Group), which he believed to be New Guinea, before returning to Batavia. In 1644 Tasman explored the southern coast of New Guinea and charted the Gulf of Carpentaria and the entire north coast of Australia.

Abel Tasman is regarded as the true discoverer of Australia. He was the first seaman to circumnavigate the continent. The largest island to the southeast of Australia and the sea between eastern Australia and New Zealand bear the name of this important seafarer.

Further reading
Sir J. Narborough, An Account of several late voyages to the south and north towards the Straits of Magellan, the South Seas ... London 1694
J. Harris, The Voyage of Captain A. J. Tasman for the Discovery of Southern Countries taken from his original journal. London 1744
Journal van de Reis naar het onbekende Zuidland, in die jare 1642. Medegedeeld en met Aanteekeningen voorzien, door J. Swart. Amsterdam 1860
C. M. Dozy, Abel Janszoon Tasman. Amsterdam 1894 (?)
C. G. Henderson, The Discoverers of the Fiji Islands: Tasman, Cook, Bligh, Wilson, Bellingshausen. London 1933

TERESHKOVA, VALENTINA VLADIMIROVNA

Soviet cosmonaut, born 1937 in Masslenikovo (Yaroslavl area).

On 16 June, 1963, Valentina Tereshkova was the first woman in space at the age of only 26 when she traveled on board the "Vostok 6". During the next three days she orbited the earth 48 times – more than the six American "Mercury" astronauts who had been in space before her.

During her flight, Tereshkova made television broadcasts for the Soviet public and maintained radio contact with the cosmonaut Valery Bykovsky, who was in space at the same time on board "Vostok 5". At one point, the spaceships passed each other at a distance of only 5 km (3 miles) and they both returned to earth on 19 June, 1963. Originally, Tereshkova's mission was only supposed to last 24 hours but due to her favorable physical condition it proved possible to prolong the journey to three days, during which time she did not leave her seat. The tasks of the mission were to study the influence of extended space travel on the female organism and comparative analyses of the consequences for males and females. Cosmonaut Tereshkova proved with her flight that with the appropriate preparation, women are just as suitable for space travel as men.

The decision to include women in the USSR space missions was made in the summer of 1961.

The Twelve Apostels,
near Port Campbell,
southeastern Australia

The Scottish explorer of Africa Joseph Thomson traveled through Morocco in his later years. This picture shows Benhaddou.

The 3,645 meter (11,960 foot) Mount Sabinjo seen from the south.

Yuri Gagarin was a member of the selection commission. Amongst hundreds of young women who wanted to become a cosmonaut, five candidates were chosen from various aviation clubs. Two of the criteria were that the women had to be unmarried and have no children. One of the women chosen was Valentina Tereshkova, who until then had worked as a textile technician and parachutist. The training programs for the male and female cosmonauts were almost identical and included the study of spaceship technology, navigation and geophysics, the study of weightlessness, periods spent in trial chambers, sport and parachute jumping. The decision as to which of the women was eventually allowed to fly on board the spaceship was only made a week before the launch. After the mission of "Vostok 6" the group of women still existed for another six years and prepared for possible new flights, e.g. from the middle of the 1960s for a "Soyuz" mission. However, this plan did not meet with universal approval, so the women were dismissed in October 1969. No new female cosmonauts were selected until 1980.

Valentina Tereshkova is regarded as one of the most important figures in the Soviet women's movement, and she also pursued a political career. In 1974 she became a member of the Central Committee and was elected into the Congress of the People's Deputies in 1989.

Further reading
M. Sharpe, This is "Seagull!". Without place of publication 1975

THOMSON, JOSEPH

Scottish explorer of Africa, born 1858 in Penpont (Scotland), died 1895 in London.

After studying geology, in his capacity of geologist Thomson took part in an expedition to east Africa which was financed by the African

Exploration Fund Committee and directed by Keith Johnston. When Johnston died during the expedition, Thomson assumed leadership. After various difficulties he reached Lake Tanganyika and the Congo River, but had to interrupt his journey due to the hostility of the natives. In 1880 he returned to the east African coast via Lake Leopold II.

In 1882, Thomson undertook a second expedition to central Africa on behalf of the Royal Geographical Society. From the east African, coast he reached Lake Tanganyika, continued on to Mount Kilimanjaro and Mount Kenya and once more confirmed the existence of these snow-covered central African mountains. After exploring the area of the Masai, a nomadic tribe in what is today the northeast of Tanzania and the south of Kenya, he returned to his point of departure. Three years later he traveled to Nigeria, Morocco and Nyassaland (present-day Malawi).

Thomson's merits are his thorough exploration of the Masai area and of the east African fauna and flora. A town in western Kenya, the nearby waterfalls and a species of gazelle were named for this Scottish explorer.

Further reading
J. Thomson, To the Central African Lakes and Back. Narrative of the Royal Geographical Society's East Central African Expedition 1878-1880. London 1881
–, Through the Masai-Land. London 1885
–, Travels in the Atlas and Southern Morocco. A Narrative of Exploration. London 1889

TINNÉ, ALEXANDRA PETRONELLA FRANCINA

Dutch explorer of Africa, born 1839 in 's Gravenhage (The Hague), died 1869 in Fessan (South Tripoli Province).

Alexandra Tinné came from a well-to-do family. After returning from a journey throughout Europe and the Middle East, she settled in

Alexandra Tinné

Cairo and devoted her time to the exploration of Africa and the fight against slavery. From the Egyptian capital she undertook her first large-scale expedition into Sudan, reached Khartoum and there paid for the release of one hundred slaves. Accompanied by her mother and the two scientists T. von Heuglin and Dr. Steudner, she journeyed into the still unexplored area of Bahr el-Ghasal, a left tributary of the White Nile in the south of Sudan. During this journey both her mother and Dr. Steudner fell victim to the unrelenting climate. On her return journey Alexandra

Tinné wandered through the Sahara and reached Cairo via Khartoum.

Alexandra Tinné studied Arabic history and the Koran in the Egyptian capital and assumed Muslim customs and way of life (a "female Lawrence of Arabia").

During an extended journey through the Mediterranean on her private yacht, Alexandra Tinné went ashore in Tripoli and, together with three Europeans and an impressive caravan, undertook an expedition to Lake Chad. Not far from Buirgiz, a village in Fessan, she was murdered by a Tuareg tribesman.

Tinné's principal merit was not so much her scientific exploration of the Bahr el-Ghasal region, but her courageous fight against the slave trade in eastern Africa.

Further reading
W. Wells, The Heroine of the White Nile. A sketch of the travels and experiences of Miss A. Tinné. New York 1871
W. Sutherland, Alexandra Tinné. Haar leven en reizen. Amsterdam 1935

TITOV, VLADIMIR GEORGYEVICH

Soviet cosmonaut, born 1947 in Stretensk (Chita region).

For the first time in the history of space travel, together with Musa Manarov, Vladimir Titov spent more than a year in space.

Originally Titov wanted to become a radio technician, but in 1965 he failed the entry examination. In 1967 he joined the Soviet air force and was selected in 1976 for the cosmonaut group.

In September 1983 Titov narrowly escaped death. A kerosene leakage on the Baikonur launching site caused a Soyuz rocket to explode. However, after a five-minute flight, the shortest of a manned USSR spaceship, the cosmonauts' capsule landed safely on the Cosmodrome with the uninjured Titov and Gennadi Strakalov.

In 1992, Vladimir Titov was nominated as a candidate for a flight on board the US Space Shuttle.

TYSON, GEORGE EMORY

Canadian whaler and Arctic explorer, born 1829, died 1906.

In the course of a polar expedition under the leadership of Charles Francis, Tyson and 17 other participants were set adrift on an ice floe in October 1872 and drifted until April 1873. He and his companions were picked up on the coast of Labrador by Isaac Bartlett in the "Tigress". In 1877 George Tyson set out on an expedition to Cumberland Sound and Baffin Land with the objective of founding a settlement on Ellesmere Land. This was intended to be a base for future polar expeditions. Although all the preparations and examinations were successfully completed, the settlement was not founded, because Congress refused to make the necessary funds available. A permanent settlement was not established until 1950.

Facing page: Alexandra Tinné on one of her expeditions, as viewed by her contemporaries

V

VAMBÉRY, ARMIN HERMANN BAMBERGER

Hungarian Turkologist and explorer of Asia, born 1832 in Dunaszerdahely (Dep. Pozsony), died 1913 in Budapest.

Even as a child, Armin Vambéry showed an immense talent for languages. Despite the poverty of his parents, he managed to attend university and speak most major European languages fluently by the age of twenty. From 1857 to 1863 he worked as a French teacher in Istanbul (Constantinople); during this time he also took up the study of oriental languages. In 1860 he became a correspondent to the Hungarian Academy of Sciences.

Three years later he set out on his large-scale journey through Asia. On behalf of the Hungarian Academy he was commissioned to establish linguistic relationships between the oriental languages and Hungarian. Dressed as a Dervish he traveled through still unexplored regions of Asia. Via the Caspian Sea he reached the Turkmen, the inhabitants of the Seljuk empire, and further via the Hyrkan desert to Chiwa, a town in an oasis on the lower Amu-Darja and an important center of trade for central Asia (annexed by Russia in 1873). From there he continued to Buchara in the sandy desert of Kysylkum, which had almost been completely destroyed under Genghis Khan and had been conquered by Russian troops in 1868; he then reached Samarkand in the river oasis of Serah Tsahan. Subsequently, Vambéry traveled through Afghanistan, having explored Persia. When he returned from his large-scale scientific expedition, Vambéry was appointed Professor of Oriental Languages in Budapest.

His work had a major influence on the geography, ethnography and linguistics of central Asia. In 1876 Vambéry became a member, in 1893 an honorary member and in 1894 a director of the Hungarian Academy of Sciences.

Further reading
A. Vambéry, Reise in Mittelasien, 2nd ed.
Without place of publication 1865
–, Meine Wanderungen und Erlebnisse in Persien.
Budapest 1868
–, Geschichte Bucharas und Transoxaniens,
2 vols. Without place of publication 1872
–, Etymologisches Wörterbuch der turkotarischen Sprachen. Without place of publication 1878
–, Der Ursprung der Magyaren. Without place of publication 1882
–, The story of my struggles, Memoirs. 2 vols.
London 1904

VANCOUVER, GEORGE

British seafarer and explorer, born 1757 in King's Lynn, died 1798 in Richmond (Surrey).

George Vancouver joined the Royal Navy at the age of thirteen and accompanied Captain James Cook on his second and third Pacific voyages. After serving for a period of nine years in the West Indies, Vancouver was instructed to take the "unlawfully" acquired areas from the Spanish, who by that time had penetrated far beyond San Francisco. In addition he was commissioned to explore the west American coast from 30° N to Cooks River, in order to find the sea route from Alaska to Hudson Bay and to establish the true significance of the discovery of the Spaniard Juan de Fuca (the "Juan de Fuca Strait").

On 1 April, 1791, Vancouver left the port of Falmouth on board the "Discovery" (not Cook's old ship) and the "Chatham", rounded the Cape of Good Hope, headed for the west coast of Australia, explored the Great Australian Bight, headed towards New Zealand, discovered the small island of Oparo, went ashore in Tahiti and, by taking a northern course, reached Hawaii and in April 1792 the North American coast. There he negotiated with the Spanish authorities. Subsequently, Vancouver explored the bays and channels of the North American west coast to Georgia Bay and the island that bears his name; he confirmed the discovery of Juan de Fuca and reached a latitude of 52° 18' N. Another sojourn in Hawaii followed (1793). In the course of the next year, Vancouver explored Cook Island a second time, visited San Francisco, rounded Cape Horn and returned to London in October 1794 via St. Helena.

Vancouver died at the age of 41; he was not able to complete his geographical travel reports. A town in the District of Columbia in western Canada as well as a 40,000 square kilometer (15,500 square mile) island were named for this great seafarer and geographer.

Further reading
J. Vancouver (brother of George), A Voyage of Discovery to the North Pacific Ocean and Round the World. 1790-1795, 3 Vols. With an Atlas of maps and plates. 1798
G. H. Anderson, Vancouver and his Great Voyage. The story of a Norfolk Sailor. Captain Geo. Vancouver. R. N. 1757-1798. London 1923
G. S. Godwin, Vancouver: A Life. London 1930

George Vancouver landed on the picturesque island of Tahiti.

On one of his travels, George Vancouver visited San Francisco. This representation of the town dates from 1846.

Amerigo Vespucci on the frontispiece of a leaflet comprising an account of his second voyage to Brazil

VESPUCCI, AMERIGO

Italian seafarer, born 1454 (?) in Florence, died 1512 in Seville.

Vespucci came from a Florentine family of patricians. At the age of 30, Vespucci went to Seville to take over the management of a trading house founded by Berardi, also from Florence. In 1497 he equipped Columbus' fleet for its voyage to the New World.

According to Vespucci's own statements, he undertook a total of four expeditions to America. On behalf of the Spanish king, Vespucci left

Cadiz on 10 May, 1497 for South America and reached the mainland one year before Columbus. (The facts of this journey are disputed.)

On his second crossing between 1499 and 1500, which he undertook together with the Spanish seafarer V. Y. Pinzón, he discovered the mouth of the Amazon, and on his third journey he explored the Brazilian coast to 52° S. In 1502 he undertook his fourth journey. On his return, accompanied by the Portuguese seafarer N. Coelho, he brought back a large shipment of dyeing woods to Lisbon.

Renowned historians have put all of Vespucci's voyages into question and have endeavored to prove that his reports were not well founded. Since the ships' documents are no longer available, it is very difficult today to investigate Vespucci's claims. The German scholar Waldseemüller named the newly discovered continent for Vespucci's first name: America.

Further reading
A. Busiri-Vici, I tri celebri navigatori italiani del seculo decimosesto (i. e. Columbus, Vespucci, Andrea Doria). Rome 1892
G. Conti, Amerigo Vespucci. Florence 1898
A. M. Bandini, Vita de Amerigo Vespucci. Bibliografica delle opere concernenti Amerigo Vespucci per G. Fumagalli. Florenz 1898 (1st ed. Florence 1745)
A. Magnaghi, Amerigo Vespucci. Rome 1924
R. Eger, Amerigo Vespucci. Zurich 1945
N. Besio Moreno, El Meridiano de Tordesillas y el descubrimiento del Rio de la Plata por Vespucci. 1952
A. Vespucci, Berichte über meine Reisen und Entdeckungen in der Neuen Welt, ed. W. Irving. Hamburg 1992

VICTOR, PAUL-EMILE

French polar explorer and navy officer, born 1907 in Geneva, died 1995.

Paul-Emile Victor studied mathematics, ethnology and literary science. On completing his engineering degree, he became an officer in the French Navy.

In 1934, Victor undertook his first scientific Arctic expedition. On behalf of J. B. Charcot, an Arctic explorer, and accompanied by three fellow countrymen, he spent a year amongst the Inuit of Angmagssalik on the east cost of Greenland. In 1936 he crossed the Greenland interior ice from west to east with three companions on sledges drawn by huskies. He then lived with an Inuit family for fourteen months and thoroughly studied their way of life; he brought back revealing information from this sojourn in Greenland.

In 1938-39 he explored Lapland and founded the "Expéditions Polaires Françaises" in Greenland in 1947 and became the director of these expeditions. He was head of the International Glacier Expedition in Greenland and president of the Scientific Committee on Antarctic Research. He also played an important role during the International Geophysical Year in 1957-58.

Paul-Emile Victor was one of the greatest French and European Arctic explorers of the

Paul-Emile Victor

The Yang-tse Kiang, which Marco Polo admiringly called the "king of rivers".

twentieth century. He undertook a total of 38 polar expeditions and wrote more than 300 scientific papers, most of them on the Arctic.

Further reading
P. E. Victor, Pilote de Terre d'Adélie. Without place of publication 1963
–, Pôle-Nord. Without place of publication 1963
–, Pôle-Nord, Pôle-Sud. Without place of publication 1967
–, Sur la piste blanche. Without place of publication 1968
–, Terres polaires, terres tragiques. Without place of publication 1971

VILKITSKI, BORIS ANDREYEVITCH

See Wilkitski.

VRAZ, ENRIK STANKO

Czech explorer, born 1860 in Trnovo (Bulgaria), died 1932 in Prague. Overcome with a passion for travel, Vraz went to Morocco for three years in 1880. Subsequently he crossed the Sahara in the direction of the Gambia River, which he reached at the end of 1885. During the next two years Vraz explored the coast of Sierra Leone, Liberia, Ghana and the Gold Coast.

In 1889 he turned towards the exploration of Central and South America and visited the islands of Guadeloupe, Martinique, Trinidad and then reached Venezuela. In 1892-93 this Czech traveler explored the Orinoco and the Amazon, crossed the Andes and reached the Pacific Ocean. In 1895 he traveled to Japan, central China, Indonesia, Indochina, Java, Bali, Lompoc, Celebes, New Guinea, Borneo and returned to Bohemia via Aden on the Persian Gulf and Suez.

Two years after his return, Vraz headed for Central America, climbed the Popocatepetl, a 5,452 m (17,887 foot) volcano 60 km (40 miles) south of Mexico City. In 1900 he again explored China, Manchuria and Korea, visited Vladivostok (the terminus of the Trans-Siberian Railway), sailed on Lake Baikal (the world's deepest lake) and once again visited America. In 1903 he visited various places on the Pacific and Atlantic Oceans and then traveled a second time through Mexico and the Central American isthmus.

Apart from Holub, Vraz is the most significant explorer from the former Czechoslovakia.

Further reading
E. S. Vraz, travers l'Amérique centrale. Itinéraire du voyageur. Prague 1900
–, Siam, le pays de l'éléphant blanc. Itinéraire du voyageur. Prague 1901
–, Chine. Itinéraire du voyageur. De Pékin pour Vladivostok. Prague 1904

A junk on the beach of Tsingtau, a town and peninsula in China

Chinese rikshaws in a hand-colored black and white photograph from 1900.

WALLACE, ALFRED RUSSELL

British scientist and explorer, born 1823 in Usk, died 1913 in Broadstone.

From an early age, Alfred Wallace was interested in botany and zoology. The well-known scientist W. Bates introduced him to entomology in 1844.

In 1850 he traveled to Brazil and studied the flora and fauna of the region of the Rio Negro and the Rio Uaupés (two rivers in Columbia and

Alfred Russell Wallace

Brazil). On his return journey he lost most of his extensive collection in a fire on board his ship.

From 1854 to 1862 he explored the Malayan archipelago and accumulated a vast collection of exotic plants and animals.

Wallace excelled in the field of animal geography and is regarded as the co-founder of the theory of evolution, which he formulated at the same time as Charles Darwin.

Further reading
A. R. Wallace, A Narrative of travels on the
Amazonas and Rio Negro. London 1853
–, The Malay Archipelago. London 1869
–, Geographical Distribution of Animals. 2 vols.
London 1876
–, Island Life. London 1880
–, Der Malayische Archipel, ed. P. Simons.
Frankfurt/M. 1983

WARBURTON, PETER EGERTON

British explorer of Australia, born 1813, died 1889.

Following an extensive period of military training spent in India, Peter Warburton traveled to Australia in the year 1853. In 1872 he led an expedition across the south of the continent, from Adelaide to Perth. This arid region of Australia, the Nullarbor Plain (meaning in Latin a plain "devoid of trees"), was practically unknown at the time. The objective of this expedition was to establish an overland route across the desert to Perth on the southwest coast. Although this aim was not achieved (since the route had to be modified due to lack of water), Warburton received numerous honors and was granted some farmland as a reward for his tribulations.

For reasons of age, Peter Warburton was not able to write an extensive account of his travels. Only a few of his sketches have survived to the present day; these were published in 1875.

WEDDELL, JAMES

British seafarer, born 1787 in Ostend (Belgium), died 1834 in London.

Weddell participated in long voyages from an early age. In 1810 he became a ship's mate on the "Firefly", then on the "Hope". Nine years later he penetrated into Antarctic waters in search of whaling grounds, sailed into the "Weddell Sea", cruised near the South Orkney and South Shetland Islands and reached 74° 15' S on 23 February, 1823. In July 1824 he returned to England.

The news of his advance was doubted by various scientists. His assertion that Antarctica could be reached on the open sea was only later confirmed by Bruce (1904) and Filchner (1912).

Further reading
J. Weddell, A voyage towards the South Pole in 1822-1824. London 1825

WEGENER, ALFRED LOTHAR

German geophysicist, meteorologist and Arctic explorer, born 1880 in Berlin, died 1930 in Greenland.

From 1906 to 1908, Alfred Wegener participated in the Danish "Danmark Expedition" to northeast Greenland. During this venture he learnt the art of traveling by dog sledge and studied Arctic technology. Wegener participated in three great sledge journeys: from Danmarkshaven (eastern Greenland) to Sabine Island and back (almost 600 km or 370 miles); from Danmarkshaven to the northeastern coast of Greenland ; from Danmarkshaven to Dronning Louise Land. The first two journeys were performed with dog sledges, the last using hand-drawn sledges.

In 1912, Wegener undertook a journey by horse sledge together with L. P. Koch from the

Peter Warburton on an expedition with camels through the arid Nullarbor Plain of southern Australia

351

The German Arctic explorer Alfred Lothar Wegener

In 1930, Wegener was once again drawn to Greenland. After erecting the "Eismitte" base (approximately on the line of Sandodden and Godhaven) he continued in a westerly direction, accompanied by the Inuit Rasmus Villumsen, to reach the coast. Half way along their journey they were both killed.

Wegener's theories about the continental drift, his papers on the thermodynamics of the atmosphere and about cloud physics, his attempts to interpret halo phenomena and especially his explorations of the cap of the Greenland interior ice already earned him the status of a significant European scientist during his lifetime.

Further reading
A. L. Wegener, *Thermodynamik der Atmosphäre. Leipzig 1911*
– (and Koch), Durch die weiße Wüste. Berlin 1911
A. L. Wegener, *Die Entstehung der Kontinente und Ozeane. Braunschweig 1920*
–, Mit Motorboot und Schlitten durch Grönland. Mit Beiträgen von J. Georgi, Fr. Loewe und E. Sorge. Bielefeld and Leipzig 1930
Wissenschaftliche Ergebnisse der dänischen Expedition nach Dronning Louise-Land und quer über das Inlandeis von Nordgrönland 1912-1913. Meddelelser om Grönland, Vol 75. Copenhagen 1930
E. Wegener, F. Loewe, *Alfred Wegeners letzte Grönlandfahrt. Leipzig 1933*
J. Georgi, *Im Eis vergraben. Erlebnisse auf "Station Eismitte" der letzten Grönlandexpedition Alfred Wegeners 1930-1931. Munich 1933*
E. Wegener, *Alfred Wegener. Tagebücher, Briefe, Erinnerungen. Wiesbaden 1960*

winter base "Borg" (east of Danmarkshaven) through Dronning Louise Land, crossed the Greenland interior ice and reached Upernavik on the west coast of Greenland.

From 1919 to 1924 he taught geophysics and meteorology in Hamburg and from 1924 to 1929 in Graz.

WEYPRECHT, KARL

German-Austrian Arctic explorer, born 1838 in Darmstadt, died 1881 in Michelstadt.

In 1856, Weyprecht joined the Austrian-Hungarian military navy. In 1866 he participated in the sea battle of Lissa, where the Italian fleet was defeated by the Austrian admiral Tegetthoff.

Weyprecht was a member of the "Isbjörn Expedition" (1871) into the then unknown ocean regions of the northern Barents Sea.

In 1872 the scientifically highly gifted naval officer was instructed by the government to undertake a major Arctic expedition. This expedition mainly came about due to the financial support of Count Wilczek. On 14 July, 1872, Weyprecht left the Norwegian port of Tromsö on board the "Tegetthoff", a ship especially built for the Arctic Sea; his aim was to reach Nowaya Zemlya and from there to continue to the North Pole. On 21 August, the "Tegetthoff" was enclosed by pack ice between Novaya Zemlya and Franz Joseph Land. During the dramatic drift journey which then ensued, Weyprecht discovered a region which he called "Franz Joseph Land". He also discovered Hall, Hohenlode, Prinz Rudolf and McClintock Islands. On another exploratory mission the explorers reached a latitude of 82° N, further north than any other polar explorer before them. They abandoned the "Tegetthoff" and were rescued by the Russian captain Voronin in Dune Bay off Novaya Zemlya (1874).

The Austrian-Hungarian expedition in which Weyprecht participated brought valuable scientific news about the Arctic region and about the nature of Franz Joseph Land.

Further reading
K. Weyprecht, Österreichisch-Ungarische Arktisexpedition 1872-1874. Metamorphosen des Polarkreises. Vienna 1879
–, Praktische Anleitung zur Beobachtung der Polarlichter und der magnetischen Erscheinungen in hohen Breiten. Vienna 1881
H. v. Littrow, K. Weyprecht, der österreichische Nordpolarforscher. Erinnerungen und Briefe. Vienna, Pest, Leipzig 1881
G. v. Brosch, 1872-1874. Die österreichischungarische Polarexpedition unter Weyprecht und Payeer. In: Gedenkblätter der k. u. k. Kriegsmarine. Vol. IV, 2nd ed. Pola 1910
K. Linke, Die österreichische Nordpolfahrt von Payer und Weyprecht in den Jahren 1872-1874. Vienna 1946

Only the roof of the station "Westküste" remains visible; the rest of the building is completely covered in snow. From here, Wegener marched to the station "Eismitte".

WILKINS, SIR GEORGE HUBERT

Australian polar explorer, born 1888 in Mount Bryan East (Australia), died 1958 in Famingham (Mass.).

Wilkins studied at the School of Mines and Industries in Adelaide. In 1912-13 he participated in the First World War as an amateur photographer and war correspondent in the Balkan operations. From 1913 to 1917 he was a photographer for the Canadian Arctic expedition of the explorer V. Stefansson. In 1917 he again participated in the First World War as a member of the Australian Flying Corps and carried out dangerous exploratory flights for the French above German lines.

In 1920-21 he accompanied the British Imperial Antarctic Expedition. In his capacity as a natural scientist he accompanied the polar explorer E. Shackleton into Antarctica in 1921. Two years later he explored the tropical region of Australia on behalf of the British Museum.

In April 1928, Wilkins proved his special aptitude for polar flights. Together with the pilot C. B. Eielson, he flew from Point Barrow in

Alaska to Spitsbergen. They covered this polar route of approximately 3,380 km (2,100 miles) in 20 hours. Later the same year, Wilkins was nominated head of the Wilkins-Hearst Expedition. During this venture, an aircraft was used in Antarctica for the first time. Again accompanied by Eielson, he carried out geographical exploratory flights above Palmer Peninsula and took the first high-quality aerial photographs of Antarctica. In 1931, Wilkins set out to reach the North Pole on board the "Nautilus" submarine but could advance no further than the edge of the pack ice. From 1933 to 1939, Wilkins was advisor to the Antarctic expeditions of the polar explorer and pilot Ellsworth. In 1935 he flew from the Falkland Dependencies via western Antarctica to the Ross Sea. During the International Geophysical Year 1957-58, Sir George Wilkins visited Antarctica for the last time. Wilkin's merits are the first high-quality aerial photographs of Antarctica. An area in western Antarctica is named after this important polar pilot.

Further reading
G. H. Wilkins, Flying the Arctic. London and New York 1928
–, Undiscovered Australia, being an account of an expedition to tropical Australia to collect specimen of the rarer native fauna for the British Museum 1923 to 1925. London 1928
–, Under the North Pole, the Wilkins-Ellsworth Submarine Expedition. New York 1931
H. M. Sherman, Thoughts of Space. New York 1942

WILKITSKI (VILKITSKI), BORIS ANDREYEVITCH

Russian polar explorer, born 1855 in Russia, died 1951 in Brussels.

Wilkitski was an officer in the Imperial Russian Navy. Promoted to rear admiral and commander of the huge ice-breakers "Taymyr" und "Vaygach", he was instructed in 1913 to conquer the Northeast Passage from east to west.

From Anadyr on the east Siberian coast, Wilkitski rounded Cape Deshnev, crossed the East Siberian and Laptev Seas in the direction of the Taymyr Peninsula, but on 1 September was already prevented from traveling any further by masses of ice near Cape Chelyuskin. He took the northeastern route and discovered a group of islands that he named "Nicholas II Land" in honor of the tsar (today: Zvernaya Zemlya = North Land). In the meantime the masses of ice had grown to such an extent that Wilkitski decided to return.

After staying over winter in Petropavlovsk, a port on Kamchatka, he made a renewed attempt in 1915 during the First World War and reached Archangel on the White Sea without any difficulties.

Wilkitski was the first person to traverse the Northeast Passage from east to west. During this journey he took extensive hydrographical measurements along the north Siberian coast.

Further reading
B. A. Vilkitski, The Nordic Seaway (in Russian). St. Petersburg 1912

WISSMANN, HERMANN VON

German explorer of Africa, born 1853 in Frankfurt/Oder, died 1905 in Weissenbach (Styria).

From 1880 to 1882, Wissmann, accompanied by the Africa explorer Dr. P. Pogge, undertook an expedition from Luanda, the capital of Angola, via Malanje in Angola to the Kasai River, a tributary of the Congo River, and reached Nyangwe on the C<ongo. This was the first successful crossing of equatorial Africa from west to east.

From 1884 to 1886, Wissmann explored the Kasai and Congo Rivers, this time together with H. Müller, C. v. François, L. Wolf and others. He founded Luluaburg on the Middle Lulua River, a right tributary of the Kasai River.

In 1888, Wissmann was appointed Imperial Commissioner, in 1895-1896 Governor of German East Africa.

v. Wissmann

75 Pf.

75 Pf.

Gedenkt unserer Kolonien

A necessity bank note from c. 1920/21 depicting the German Africa explorer Hermann von Wissmann

After a journey through Asia, Wissmann withdrew to his property in Styria and devoted himself to travel literature. He died on June 15, 1905 as the result of a hunting accident.

Hermann von Wissmann's principal achievement is the geographical exploration of equatorial Africa.

Further reading
H. v. Wissmann, L. Wolf, C. v. François,
H. Müller, Im Innern Afrikas. Leipzig 1888
H. v. Wissmann, Meine zweite Durchquerung
Äquatorialafrikas vom Kongo bis zum Sambesi.
Frankfurt/O. 1890
–, In der Wildnis von Afrika und Asien. Jagd-
erlebnisse. Berlin 1901
R. Schmidt, Hermann von Wissmann und
Deutschlands koloniales Wirken. Berlin-
Grunewald, without year of publication.
H. v. Wissmann, Deutschlands größter
Africaforscher. Sein Leben und Werk mit
Benutzung des Nachlasses, dargest. v. C. von
Perhandt, G. Richelmann, Rochus Schmidt.
Berlin 1906

WRANGEL, FERDINAND PETROVICH BARON VON

Russian admiral and Arctic explorer, born 1796 in Pskov, died 1870 in Dorpat.

In 1817, Wrangel took part in an expedition led by Captain Golovnin to extend the Russian colonies in Alaska and to carry out hydrographical investigations in the Bering Strait.

In 1820, the Imperial Russian Navy instructed Wrangel, who by this time had acquired some fame, to establish the precise geographical position of Cape Shelagin, to explore the Medvezhi Islands and from there to continue to the North Pole. On 2 November, Wrangel sailed from St. Petersburg to the Barents Sea, reached Cape Shelagin with dog sledges, explored the Medvezhi Islands and undertook a 46-day trek through the Russian Arctic towards the North Pole.

In 1822, Wrangel explored Kolyma Bay and the land of the Chuktchen in the far northeast of Siberia.

Next double page: The German explorer Hermann von Wissmann (seated at left) with Sudanese soldiers in Cairo in the year 1889

Ferdinand Petrovich Baron von Wrangel

In February 1823, the Arctic explorer reached a latitude of 70° 5' N on a further Arctic voyage and sighted an island in the East Siberian Sea which today bears his name. Wrangel only returned from this successful venture one and a half years later.

After his circumnavigation of the world in 1827, Wrangel was named governor of the Russian colonies in the northwest of North America. In 1847, he became an admiral, and from 1853 to 1858 he was the Russian Naval Minister.

The principal achievement of this capable Arctic explorer was the geographic and ethnographic investigation of the as yet practically unexplored northeast of Siberia.

Further reading
Narrative of an Expedition to the Polar Sea, in the years 1820, 1821, 1822 and 1823 commanded by F. Wrangel. (Translation from G. Engelhardt's German version of the original Russian by Mrs. Sabine) London 1840

A milestone in the conquest of the skies: The Wright brothers were the first to demonstrate with a motor-powered "flying machine" that man could move about in the air like a bird.

F. v. Wrangel und seine Reise längs der Nord-
küste von Sibirien und auf dem Eismeere,
ed. L. v. Engelhardt. Leipzig 1885
Ein Kampf um Wahrheit. Leben und Werk
des Admirals Baron F. v. Wrangel, ed. Baron
Wilhelm von Wrangel. Stuttgart 1939

WRIGHT, ORVILLE AND WILBUR

American aviation engineers. Orville born 1871 in Dayton, died 1848 in Dayton; and Wilbur, born 1867 in Henry Country, died 1912 in Dayton. Following Otto Lilienthal, the two brothers undertook trials with model planes and in 1900-1902 with gliders. On 17 December, 1903, Orville Wright managed to fly for 12 seconds in a biplane. This craft had been built by the two brothers in 1899 and had undergone constant improvement. It was driven by a 12 horsepower gasoline engine. On 20 September, 1903, Wilbur Wright undertook his first sightseeing flight with "Flyer 2", powered by a 16 horsepower engine.

The Wright brothers solved the problem of how man can untertake artificial flight.

Further reading
H. Combs, Brüder des Winds. Orville und Wilbur
Wright. Without place of publication 1981
A. Sproule, Die Brüder Wright. Die Anfänge der
Fliegerei. Recklinghausen 1992

The brothers Wilbur and Orville Wright, famous American pioneers of aviation

YZ

YERMAK, TIMOFEYEVICH

See Jermak.

YOUNG, JOHN WATTS

US American astronaut, born 1930 in San Francisco.

John Young is one of the most experienced of all astronauts, since he took part in six space missions. In 1965 he was on board "Gemini 3", the first manned flight in this space program. He was also a member of the crews of "Gemini 10", "Apollo 10" and of "Apollo 16"; during this mission he spent three days on the moon. Young and Robert Crippen were the first astronauts on board the space shuttle "Columbia" in April 1981. From 28 November to 8 December, 1983, John Young was commander of shuttle mission "STS-9"; Ulf Merbold was also a member of the six-strong crew. The was Young's last flight, since the space shuttle flights were discontinued after the "Challenger" disaster in 1986, to be resumed only in September 1988.

Young spent a total of 835 hours in space and today works as an advisor to NASA.

Count Ferdinand von Zeppelin

YOUNGHUSBAND, SIR FRANCIS EDWARD

British explorer of Asia and Africa, born 1862 in Murree (today Punjab/Pakistan), died 1942 in Lytchett Minster (Dorset).

Younghusband joined the British Army, became an officer and was detached to India in 1882. In 1886, he accompanied a British expedition into Sinkiang province; during this expedition he crossed the Taklamakan desert. From 1890 to 1897, he explored the Pamir Mountains. In 1896 and 1897 he traveled through Transvaal and the former Rhodesia (present-day Zimbabwe) as a correspondent of the "Times".

In 1903, the British government again called him to India. Together with General MacDonald, he headed the British military expedition to Lhasa in order to drive back the Russian influence. Access to Lhasa was forced by the British. From 1906 to 1909, Younghusband was British ambassador to Kashmir.

Younghusband's expeditions were of scientific and political significance.

Further reading
F. E. Younghusband, Heart of a Continent.
London 1896
–, India and Tibet. London 1910
–, The Epic of Mount Everest. London 1927
–, Dawn in India. London 1930

ZEPPELIN, GRAF FERDINAND VON

German inventor, born 1838 in Constance, died 1917 in Berlin.

Zeppelin invented the maneuverable rigid airship, which he had begun to develop in 1874. From 1892 he devoted all his time to this plan, supported by the engineer T. Kober. After having rejected government support, Zeppelin founded a "public limited company for the promotion of airship travel" in 1898, contributing more than half of the capital from his private fortune. The first Zeppelin airship (LZ 1) was constructed on Manzell Bay near Friedrichshafen; it took to the air on 2 July, 1900. This airship already had all the special features of the subsequent 129 Zeppelin airships. After the destruction of LZ 4 near Echterdingen in 1908, a national donation created the financial basis for the further development of the Zeppelin. In the same year, the "Luftschiffbau Zeppelin" company was founded in Friedrichshafen.

Zeppelin already had the idea of flying across the Arctic in 1910; however, this plan could not be realized in his lifetime. It was not until 24 July, 1931, that a Zeppelin was launched in Friedrichshafen. Via Berlin, Königsberg, Riga, Reval and Helsinki, it traveled to Leningrad, where the actual Arctic flight started. On board was the Russian Arctic explorer Samoilovich, who had determined the route and the Arctic regions to be explored. After flying over Archangel, the vast trading center for timber, the airship reached Franz Josephs Land, where it landed on 27 July. After surveying large areas of the Norwegian Arctic base, the airship headed for the Novaya Zemlya Islands which, however, could not be found due to dense fog. But aerial photographs could be taken of the North Land Islands. Via Cape Chelyuskin, LZ 127 reached the Taymyr peninsula and at Cape Dixon the Artic Sea. Only then could the double island of Novaya Zemlya be surveyed. Via Archangel and Leningrad, where the airship could not land due to a thunderstorm, the crew flew directly to Berlin.

The scientific results of this Arctic flight were of great importance for the meteorology and geology of the Arctic region.

Further reading
Kapitän H. v. Schiller, Zeppelin. Wegbereiter des Weltluftverkehrs. Bad Godesberg 1966
K. Grieder, Zeppeline. Giganten der Lüfte. Without place of publication 1971.
R. Italiaander, Ferdinand Graf von Zeppelin. Reitergeneral, Diplomat, Luftschiffpionier, 2nd ed. Konstanz 1986.

H. v. Schiller, Zeppelin. Aufbruch ins 20. Jahrhundert. Without place of publication 1989
K. Grieder, Zeppelin Dornier Junkers. Markantes aus der deutschen Luftfahrtgeschichte. Disentis/Schweiz 1989
M. Bélaf, Graf Ferdinand von Zeppelin, 3rd ed. Leipzig 1990

The North Land Islands and Nowaja Semlja as seen from an airship

THE WORLD OF ATLASES

Very early on in the history of mankind, it became obvious that the world had to be recorded graphically in order for people to be aware of their own location in comparison to the rest of the world. After all, written records, sketches of routes and representations of local conditions were indispensable as an orientation aid for travelers. The urge to sail into the wide world and to explore unknown lands and the natural riches of the planet Earth also made it necessary to prepare atlases. In order to do so, the New World first had to be explored.

THE WORLD VIEW OF CLAUDIUS PTOLEMY

The history of cartography has accompanied the history of the discovery of our planet almost from its very beginning. In the 2nd century AD in his eighth book "Geography", Claudius Ptolemy described how the entire planet could be represented using a system of maps. He included the first 26 maps with his book.

Around 800 AD Ptolemy's work was translated into Arabic. However, this was not a significant advance for the science of cartography. It was not until this work was translated into Latin in 1409 that the concept of atlases started to gain acceptance. In the period following this, numerous variants appeared with and without maps. However, as these were all drawn by hand, which was of course a time-consuming process, the spread of the atlas was subject to restrictions. The invention of the printing press ensured that the atlas could be reproduced accurately in large numbers and that it could be altered, improved or supplemented from one edition to the next. The first such volume was published in 1477 in Bologna.

Printers strove to ensure that their work was always up to date, and thus there appeared a constant stream of new map variants that translated the information brought home by the travelers and explorers into a cartographic representation.

ABRAHAM ORTELIUS, THE FATHER OF THE WORLD ATLAS

Up until this point, the individual maps were put together in a rather haphazard manner: The printers made use of whatever cartographic material happened to be available. The individual pages of an atlas were compiled at the whim of the printer – there was no standard system.

The first significant prototype of a world atlas appeared in the form of the "Theatrum orbis terrarum", compiled by Abraham Ortelius. The first edition from 1570, which already contained 53 cartographic tables, was printed in Latin. This was followed by editions in German, Spanish, French and Italian. The last editions, the scope of which was constantly extended, comprised no less than 128 tables.

Abraham Ortelius, the creator of the modern world atlas, was born in Antwerp in 1528. His grandfather had also been born in this city. When his father died when Abraham was just eleven years old, his uncle Jacobus van Meteren assumed responsibility for him and his two sisters. The young Abraham was interested in geography and history from an early age, but the main concern was for him to earn money to sustain the family. Together with his sisters he worked as a "Kaartenafzetter," in other words he colored maps – an exacting artistic task that was very much in demand at that time. However, he mainly dealt in books and coins; his cartographic work was more of a supplementary income.

AN UNTIRING TRAVELER

Buying and selling books, maps and other antiques meant that Abraham had to travel a lot; this was probably one reason why he never married. Besides his other work, Ortelius drafted a few maps – of the world (1564), of Egypt (1565) and of Asia (1567). Today, however, these maps are not regarded as anything special and they differ little from other maps that were on sale at that time. Ortelius' many travels, for example to Italy, Germany and France, are certain to have played some part in his later career as a cartographer, as they constantly broadened his experience and provided him with all news of the adventurers and explorers that reached Europe at that time. However, one important factor in determining the course of his later career was his friendship with Gerardus Mercator, whom he had met at a trade fair in Frankfurt in 1554. In 1560 Ortelius and Mercator traveled together through France.

The restless life of a tradesman left Ortelius little time for other activity, but during these years he collected numerous books, above all atlases – a valuable collection that he would need later for his work and which motivated him to take up his future career.

The market was flooded with maps of differing quality; demand was enormous. The large trading companies in Antwerp urgently required accurate maps and Ortelius had the contacts and the knowledge to provide these important customers with the material they needed. In this way he became a specialist to whom everyone turned for advice – and not only in matters of cartography. Ortelius also provided his clients with business advice. He undertook numerous journeys for the most important tradesman in Antwerp at that time, Gilles Hooftman, to pave the way for trade relations with other countries. Eventually, Gerardus Mercator encouraged Ortelius to create a world atlas, which turned out to be much superior to everything before it. He worked for over two years on the first 53 pages of this atlas.

MAPS FOR TRADE WITH FOREIGN COUNTRIES

Religious persecution drove Ortelius to England in 1576. From here he traveled to Liege to wait for more peaceful times before he could return home.

Ortelius' friend Mercator further developed the science of atlas cartography with his "Atlas sive cosmographicae meditationes de fabrica mundi et fabricati figure" ("Atlas or cosmographic observation of the creation of the world and the form of the creation"), which was published in 1595. Ortelius' work was characterized by its topicality, while scientific accuracy and uniformity of representation seemed less important to him. He also worked very quickly. Ortelius was more commercially minded, almost pragmatic: His atlas was intended for day-to-day use in international trading business. Mercator saw the task from a completely different viewpoint: He was a scientist and strove to be as accurate and uniform as possible. Although Mercator also had to live from the proceeds of his work, his actual interest was not determined by economics. As a result, Mercator's work took over from Ortelius' world atlas and from that time onwards was regarded as the authoritative volume. The descendants of these two cartographers continued to print the works for many years, but the material was only updated where absolutely necessary. This of course brought about a constant reduction in the quality of the atlases.

NEW IMPULSES FROM FRANCE

The 17th and 18th centuries saw new impulses in atlas cartography, especially from France. The Sanson family were regarded as leaders in this field for almost a hundred years. Since the atlas-makers refined and perfected the science of surveying, the maps became increasingly accurate. Many blank spots on the maps were filled in thanks to the urge for discovery of the explorers who ventured into the rainforests, deserts and icy seas of our planet.

Interesting atlases also appeared on the market in Germany. Publishers such as Johann Baptist Homann from Nuremberg (who published his first atlas in 1707), and Matthias Seutter from Augsburg (whose first work was published in 1728) surprised the public with constant improvements in quality. In addition to this, continuous improvements were being made in printing technology; this was of course reflected in the quality of the atlases.

Right from the outset the world atlas served as an aid for astronomical and geographical orientation. The geographic sheets were later supplemented with topical maps, which were intended to make the works more attractive also made them more dependent on being up to date.

Some of the most beautiful maps from the first atlas by Abraham Ortelius, "Theatrum orbis terrarum" from 1573, are shown on the following pages.

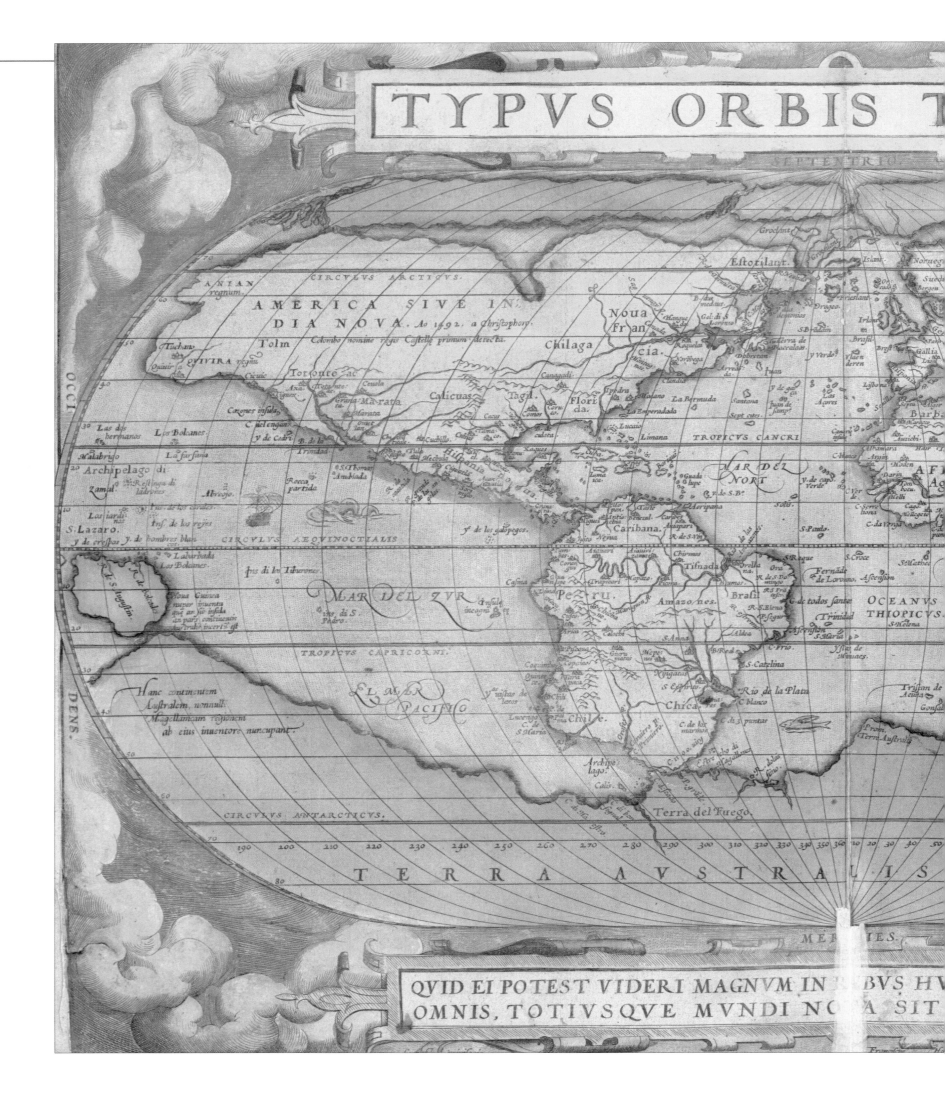

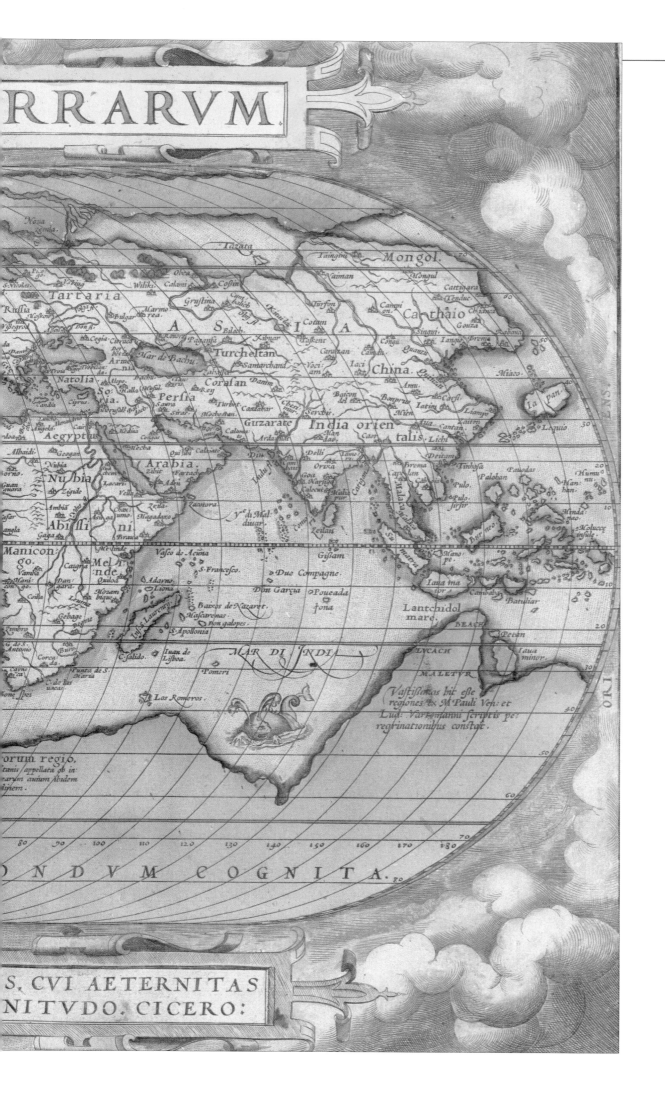

The first map from the celebrated atlas of Abraham Ortelius shows the Earth and all countries known at the time. The maps were all colored by hand, since color printing had not yet been developed.

Europe, shown on this map, was naturally the best explored continent at the time, and this map thus contains a great deal of information.

FLANDRIA

MARIS GERMANICI

SEP. OC OR MER.

PARS PICARDIÆ

Notarum explicatio.

Vrbes
Arces
Monasteria
Pagi

Milliaria Flandrica, parua,
mediocria, & magna.

Gerardus Mercator
Rupelmundanus
Describebat

camp veldt

The area of the historial Flanders, the region on the northern Atlantic coast, today includes parts of Belgium, France and the Netherlands. This detailed map is surprisingly accurate; nevertheless, there were still blank spots which were filled with opulent illustrations.

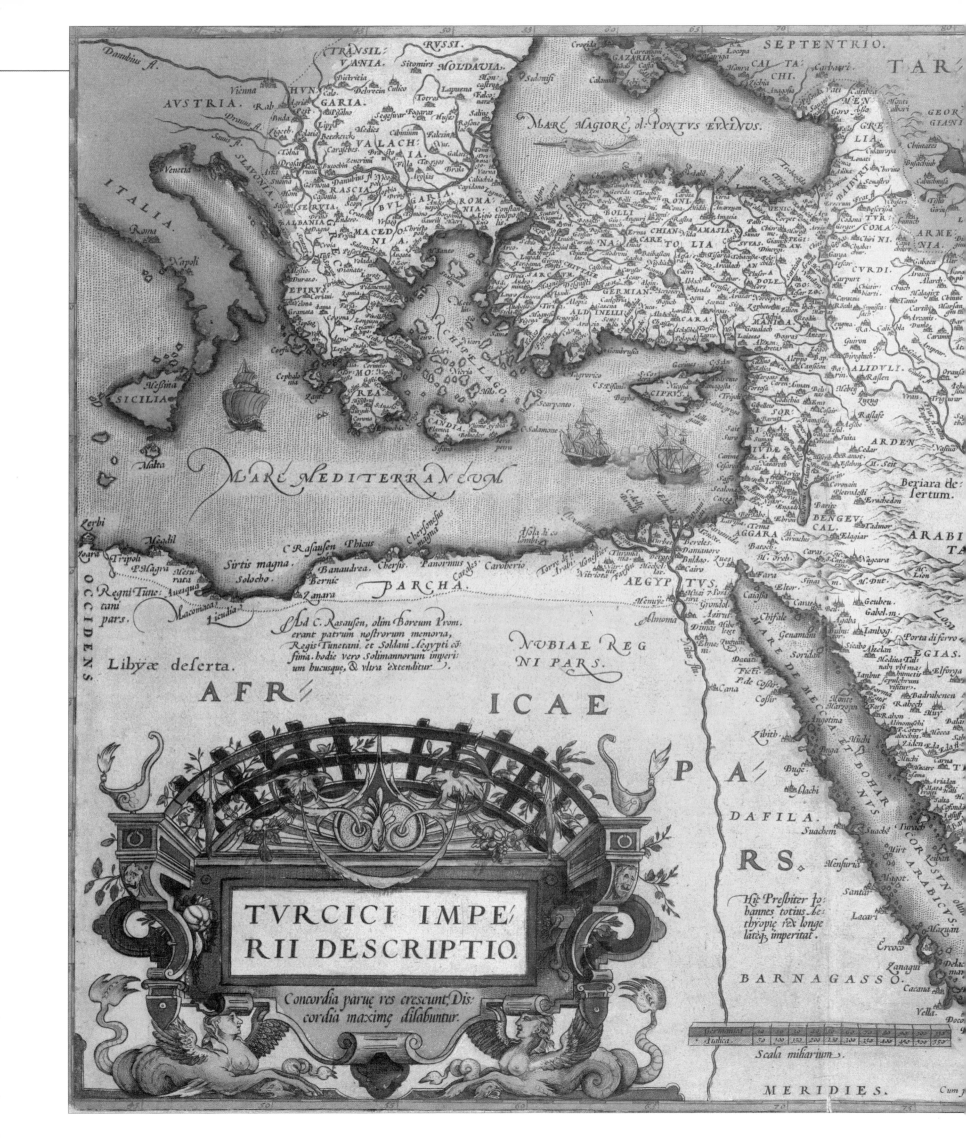

TRANSIL/ VANIA. RVSSI *Croisila* GAZARIA SEPTENTRIO.
Sitomirs MOLDAVIA. CAI TA: CHI Carbauri TAR/

Vienna HVN GARIA. *castrum* MEN GEOR
AUSTRIA. Rab. Egria Pest GRE GIANI
Buda Lippa LIA.

VALACH Cibinium Falcin MARE MAGIORE, ol: PONTVS EVXINVS.
SLAVONIA IA. RONI BATBVR
RASCIA BOLLI AMASIA COMA
SERVIA ROMA CHIAN TO LIA ARME
ALBANIA NIA. NA CARE SVAS NIA
MACEDO GERMAN CVRDI
NIA. ALD INELLI CARA MANIA

EPIRVS SARCVM DOLE BO:
Corinti MAGNESI CANDELORO

Corfu ARCHIPELAGO NICOSIA ALIDVLI
CIPRVS Raslen

Napoli REA Milo Scanderona
CANDIA C.S. Pisani Baphe SOR
Bapha Damasco Raslafe
ARDEN

MARE MEDITERRANEVM IVDÆA. M. Seit

SICILIA Messina Beriara de
sertum.

Zerbi Isola di co lombi. BENGEV ARABIA
Meadil C Rasausen Phicus Chersi. CAL. TA
Sirtis magna. Banaudrea. Panormus M. Ireb.
Tripoli Solocho. Bernic Zamara BARCHA. Cairo Ques AEGYPTVS. H. Lion
Regni Tune: tani pars. Nitriota EGIAS.
Macomiaes? Licidia? Ad C. Rasausen, olim Boreum Prom. Porta di ferro
erant patrum nostrorum memoria, Ianbog.
Libyæ deserta. Regis Tunetani, et Soldani Aegypti cō= NVBIAE REG
finia, hodie vero Solimannorum imperi= NI PARS. Sicabo
um hucusque, & vltra extenditur. MARE DE MECCA
AFR/ ICAE Dacari Badrihenen
Chifale Ficti. Cana Rabech
Cosir Farsi Huy
Zibith P/ Michi
Buge Zaden
Islachi THOBOR Micha
Tasama ARS. ARIADAN
DAFILA. COR SVN
Suachem Suacheb Tinuch
Mensurin Zeilam ARABICVS
Magot.
Santar BARNAGASSO.
Hic Presbiter Io=
hannes totius Ae= Ercoco
thiopiæ rex longe
latéq, imperitat. Zanaqui Lacari Delaca mar
Cacana
Vella.

TVRCICI IMPE/ RII DESCRIPTIO.

Concordia paruæ res crescunt, Dis= cordia maximæ dilabuntur.

Germanica Scala miliarium.
Italica.

MERIDIES.

This map entitled Description of the Turkish Empire ("Turcici Imperii Descriptio") shows at its center today's countries of Greece, Turkey and the Arabian region. The outlines of the Black Sea and the Caspian Sea (in the upper part of the map) betray the inevitably sparse geographical knowledge of that time.

373

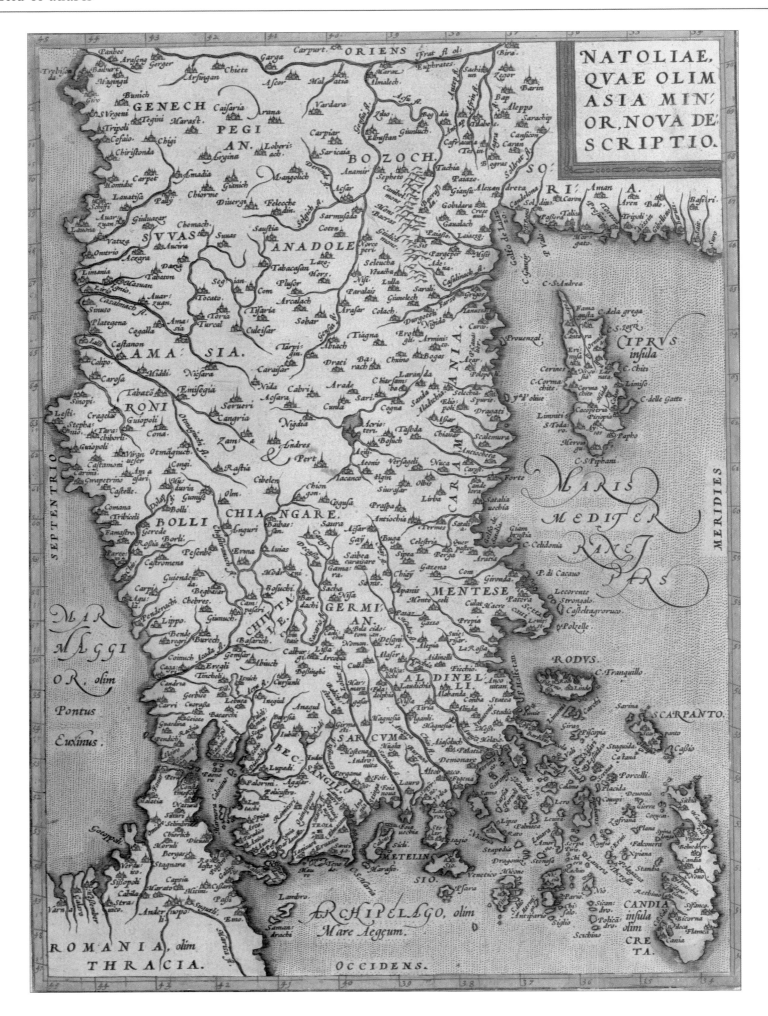

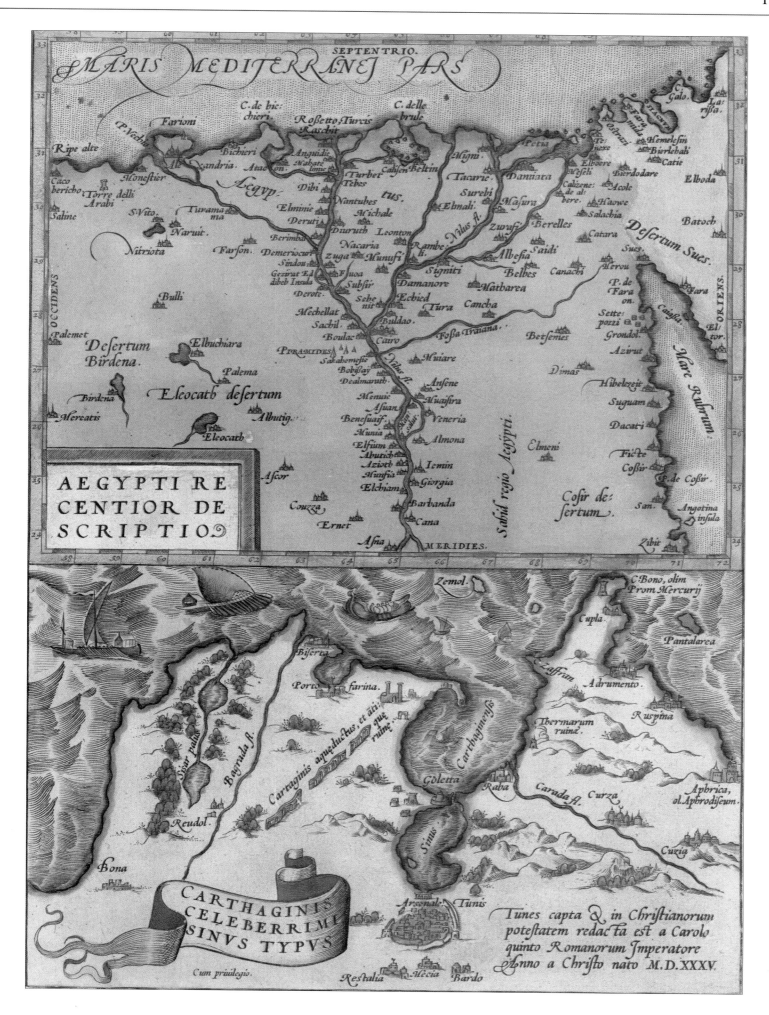

The map on the facing page – with east at the top – depicts Anatolia, a region of Turkey. The islands of Crete, Rhodes and Cyprus are shown on the right. The map on this page represents the Nile Delta and below the regions of Carthage and Tunis, present-day Tunisia.

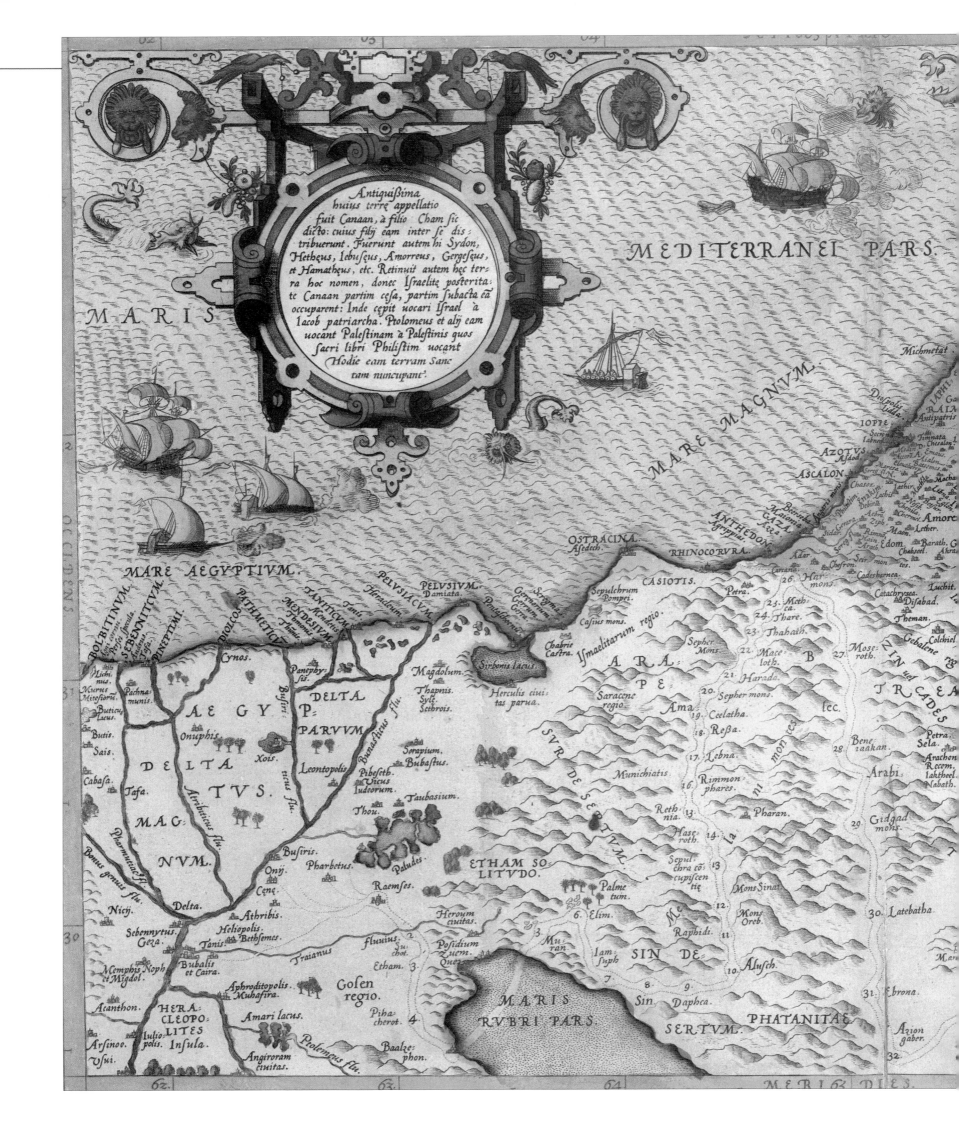

MEDITERRANEI PARS.

MARIS

MARE MAGNVM.

Antiquißima
huius terrę appellatio
fuit Canaan, à filio Cham sic
dicto: cuius filij eam inter se dis-
tribuerunt. Fuerunt autem hi Sydon,
Hethęus, Iebusęus, Amorreus, Gergesęus,
et Hamathęus, etc. Retinuit autem hęc terra hoc nomen, donec Israelitę posterita-
te Canaan partim cesa, partim subacta ea
occuparent: Inde cępit uocari Israel à
Iacob patriarcha. Ptolomeus et alij eam
uocant Palestinam à Palestinis quos
sacri libri Philistim uocant
Hodie eam terram Sanc-
tam nuncupant.

Michmetat

Dialpoli
Lidda

IOPPE

BAIA
Antipatris

Timnata
Chessalon
Accor

AZOTVS
Asdod.

ASCALON

Chaser

Lachis

Beerseba
Maiuma
GAZA

ANTHEDON
Agrippias

Amor

Sidcr

Edom

OSTRACINA.
Asedech.

RHINOCORVRA.

Adar.

Seir mon
tes.

Cadesbarnea.

MARE AEGYPTIVM.

PELVSIVM.
Damiata.

PELVSIACVM.

Heracleum.

Germanium
Gerra

Scytha

CASIOTIS.

Petra.

Carcana.

26. Har-
mons.

Catachrysea.
Disabad.

Luchit.

Theman

TANITICVM.

MENDESIVM.

Thmuis.

Tanis.

Pentascheno

Sepulchrum
Pompei.

25. Meth-
ca.

24. Thare.

BOLBITINVM.

SEBENNITICVM.

PATHMETICVM.

Casius mons.

23. Thahath.

Moses
roth.

Gebalene
reg

Colchiel

DIOLCOS.

Cynos.

Panephy-
sis.

Chabrie
Castra.

Ismaelitarum regio.

Sepher
Mons

22. Mace
loth.

B

27.

ZIN uel

Michi-
nus.

Murnt
Mitefiorú

Pachna-
munis.

Busiri

DELTA.

Magdolum.

Sirbonis lacus.

Herculis ciui-
tas parua.

ARA-
PE

Saracene
regio

21.

Harada.

ARCADES

Butica
Lacus.

AEGYP-
PARVVM

Thapnis.
Syle.
Sethrois.

Ama

20. Sepher mons.

19. Ceelatha.

Petra
Sela.

Butis.

Onuphis

Xois.

Bunasticus flu.

Sorapium.
Bubastus.

SVR DESE

18. Reßa.

Arachon
Recem.
Iahtheel.

Sais.

Leontopolis

Pibeseth
Vicus
Iudeorum.

Munichiatis

17. Lebna.

16. Rimmon
phares.

Arabi.

Nabath.

Cabasa.

DELTA

 SEPTVM

Tafa.

TVS.

Thou.

Taubasium.

Reth-
nia.

13

Pharan.

MAG-

Atribiticus flu.

ni montes

Buniris gratus fl.

Busiris

Hase-
roth.

14.

la

Gidgad
mons.

NVM.

Onij.

Pharbetus.

Paludes.

ETHAM SO-
LITVDO.

Pharmeticae fl.

Cenę.

Raemses.

Sepul-
chra tő
cupiscen-
tię

13

Mons Sinai

Nicij.

Delta.

Palme-
tum.

Me

12.

Mons
Oreb.

30. Latebatha.

Athribis.

Heroum
ciuitas.

3.

Mu-
ran

6. Elim.

Raphidi

11

Heliopolis
Bethsemes.

Fluuius
Su-
chot.

Posidium
Zuem
Quem

SIN DE-

Sebennytus.
Geza.

Tanis.

Traianus.

Etham. 3.

Iam
suph

10. Alusch.

Memphis Noph
et Migdol.

Bubalis
et Caira.

Aphroditopolis
Muhafira.

Gosen
regio.

7.

8.

9.

Sin Daphca.

31. Ebrona.

Acanthon.

HERA-
CLEOPO-
LITES

Amari lacus.

Piha-
cherot. 4

MARIS
RVBRI PARS.

SERTVM.

PHATANITAE

Azion
gaber.

Arsinoo.

Iulio-
polis.

Insula.

Baalze-
phon.

32.

Vsui.

Angiroram
ciuitas.

Ptolemeus flu.

MERIDIES.

It is surprising that even in the 16th century the geographical knowledge of Palestine – the region of present-day Israel and Lebanon – was so detailed.

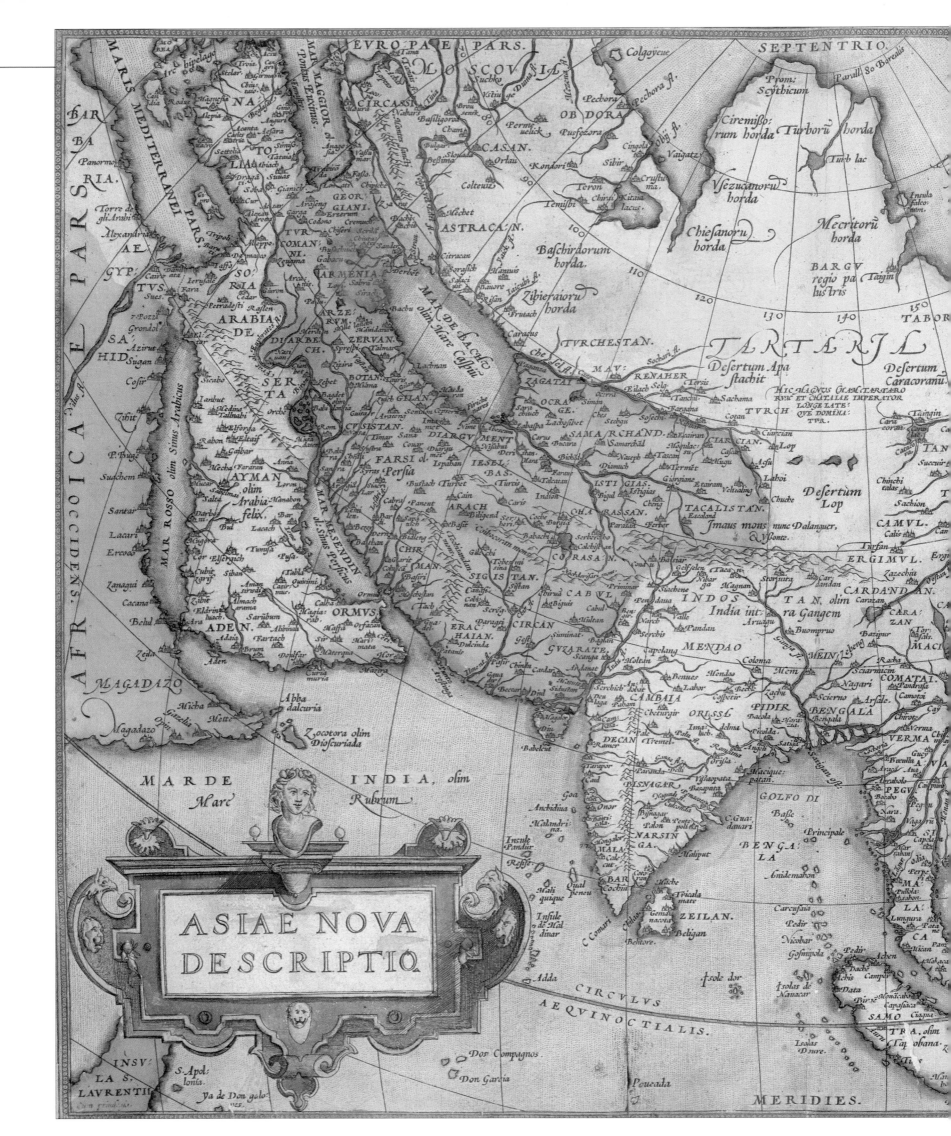

EVROPAE PARS.   SEPTENTRIO.

MARIS MEDITERRANEI PARS.

Pontus Euxinus.   MARI MAGGIOR ol.

MOSCOVIA

Colgoyeue

Parall. 80 Borealis

Prom: Scythicun

NA   Arc hipelago

CIRCASSI

OB DORA

Ciremisso; rum horda   Turboru horda

BAR BA

TO LIA

CASAN.

Turb lac

RIA.

ASTRACAN.

GEOR GIANI.

Vsezucanoru horda

Insula falco: nu.

AE GYP TVS.

SO RIA

ARMENIA.

Chiesanoru horda

Mecritoru horda

ARABIA DE

DIARBE CH.

ARZE RVM.

ZERVAN.

MAR DE BACHV olim Mare Caspiu

Baschirdorum horda

Zibieraioru horda

BARGV regio pa lus tris   Taigin

TVRCHESTAN

TARTARIA

Desertum Apa stachit

Desertum Caracoranu

130   140   150   TABOR

SER TA.

BOTAN.

ZAGATAI

MAV: RENAHER

HIC MAGNVS CHAM TARTARO RVM ET CHITALAE IMPERATOR LONGE LATE QVE DOMINA TVR.

AFRICA E PARS.   Indus fl.

MAR ROSSO olim Sinus Arabicus

GILAN.

OCRA GE.

SAMA RCHAND.

CIARCIAN.

Taigin

CVSISTAN.

DIARGV MENT.

BAS.

CIARCIAN.

Desertum Lop

TAN

AYMAN olim Arabia felix.

FARSI ol. Persia

IESEL.

ISTI GIAS. ISTIGIAS.

CHA BASSAN.

TACALISTAN.

CAMVL.

ERGIMVL.

MAR MESENDIN al: Sinus Persicus

ARACH

Smaus mons nunc Dalanguer, Vsonte.

CORASAN.

CARDANDAN.

CARA ZAN

CHIR

MAN

SIG IS TAN.

CABVL

INDOS TAN, olim ra Gangem

India int

ORMVS.

ERAC HAIAN.

CIRCAN

GVZARATE.

MENDAO

MACI

ADEN

Zocotora olim Dioscuriada

CAMBAIA

ORISSL

PIDIR

BENGALA Bengala

VERMA

MAGADAZO

INDIA, olim Rubrum

DECAN

BISNAGAR

GOLFO DI Basse

Principale

PEGV

Magadazo

MARDE Mare

NARSIN GA.

BENGA LA

MALA cut

VA

ZEILAN.

MA

LA

CA

ASIAE NOVA DESCRIPTIO.

C Comari

Nicobar

Gosnipola

Achen

SAMO

TRA, olim Taprobana.

AEQVINOCTIALIS.

CIRCVLVS

A sole dor

Isolas de Nauacar

MERIDIES.

INSV LAS S. LAVRENTII

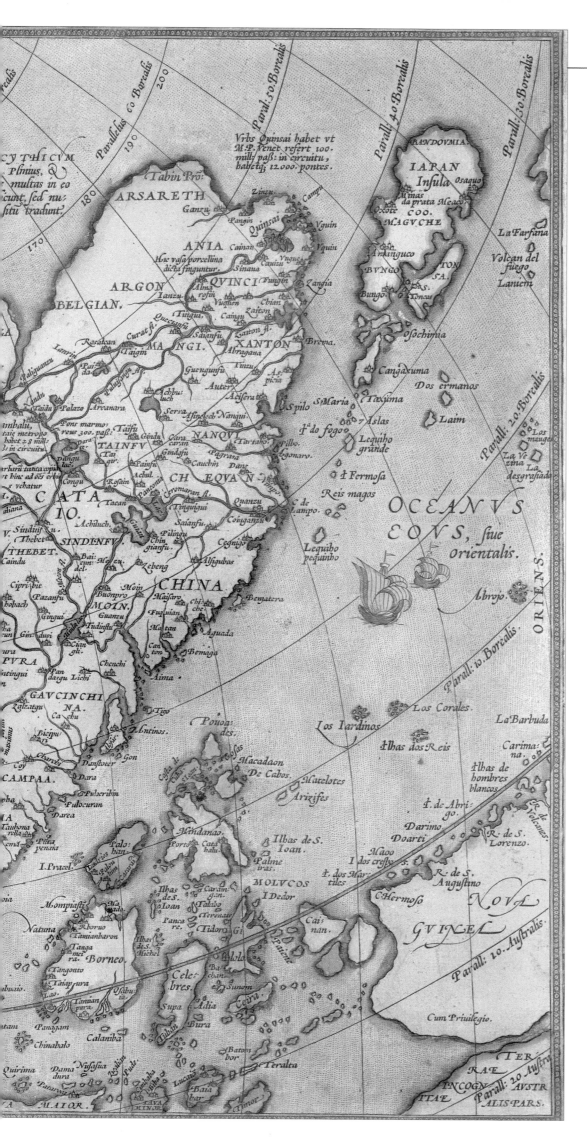

This map is entitled Description of the New Asia ("Asiae nova descriptio"). If one compares a contemporary map of the Far East with this work of Ortelius, one cannot help but wonder at the detailed geographical knowledge the cartographer already had at the time. By collecting maps of varying quality over the years, he had at his disposal a vast fund of contradictory information. The importance of Ortelius' work lies in his capacity to produce a map such as this.

379

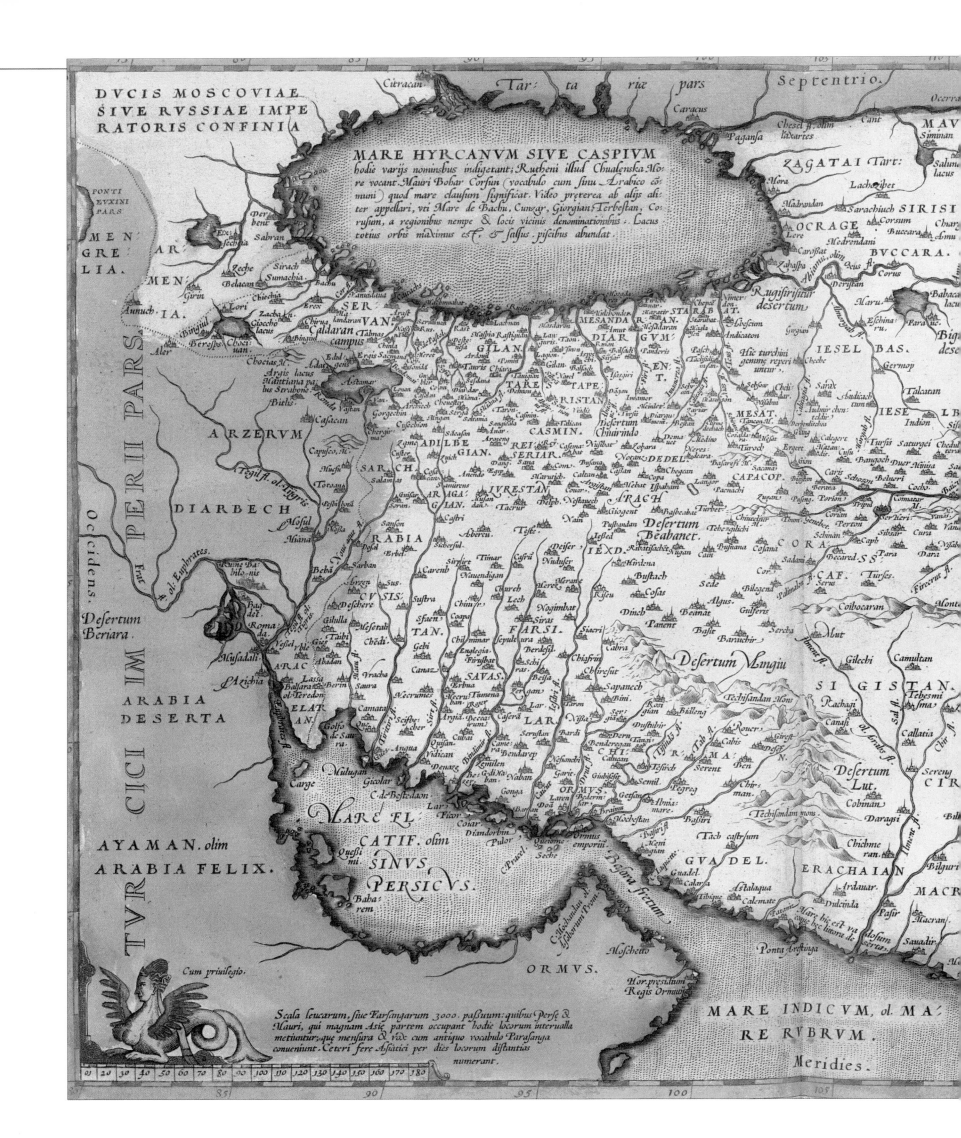

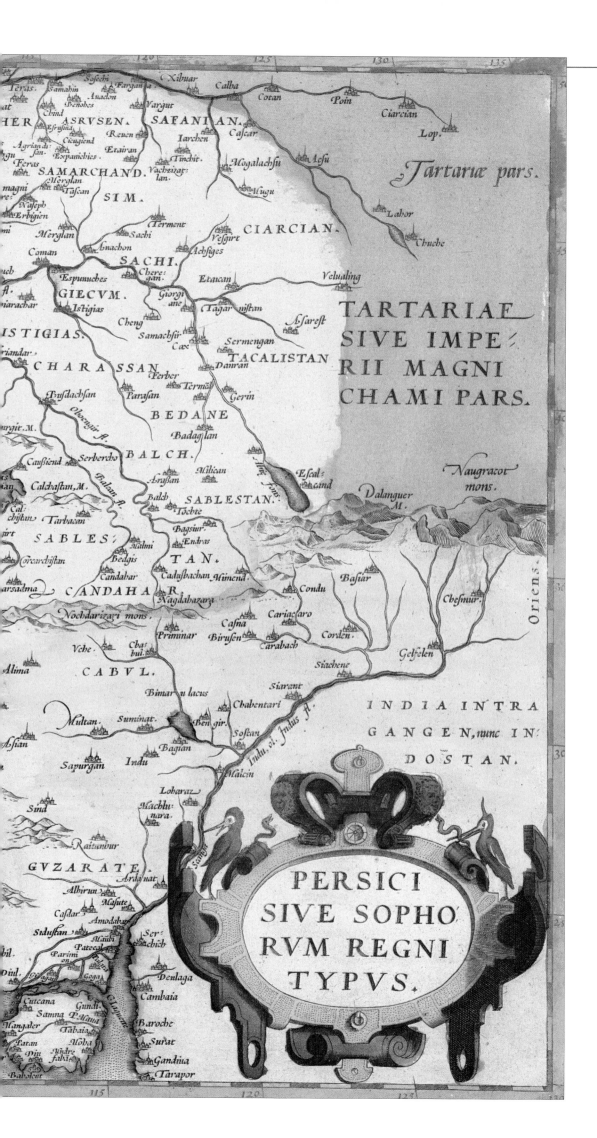

This map of Persia is also impressive by virtue of its richness of geographical detail. The actual form and size of the Caspian Sea, however, only vaguely correspond with its geograhical placement. A more accurate representation is that of the Persian Gulf and the Strait of Hormuz. The Tartar Empire (at the upper right in this map) stands for Russia.

381

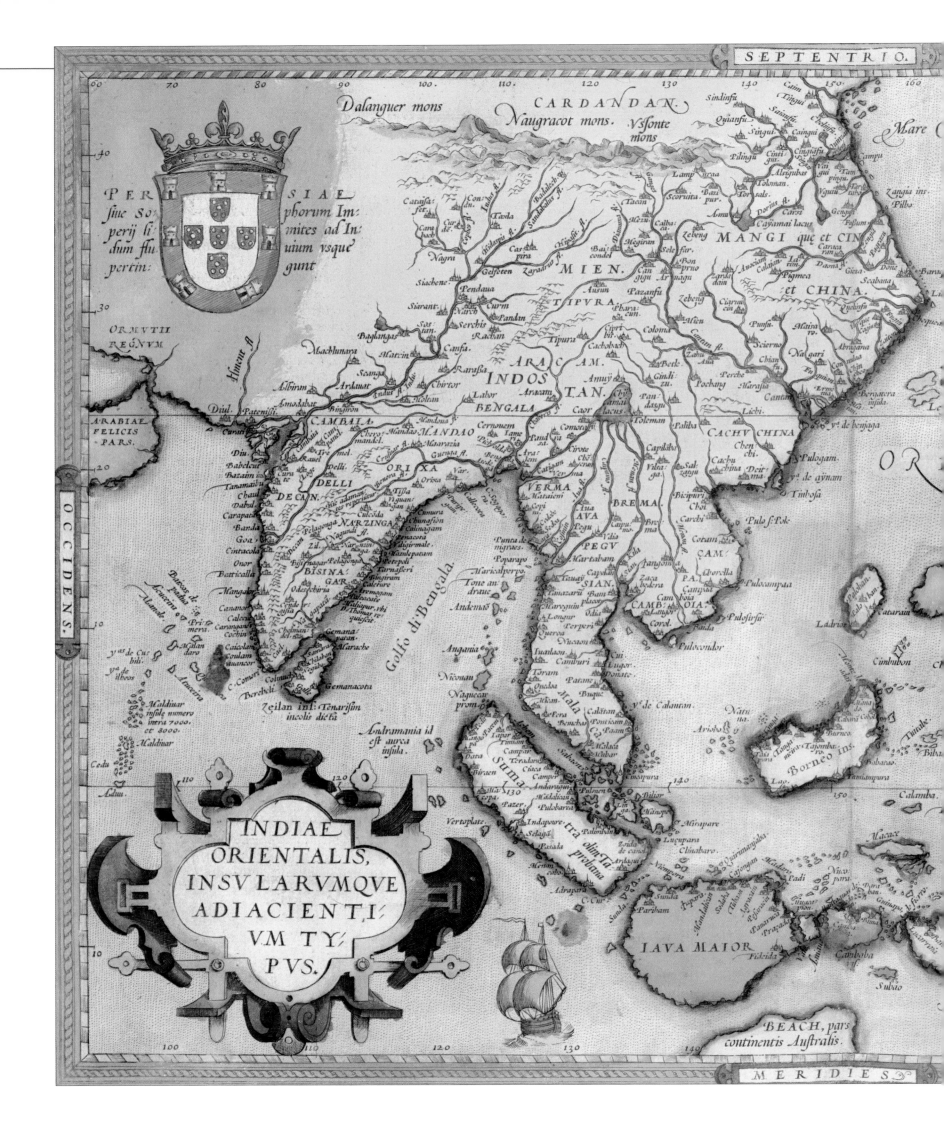

Dalanguer mons   CARDANDAN.   Sindinsu
Naugracot mons.   Ussonte mons

PER SIAE
siue So phorum Im:
perij li mites ad In:
dum flu uium usque
pertin: gunt

ORMVTII REGNVM

MANGI que et CIN et CHINA

ARABIAE FELICIS PARS.

CAMBAIA   MANDAO   CACHV CHINA

ORIXA

DELLI   DE CAN   VERMA   BREMA   ÇAM
NARZINGA   AVA   PEGV   CAMB OIA
BISINA GAR   SIAN.   PA.

Golfo di Bengala.

Maldiuar insulæ numero intra 7000. et 8000.

Zeilan insi: Tenarisin incolis dicta

Andramania id est aurea insula.

Suma tra olim Ta probana

Borneo ins.

INDIAE
ORIENTALIS,
INSVLARVMQVE
ADIACIENTI;
VM TY;
PVS.

IAVA MAIOR

BEACH, pars continentis Australis.

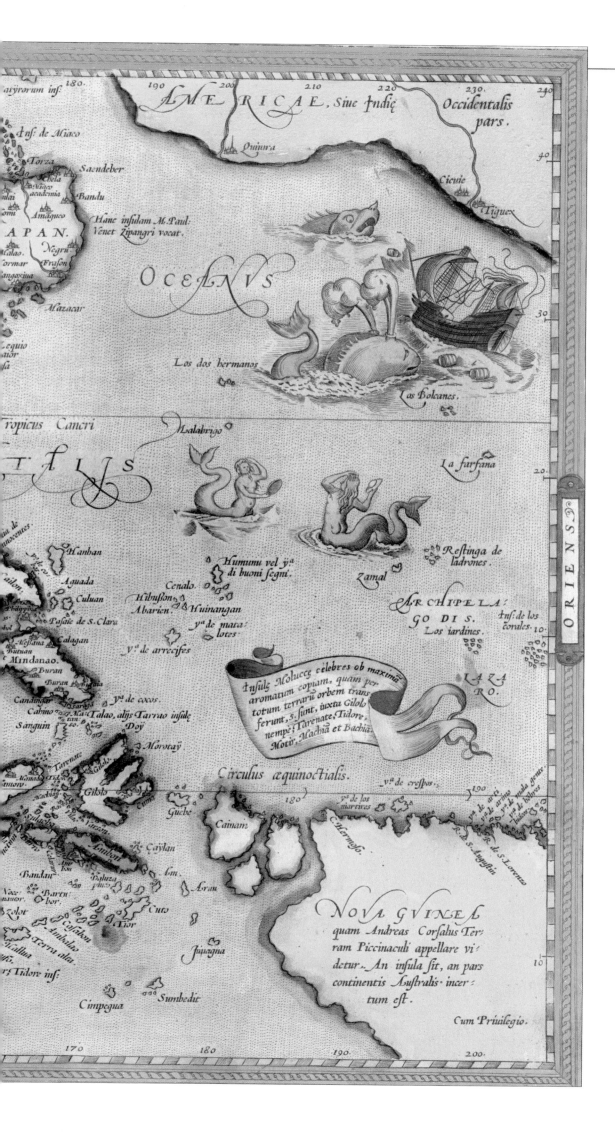

The navigators also reached the exotic regions of Asia and brought a wealth of information back to Europe. For this reason, Ortelius was able to draw this surprisingly correct map of India and Japan. Nor did he forget the islands of Sumatra, Borneo and the Philippines. The cartographer filled in the blank areas on the map with proud vessels, sea monsters and mermaids.

383

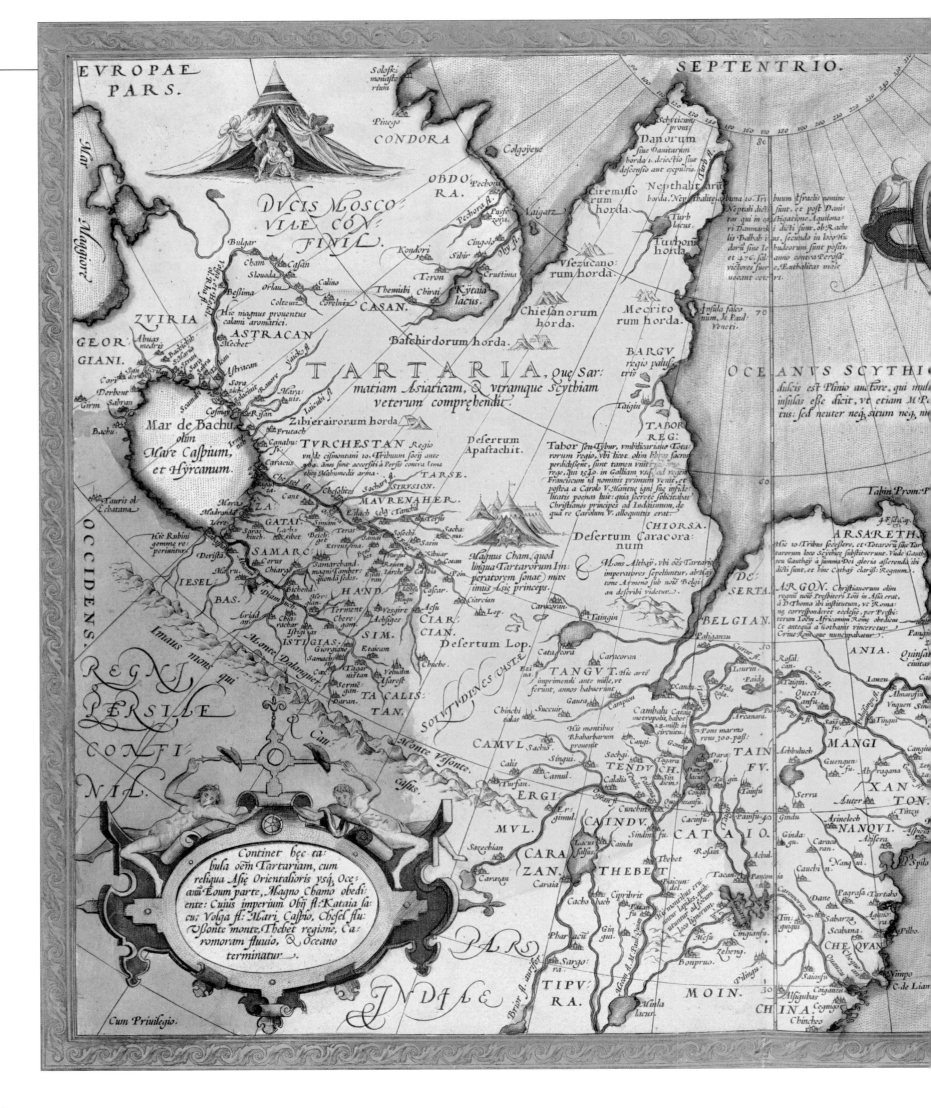

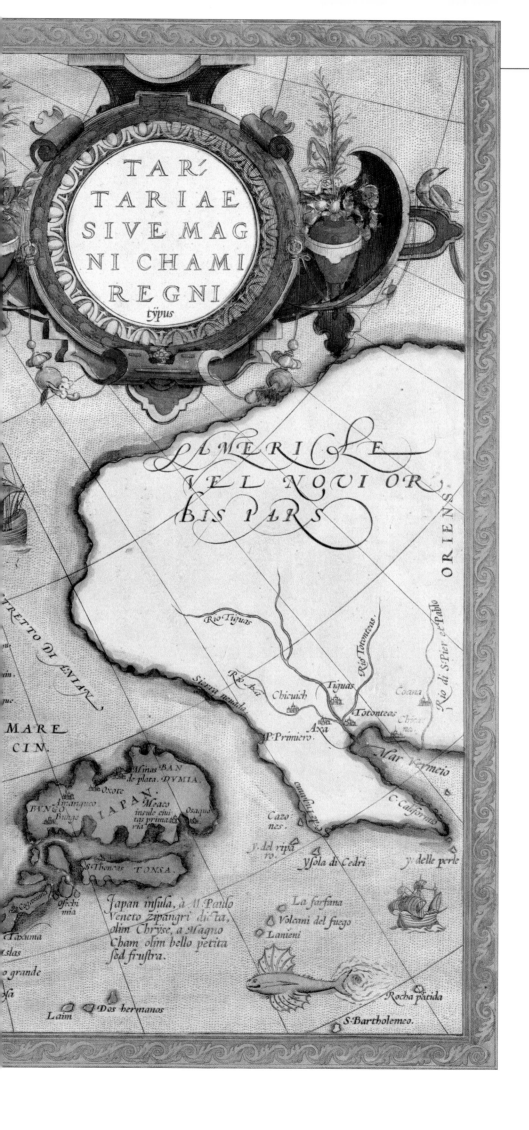

For Ortelius, the region of Russia, China, Japan and the Arctic Ocean with the North Pole was "terra incognita". Nevertheless, his vague impression was more or less correct.

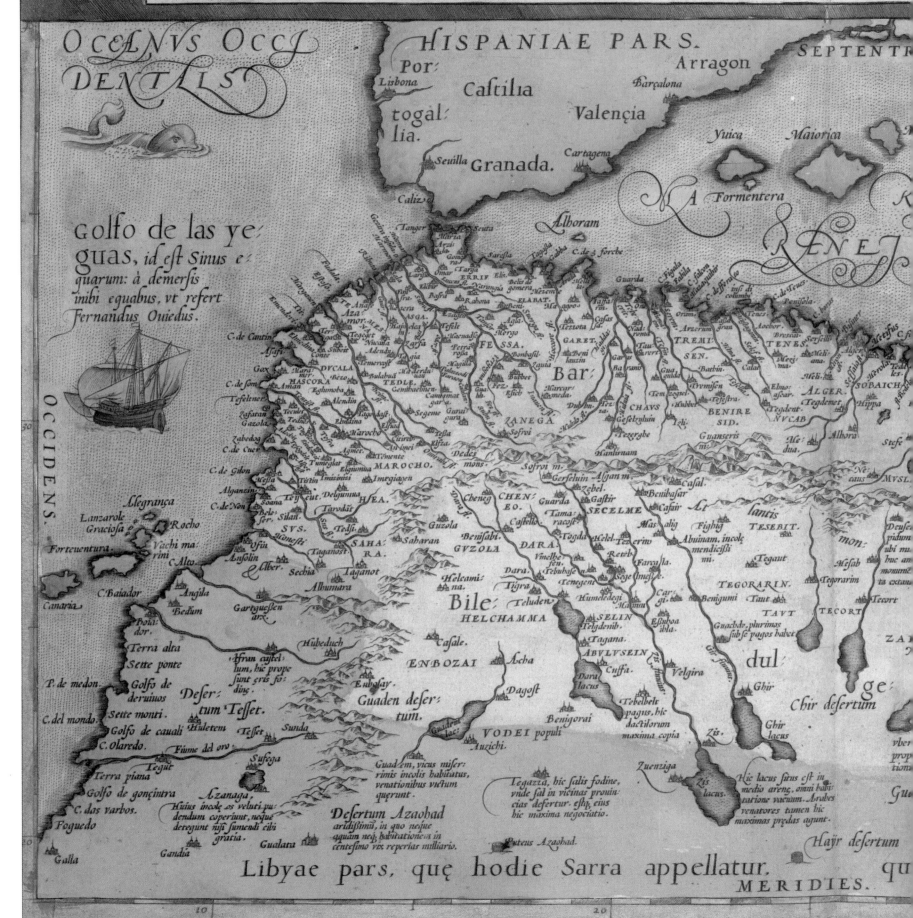

OVA DESCRIPTIO.

die vocatur
totus ille Africæ
tractus maritimus
qui olim vtramq. Mauri=
taniam, et Africam minorem
continebat.

x, idem quod desertum significat.

The North African coast was well explored: Although the sailors rarely ventured far inland, they sailed close to the coastline.

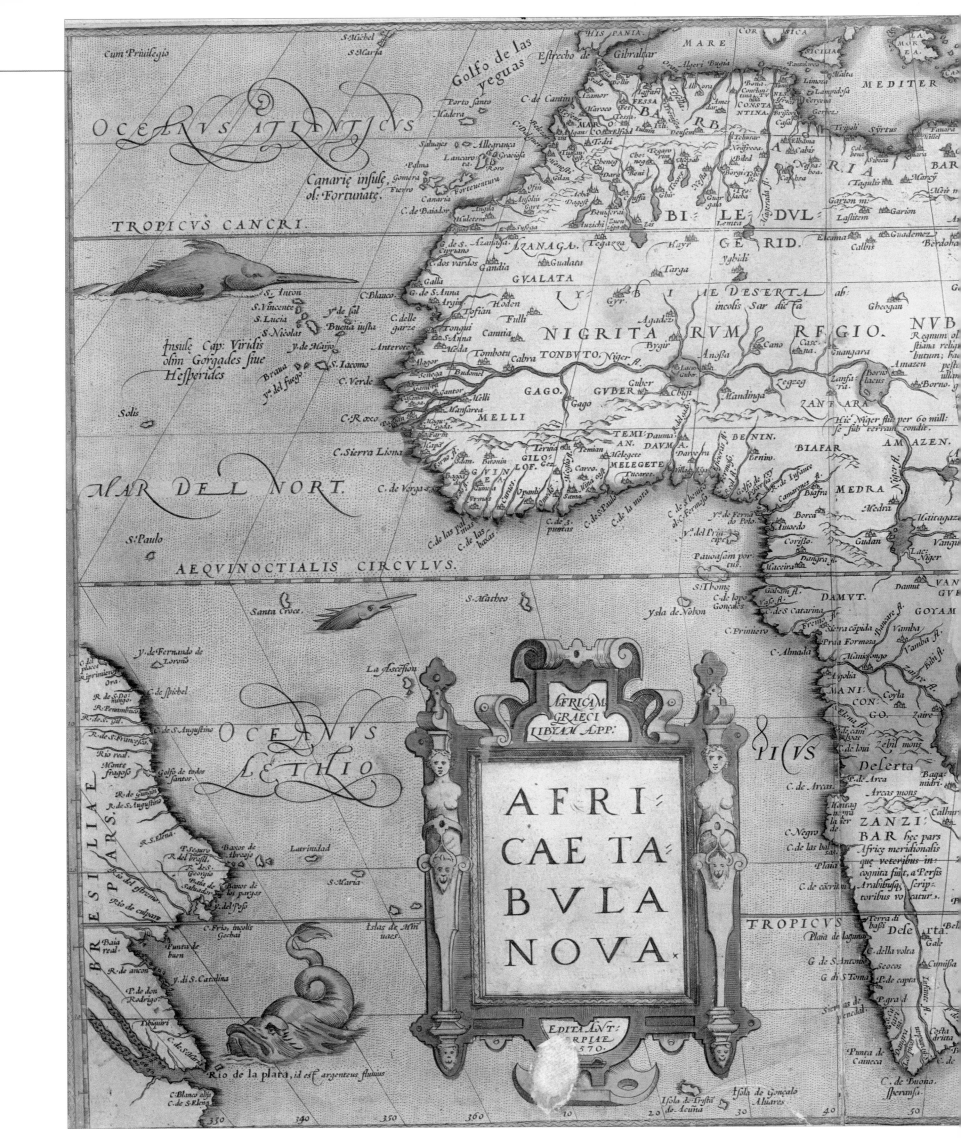

This representation of the African continent was considered a special treat by Ortelius' contemporaries. He had painstakingly collected all the information available to him and created a remarkably correct picture of the continent. At the lower right, the armada of explorers can be seen forging ahead with billowing sails.

389

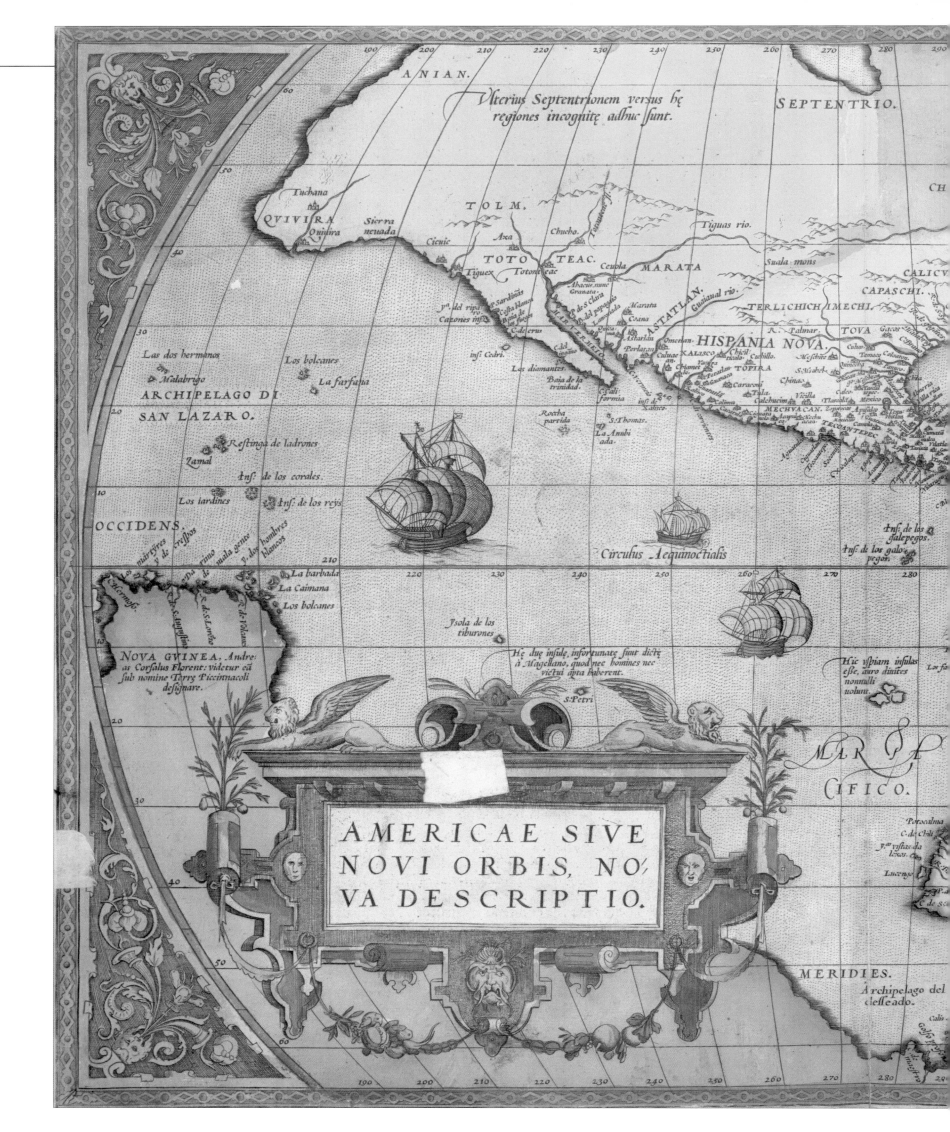

ANIAN.

Ulterius Septentrionem versus hę
regiones incognitę adhuc sunt.

SEPTENTRIO.

Tuchana

QVIVIRA
Quiuira
Sierra
neuada

TOLM.

Cicuic
Axa
Chucho
Tiguas rio.

TOTO TEAC.
Tiguex Totonteac
Ceuola MARATA
Suala mons

Abacus nunc
Granata
S. de s clara
Marata

yn. del rio
Cazones inf.
P. Sardinas
Costa blanca
Baia de
los fuegos
del papagaio
Oniza
nat.
Casana
Astatlan

CALICV
CAPASCHI.

TERLICHICH IMECHI.

R. Palmar.
TOVA
Gacos

Las dos hermanos
Malabrigo

Los bolcanes
La farfana

ARCHIPELAGO DI

SAN LAZARO.

Restinga de ladrones.
Zamal

inf. de los corales.

inf. Cedri

Los diamantes.
Baia de la
trinidad.

Cali
formia
inf d.
Xalisco.

Rocha
parrida
S. Thomas.
La Anubi
ada.

Astatlan
Ometan
Perlaran
Culuac
an.
KALASCO Chicil
cricula.
HISPANIA NOVA.
Cubillo.
TOPIRA
Meschice
S. Michel
Cuhz
Tamacy
Quinira
Tlacoapa

Colima
Caraconi
Tula
Calchuein
Vicilla
MECHVACAN.
Mexico
TECANTEPEC.

Los iardines
inf. de los reys

OCCIDENS.

martires
y de creffos
P. dos hombres
blancos

inf. de los
galepegos.
inf. de los galo
pegos.

Circulus Aequinoctialis

La barbada
La Caimana
Los bolcanes

hermofo.

Ysola de los
tiburones

NOVA GVINEA, Andre:
as Corfalus Florent: videtur eā
sub nomine Terrę Piecitnacoli
defignare.

Hę duę insulę, infortunatę funt dictę
à Magellano, quod nec homines nec
victui apta haberent.

S. Petri

Hic uspiam insulas
efse, auro dinites
nonnulli
uolunt.

MAR PA

CIFICO.

AMERICAE SIVE
NOVI ORBIS, NO-
VA DESCRIPTIO.

Poroculma
C. de Chili
y de vistas da
locas Ca.

Lucenso

MERIDIES.

Archipelago del
defseado.

Although Columbus had already discovered the Americas a century earlier and the New World was of great importance to Europe, cartographical knowledge of this immense continent seems to have been sparse at the time that Ortelius put forth his new description of America.

391

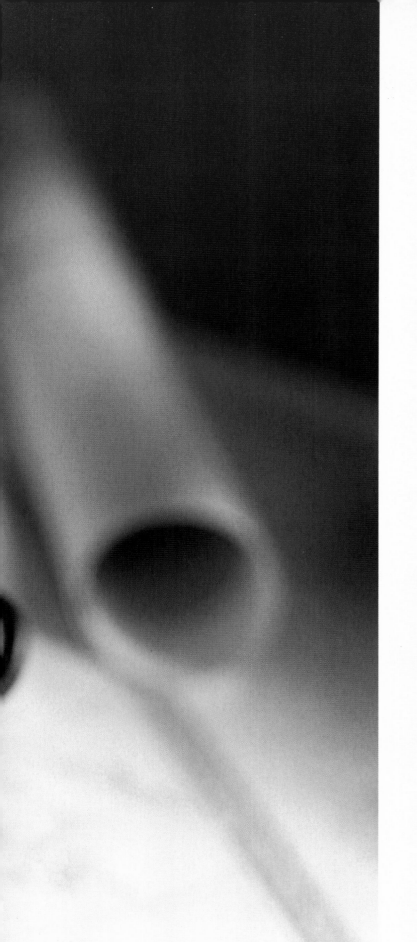

T IMELINE

The following chronological table gives an overview of mankind's achievements over the course of the millennia in the exploration of the Earth – and, most recently, of further heavenly bodies. It provides documentation of astounding advances in knowledge from the concept of a flat Earth up to today's detailed information of every point on our globe.

THE PRE-CHRISTIAN ERA

c. 3000 BC — Trade journeys of the Egyptians to the Land of Punt (on the Somalian coast?): incense, resin, precious woods.

2000-1500 BC — The Cretans maintain extensive trade relationships with the countries of the eastern Mediterranean. They establish colonies in Spain and reach the Atlantic Ocean via the Strait of Gibraltar.

c. 1500 BC — After the Cretans, the Phoenicians rule the Mediterranean.

c. 945 BC — Expedition to Ophir (eastern Sudan?) commissioned by King Solomon and supported by the Phoenicians.

c. 800 BC — Madeira and the Canary Islands are discovered by the Phoenicians.

596-594 BC — From the Red Sea the Phoenicians presumably circumnavigated Africa.

c. 500 BC — The Carthaginians possess colonies in Sardinia, Sicily, Spain, Gaul and on the west coast of Africa.

4th century BC — The Carthaginians reach the Azores.

334-323 BC — Alexander the Great reaches India by the overland route and rules over the entire world known at the time to the Greeks.

c. 330 BC — Pytheas of Massalia (Marseille) travels from Marseille via Cadiz to the British Isles, to Thule, the legendary country of the far north, to the German Bight and to the Baltic.

325-321 BC — Nearchos explores the sea route from the Indus to the Euphrates.

c. 5 BC — A Roman fleet reaches southern Scandinavia.

The Canary Islands

7th–9th CENTURY

c. 670 — The Faroe Islands are discovered by Irish monks.

c. 795 — Iceland is visited by Irish-Scottish monks.

860-870 — According to the Norwegian chronicles and sagas, the Norwegian Vikings Floki, Gardar and Nadod are said to have rediscovered Iceland.

c. 870 — Ottar, a Norwegian seafarer, circumnavigates the North Cape and reaches the mouth of the Dvina River (present-day Archangel).

876 — The Icelander Gunnbjörn Ulfson is thrown off course by a storm and lands on the southern tip (Cape Farvel) of Greenland, where he spends the winter.

10th–11th CENTURY

953   Ibn Haukal, an Arabic traveler, explores the Indus valley (present-day Bahawalpur, Khanpur and Sindh).

982   Eric the Red starts the colonization of Greenland from Ireland.

983   Establishment of the settlements of Westbygd and Ostbygd on the west coast of Greenland by Eric the Red.

999   Leif, Eric's son, lands on the coast of Nova Scotia in northeast America and stays there over winter.

1003   The Norwegian Karlsemme Torfinn establishes a settlement in Markland (probably Labrador). After an attack by the Skraelings (American natives) the colony is abandoned.

12th CENTURY

1165-1173   Journey of the Spaniard B. de Tudela to the south of France, Italy, Cyprus, Syria, Mesopotamia, Persia, Arabia and Egypt.

1170-1185   The Arabian globetrotter Ibn Djobeir undertakes several journeys through the Near East.

A rock temple on the left bank of the Nile, Egypt

13th CENTURY

1245-1247   Giovanni di Piano Carpini, a Franciscan monk from Umbria, undertakes a large-scale diplomatic journey into the east on behalf of the Council of Lyon. Accompanied by his brother, he crosses the vast steppes and deserts of southern Russia and Western Turkestan (Khanates of the Golden Horde and Chaghati) north of Lake Kaspi and the Aral Sea, through the Dzungarian Gate and reaches Qara-Qorum (Karakoram), the residence of the Great Khan Kuyuk.

1253-1256   Journey of the Lower German Franciscan monk Wilhelm von Rubruk (Ruysbroek) on behalf of Ludwig the Holy from Akkon (Palestine) through the Khanates of the Golden Horde, passing the Aral Sea on the north, via Balaga-sun (Khanate Chaghati) to Qara-Qorum, the residence of the Great Khan Mangu.

1270   Rediscovery of the Canary Islands by the Genoese seafarer Malocello.

1271-1295   Marco Polo, globetrotter from Venice, travels via Constantinople through the empire of the Ilkhane (Iraq and Iran), visits the towns of Hormuz, Kerman, Balch, Khotan and reaches Khanbalik (Beijing). After a 17-year sojourn at the court of the "Middle Kingdom" he returns via Java, Ceylon, Calicut (Malabar coast), Tabriz, Trapezunt (Turkey) and Constantinople to Venice.

1291   Vadino and Ugolino Vivaldi, Italian seafarers, attempt to reach the Indian coast. They founder not far from Mogadishu (Somalia).

14th CENTURY

1300   The first Portulanes (detailed port and coast descriptions) are published.

1312   Lancelot of Maloisel, a seafarer from Genoa, rediscovers the Canary Islands, which had fallen into oblivion. However, they are not colonized.

1313-1316   Oderich of Pordenone (Friaul), a Franciscan monk, travels through Persia, the Malabar coast, Ceylon, Sumatra, Borneo, the Mekong Delta, China (to the "world port" of Hangchu). On his return journey he crosses Turkestan and Tibet.

1314   G. de Carignano, Italian traveler, explores the northern Sahara desert.

1326-1349   Ibn Battuta, Arabic scholar and pilgrim, travels as far as Beijing.

1341   Alfonso IV, king of Portugal, instructs N. da Recco and A. del Teggio de Corbizzi to undertake an expedition to the Canary Islands.

1342-1347   The Italian Franciscan monk Marignolli is guest at the court of the Great Khan in Beijing.

1344   Pope Clement VI grants the Catalan L. de la Cerda the Canary Islands for an annual remuneration.

1345   Count L. de la Cerda undertakes a voyage to the Canary Islands.

1346   Expedition of the Spaniard Jaime Ferrer to the Canary Islands.

1351   The Azores and Madeira are already included in the atlas of the Medici. The Laurentinian map shows the islands of Madeira and Porto Santo under the name of "Isola de leghame", the Azores under the name of "Insulae de Cabrera de Columbis de Corvis marinis". Africa ends with Guinea.

1352   Ibn Battuta crosses the Sudan and reaches the legendary city of Timbuktu.

1375   First map of the Sahara.

1385   The Portuguese defeat the Castilians. Start of colonial expansion.

1394   Henry the Seafarer is born.

The Sahara Desert

15th CENTURY

1402   Béthancourt, a Norman, undertakes the first systematic settlement of the Canary Islands.

1415   The Portuguese storm the Moorish citadel of Ceuta and set out on their campaign of conquest in North Africa.

1418-1420   Tr. Vaz Teixeira and G. Zarco, Portuguese seamen, initiate the colonization of Madeira and Porto Santo. B. Perestrelo, a Portuguese nobleman, receives Porto Santo as a fief.

1419   Henry the Seafarer establishes a nautical college on Cape São Vivente and organizes the Portuguese voyages of discovery from there.

1424   N. Conti, a traveler from Venice, is the first European to visit the island of Ceylon.

1439-1444   N. Conti travels via Damascus and Hormuz on the Persian Gulf to India and then visits Ceylon, Bengal, Burma, Java and Borneo.

1440   The caravel, a long three or four-master, takes the place of the "Barcha" in the traffic across the Atlantic.

1441   The Portuguese seafarer N. Tristão rounds Cape Blanco on the west coast of Africa; it had probably already been reached by the Arab Ibn Fatima during the Middle Ages.

1443   Advance of N. Tristãos into the Arguin Bay on the west African coast.

1444   First business contacts with Black Africa by the Portuguese Diaz and Tristão.

1445   The Portuguese L. Goncalves reaches the Rio do Ouro (western Africa). João Fernandes, a Portuguese adventurer, ventures 100 km (60 miles) into the Sahara from western Africa.
Alvaro Fernández rounds Cape Verde and sails to Cabo dos Mostos.

1447   Malfante, a Genoese merchant, spends time in Tuat (Sudan) on instruction of the Centurione Genoa bank.

1451   Christopher Columbus is born.

1455-1456   A. da Ca da Mosto, an Italian seafarer in Portuguese services, undertakes a large-scale expedition to the Cape Verde Islands and to the west coast of Africa, travels through Senegal and Gambia and establishes trade relationships with the black leader N. Mansa.

1460   Henry the Seafarer dies.

1462   The Portuguese seafarer Pedro de Sintra reaches Cape Mesurado on the west African coast.

1479   The Canary Islands belong to Spain.

1482   Construction of the Mina citadel (Gold Coast) and initiation of trade with central Africa.

1485   Diego Cão, a Portuguese seafarer, reaches the mouth of the Congo River and establishes relations with the ruler Mani Congo (hence the name of the river).

1486-1488   The Portuguese B. Diaz rounds the "Cape of Storms" (Cabo tormentoso) and

A typical 15th-century vessel

arrives at Mossel Bay. This cape is henceforth called "Cape of Good Hope" (Cabo da boa esperanza).

1487   The Portuguese Pero da Covilha reaches India (via Alexandria, Aden, Calicut, Goa) on an overland route. A. Paiva, a Portuguese, visits Somaliland and Abyssinia (Ethiopia).

1490   The Spanish conquer Palma (Canary Islands).

1492   Granada is conquered by the Spanish, and colonial expansion is initiated. Columbus undertakes his first voyage to the Central American islands and discovers San Salvador, Cuba and His-paniola.

1493-1496   Columbus sails to the "New World" for the second time and discovers the islands of Dominica, Marie-Galante, Guadeloupe, Puerto Rico, Antigua and Jamaica.

1494   Treaty of Tordesillas: Under the direction of Pope Alexander VI, the Spanish and Portuguese establish their rights both for known countries and for those yet to be discovered.

1495-1498	J. F. Labrador, a Portuguese seafarer, sails to Greenland with P. de Barcelos.
1497	J. Cabot, a Genoese seafarer, sails to North America on behalf of the English king Henry VII, explores Labrador and Newfoundland and reaches Cape Breton.
1497-1499	Vasco da Gama establishes the first direct connection by sea between Lisbon and Calicut on the Malabar coast.

1498-1499	A. de Ojeda and A. Vespucci explore the South American coast from French Guyana to Venezuela.
1498-1500	Columbus' third journey to Central America. Near the mouth of the Orinoco, he unwittingly sets foot on the South American mainland for the first time.
1499	A. Vespucci sails along the Brazilian coast but does not go ashore.

16th CENTURY

1500	P. A. Cabral, Portuguese seafarer, lands in Brazil on the latitude of the Easter Mountain (Monte Paschoal). Exploration of Labrador on the Canadian east coast by the Portuguese Miguel and Gaspar Cortereal.
1501	Columbus sails to the "New World" for the fourth and last time. J. da Nova discovers the Atlantic Island of Ascension.
1502	Vasco da Gama sets out on his second journey to India. J. da Nova discovers St. Helena (South Atlantic). Amerigo Vespucci sails from Rio de Janeiro to South Georgia (southwest Atlantic).
1502-1503	Columbus explores the Honduran coast.
1505	Albuquerque, Portuguese general, conquers Hormuz on the Persian Gulf.
1506	D. Diaz, Portuguese seafarer, discovers the island of "Saint Laurentius" (Madagascar).
1507	De Almeida, Portuguese governor of Goa, conquers the combined fleet of Egyptians and Indians off Diu (a port on the west coast of India). The German cartographer Waldseemüller gives the continent discovered by Columbus on his third voyage the name of "America". Portuguese colonists establish the first European settlement in Black Africa on the island of Mozambique (East Africa).

1507-1508	V. Y. Pinzón reaches the Mexican peninsula of Yucatan.
1508	F. de Almeida discovers the Maldives (Indian Ocean).
1509	Sequeira from Portugal conquers Molucca and reaches the Philippines.
1510	Foundation of Santa Maria de la Antigua, the first European settlement on the South American subcontinent. Albuquerque conquers Goa on the Malabar coast (India).
1510-1513	Pizarro travels across Panama.
1511	Abreu, a Spanish seafarer, explores the coast of New Guinea, without realizing that it is an island.
1513	Ponce de Léon, a Spanish conquistador, discovers Florida. The Spanish explorer Balboa crosses Panama, discovers the land connection

Uxmal, religious center of the Mayan culture in Yucatán, Mexico

between the Atlantic and the Pacific and reaches the Pacific Ocean.

1514   A. Fernández, a Spanish adventurer, sets out from Sofala (eastern Africa) to explore Rhodesia as well as the area ruled by the black potentate Monomotapa.

1516   The Spanish explorer J. D. de Solis discovers the mouth of La Plata. The Portuguese R. Perestrello reaches the Chinese city of Canton in a junk.

1517   Córdoba, a Portuguese adventurer, is commissioned to explore the Bay of Campeche (Mexico). Balboa is beheaded. The Spanish adventurer Díaz explores the coast of Yucatan (Mexico).

1518   J. de Grivalja, a Spanish adventurer, reaches the Panuco River (Mexico).

1519   Magellan circumnavigates the world from west to east.
The Spaniard A. de Piñeda sails from Isla de Santiago (Jamaica) along the coast of Florida to Tampico (Mexico). The Spanish conquistador Hernando Cortez lands in Mexico and occupies the Aztec capital of Tenochtitlán.

1520   Magellan discovers the southern passage from the Atlantic to the Pacific ("Magellan Strait"). The passage takes from 18 October to 8 November.
In the "Noche triste", the "night of sorrow" of 1 July, Aztecs drive the Spaniards out of Tenochtitlán.

1521   The Aztec Empire (Mexico) is destroyed. Magellan is killed by natives on the Philippines.

1522   P. Andagoya, a Spanish conquistador, reaches Peru. An accident forces him to abandon his plan of continuing south.

1524-1528   Pizarro explores the coast of Ecuador and Peru and discovers the Inca empire.

1525   The Portuguese seafarer E. Gomez explores the North American coast as far as Cape Cod (to the south of Boston) on the commission of the Spanish king.

View of the Pacific on the American west coast

1526   Merchants from Dieppe land on the island of Madagascar and attempt to establish economic relations with the local inhabitants. The Italian seafarer S. Cabot is commissioned by the Spanish to repeat Magellan's journey. He is unsuccessful. The coast of New Guinea is explored by the Portuguese J. de Menezes. At the same time his pilot, Caetano, discovers the Sandwich Islands (northeastern Pacific).

1527-1528   Saavedra, Pizarro's comrade-in-arms, discovers the Ladrone Islands (Marianas) from the west coast of America.

1528   P. de Narvaez, a Spanish adventurer, explores the eastern American coast and advances as far as the Appalachian village of Tallahassee.

1529   The French seafarers Jean and Raoul Parmentier land on Sumatra. Both are killed during a battle with the natives.

1530-1531   The German conquistador N. Federmann, governor of the Welsers in Venezuela, advances from Coro (northwestern Venezuela) into the interior of the country.

1530-1536   Accompanied by Estebanico the Spanish A. N. Cabeza explores the region around the Mississippi, Arkansas and Colorado and the area that was later to become the states of New Mexico and Arizona.

Grand Canyon, USA

1531   A. Ehringer reaches the Rio Magdalena and Rio Cauca. The Portuguese reach the Zambezi (southeastern Africa).

1533-1534   Pizzaro destroys the Inca culture.

1535-1536   J. Cartier, a French seafarer, is commissioned by the French king Francis I to carry out an expedition to North America and sails up the St. Lawrence River to the village of Stadacone (today Quebec).

1535   Foundation of Buenos Aires at the mouth of La Plata by the Spaniard Mendoza. Foundation of Lima (Ciudad de Los Reyes) by Pizarro.

1535-1537   The Spaniard Almagro conquers what is today Chile.

1535-1538   G. Hohermut and P. v. Hutten, German conquistadors and governors of the Welsers in Venezuela, travel via the Cordillera de Merida and reach the upper course of the Rio Guaviare (left tributary of the Orinoco).

1536-1538   With a small army, the Spaniard G. J. Quesada subjugates the Chibcha (an Indian people in central Columbia).

1537   The Spaniard D. M. de Irala explores the Rio Pilcomayo. Foundation of Asunción (today the capital of Paraguay).

1539-1542   H. de Soto, a Spanish conqueror, searches for precious metals in Florida in vain, crosses what is today the US state of Alabama and reaches the Mississippi (at what is today Memphis). He is the first white man to have crossed the vast North American prairies.

1540   The Spaniard F. de Coronado reaches the Grand Canyon (Colorado) and visits the Suni Indians. He does not find the legendary seven cities of Cibola.

1540-1541   P. de Valdivia, an adventurer from Spain, travels from Cuzco to central Chile and founds Santiago.

1541-1542   The Spaniard F. de Orellana sails the entire Amazon from Peru to the Atlantic. In doing so, he prepares the ground for the conquest of Brazil. J. Cartier and S. de Robeval (French seamen) sail to North America to conquer the legendary land of "Saguenay" (Canada), which had been described by the Indian chieftain Donnaconna. The rock samples they bring back to London prove to be worthless.

1542   In Lisbon a report is published according to which the Portuguese have discovered Australia.

1549   The missionary Franz Xaver lands in Kagoshima (Japan).

1553   Willoughby, a British seafarer, reaches Novaya Zemlya (West Siberian Arctic Sea), spends the winter on the Kola Peninsula and dies there along with 50 companions. S. Cabot sails to North America in an unsuccessful attempt to find the Northwest Passage.

1556   Burrough, a British seafarer, attempts to pass through the Kara Sea (between the islands of Novaya Zemlya and Vaygach); he does not succeed.

1557-1558 The English seafarer Jenkinson sets out from the mouth of the Dvina in Russia in the direction of the Caspian Sea and reaches Buchara.

1558 The Spaniard J. Ladrilleros is the first to sail through the Magellan Strait from west to east.

1560 D. G. da Silveira, a Jesuit priest from Goa, explores the region around what is today Salisbury (Rhodesia) and attempts to convert the ruler Monomotapa to Christianity. The Portuguese is killed.

1564-1567 Legazpi, a Spanish seafarer, conquers the group of islands in the West Pacific which he names the "Philippines" in honor of the king.

1569 F. Barreto unsuccessfully attempts to seize South Africa for Portugual.

1576 While searching for the Northwest Passage, the British seafarer Frobisher explores the coast of Labrador and reaches a latitude of 63° N.

1577 F. Drake, a British seafarer and pirate, undertakes his first circumnavigation of the world from west to east and returns to England with a large booty.

1579 Drake takes possession of New Albion (north of San Francisco) for Britain.

1580 A. Pet and C. Jackman, English seafarers, attempt to reach the Kara Sea through the Yugor Strait. They are prevented from doing so by ice masses. Jackman dies on this mission.

1581-1582 The Cossack Yermak conquers Sibir, the "capital" of the Tartars. Soon the entire region to the south of the Urals is known as Siberia.

1587 The Englishman Davis sails reaches 72° 12' N (today Baffin Bay). The city of Tobolsk is founded. The entire region from the Urals to the Ob is in the hands of the czars.

1592 Houtman, a Dutch seafarer, rounds the Cape of Good Hope and sails directly to Sumatra (Indonesia). Davis visits the Islas Malvinas (Falkland Islands).

1595 Sir Walter Raleigh, a British seafarer, explores the Orinoco.

1595-1597 On their second and third journeys the two Dutchmen Barents and Rijp discover the Medvezhi Islands, Spitsbergen, they circumnavigate the island of Novaya Zemlya and spend the winter there.

1597 Barents freezes to death on Novaya Zemlya.

1598-1600 The Dutchman Van Noort circumnavigates the world.

1599 The Dutch settle in Japan. Gerrits, a Dutch seafarer, discovers Graham Land (Antarctica).

17th CENTURY

1601 The Dutch settle in Annam (Indochina).

1603 Bento de Goes, a Portuguese missionary, travels from Agra (India) via Lahore, Peshawar, Kashgar and Hami to Su tzu in central China.

1603-1604 Champlain, a French researcher, undertakes his first journey to North America and explores the coast of Nova Scotia.

1605-1606 Setting out from Lima, the Spanish seafarer Quiroz discovers the island of Tahiti ("Sagittaria"), the Torres Strait and the largest of the New Hebrides Islands, which he names "Austrialia del Spíritu Santo".

1606 Torres, a Spanish seafarer, sails through the body of water between Australia and New Guinea and names it after himself. W. Janszoon, a Dutch seafarer, sailing from the island of Java, lands on the York Peninsula in Australia and explores the Gulf of Carpentaria (northeastern Australia).

1607-1610   H. Hudson, a British seafarer and explorer, undertakes three journeys to Greenland, Spitsbergen, "Jan Mayen" island (European Arctic Sea) and the "Hudson River". He reaches 80° 23' N.

1608   Champlain explores and charts the Canadian west coast and founds the city of Quebec (Indian village of Stadacona).

1609   J. dos Santos, a Dominican priest from Portugal, spends time in Sofala (on the East African coast), visits the Comoros, Madagascar, Mombassa (eastern Africa) and Axum, the old capital of Abyssinia. Dutch merchants establish a trading post in Hirado (Japan). Establishment of a Dutch post on the Hudson River.

1610   Hudson explores the bay that is named after him; together with nine companions, he is forced to leave his ship.

1611   The British seaman Burton sails to Hudson Bay and spends the winter at "Port Nelson", where Hudson and his companions had been left. However, he is unable to find any trace of them.

1612   The Dutchman Peter Minuit founds New Amsterdam on the east coast of North America (later to become New York).

1613-1623   English trading post in Japan.

1615   P. Paez, a Portuguese missionary, discovers the sources of the Blue Nile.

1616   D. Hartog, a Dutch seafarer, lands on the west coast of Australia. The Portuguese traveler G. Bocarro discovers Lake Nyassa 200 years before Livingstone. He covers around 1,500 km (930 miles) within two months. His journey ends in Kilwa (east African coast). While trying to find the Northwest Passage, the Britons Baffin and Bylot reach 78° 10' N. The Dutch seafarers Le Maire and Schouten discover a safe passage between the Atlantic and the Pacific to the south of the Magellan Strait, called the "Le-Maire Strait".

Indonesia

1619   Foundation of the Dutch trading post in Batavia (Indonesia).

1620   The crew of the "Mayflower" found the British settlement of Plymouth on Cape Cod. The British transport the first slaves from Black Africa to North America.

1622   The Dutchman Nuytz explores the Great Australian Bight. The Portuguese are forced to give up Hormuz.

1623   Carstenz, a Dutch seafarer, explores York Peninsula (northern Australia), erroneously describing it as "New Guinea".

1627   P. Nuytz charts over 1,600 km (1,000 miles) of the southern Australian coast.

1632   Foundation of the British colony of Maryland in North America. The Dutch settle in Curacao (north of Venezuela). Yakutsk on the Lena is conquered by Cossacks.

1635   The French occupy the Caribbean island of Guadeloupe.

1637   Foundation of the Siberian Ministry ("Sibirsk Prikaz") for the conquest and colonization of the entire east of Russia.

1638   Via the lower Tunguska (a tributary of the Lena), the Cossacks reach the Sea of Okhotsk (Pacific).

1639   English merchants found a trading post in Madras (India).

1642-1644   Commissioned by Governor Van Diemen, A. J. Tasman undertakes a major exploration of the Pacific. Setting sail from the island of Mauritius, he discovers

"Van Diemen's Land" (Tasmania), lands on the west coast of New Zealand, sails around the waters of the Tonga and Fiji islands and, via New Guinea and New Britain (Bismarck Islands), sails to Batavia (Java). Without knowing it, he has circumnavigated Australia.

1643   The Dutch seafarer De Vries discovers the Kuriles, Sachalin and the Japanese island of Hokkaido.

1643–1646   The Russian Poyarkov explores the region from Yakutsk to the mouth of the River Oulia (Sea of Okhotsk).

1644   Foundation of a Russian settlement on the Kolyma (northern Siberia).

1648   Deshnev, a Cossack seafarer, sails from the mouth of the Kolyma and rounds the outermost tip of Siberia (Asian North Cape) and sets up a camp on the River Anadyr. His report is only discovered in 1736 in Yakutsk by the German-Russian historian G. F. Müller.

1649–1650   Khabarov, a Russian conquistador, explores the Lena and Olekna Rivers and conquers the entire Amur region.

1651   The Persians acquire Maskat on the Gulf of Oman. The Portuguese supremacy over the Persian Gulf is over.

1652   The Dutch wrest the Cape of Good Hope from the Portuguese and, under the leadership of J. v. Riebeck found the "cape colony". The missionary Monte-sarchio explores the Congo as far as the "Stanley Falls".

1653–1655   The Canadian woodsmen P. Radisson and de Groseilliers explore the Ottawa River, Lake Huron and establish trade relations with the Sioux.

1654   The Russian Baikov travels to China; he is the first European to reach Peking from the north.

1655   England occupies the island of Jamaica.

1658   The Portuguese are driven out of Ceylon by the Dutch.

1667   The Frenchman C. de la Salle explores the Ohio up to the "Louis Falls". Holland purchases Guyana (South America).

1669   T. Bowrey, a British geographer, charts a large part of the Indian subcontinent.

1670   Prince Rupert of England founds the Hudson Bay Company.

1673   The French Jesuit Marquette and the woodsman Jolliet explore the Mississippi.

1682   La Salle is the first to reach the mouth of the Mississippi from the Great Lakes.

1687   La Salle sets out once more for the Mississippi to relieve Fort Louis. He is killed by two of his fellow countrymen.

1690–1692   The German adventurer E. Kaempfer visits Ceylon, Sumatra, Java, Siam in the service of the Dutch East India Company and spends two years in Yeddo (Japan).

1697–1698   The Cossack Atlassov occupies Kamchatka Peninsula (eastern Asia).

1699   The Canadian le Moine d'Iberville rediscovers the mouth of the Mississippi. Two Frenchmen, the physician Poncet and the priest Bénévent, reach the heart of Abyssinia. The priest dies in Gondar.

Kamchatka Peninsula

Poncet brings back the first accurate description of the country to Europe. The Englishman William Dampier sails round the Cape of Good Hope in the direction of the west coast of Australia; he finds the passage between New Britain and New Guinea.

18th CENTURY

1716 Desideri, an Italian Capuchin monk, enters Lhasa and spends five years in the city of the "Holy Books".

1722 Roggeveen, a Dutch seafarer, discovers Easter Island (Pacific) on Easter Monday.

1725-1727 The Dane v. Bering, in the service of Russia, discovers the strait that bears his name between Siberia and Alaska and explores Kamchatka Peninsula.

1737-1745 The Frenchman La Condamine leads the first major scientific expedition in South America.

1738 Martin Spanberger, Bering's lieutenant, reaches the Kuriles and establishes contact with Japan.

1739-1741 The Russian Laptev explores the Siberian coast from the Lena to Yenissei.

1740-1741 Bering sails from Okhotsk (east Siberian coast) to Alaska and is the first European to set eyes on Mount St. Elias.

1740-1744 Anson from England undertakes a major exploratory expedition in the Pacific.

Alaska

1742 On a sledge, the Russian Chelyuskin reaches the cape that bears his name (77° 41' N).

1759 The Scottish Africa explorer R. Gordon, in the service of Holland, establishes the connection between the South African rivers Oranje and Vaal (a tributary).

1761-1767 Commissioned by the king of Denmark, the German traveler Carsten Niebuhr sets out from Cairo to explore the Arabian Peninsula. He visits Medina, Mecca, Sana (Oman) and Hormuz and on his return journey visits Persepolis, Baghdad, Aleppo and Constantinople.

1763 Foundation of the first French settlement on the Falkland Islands by the seafarer Bougainville. The following year, France is forced to cede this colony to Britain.

1766-1769 The Frenchman Bougainville undertakes a major pacific expedition. He discovers an island belonging to the Solomon group which later bears his name.

1764-1766 Byron, a Royal Navy officer, discovers the Gilbert Islands (west Pacific).

1767 The English seafarer Wallis explores the Pacific island of Tahiti.

1768-1771 The Englishman James Cook undertakes his first circumnavigation of the world from west to east. He discovers and explores the part of Australia now named New South Wales, drops anchor in New Zealand and finds the passage between the north and south islands ("Cook Strait").

1768-1773 J. Bruce, a Scottish adventurer, rediscovers the sources of the Blue Nile and travels through most of Ethiopia.

1768-1774 On commission of Catherine II of Russia, the German scientist Pallas explores Siberia and reaches Amur.

1770 The Spanish build Fort San Francisco.

1771-1772 The British naval officer S. Hearne explores the Coppermine River to its mouth on the Canadian Arctic coast.

1772 Y. de Kerguélen, a French seafarer, discovers an island in the Indian Ocean that now bears his name.

1772-1775 J. Cook's second circumnavigation of the world. From South Africa he becomes the first European to cross the

Antarctic Circle he lands on New Zealand, discovers New Caledonia and returns to England via Cape Horn.

1776 The Spanish monks Escalante and Domínguez explore the Colorado and the Green River and reach 37° N.

1776-1779 James Cook's third circumnavigation of the world. He is killed during a confrontation with natives on Hawaii.

1781-1783 The Frenchman Le Vaillant is the first European to set foot on Namaqua Land (southwestern Africa).

1783-1793 The Spaniard A. R. Ferreira sails the entire Amazon from Peru. During this extended journey he explores the tributaries of the Amazon, the Rio Negro, Rio Branco, Madeira, Guapore, Cuyaba and the San Lorenzo.

1785-1788 La Pérouse, a French seafarer, is commissioned by the French king Louis XIV to carry out a scientific circumnavigation of the world. He dies in unclear circumstances not far from the Pacific island of Vanikoro.

1787-1788 The British captain A. Philipp transports 1,000 convicts to the east coast of Australia. Sydney is founded ("Botany Bay").

1788 Foundation of the British "Association for the promotion of the interior of Africa", called the "African Association" (later the Royal Geographical Society, London).

1789-1793 A. Mackenzie, a Scottish fur trader, sets out from Fort Chippewa on Lake Athabaska to explore the river that now bears his name. Crossing the Rocky Mountains, he reaches the Pacific on 22 July, 1793 and is thus the first European to cross the North American mainland from east to west. The overland east-to-west passage is established.

1791 The Spanish establish the missionary station of Los Angeles.

1791-1794 Malaspina, a Spaniard of Italian ancestry, explores the North American Pacific coast as far as Mount St. Elias (Alaska).

1794 The first trading route from Alaska to Okhotsk (Siberian east coast) is opened.

1795-1797 Mungo Park's first journey to the Niger (Sudan) on commission from the "African Society".

1798 The English seafarers M. Flinders and G. Bass circumnavigate Tasmania in fourteen weeks, thus proving that it is an island. J. M. Lacerda, a Portuguese traveler, unsuccessfully attempts to cross the Indian Ocean from Mozambique.

1798-1801 The German Africa explorer Hornemann is the first European to cross the eastern Sahara from Egypt to Bornu.

1799-1804 A. v. Humboldt and A. Bonpland set out to explore South America from the mouth of the Orinoco to Bogotá and Quito.

19th CENTURY

1800-1802 The French seaman Naudin explores the South Australian coast between Nuytz Land and Tasmania.

1800-1806 Mungo Park is commissioned by the African Society to explore the Niger meander; he reaches the "Bussa Falls".

1801 The Englishman M. Flinders circumnavigates Australia in a sloop and charts the contours of the continent.

1802-1810 The Portuguese explorers A. José and P. Baptista set out from Angola to investigate Portuguese East Africa (Mozambique) and South Africa. They are held captive for four years by King Kazembe of Luanda.

1803-1806 Russian explorer and seafarer A. J. v. Krusenstern's first circumnavigation of the world.

1811   Disguised as a Chinese, the English traveler T. Manning reaches Lhasa.

1814   The Swiss researcher J. L. Burckhardt travels to Mecca and Medina.

1814-1817   The German scientist Prince zu Wied-Neuwied explores the Brazilian coast.

1816   Tuckey, a British explorer, explores 4,100 km (2,550 miles) of the Congo.

1817-1819   The German scientists Spix, Martius, Pohl and Natterer undertake a scientific expedition to the Amazon region and the mountains of Brazil.

1817-1820   The French scholar Freycinet circumnavigates the world, accompanied by the hydrographer Dupérey.

Giant tree in the Amazonian forest

1818   The Englishman J. Ritchie sets out from Tripoli to cross the Sahara and reaches Mursuk, the capital of the Fessan.

1819-1821   German-Russian F. G. v. Bellingshausen discovers "Peter I Island".

1821-1829   The Dane Raah explores the west coast of Greenland from Cape Farvel to Upernavik and the east coast as far as Dannebrog Island.

1826   Major Laing, a Scottish Africa explorer, reaches the legendary city of Timbuktu.

1829   A. v. Humboldt explores the Chinese Dzungaria and the Caspian Sea.

1829-1833   James Ross, a British polar explorer, spends three winters in the Arctic. He reaches the North Magnetic Pole and discovers "Boothia Felix" Land.

1830-1831   The brothers R. and J. Lander explore the entire course of the Niger.

1831-1835   R. Fitzroy, a British seafarer and astronomer, accompanied by the young Charles Darwin, explores Patagonia and Tierra del Fuego (South America).

1832-1834   Maximilian Prince zu Wied-Neuwied explores the Mississippi and Missouri.

1836   The Englishman Davidson advances deep into the Sahara from North Africa.

1839-1842   Three Egyptian expeditions explore the White Nile.

1840   The French explorer and seafarer Dumont d'Urville discovers "Adélie-Land" (Antarctica). C. Wilkes, an American polar explorer, investigates 2,700 km (1,680 miles) of the Antarctic coast.

1840-1841   J. Eyre, a British researcher, crosses South Australia from east to west.

1842-1844   The American J. C. Frémont explores North America between the Mississippi and the west coast on five expeditions.

1843-1847   The French scholar Castelneau and the mining engineer Orserey carry out an exploratory journey to Brazil, Bolivia and Peru accompanied by the British botanist Weddell. They discover the sources of the Paraguay.

1845   Unsuccessful quest for the Northwest Passage by the English Arctic explorer J. Franklin, who loses his life along with his entire crew.

1847   The German Africa explorers Krapf and Rebmann investigate Kenya.

1848   Rebmann is the first European to discover the snow-covered Kilimanjaro (the highest mountain in east Africa).

1849   D. Livingstone reaches Lake Ngami (Bechuanaland, South Africa).

1850   Panet, a French Africa explorer, travels across the Sahara from St. Louis de Sénégal to Mogador (Morocco).

1850-1855 The Germans H. Barth, A. Overweg and the Englishman Richardson explore the central Sahara.

1853 The American E. K. Kane sails with a crew of 17 through Smith Sound in Rensslar Bay (Greenland) and spends the winter there. They explore the 36 km (22 mile) Humboldt Glacier.

1855 D. Livingstone explores Central Africa and discovers the Victoria Falls.

1856 During his attempt to advance into the eastern Sahara from Lake Chad, the German explorer of Africa E. Vogel is murdered near Lake Chad.

1858-1859 The English Africa explorer J. H. Speke discovers Lake Victoria together with Burton.

1859 D. Livingstone discovers Lake Nyassa.

1860 The American C. F. Hall advances into the Arctic in the "Polaris" and reaches a latitude of 82° 16' N. On Speke's second expedition, this time accompanied by Grant, he discovers the Kagara, which flows into Lake Victoria.

1860-1861 R. O. Burke, an Irish traveler, and the Englishman W. Wills are the first to cross Australia from south to north.

1862 The Scot J. McDonald Stuart is the first to cross Australia from south (Adelaide) to north (Darwin) and returns by the same route. G. Rohlfs, a German explorer of Africa, investigates the as yet unknown High Atlas and reaches the oases of Tafilalet (southern Morocco). J. H. Speke solves the mystery of the Nile sources.

1864 S. Baker, a British researcher, accompanied by his wife, discovers Lake Albert.

1869 A. Tinné, a Dutch explorer of Africa, is murdered by a Tuareg during her attempt to reach Timbuktu. German expedition to Greenland in the two ships "Germania" and "Hansa" under the leadership of Koldewey and Hegemann.

Alexandra Petronella Francina Tinné

G. Schweinfurth, a German explorer of Africa, investigates Sudan.

1869-1870 The German G. Nachtigal travels to Tibesti, mountainous country of the central Sahara.

1872-1874 Arctic expedition by the Austrian J. Payer. "Franz Joseph Land" is discovered.

1873-1875 The English officer V. L. Cameron explores the entire Congo basin. The Russian G. Potanin crosses eastern central Asia several times.

1873-1876 H. M. Stanley circles Lake Victoria and Lake Tanganyika and discovers Lake Edward and the Ruwenzori Range.

1877 H. M. Stanley explores the Congo to the Atlantic. The German Sahara explorer Erwin v. Bary explores the Aïr, a massif of the central Sahara.

1878-1879 G. Rohlfs, with five companions, is commissioned by the German Africa Society to undertake an expedition to study the mysterious oasis group of Kufra (Libyan desert), Rohlfs enters the Taiserbo oasis on his own.

1878-1880 The Swede A. E. Nordenskiöld conquers the Northeast Passage.

1879-1881 Journey of the American navy lieutenant G. W. de Long in the northern Arctic Sea. His ship, the "Jeanette", is crushed by ice masses. De Long and almost all his companions die.

Desert landscape in Africa

1882-1883　The first International Polar Year, in which ten nations take part and 15 polar stations are established.

1883-1884　The Frenchman C. de Foucauld explores the oases of Laghuat, Ghardaïa, El Goléa, Ouargla and Touggourt.

1886　M. Palat, a French officer and Sahara explorer, is murdered during his attempt to explore southern Oranais (Algeria).

1887　The Frenchman C. Douls is murdered during his attempt to reach Timbuktu via Tafilalet and Tuat.

1888　Norwegians F. Nansen and O. Sverdrup cross the 560 km (350 mile) long and almost 3,000 km (1,860 mile) high inland ice fields of Greenland in 40 days on snowshoes.

1890-1892　Captain Monteil, a French Sahara explorer, crosses the desert from St. Louis de Sénégal to Tripoli.

1891　O. Lilienthal carries out flights with self-made hang gliders. R. E. Peary, an American polar explorer, crosses the Greenland interior ice shelf from west to east, explores the Inglefield Gulf and the Robeson Channel, which separates Greenland from Ellesmere Land.

1891-1893　The German explorer E. D. von Drygalski undertakes an expedition to the ice fields of Greenland.

1893-1896　F. Nansen drifts through the Arctic Sea in the "Fram". He discovers the Taymyr Peninsula and the islands "Sverdrup" and "Nordenskiøld".

1894-1897　The first major Asian expedition by the Swedish researcher S. Hedin. He crosses the Takla-Makan Desert, the Pamir mountain range and the Tarim Basin.

1895-1897　Jackson from England explores the entire "Franz Joseph Land".

1897　Swedish engineer S. A. Andrée's attempt to reach the North Pole from Spitsbergen in a balloon is unsuccessful.

20th CENTURY

1900　The Italian Arctic explorer Cagni, from the Duke of Abruzzia's expedition, reaches 86° 33' N (803 km or 499 miles from the North Pole). France occupies the In-Salah oasis and paves the way for a military penetration of the Sahara. The first Zeppelin airship (LZ 1) takes to the air on 2 July in the Bay of Ranzell near Friedrichshafen.

1902　300 Tuaregs are killed by the French lieutenant Cottenest in an armed conflict. The Hoggar (massif in the southern Algerian Sahara) becomes French territory. The whole of Sudan is under the control of the French government. E. v. Drygalski discovers "Kaiser Wilhelm II Land" and the ice-free extinct Gauss Volcano (Antarctica).

1902-1904 The members of the "Discovery" expedition, under the leadership of R. F. Scott, reach 82° 17' S in the Antarctic during a sledge journey on the shelf ice. Scott discovers "King Edward VII Land".

1902-1905 The French general and Sahara specialist Largeau explores the region around Lake Chad.

1903 The Russian lieutenant Kolchak and the engineer Brousnen complete a crossing of the North Siberian Islands on foot. Bennett Island is thoroughly explored. The French General Laperrine carries out an expedition to the as yet unexplored Moudyr and Aknet massifs (Sahara). W. Wright succeeds in making his first flight in "Flyer 2" on 20 September.

1903-1906 R. Amundsen, a Norwegian polar explorer, is the first to conquer the Northwest Passage.

1904 The two French Sahara specialists C. de Foucauld and Laperrine undertake a major geographical, geological and geodetic scientific expedition across the Sahara.

1904-1905 Large-scale expedition by Frenchmen Flye-Sainte-Marie, Nieger, Mussel, Rouzade and Taillade through the western Sahara. A 2,300 km (1,430 mile) stretch is charted.

1905 In the Hoggar C. de Foucauld establishes a hermitage on the 2,700 meter (8,860 foot) Asekrem peak.

1906 Dr. H. Rice, an American researcher and rector of Harvard University (USA), explores the Rio Negro and the Rio Branco (Amazon).

1906-1907 Greenland expedition by the Dane Mylius-Erichsen with the ice-resistant ship "Danmark".

1906-1914 Fawcett, a British major, explores the Amazon and its tributaries.

1907 Arctic journey of the "Belgica" under the leadership of the Belgian Arctic explorer A. de Gerlache. The aim of this expedition is to reach the Bering Strait; however, it has to be abandoned because of extensive ice masses in the Kara Sea.

1909 The American polar explorer R. E. Peary sails round the north coast of Greenland and is the first to reach the North Pole. E. H. Shackleton, an Irish polar explorer, is the first to penetrate as far south as 88° 23'. He is forced

Amundsen and his companions at the South Pole

to turn back just 178 km (111 miles) from the Pole.

1911 On 14 December Amundsen is the first to reach the South Pole, where he raises the Norwegian flag.

1912 The Swiss meteorologist A. de Quervain crosses Greenland's interior ice fields in the far north from east to west. K. J. von Rasmussen and a companion cross Greenland's interior ice from Melville Bay to Denmark Bay.

1912 On 17 January, R. F. Scott is the second to reach the South Pole from McMurdo Sound. He and his four companions die just short of completing their return journey.

The midnight sun

1912-1922 The French Africa explorers Nieger and Laperrine undertake a series of extensive journeys in South Oranais, Saura, Tuat and Aïr, a massif in the central Sahara.

1913 General Tilho, a French Sahara specialist, explores the Tibesti and the Ennedi. Capt. Cortier, a French Sahara specialist, crosses Sudan from north to south. The Dane J. P. Koch and the meteorologist Wegener cross Greenland's interior ice from east to west.

1914 The Russian J. Nargurski attempts the first Arctic flight in a seaplane. However, after flying over Novaya Zemlya for three hours he is forced to turn back over the Barents Sea.

1914-1936 The French researcher Dr. Charcot undertakes a major expedition to Greenland.

1916 The French Sahara explorer Ch. de Foucauld is murdered in Tamanrasset, the main town of the Hoggar massif.

1920 Englishwoman J. R. Forbes, accompanied by the Egyptian diplomat and researcher Hassanein bey, is the first European woman to set foot in the Kufra oasis group in the Libyan Desert.

1921-1922 K. Rasmussen crosses the North American coastal region from Melville Peninsula to the Bering Strait by sledge and boat.

1922-1923 Egyptian Hassanein bey explores all the oases of the Kufra group and the Arken and El-Aounat massifs.

1922-1925 Ten French Sahara explorers are the first to cross the Sahara in five tracked vehicles ("croisière noire").

1923 W. Mittelholzer, a Swiss Alpine aviator, undertakes three daring flights in the Arctic.

1924 Frenchman Bruneau de Laborie reaches the Kufra Oases from the southwest.

1925 R. Amundsen attempts to fly over the North Pole in two Dornier-Wal flying boats. He is forced to make an emergency landing eight hours into the flight.

1926 R. E. Byrd, an American Arctic explorer, is the first to fly over the North Pole on 9 May, setting out from Spitsbergen. He requires 15 hours for the flight. Amundsen and the Italian Nobile fly over the North Pole in the airship "Norge".

1927 On 21 May, C. Lindbergh makes the first solo flight over the Atlantic in his "Spirit of St. Louis".

1928 The Australian Wilkins makes a successful flight in the Arctic from Alaska to Spitsbergen. The Italian U. Nobile reaches the North Pole on 25 May in his airship "Italia". The airship crashes during the return flight. Nobile and his crew are rescued.

1929 Byrd is the first to fly over the South Pole on 28 November.

1931 On the initiative of the car manufacturer A. Citroîn, a major scientific expedition called "croisière jaune" travels from Beirut through the whole of Asia to Peking in tracked vehicles. The expedition covers 12,115 km (7,530 miles), and 5,000 photographs are taken. The Jesuit P. Teilhard de Chardin and a group of specialists take part in this journey.

1932-1933 The second International Polar Year: 15 countries participate and erect more than 500 stations in the polar regions.

1933 O. Lilienthal dies.

1934 The Englishman Lindsay crosses Greenland on the B. von Jakobshavn. On 15 August Beebe and Barton reach a depth of 923 meters (3,028 feet) near the Bermuda islands in a self-made ball of steel.

1935 The American pilot Ellsworth flies over western Antarctica.

1936 The last major scientific expedition to the western Sahara is undertaken by the French scholar T. Monod, accompanied by lieutenant Brandstetter and three natives. The French Arctic explorer P. E. Victor crosses Greenland at the Angmagssalik latitude.

1937-1938 Drift journey by the Russian I. D. Papanin through the Arctic Sea on an ice floe.

1937-1940 Three-year drift by the "Sedov" in the Arctic Sea under the command of the Russian Balyguin.

1938 H. Harrer and A. Heckmair are the first to climb the notorious north face of the Eiger.

1938-1939 Using a catapult start, German aviators undertake flights in the Arctic over New Swabia.

1946-1947 Research is carried out in Antarctica by the Byrd expedition.

1947 In his "Kon-Tiki", T. Heyerdahl demonstrates that it would have been possible to reach Polynesia from the west coast of America in a balsa boat.

1953 Edmund Hillary (together with Sherpa Tensing Norgay) is the first person to climb Mount Everest. Auguste Piccard reaches a depth of 3,150 m (10,335

In the 20th century, the Earth became too small for the explorers. Now is the time for the conquest of outer space.

feet) in his deep-sea diving device, the "Bathyscaphe".

1956 The French ethnologist H. Lhote discovers 800 rock drawings of Tassili N'jjer (eastern Sahara).

1957-1958 International Geophysical Year (IGY). A transantarctic scientific expedition commissioned by the British Commonwealth under the leadership of V. E. Fuchs and the first crossing of the Antarctic continent by land via the South Pole.

1958 The US submarine "Nautilus" sails beneath the frozen surface of the North Pole from 1–5 August.

1960 The Swiss diver Jacques Piccard sets a record in the West Pacific Mariana Trench, reaching a depth of 10,912 meters (35,801 feet).

1961   Soviet Yuri Gagarin is the first person to orbit the Earth in the "Vostok 1".

1962   H. Harrer crosses the tropical island of New Guinea and is the first to climb 32 snow-covered peaks. He also discovers the source of the stone axes ("Je-Li-Me").

1963   Soviet cosmonaut Valentina Tereshkova is the first woman in space.

1965   Soviet cosmonaut Alexei Leonov is the first person to leave a space capsule in space.

1968   "Apollo 7" is the first manned spaceship of the Apollo series. On board are astronauts R. Cunningham, D. Eisele and W. Schirra. US American astronauts W. Anders, F. Borman and J. Lovell are the first to circle the moon in "Apollo 8".

1969   US astronaut Neil Armstrong descends from "Apollo 11" and is the first human being to set foot on the moon. He is followed 20 minutes later by Edwin Aldrin.

1970   In the papyrus boat "Ra II", T. Heyerdahl sails from the west coast of Morocco across the Atlantic to the island of Barbados.

1975   The first joint American-Soviet space mission. The two spaceships "Apollo" and "Soyuz 19" connect. On board are astronauts T. Stafford/D. K. Slayton and cosmonauts A. Leonov/W. Kubassov.

1977-1978   In the "Tigris" T. Heyerdahl reaches Djibouti sailing from Basra through the Persian Gulf, thus demonstrating that the Sumerians may have reached Africa in boats driven by wind and the ocean's currents.

1978   S. Jaehn is the first German in space on board the Soviet space capsule "Soyuz 31". R. Messner and P. Haberer are the first to climb Mount Everest

Reinhold Messner

without the aid of high-altitude breathing apparatus.

1981   The start of the first space shuttle mission. On board are US astronauts R. Crippen and J. Young.

1983   Sally Ride is the first American woman in space. The German U. Merbold is the first non-American in space on board a space shuttle ("Columbia"). T. Heyerdahl discovers ruins of an ancient culture on the Maldives.

1986   The space shuttle "Challenger" explodes shortly after lift-off. All seven astronauts are killed. R. Messner is the first person to climb all 14 eight thousand meter (26,250 foot) mountains on the planet without using high-altitude breathing apparatus.

1988   The Soviet cosmonauts M. Manarov and V. Titov are the first to spend more than a year in space, on board the space station "Mir".

1989-1990   R. Messner and A. Fuchs cross Antarctica on foot in 92 days.

1992   U. Merbold is again in space for eight days on board the "Discovery".

1994   U. Merbold takes part in the space mission "Euromir". This space flight takes four weeks and is carried out in cooperation with Russian cosmonauts.

1995   The US space shuttle "Atlantis" docks with the Russian space station "Mir".

1997   The US space probe "Pathfinder", equipped with a remote-controlled exploration vehicle, lands on Mars.

1998   Contracts are drawn up for all preparatory work for the International Space Station (ISS). In the summer, American and Russian modules are launched into orbit, and on 10 December the first ISS crew commences activity on board. The International Space Station is the largest technological project ever undertaken in the history of mankind. At the age of 77, John Glenn once more flies into space on board the "Discovery", thus setting an age record for an active astronaut.

1999   The Mars exploration vehicle commences operation.

21st CENTURY

2000   From the spaceship "Endeavour", 113 million square kilometers (44 million square miles) of the Earth's surface are scanned by means of high-resolution radar devices. The three-dimensional images are 30 times more precise than any previously generated.

2001   In the course of the "2001 Mars Odyssey" mission, lasting from April to October, the surface of the red planet is investigated. In March 2001, the space station "Mir" crashes into the South Pacific as planned, after orbiting the Earth 86,331 times.

The Earth as seen from space

BIOGRAPHICAL INDEX

GEOGRAPHICAL INDEX

ILLUSTRATIONS

Archiv für Kunst und Geschichte, Berlin: pp. 161, 199, 200/201, 301, 302, 304/305, 308/309, 310, 311, 317, 322, 339, 340, 347, 355, 356/357

dpa: pp. 57, 65, 140, 172, 222, 225, 227, 250, 251, 270 left, 286

Deutsches Literaturarchiv, Marbach: pp. 70 right, 96, 129, 193, 194, 196

Deutsches Museum, München: pp. 85 left, 150, 318, 334, 350, 352, 359, 360

Thor Heyerdahl: Kon-Tiki, Oslo 1948: pp. 186, 187 (both)

Landesbibliothek Baden-Württemberg: pp. 8, 9 (both), 22, 26, 366–391, 25, 28/29, 30/31, 34, 39, 43, 45, 56, 99 (both), 109 left, 114, 115, 145, 147, 148, 169 bottom, 197, 204, 206/207, 210, 211, 213, 277, 293, 299, 312, 321, 343, 358 top

MEV: pp. 7, 58, 75, 81, 82, 113, 120/121, 156, 254, 272, 274, 295, 297, 330, 332/333, 335, 336/337, 394, 395, 396, 398, 399, 400, 402, 404, 408

PhotoDisc: pp. 6, 54/55, 66, 67, 93, 232/233, 240, 392/393, 411, 413

Collection WZ Media: pp. 10, 13, 14, 27, 41, 47, 48, 49, 50, 51, 59, 60, 61, 62, 63, 64, 70, 71, 76, 78, 79, 80, 84, 85 rechts, 86, 87, 95, 98, 102, 103, 105, 106, 107, 109 right, 118, 122, 123, 124 top, 124 bottom, 125, 126, 127, 130, 131, 132, 133, 135, 136, 142, 143, 146, 152/153, 154, 155, 159, 165, 166, 167, 168, 169, 170, 171, 173, 174, 178, 179, 179, 180, 181, 182, 183, 184, 185, 203, 215, 216, 217, 219, 228 top, 228, 229, 230, 231, 235, 236, 237, 244, 245, 247, 252, 258, 259, 260, 261, 262, 264, 265, 266, 267, 268, 269, 270 right, 271 top, 278, 279, 280, 281, 282, 283 left, 284, 287, 288, 289, 290, 291, 292, 294, 296, 306, 307, 319, 320, 323, 324, 325, 326, 327, 328, 329, 331, 338, 348, 349, 351, 353 top, 358 bottom, 397, 409, 410

Silvestris Fotoservice: pp. 52, 69, 73, 111, 137, 139, 140/141, 151, 177, 189, 191, 209, 257

Staatsbibliothek Bamberg: pp. 15, 16/17, 18/19, 21, 23, 24, 33, 97, 202, 239, 273, 300, 346

W. Waldmann: pp. 4/5, 6, 7, 37, 89, 90/91, 100/101, 116/117, 119, 220/221, 243, 248/249, 344/345, 362/363

Else Wegener: Alfred Wegeners letzte Grönlandfahrt, Leipzig 1932: p. 352

Zeppelin Museum, Friedrichshafen: p. 361

Although every effort has been undertaken to ascertain the sources of the pictorial material, we have not been successful in all cases. We should be grateful for any relevant information submitted.